# STUDYING THE ENGLISH LANGUAGE

Other books by the author

*Debating Dialect: Essays on the Philosophy of Dialect Study* (editor)
*Gowerland and its Language*
*The Anglo-Welsh Dialects of North Wales*

# Studying the English Language

## 2nd Edition

ROB PENHALLURICK

First published 2003 by
PALGRAVE MACMILLAN
Second edition published 2010 by
PALGRAVE MACMILLAN

Palgrave Macmillan in the UK is an imprint of Macmillan Publishers Limited, registered in England, company number 785998, of Houndmills, Basingstoke, Hampshire RG21 6XS.

Palgrave Macmillan in the US is a division of St Martin's Press LLC, 175 Fifth Avenue, New York, NY 10010.

Palgrave Macmillan is the global academic imprint of the above companies and has companies and representatives throughout the world.

Palgrave® and Macmillan® are registered trademarks in the United States, the United Kingdom, Europe and other countries.

ISBN 978–0–230–20014–2 hardback
ISBN 978–0–230–20015–9 paperback

This book is printed on paper suitable for recycling and made from fully managed and sustained forest sources. Logging, pulping and manufacturing processes are expected to conform to the environmental regulations of the country of origin.

A catalogue record for this book is available from the British Library.

A catalog record for this book is available from the Library of Congress.

10   9   8   7   6   5   4   3   2   1
19  18  17  16  15  14  13  12  11  10

Printed and bound in China

# Contents

# List of Figures

# Preface

This book is an introduction to the English language, its history, and use. It is also an introduction to the study of English, to theories and views on English and on language in general. Many of these views come from modern linguistics, but the book also draws on classic work in other disciplines, such as semiotics, cognitive science, anthropology, communication theory, and critical theory. It is in this way distinctive as an introduction, placing a wealth of information about English in the context of a guide to language theory, and vice versa. It can be used by teachers and students as a course book or by the general reader.

The design and style of the book emphasize readability. It consists of 18 short chapters, each of which can be read without difficulty in one sitting. Although the chapters have a certain progression, you can in fact read them in any order, and each is self-contained. You do not have to consult other chapters in order to understand fully the one you are reading. It is true, however, that the more chapters you complete, the more you will become aware of their interconnections, and the bigger picture will emerge. Topics mentioned in one chapter are developed further or supplemented in others. Key terms are highlighted in bold and are glossed where they occur in the text. A comprehensive index allows you easily to locate key terms and their definitions. At the start of each chapter, there is a brief summary of its contents. At the end of each chapter there are carefully selected suggestions for taking your reading to the next stage, and at the end of the book there is a bibliography of all the works referred to, as well as a 'webography'.

This new edition has been thoroughly updated in light of developments since the first edition. The book's coverage is unusually wide-ranging. It describes the diversity, history, and pre-history of English, and analyses debates about language and reality, language and gender, language reform, and about the evolution of language; it looks at the nature of Standard English, at attitudes towards dialects and accents, and at language planning in relation to English; it provides guides to the semiotic view of language, to discourse analysis, to models of communication, and to the reasons for slips of the tongue. Three new chapters have been added which broaden the scope of the book further: on

American English, on English as a global language, and on the work of Noam Chomsky.

My intention is that the book gives a clear, reliable, and accessible introduction to knowledge about the English language. I enjoy observing language everywhere, I enjoy thinking about it, I enjoy playing with it, and I enjoy rummaging around in scholars' explanations of it. I hope that this book adds to and stimulates your enjoyment of the same.

RP

# Acknowledgements

The author and publishers wish to thank the following for permission to reproduce material:

Aardman Animations Ltd for the Wallace and Gromit illustration (ACS/NSG/48/0). Copyright © Aardman/Wallace & Gromit Ltd 1995;

The French Ministry of Culture and Communication, Regional Direction for Cultural Affairs (Rhone-Alpes region) and the Regional Department of Archaeology, for the photograph taken in Chauvet Cave;

Walter de Gruyter GmbH & Co KG for figures from N. Chomsky, *Syntactic Structures* (1957), pp. 19, 27 (State and Tree diagrams); and W. Labov, S. Ash and C. Boberg, *The Atlas of North American English Phonetics, Phonology and Sound Change* (2006), p. 148;

Indiana University Press for Figure 13 from Thomas A Sebeok, *A Sign is Just a Sign* (1991), p. 29;

Scoop, on behalf of *Paris Match* for the front cover of their 25 June–2 July 1955 edition [no. 326];

The University of Illinois Press for figure from Claude E. Shannon and Warren Weaver, *The Mathematical Theory of Communication* (1949), p. 5. Copyright © 1949, 1977 by the Board of Trustees of the University of Illinois;

The University of Michigan Press for Figure 4 from Hans Kurath, *A Word Geography of the Eastern United States* (1949, 1967), Fig. 141;

Every effort has been made to trace the copyright holders but if any have been inadvertently overlooked the publishers will be pleased to make the necessary arrangement at the first opportunity.

# Abbreviations

Abbreviations are glossed in the text when used for the first time. For the reader's further convenience, here is a list of specialized abbreviations used.

| | |
|---|---|
| AAE | African American English |
| AAVE | African American Vernacular English |
| *ANAE* | *Atlas of North American English* |
| Aux | auxiliary |
| CDA | critical discourse analysis |
| CDS | critical discourse studies |
| CI | conceptual-intentional |
| *DARE* | *Dictionary of American Regional English* |
| EFL | English as a foreign language |
| en | passive verb-element |
| ENL | English as a native language |
| ESL | English as a second language |
| FL | faculty of language |
| FLB | faculty of language–broad sense |
| FLN | faculty of language–narrow sense |
| FOXP2 | forkhead box P-group number-2 (gene) |
| HRT | High Rising Terminal or Tone |
| IPA | International Phonetic Alphabet |
| L | language |
| L1 | first-language |
| L2 | second-language |
| LF | Logical Form |
| LSA | Linguistic Society of America |
| MP | Minimalist Program |
| N | noun |
| NP | noun phrase |
| *OED* | *Oxford English Dictionary* |
| PF | Phonetic Form |
| PIE | Proto-Indo-European |
| pl | plural |

| | |
|---|---|
| RP | Received Pronunciation |
| S | sentence |
| SAE | Standard Average European |
| sing | singular |
| SM | sensory-motor |
| SMCR | source-message-channel-receiver |
| SVO | subject-verb-object |
| T | the |
| UG | universal grammar |
| VP | verb phrase |

# 1 Space
## The Diversity of English

This chapter includes the following:
- Should we say **English** or **Englishes**?
- What is the difference between a **dialect** and a **language**?
- Definitions of the terms **accent** and **variety**.
- An introduction to **pidgins** and **creoles**.

## Introduction

One summer, when I was very little, we went on a family holiday to Scotland. We drove from southern Britain and our journey took us through the outskirts of Glasgow. We got lost, so lost that my father actually felt the need to ask for directions. While we waited at a set of traffic lights, he wound down the car window, gestured at the driver of the truck next to us, and asked for help. The man replied, at some length, my father thanked him and we drove off, back on our way. I was amazed, because I had not understood a word that the truck driver had said. I thought he must be speaking another language. I must have said something about this, because I remember my father explaining to me that the man really had been speaking English, but in a strong Scottish dialect – in all likelihood the local Glasgow dialect. This was a weird and new phenomenon to me, made all the more perplexing because it seemed that my father, unlike me, *had* understood what the Glaswegian was saying. The incident obviously made an impact on me. I suppose I found it bizarre that there were people in the world who spoke the same language as me in such a way that it sounded totally unlike my language.

I need not have worried. Ferdinand de Saussure (1857–1913), perhaps the most influential of modern linguists, said, 'The most striking thing about the study of languages is their diversity – linguistic differences that appear when we pass from one country to another or even from one region to another. Divergences in time often escape the observer, but divergences in space immediately force themselves upon

1

him' (1916, p. 191). The geographical diversity of language is one of its most basic and conspicuous characteristics. This diversity presents us with separate languages, and within each language we encounter regional dialects. Language changes in space. This chapter looks at the geographical diversity of the English language, and English is an especially diverse language, so diverse that the question of its 'one-ness' arises. Should we talk not of *the English language* but of *the English languages*? Indeed, one book on English first published in the 1990s was called *The English Languages* (McArthur, 1998), and the terms *world Englishes* and *new Englishes* have become widely used. The basic question here is whether we should look upon English as a huge, worldwide agglomeration of regional dialects, or as a 'family' of closely related languages (each one consisting of dialects, needless to say), a bit like the family of Romance languages (French, Italian, Spanish, and so on). This issue entails working out the essential difference between a **dialect** and a **language**, if in fact there is an essential difference.

With this in mind, I have assembled a small sample of short texts, and I have the same question to ask about each one: Is it English?

## Geographical variety in English

Here is my first short text:

(i) The gymanfa ganu at this year's National Eisteddfod will be conducted by the musical director of Morriston Orpheus Choir.

Is it English? Plainly it is – though there may be some element of doubt. It is an extract from a news item in my local newspaper, and if we were to look at the rest of the article we would see clearly that it is written in **Standard English**, the variety of English usually employed by newspapers in Britain. Standard English developed out of fifteenth-century, educated London English into a supraregional variety used for most written English, and associated with high social prestige in its spoken form. As well as being **supraregional** (that is, not restricted to a geographical locale), Standard English is often perceived to be the core variety of English, almost synonymous with the English language itself (though this is a problematic viewpoint, which overlooks the great diversity of English), because it has been treated as a model of usage. However, there are some noticeably un-English, foreign-looking words in the extract above, particularly *gymanfa, ganu,* and *Eisteddfod,* and in truth these are not English but Welsh words. A *gymanfa ganu* is a singing festival (literally, it means 'festival (of) singing'), and an *Eisteddfod* is a festival of literature and music. These words refer to cultural events of a peculiarly Welsh character, to the extent that the Welsh names are used even when the text as a whole is written in Standard English. Given that the text is from a local newspaper, we should not be surprised that its English contains a little added local colour. Compare it with, for example, the following:

> Beginning this season, intentional grounding will result in a loss of down at the spot of the foul.

This is from a sports news item on 'College Football', in a local newspaper from the United States. It is not as incomprehensible to me as the Glasgow truck driver was all those years ago, because it is recognizably written in the vocabulary of Standard English, but nevertheless I have had to seek native assistance in order to understand the local linguistic colour, here specifically in the form of word-senses relating to *college football* (American football played at the college, that is, university level). When a team is on *offense*, it has four goes or chances or *downs* to make ten yards. If successful, the team gets another four downs. *Intentional grounding* is when the *quarterback* deliberately throws the ball down hard rather than lose yardage by being tackled. Under the new rule referred to, play resumes at the spot of the intentional grounding. What we are finding so far, then, is that even in written Standard English (which is the most homogenized type of English) there can be localized diversity. (You can read more about American English in Chapter 4, and about the notion of an American Standard English in Chapter 12.)

Also, there are more intruders than just the Welsh words in my first short text above. *Orpheus* (a name from Greek mythology) is another easily identified foreign word in (i), but more surprising is the fact that exactly 50 per cent of the vocabulary in the text is of foreign origin. *National, conducted, musical, director,* and *Choir* all entered the English language from French during the late medieval period (most of them can be traced yet further back to Latin), and have subsequently became 'naturalized' into English, so that we no longer notice their foreignness. Words such as these are called **loanwords** or **borrowings**, both slightly misleading terms in that the words involved are not so much 'loaned' or 'borrowed' but *copied* from one language into another. Borrowing is a very common process that occurs when communities of speakers of different languages come into sustained contact with each other. The examples above are among the several thousand French loans that came into English after the Norman Conquest of England in 1066 (the Normans spoke French). Throughout its history English has borrowed words from other languages, thousands upon thousands of words from over a hundred different languages. The words *gymanfa*, *ganu*, and *Eisteddfod* are not loanwords – not in the context of Standard English – because their foreignness is too visible. They are **foreignisms**. The remaining words in the text (setting aside the place-name *Morriston*) all go back to the early centuries of English, before the Norman Conquest, to the period in the history of the language known as **Old English**, and they are all native English words.

This first short text (i) and the US clip show us that the standard variety of English (here in its written form) can incorporate local linguistic colour, in the shape of words from another language or in the shape of local and specialized English words and meanings, and that even Standard English, apparently the most core variety of English, possesses a considerable integrated foreign element.

Here is the second short text:

(ii) There was a particular way ... of ... churning, you see, by handle in them days to get the ... correct slap on the contents ... from ... what was inside, you see. And then when we were churning ... the first thing ... [er] ... my mother used to do – when we were in the croft – to fasten it up tightly ... and pour ... a kettle full of water into it ... [er] ... to warm it up for the ... separating purpose as it was termed, you see, then the butter used to come in small lumps. [...] And then she had another ... [er] ... gadget, like a plate, called *y gwpan denau* ... 'the thin cup' ... translating it into English – that was of sycamore 'ood ... and then it was with this *gwpan denau* ... she used to squeeze the buttermilk ... from ... [er] the butter lumps that'd come from the churn, you see.

Is it English? Yes, again clearly it is, but not Standard English, although the vocabulary is mostly standard. If we were to listen to the whole of the interview from which this extract comes, we would conclude that the interviewee above was speaking a variety of **non-standard English**. The text is my transcription of a small part of the interview: a pause by the speaker is represented by three periods ... and [...] indicates a short edit. The speaker is an elderly man from North Wales, whom I interviewed in 1980, describing butter-making on the small farm (or *croft*) of his youth. He spoke the regional dialect or variety

of English known as Welsh English (I was collecting samples of northern Welsh English at the time). Like all regional dialects of English,
Welsh English is characterized and defined by its non-standard features, that is, features considered out of keeping with Standard English.
However, we have already seen from the discussion of text (i) that
non-standard words can occur in written Standard English, and in text
(ii) we see the reverse of this – standard words in non-standard English.
So on what basis is the first labelled 'Standard English' and the second 'non-standard English'? The broad answer is that (when looking
at each text in its entirety) it is a matter of degree, for in practice
there is no absolute, impermeable barrier separating Standard and non-
standard English. The newspaper articles are made up *mainly* of items
considered (in the present day) standard (and they are written texts –
written English has been more subject to standardization than spoken
English), whereas the speech of my elderly informant, although it possessed standard items, was nonetheless saturated with non-standardness.
The non-standard features of the language in text (ii) occur at three
linguistic levels: pronunciation, grammar, and vocabulary.

For example, there is the pronunciation *'ood*, which is *wood* without the initial *w*-sound that occurs in the standard pronunciation. Such
**initial-*w*-loss** is a feature of traditional rural Welsh English caused by
the influence of the Welsh language, which has a comparative lack of
initial *w*-sounds. The English of my informant was full of such Welsh-
influenced pronunciation habits, though these are not easy to show in
writing without using the technical script of the International Phonetic
Alphabet (IPA). They include, for example, a **rolled** pronunciation
of *r* (that is, with the tip of the tongue tapping against the roof of
the mouth), and a tendency to **unvoice** (that is, whisper) *z*-sounds,
so that *cheese* ends with an *s*-sound. The informant also spoke with
the sing-song intonation associated with Welsh English. This involves
different patterns of pitch movement across syllables and more frequent oscillation between high and low pitch compared with standard
intonation.

As for grammar, like many Welsh-English speakers, my informant
used '-*ing* verb phrases' to describe habitual actions or states in the past
where '*used to* phrases' would occur in Standard English for this sense.
For example, at another point in our conversations he said, 'in these
crofts they were rearing a pig for domestic use'. The Standard English
version of this would be 'in these crofts they used to rear a pig for
domestic use'. These non-standard -*ing* phrases (or **progressive verb
phrases**, to use a more technical term) result from the literal translation

of Welsh grammatical constructions into English, and they are characteristic of late twentieth-century Welsh-English syntax in regions where the Welsh language continued to have a strong presence. (The term **syntax** refers to sentence or phrase structure, while **morphology**, another major area of grammar, refers to word structure.) In text (ii) above, 'when we were churning' is probably another example of a non-standard, habitual past, progressive verb phrase, equivalent to Standard English 'when we used to churn', although there is some ambiguity about this one – it can be interpreted as describing an action in progress (in the past), and therefore having the same sense that the construction would have in Standard English.

At the level of vocabulary, the text gives us *y gwpan denau*, from Welsh (literally, 'the cup thin') – probably not a local borrowing, but best classified as a local foreignism. Like most native Welsh people of his age in most of North Wales in the 1980s, my informant was bilingual in Welsh and English, and his Welsh influenced his English. However, the substantial majority of speakers of Welsh English are monolingual in English, and living in regions where the traditional, local Welsh has fallen out of use. Yet their English is characterized by influence from the Welsh language. The pronunciation habits of Welsh English throughout the greater part of Wales are heavily influenced by the pronunciation conventions of Welsh, and individuals with no Welsh nevertheless can have Welsh traces running through their accents, including rolled *r*-pronunciations, for example. Welsh-derived syntactic features, such as emphasizing a phrase by placing it at the start of a sentence (**fronting**, it is called), as in ' "Shelving wagons" they were calling them' (recorded in Parry, 1999, p. 120), occur in the Welsh English of non-Welsh-speaking areas as well as that of Welsh-speaking areas (this example also shows that Welsh-influenced progressive verb phrases can occur in non-Welsh areas). I have often heard constructions such as 'Swansea she lives' (or, for that matter, 'fronting, it is called' rather than 'it is called fronting'). A few Welsh-derived loan-words, such as *twp*, meaning 'stupid' (pronounced 'toop') are also used by non-Welsh speakers. All these features were 'copied' from Welsh into English as it spread through Wales, and they became embedded in the local English, persisting there even after Welsh itself had receded.

Contact with other languages has similarly affected, characterized and helped define English in the other Celtic areas of the British Isles, and also English across the world. For example, in their study of *English in Australia and New Zealand* (1998), Kate Burridge and Jean Mulder note (pp. 12, 159) that Maori English is a variety of

New Zealand English distinguished by pronunciation (or **phonolog-ical**) features and vocabulary (or **lexical**) features carried over from Maori into English. They also give an example of morphological trans-ference: in its second-person pronouns Maori English has a three-way distinction carried over from Maori, *you* (singular), *youse* (two), and *youse fellas* (more than two). New Zealand English and Australian English have loanwords from Maori and from Aboriginal languages, respectively (Burridge and Mulder, 1998, p. 132), such as *wahine*, 'a Maori woman or wife', and *waddy*, 'an Aboriginal war-club'. Many such loanwords have entered the mainstream of Standard English, for example, *haka* from Maori and *boomerang* from Aborigine. In North America, English has been affected by contact with Native American languages, West African languages (initially through the slave trade), and European-settler languages such as Spanish and Dutch. In South Africa, English has been influenced by Dutch/Afrikaans and by African languages. Then there are the so-called New Englishes, such as Indian English, Malaysian English, and Singapore English, characterized again by contact with local languages, and by rapidly expanding numbers of speakers. (Chapter 5 looks in more detail at 'English Across the World'.)

So we see that the geographical diversity of English is related to its spreading out of England into territories where it picked up features from other languages and cultures. This divergence was also aided in some cases by an immigrant English going through a period of com-parative isolation (for example, in North America and Australasia) from its mother dialects or varieties in Britain. Each of these regional dialects or varieties of English, across the world, is characterized by a bundle of distinguishing phonological, grammatical, and lexical features that mark it off from Standard English and other dialects of English. In so far as each remains a dialect of English, it also has sufficient features in common with other dialects of English to be generally comprehensible to speakers of those dialects, and furthermore there is a counter-trend to diversification that supports this mutual intelligibility. This counter-trend is manifested in the standardization of English, not only in its homeland (as evidenced by Standard English), but in other territo-ries (as evidenced by the emergence of newer, national standards) and globally (in a mixing and mingling of national standards into an inter-national standard), and it is manifested also in the levelling influences of mass-media English.

Thus we have arrived at what appears to be a workable distinc-tion between a **dialect** and a **language**. A dialect or variety of English remains so for as long as it shares a common core of features with other dialects or varieties of English. In other words, dialects of the same language are mutually intelligible. Different languages are not mutually intelligible.

There are one or two brief details to add to this. Linguists sometimes use the term **variety** in place of **dialect**, because of the negative connotations that *dialect* has acquired, due to the erroneous popular belief that a regional dialect is *sub*standard rather than *non*-standard. I have used these two terms pretty much interchangeably in this chapter, but in linguistics *variety* is seen as a more neutral alternative to *dialect*, and when national types of a language are being referred to (like Welsh English, Australian English, and New Zealand English), *variety* is generally felt to be more appropriate. In addition, both terms refer to matters of vocabulary, grammar, and pronunciation. The term **accent**, when used in connection with the regional variation of a language, refers to matters of pronunciation only. Some linguists, however, prefer to define **dialect** as regional vocabulary and grammar only, and **accent** as regional pronunciation. This is on the grounds that although a regional accent will 'belong' quite naturally to a regional dialect (for example, a speaker of Welsh-English dialect will have a Welsh-English accent), that accent can become detached from its 'parent' dialect (our Welsh-English speaker might, after years of external influence, end up speaking Standard English with a (usually modified) Welsh-English accent). I bear this in mind throughout this book, but when I refer to regional *dialects* or *varieties*, I use the terms to include pronunciation features (that is, their associated accents). Speakers can also become **bidialectal**, proficient in more than one dialect, and switch from one to the other depending on the formality of the social context, a practice called **code-** or **style-shifting**.

Sad to say, however, our workable distinction between dialect and language is workable only up to a point. Useful it remains, but there are some riders to add, and one can be mentioned immediately. As we have in fact already seen, mutual intelligibility can be partly a subjective business. Thinking back to my encounter with the Glaswegian truck driver, my father (who had heard Scottish dialect before) could make out what he was saying, but I could not. Mutual intelligibility depends not only on the intrinsic characteristics of a dialect but on the state of knowledge of outsiders trying to understand it, and if we take this logic far enough, we will notice that something similar applies to understanding a different language.

Let's remember also that a dialect or variety is quite an impressionistic, abstract entity. Welsh English, for example, is an abstraction.

One could take a map of Britain and draw a line somewhere to the west of the Wales–England border and say, 'This is where Welsh English begins', but it would be wrong to think that all the English spoken to the west of that line as far as the Irish Sea conforms to a single template. Northern Welsh English is distinguishable from southern Welsh English, and there are identifiable sub-varieties within these sub-varieties, including a number of areas which show relatively little influence from the Welsh language. (And there will be a non-standard/standard stratification in each region, correlated with social class.) Each regional division can be justified by the differences we identify between dialects, but within each division there is further diversity. Classifying the dialects or varieties of English involves abstraction. Furthermore, it would be a simplification to draw that line to the west of the Wales–England border, because the boundaries between dialects are not rigid, impermeable or absolute. Not only is there the 'common core' of features connecting dialects, but also there can be non-standard links. There are dialects or varieties of North American and Australasian English which have been influenced historically by the regional dialects of British English. And some of the non-standard vocabulary and grammar that my elderly Welsh-English informant used during our conversations came from English English, like *shippon*, meaning 'cow-house', a very old native, dialectal English word, which had spread into North Wales from north-western England, and demonstrative *them*, as in *them days* in the text above, a very widespread non-standard form. The boundaries between dialects are useful constructs rather than hard facts. It is also worth noting that texts (i) and (ii) above have shown that the boundaries between languages are very permeable too.

## Geographical diversity and the passage of time

My third short text tells us more about the diversity of English. It comes in two versions. Here is the first version:

(iii)  (a)
    Nu scylun hergan     hefænricæs Uard,
    Metudæs mæcti     end his modgidanc,
    uerc uuldurfadur;    sue he uundra gihuæs,
    eci Dryctin,    or astelidæ.

Is it English? It is. The text is in a regional dialect of English, but it is also about 1300 years old. It is the first half of a poem known as *Cædmon's Hymn*, dated to AD 737 and therefore one of the earliest surviving examples of Old English (which lasted from the mid-fifth century to the mid-twelfth). This version of Cædmon's Hymn (taken from Sweet, 1946, p. 166) is one of several in the Northumbrian dialect of Old English, each found in manuscripts of the monk Bede's *Ecclesiastical History of the English People*. Here is a word-for-word translation of the text into the vocabulary of present-day Standard English:

> Now must we praise of the kingdom of heaven the Guardian,
> of the Creator the might and thoughts of his mind,
> works of the glory-father; as he of the wonders of each one,
> eternal Lord, the beginning established.

Original and translation give us some idea of the kinds of changes that have taken place in the language since Old English. Some of the words in the original are no longer used, for example, *Metud* 'Creator', *modgidanc* 'thoughts of mind' (though its first part is modern *mood*), and *eci* 'eternal'. About 85 per cent of Old English words have fallen out of use, though the total vocabulary of English has actually expanded enormously since Old English – there are over a million lexical items in present-day English, not counting most non-standard words, compared with roughly 24,000 in Old English (these statistics are from Crystal, 2003a, pp. 27, 119), and a major reason for this expansion is massive borrowing. Most of the words in the hymn that do survive have changed their form, for example, *Nu* 'now', *hefæn* 'heaven', and *Uard* 'ward'. There are no letter *w*s in the text, and there is one symbol not often encountered in present-day English, *æ*, known as 'ash'. Old English manuscripts use several letters not found in present-day English, these being *þ* 'thorn' (replaced by *th*), *ð* 'eth' (*th* again today), *ʒ* 'yogh' (replaced by *g* or *gh*, or *j* or *y*) and *ƿ* 'wynn' (*w* today). And present-day English has letters not used or rarely used in Old English: *g, j, q, r, s, th, v, w, x*, and *z*. Lastly, the Northumbrian original uses different and more morphological endings (or **inflections**) compared with present-day English, including the genitive singular *-æs* in *hefænricæs*, literally 'heaven-kingdom of', *Metudæs* 'of the Creator', and *gihuæs* 'of each one', and the genitive plural *-a* in *uundra* 'of wonders'. These genitive inflections indicate possession or belonging-to, and their barely surviving remnant (at least in its correct usage) in present-day Standard English is the apostrophe *s*. Old English had a more developed inflectional system than present-day English, and in compensation for the erosion of this, tighter rules concerning the ordering of English syntax have evolved.

The effects on language of the passage of time are relevant to our interest in its geographical diversity and in the distinction between dialects and languages, as we shall see, but I have included the Northumbrian version of Cædmon's Hymn here in order also to compare it with a second version, below:

(iii)  (b)

   Nu we sculan herian      heofonrices Weard,
   Metodes mihte     and his modgeÞonc,
   weorc Wuldorfæder;     swa he wundra gehwæs,
   ece Dryhten,     ord onstealde.

Again this is the first half of the hymn, but this time it is from a version in the West Saxon dialect of Old English. There are spelling and morphological differences between the two versions, although the *w*s in the West Saxon version are modernizations by its editor, Henry Sweet (1946, p. 43). Some of the differences are due to the separate dates of the two versions – the West Saxon is over two centuries later than the Northumbrian. The *-es* and *-e* of the West Saxon (in *heofonrices*, *Metodes*, *mihte*, and *ece*), compared with the *-æs* and *-i* of the Northumbrian, are changes brought about by the passage of time. But most of the differences in spelling are regional differences, with two of them indicating different regional pronunciations: the vowels *-a-* in *Uard* and *-e-* in *uerc* in the Northumbrian beside the *-ea-* and *-eo-* in the West Saxon (the other differences in spelling do not reflect different pronunciations). (My analysis here is based on that of Brook, 1965, pp. 51–2.) Written Old English was not standardized – in the Old English period there was no supraregional standard variety of English, and scribes would have their own regional conventions to follow.

It is highly likely that the contrasts in spoken Old English were more marked still than those in written Old English. The point here is that English was a diverse language from its very beginnings. In fact, at its beginning the English language was less a language and more an assortment of related dialects (Old Englishes perhaps). These dialects were brought to England in the fifth century AD by tribes from the north-western regions of the European mainland. The archaeological record suggests that the most prominent of these incoming tribes were the Angles and Saxons, who settled in the east, the midlands, and the south of England. Another tribe, the Jutes, settled in the south-east corner of the country. There were smaller numbers of other tribes, and later waves of settlers. It took some centuries for the notion of an English nation to develop, and it took around 300 years for the idea to emerge that these tribal dialects constituted a single, *English* language. In its very essence, therefore, English is geographically diverse. Linguists have identified four chief dialects of Old English: Northumbrian, in the north of England; Mercian, through the midlands; West Saxon, through most of the south; and Kentish, in the south-east. The English of England has been subjected to much change since these early centuries, but the geographical diversity of Old English underlies the striking heterogeneity of the traditional rural dialects of England.

My fourth short text helps us make more progess in distinguishing a dialect from a language.

(iv)  Sjoch dêr sit Wopke
mei syn keale holle en syn swarte skuon
Wopke sit tichtby in grutte sleat,
mar Wopke is hiel fersichtich.
Mem hat Wopke in soad oer de sleat ferteld.
Yn 'e sleat wenje ek fisken hat Mem sein.

Is it English? No, it is Frisian. It is a poem about a character called Wopke and it was used in nursery schools in Friesland in the 1970s (according to my source, a 1979 booklet entitled *The Frisian Language*, written by K. Boelens, p. 29). Estimates of numbers of present-day speakers of Frisian vary between 400,000 and 750,000, living mainly in Friesland, a northern province of the Netherlands. Here is a Standard English translation of the poem:

Look there sits Wopke
with his little bald head and his black shoes
Wopke sits close to a broad ditch,
but Wopke is very careful.
Mother told Wopke a lot about the ditch.
Fish live in the ditch too, Mother said.
(Boelens, 1979, p. 29)

I have included the poem here because the Frisian language is the closest relative of the English language. In point of fact, *Old* Frisian and Old English were very probably mutually intelligible. There were Frisians among the continental tribes that settled in England in the fifth century AD, and Old Frisian can be considered a member of the same group of dialects that made up Old English. Boelens (1979, p. 11) thinks that 'Anglo-Saxons and Frisians of the early Middle Ages had no trouble understanding one another', and this is corroborated by the case made by the linguist James Milroy (1996, pp. 174–8) that Old English and Old Frisian 'were so similar that they were probably to a large extent mutually comprehensible' (p. 176). In other words, the differences between Old English and Old Frisian are on a par with the differences between the Northumbrian and West Saxon dialects. Subsequently, English and Frisian have diverged, though close resemblances remain. The divergence has much to do with geographical separation, but we can see now that there are non-linguistic factors that can contribute to our use of the labels **dialect** and **language**. The emergence of the English sense of nationhood is associated with the emergence of English's 'language-hood', and the separation of English and Frisian is linked with political as well as geographical distance. Similarly there are some present-day *languages* which nevertheless have a significant measure of mutual intelligibility – Danish, Swedish, and Norwegian, for example. The mutual-intelligibility test for deciding between calling something a dialect or a language is thus rather frustrated by these basically ideological factors. And even if we filter out ideology, the clear message from my example texts is that the difference between a dialect and a language is a matter of degree, or, as Saussure (1916, p. 193) put it, 'languages and dialects differ quantitatively, not by nature'. They belong to a continuum, a scale of diversity.

## Conclusion

My fifth short text provides a final, brief illustration of the main points of this chapter:

(v)  Da' girl deh don wan fuh dem chillun do nothin fuh me.

Is it English? Arguably. A translation into Standard English would be, 'That girl there does not want the/those children to do anything for me' – but translation does not mean that text (v) is not English already.

The text is a transcription by the linguist Salikoko S. Mufwene of a 1980s recording of Gullah (from Mufwene, 1991, p. 223). Gullah is a **creole**. It is also known as Sea Island Creole and Geechee (a derogatory name), and is spoken by no more than half-a-million people (Mufwene, 2008b, p. 278) along the coastal regions of the south-eastern United States, from Florida to North Carolina. Creoles are usually referred to as languages. The conventional view has been that creoles evolve out of **pidgins**, which are also usually referred to as languages. Pidgins are communication systems which arise between speakers of different languages, or as Ishtla Singh (2000, p. 12) puts it: 'A *pidgin* is a contact language formed from the meeting of at least two mutually unintelligible systems.' In a pidgin we have the mutually intelligible formed from the mutually unintelligible. It is a meeting place of languages. The conventional view is that a creole is a pidgin that has become a mother tongue for a group of speakers. There is another view, put forward (for example) by Mufwene (2008b), who argues that pidgins and creoles are different entities, rather than different stages in the same process. In this view, a pidgin is essentially a trade 'language', which can develop into an **expanded pidgin** of greater complexity. A creole, however, in this view, is a mother tongue because it is a *dialect* of a European language, a dialect that arose in colonial times as a result of sustained, local contact between Europeans and non-Europeans.

Often creoles developed out of contact between the languages of the historical colonial powers of Europe and those of the cultures they colonized and enslaved, and these European languages feature in the classification of creoles as English-based, French-based, Portuguese-based, Spanish-based, and so on. Gullah originates in the mixing of English and at least four mutually unintelligible West African languages. It is one of many English-based creoles and pidgins, which are found chiefly in the Caribbean, West Africa, and the west Pacific.

But note that term *English-based*. It implies what? – a thing which is neither inside nor fully outside English. Mufwene, a leading specialist on Gullah and on creoles generally, maintains that the labelling of English-based creoles and pidgins as languages is ideological, reflecting an essentially imperialist and racist hierarchizing of varieties of English into those within English and those outside it – 'which have been stipulated as separate languages, despite their speakers' claim that they too speak English' (Mufwene, 1997, pp. 182–3). With regard to Gullah, he says (2008a, p. 551), 'A reason commonly invoked to set Gullah apart from other North American English varieties is that it is not intelligible to speakers of other English varieties', adding, 'However, mutual intelligibility is not a reliable criterion for determining whether a particular language variety is a dialect of a language or a separate language.'

There have been various viewpoints on the precise origins of Gullah – when and where it originated, and the relative roles of African languages and English in its makeup. A consensus view is that English is its **lexifier**, that is, its primary source of vocabulary, and that its **phonology** (sound-system) and grammar show West African influence. Mufwene is one of those who argue in favour of strong non-standard English influence on Gullah overall. He also says that it began to form in the early eighteenth century 'on the large South Carolinian and Georgian coastal rice fields' (2008a, p. 552), a few decades after the British colonists and their African slaves arrived in the area. In the mini-illustration (v) above, the particular grammatical usage exemplified by the first *fuh* ('for') is shared by Gullah with other Atlantic English creoles (Mufwene, 2008a, p. 554), and probably indicates underlying West African influence (Weldon, 2006, p. 180). The **plosive** or **stop** *d*-sound found initially in *Da'*, *deh*, *dem* (rather than **fricative** *th-*) occurs in many varieties of English in the Caribbean and the United States (Schneider, 2008a, p. 394). For Mufwene (2008a, p. 551), Gullah is simply 'as much English as other non-standard dialects that evolved concurrently with it'.

What Gullah illustrates for us is the blurriness of the distinction between dialect/variety and language. All the indeterminacy conjured up by the unfailing diversity of English comes together in creoles: they are on the edge of English, either dialect or language, and they show diversity evolving out of diversity – as Mufwene (1997, p. 189) points out, the English that provided vocabulary for creoles was sometimes standard, sometimes non-standard. (It is likely that the English that most influenced Gullah in its early years was that of south-western England (Weldon, 2008, p. 193).)

What we have seen in this chapter is that English has indeed always been diverse, so that we need both a singular and a plural label for the phenomenon: **English**, which emphasizes its core unity, and **Englishes**, which emphasizes its perpetual divergences.

## Further reading

Tom McArthur's *The English Languages* (1998) is a valuable overview of the character of global English at the end of the twentieth century, and of scholars' attempt to describe the phenomenon. Without doubt, the first stop for more detail on varieties of English in Britain and Ireland is *Language in the British Isles* (2nd edn, 2007), edited by David Britain. The British Library's outstanding *Sounds Familiar?* website allows you to listen to many recordings of British English dialects and accents (including northern Welsh English) drawn from the BL's Sound Archive. It can be accessed at: http://www.bl.uk/learning/langlit/sounds/index.html. Also useful is the series of *Celtic Englishes* volumes (1997–2006), edited by Hildegard L. C. Tristram. *International English: A Guide to the Varieties of Standard English* (5th edn, 2008), by Peter Trudgill and Jean Hannah, gives an outline and taster of varieties inside and outside Britain. *World Englishes: The Study of New Linguistic Varieties* (2008), by Rajend Mesthrie and Rakesh M. Bhatt, provides a single-volume survey of English across the world, with an emphasis on 'New Englishes', particularly second-language varieties in the Caribbean, West and East Africa, and South and South-East Asia. *Pidgins and Creoles: An Introduction* (2000), by Ishtla Singh, is a helpful guide to pidgins, creoles, and **creolistics** (the study of pidgins and creoles). *Language Evolution: Contact, Competition and Change* (2008), by Salikoko S. Mufwene, is more complex, but presents an important perspective on pidgins and creoles from a leading specialist. *Changing English* (2007), edited by D. Graddol, D. Leith, J. Swann, M. Rhys and J. Gillen, gives an extended treatment to the central themes introduced in this chapter. Einar Haugen's 'Dialect, Language, Nation' (1966) is the classic essay on the terms **dialect** and **language**.

# 2  Time
## The History and Pre-history of English

---

This chapter includes the following:
- The historical periods of English – **Old English**, **Middle English**, **Early Modern English**, and **Modern English**.
- The **Indo-European** family of languages.
- A guide to processes of **linguistic change**.
- The **Great Vowel Shift** and the **Northern Cities Shift**.
- An introduction to **comparative philology**.

---

## Introduction

In this chapter we travel from *mūs* to *mouse potato*. In doing so, we look at the effects of time on language, because the journey takes us through the ancestry and history (from its origins to the present day) of the English language. *Mūs* is a word from Sanskrit, the oldest known member of the Indo-European family of languages (Sanskrit dates from before 1000 BC), and the story of *mūs* leads in due course to *mouse potato*, a modern phrase from a younger language in the Indo-European family, English.

So we shall see that there is a line of continuity that connects *mūs* and *mouse potato*, but we shall see also that this continuity entails change. The converse of this point is made by the linguist Ferdinand de Saussure in his discussion of the relationship between time and language: 'What predominates in all change is the persistence of the old substance; disregard for the past is only relative. That is why the principle of change is based on the principle of continuity' (1916, p. 74). Saussure discusses (pp. 71–8) two apparently contradictory qualities of any language: first, its **immutability**, that is, its inherent resistance to change, and secondly, its **mutability**, that is, its susceptibility to change caused by the effects of time combined with social forces. Saussure's conclusion is that the elements of any living language will be exposed to alteration precisely

17

because they perpetuate themselves. In other words, linguistic change involves continuity and linguistic continuity involves change. This is something that we shall see evidence of in this chapter, in the particular history of the changing of *mūs* to *mouse potato* and in the wider history and pre-history of English. During the telling of these histories we shall encounter and explore such concepts as Indo-European and language families, as well as some key theories dealing with linguistic change.

## The pre-history of English

Saussure was concerned with showing that there is no such thing as absolute innovation in language, but there does appear to be a type of change that brings an end to continuity, and it is best to deal with this before proceeding further. It is language death. Our modern age of communication, in which several languages (English above all) dominate internationally, threatens also to be an age of mass language extinction. The linguist David Crystal estimated that half of the world's 5000-plus languages – those with fewer than 10,000 speakers each – are in danger of extinction (Crystal, 'Death Sentence', *Guardian*: 'G2', 25 October 1999, p. 2; see also Andrew Dalby's *Language in Danger*, 2002). Nevertheless, in the case of languages, the term *death* can be something of an exaggeration. Even language death can involve continuity. Take, for example, the 'dead' language Latin. Spoken Latin did not so much die as evolve into a group of related languages, the Romance group (French, Italian, Spanish, and others), and Latin in written form persists to this day in limited use, through its association with the Christian church, science, and law. And this is not to mention the Latin or Roman alphabet, now used all over the world for writing hundreds of languages, including English.

Cornish provides a different example of linguistic life after death. The Survey of English Dialects, carried out during the mid-twentieth century (see Orton et al., 1962–71), found nearly 30 words from the extinct Cornish language being used in the English dialects of Cornwall (such as *muryans*, from Cornish *muryon*, 'ants'). Furthermore, some of these Cornish **loanwords** in English were not Cornish in origin but had been borrowed earlier into Cornish from other languages, such as French and Latin (Wakelin, 1975, pp. 180–201, lists all these Cornish loans). **Borrowing** is a process whereby linguistic items – frequently words – are copied from one language into another, something which happens as a matter of course when sustained contact occurs between separate languages, and it (borrowing) can provide a means by which vocabulary from a dead language can survive in a separate living language (though that vocabulary may undergo change as a consequence of its integration into the new host language – witness the plural -s added to Cornish *muryon*, already a plural form in Cornish). Words can outlive their original language by some considerable time, though borrowing is not the only explanation for this, as we shall see.

Saussure's view (2002, p. 102) is that 'A language never dies of inner exhaustion, after having completed its given career.' He contends that, although a language can be exterminated, annihilated by political or colonial force, the normal process is one of change and continuity not death. Thus French is merely a later stage of Latin, and Latin an earlier stage of French.

What of the other end of life's journey? Do languages get born? No – here again we have continuity and change. Saussure says (2002, p. 102), 'The actual birth of a new language has never been reported anywhere in the world', because 'we have never known of a language which was not spoken the day before or which was not spoken in the same way the day before'. (Needless to say, one could construct an argument to show that this view does not apply to artificial languages, but our subject here is natural language.) Languages do not get born, they evolve out of previously existing linguistic situations. The English language is an excellent example of this. There *is* a kind of birth-date for English and it is not entirely contrived. It is the mid-fifth century AD. It was at that time, following the withdrawal of the Roman legions from Britain by the early fifth century, that the south and east of the land began to be settled by Germanic tribes from the European mainland. The Celtic inhabitants of Britain were now joined by Angles (from the south of the Danish peninsula), Saxons (from the coastal plain to the west of the Danish peninsula), Jutes (from Jutland, in the north of the Danish peninsula), Frisians (from the coastal areas to the west of the Saxon lands), and Franks (from western Germany – it was after the Franks that France was named, following their involvement in the conquest of Gaul in the sixth century AD). These newcomers brought with them a diverse group of Germanic dialects, which by the eighth century they had labelled under the umbrella **Englisc**. Thus the 'birth' of English actually involved continuity, and it involved diversity. It took some time for the immigrants' dialects to acquire a new collective identity as English; before their arrival in Britain these dialects already possessed a lengthy Germanic and, beyond that, Indo-European history. What then of that history? And what exactly do the terms **Germanic** and **Indo-European** mean when applied to language? Oddly, this story begins in the late eighteenth century.

In September 1783, the judge and scholar of oriental culture William Jones (1746–94) took up an appointment in Calcutta, India. Some two years later he began to study Sanskrit. Sanskrit is an ancient language of the Indian subcontinent, associated in particular with learned and religious texts. On 2 February 1786, Jones delivered his Third Anniversary Discourse to the Asiatick Society, which contained the following passage:

> The *Sanscrit* language, whatever be its antiquity, is of a wonderful structure; more perfect than the *Greek*, more copious than the *Latin*, and more exquisitely refined than either, yet bearing to both of them a stronger affinity, both in the roots of verbs and in the forms of grammar, than could possibly have been produced by accident; so strong indeed, that no philologer could examine them all three, without believing them to have sprung from some common source, which perhaps no longer exists: there is a similar reason, though not quite so forcible, for supposing that both the *Gothick* and the *Celtick*, though blended with a very different idiom, had the same origin with the *Sanscrit*; and the old *Persian* might be added to the same family.

With these observations Jones effectively set the agenda for language studies in Europe for the following century, right up until the publication in 1916 of Saussure's *Cours de linguistique générale*. **Comparative philology** (or sometimes simply **philology**), as it became known, was the dominant trend in nineteenth-century language studies, and was concerned with examining correspondences and similarities in the vocabularies, grammars, and pronunciation patterns of different languages, with the aim of developing Jones's two main claims: that there were important connections between many of the languages of Europe and south-western Asia, and that a major reason for this was a common, single source for all these languages.

To take one tiny example, *mūs* or *mūsh*, a Sanskrit word which means 'mouse' – it has the same root as a term meaning 'stealer, thief' and possibly its earliest sense is 'the stealing animal'. It is noticeably similar to the English word *mouse*. How come? English *mouse* could be a borrowing, but borrowing is not a particularly plausible explanation for the resemblance between *mūs* and *mouse*. Certainly direct borrowing from Sanskrit to English is out of the question, given that Sanskrit is primarily a language of writing and that there has never been sustained contact between Sanskrit and English. However, could *mūs* have been plucked from Sanskrit by some scholarly English writer and used in an English text, thereafter starting a new (English) life? This is, after all, how thousands of words from Latin, Greek, French, Italian, and Spanish were drawn into English during the sixteenth and seventeenth centuries, under the influence of the Renaissance. No. *Mouse* belongs to the core, native word-stock of English. It can be traced back to **Old English**, the period in the history of the language that stretches from the mid-fifth century AD to not long after the Norman Conquest of England. It is not a borrowing into English, though it is a much-travelled little thing. Versions of *mouse* turn up in many languages. For example, German has *Maus*, which can be traced back to Old High German, a period covering approximately AD 700–1100; Frisian has *mûs*, which goes back to Old Frisian, which lasted from the fifth century AD to the end of the fifteenth; and Dutch has *muis*, which can be traced back to Medieval Dutch. Danish, Swedish, and Icelandic have *mus*, which can be traced back to Old Norse, which lasted from the third to the fourteenth centuries AD. Greek has *mûs* and Latin has *mūs*. Russian has *mysh'* and Polish has *mysz*, both of which can be traced back to Old Slavonic, which dates from the ninth to the end of the fourteenth centuries AD (roughly). And Persian has *mūsh*. *Mūs* therefore looks like a word which has travelled, through time, across considerable distances. The most plausible explanation for the wide occurrence of versions of *mouse* is that, ultimately, they had a single, common source, from which the various forms have gradually, progressively evolved. Hence the word has been given a hypothetical **Indo-European** original form: *\*mūs*. (It is conventional to mark hypothetical, reconstructed forms with an asterisk.)

This, then, is comparative philological thinking in microcosm. Accumulation of great amounts of such data, charting correspondences across many languages, enabled scholars to reconstruct the earliest histories of individual features, and of the languages to which they belong. Of particular interest are **cognates** – words that are 'born together', such as *mouse, Maus, mûs, muis*, and so forth – that is, words which are essentially, historically speaking, the same word, originating in the one source. From this work philologists postulated a common, original source language, known as **Proto-Indo-European** (**PIE**) or **Indo-European** (the latter is the older term, coined by Thomas Young in a book review in 1814). No PIE texts actually exist. It is a hypothetical language, a construct based on the evidence provided by its descendent languages, and its descendent languages are described as members of 'the Indo-European family'. The Indo-European family is just one of between 17 and 30 **language families** (the number depends on the classification method one follows) that have been identified in the world, but it is a family which now embraces about half the world's population. It has many branches, and its genealogy can be shown in the form of a family tree. It was the philologist August Schleicher (1821–68) who first developed (in 1863) the **family-tree model** of Indo-European (he also pioneered the reconstruction of early, hypothetical linguistic forms). Within the family, languages have been placed in smaller groupings, based on the closer resemblance that exists between them. Taking the *mūs*-bearing languages above, English, German, Frisian, and Dutch are four members of the **Germanic** branch of Indo-European. Danish, Swedish, and Icelandic also belong to the Germanic branch, but more specifically to the North Germanic group, while English, German, Frisian, and Dutch belong to West Germanic. Greek is in a group of its own, while Latin belongs to the Italic branch. Russian and Polish are two Slavic languages, and Persian belongs to the Iranian branch. See Figure 1 for my own (simplified) version of the Indo-European family tree.

In the nineteenth century another, broad division between western and eastern Indo-European languages was made, known as the **centum–satem division**. *Centum* is the Latin word for 'hundred', *satem* is the Avestan (an ancient Iranian language) word for 'hundred'. *Centum* begins with a *k*-sound, *satem* with an *s*-sound. It was found that the Indo-European languages could be split into two broad groups: a western group with *k* in its 'hundred'-words, and an eastern group with an *s*-type sound. Of these two variants it is thought that *k* is the original PIE form and *s* a later development which occurred in the east (later still a similar sound change occurred in some *centum* languages, for example, Latin *centum* became French *cent*, with *s*, and Spanish *cento*, with *th*). The neatness of this pattern was unravelled rather by the discovery around the turn of the nineteenth and twentieth centuries of two new geographically eastern branches, Anatolian and Tocharian, which nevertheless proved to be linguistically western, that is, members of the *centum* group. There is a respectable explanation for this discrepancy, and we shall deal with it soon, but the family-tree model by itself cannot account for these exceptions to the *centum–satem*/west–east division.

Another prominent discovery of comparative philology, also concerning regular sound change, is known as **Grimm's Law**, after its chief formulator, the philologist and folklorist Jacob Grimm (1785–1863). Grimm's Law (1822) gave a systematic account of correspondences between certain consonants in the Germanic languages and in other

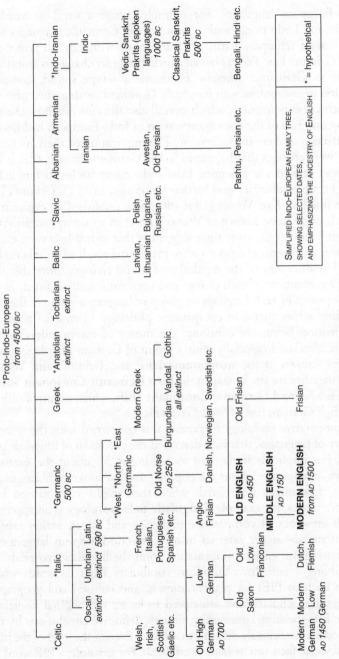

FIGURE 1  SIMPLIFIED INDO-EUROPEAN FAMILY TREE

SIMPLIFIED INDO-EUROPEAN FAMILY TREE,
SHOWING SELECTED DATES,
AND EMPHASIZING THE ANCESTRY OF ENGLISH

* = hypothetical

*Proto-Indo-European
from 4500 BC

*Anatolian
extinct

Tocharian
extinct

Greek

Greek
Modern Greek

*Germanic
500 BC

Gothic
Burgundian Vandal
all extinct

*East
Germanic

*North
Germanic
Old Norse
AD 250

Danish, Norwegian, Swedish etc.

*West
Germanic

Old Frisian
Frisian

Anglo-
Frisian

OLD ENGLISH
AD 450

MIDDLE ENGLISH
AD 1150

MODERN ENGLISH
from AD 1500

Low
German

Old
Low
Franconian
Dutch,
Flemish

Old
Saxon

Modern
Low
German

Old High
German
AD 700

Modern
German
AD 1450

*Italic

Oscan
Umbrian
extinct

Latin
590 BC

French,
Italian,
Portuguese,
Spanish etc.

*Celtic

Welsh,
Irish,
Scottish
Gaelic etc.

*Indo-Iranian

Indic

Vedic Sanskrit,
Prakrits (spoken
languages)
1000 BC

Classical Sanskrit,
Prakrits
500 BC

Bengali; Hindi etc.

Iranian

Avestan,
Old Persian

Pashtu, Persian etc.

Armenian

Albanian

*Slavic

Polish
Bulgarian,
Russian etc.

Baltic

Latvian,
Lithuanian

Indo-European languages. For example, where a word in Sanskrit, Greek, and Latin began with a *p*-sound, the Germanic languages have an *f*-sound (compare Latin *pater* and *piscis* with English *father* and *fish*). Grimm's Law also explained a further regular change to 'hundred'-words in Germanic, whereby *k* became a *h*-type sound (compare, needless to say, *centum* with *hundred*). Grimm's Law described nine sets of such correspondences, which overall also demonstrate how changes in any one area of the consonant system of Indo-European had knock-on effects elsewhere in the system. The implication of the Law is that these were changes that happened in the Germanic branch after it had emerged or as it was emerging from Indo-European but before it had itself begun to diversify into further groupings. In 1875, Grimm's Law was refined by Karl Verner (1846–96), who published an explanation (which came to be known as **Verner's Law**) of apparent exceptions to Grimm's Law, at the same time suggesting that sound-laws were exceptionless: (apparent) exceptions were merely the result of an incomplete law. The discovery of the regularity of sound changes (once the phonetic environment of each change had been sufficiently defined) in the development of each language or group of languages is one of the outstanding achievements of comparative philology. (Two brief points of information before we continue: the theory of exceptionless sound-laws is associated especially with a group of German philologists who became known as the **neogrammarians**; and Grimm's and Verner's Laws together are also known as the **First Germanic Consonant Shift** – there is a **Second Germanic Consonant Shift**, which occurred only in the High German line of West Germanic.)

Comparative philology in general was concerned with the internal history of languages, that is, it described the evolution of linguistic patterns, but implicitly it also had something to say about the 'external' history of languages: about the populations that spoke early languages, where they might have lived, when they might have moved into new territories, for example. **Linguistic palaeontology** is an approach which grew out of comparative philology and which makes explicit statements about the external history of Indo-European languages – by drawing out cultural information from the linguistic materials. By assembling a core Indo-European vocabulary (that is, words which all go back to PIE) for plants, animals, and cultural and geographical features, scholars have attempted to locate the original homeland of the PIE-speaking community, though definitive conclusions by this method are notoriously difficult to achieve. Even at the level of the individual word, facts can be hard to establish. For example, a PIE word for 'beech' has been reconstructed, *$bheh_{a}\hat{g}\acute{o}s$ (Mallory and Adams, 2006, pp. 170–1). It was once thought that the existence of this word in PIE indicated that the homeland of the PIE speakers could not be on the Russian or Asian steppe, because it was thought that the beech tree did not grow east of a line running from the Baltic Sea to the Black Sea, the logic being that if the 'Proto-Indo-Europeans' had a word for the beech then they must have lived in a region where it grew. However, scholars disputed whether a word for beech could be taken back to PIE, and the word-form (arguably) descended from *$bheh_{a}\hat{g}\acute{o}s$ did not uniformly refer to beech in every language (for example, Russian *buzina* means 'elder'), and, moreover, species of beech other than the common beech did occur further east. Other PIE reconstructions have proved similarly problematic. At least we can be pretty sure that the original Indo-Europeans were familiar with mice.

**Glottochronology** (or **lexicostatistics**) is an approach to dating PIE, a kind of 'linguistic version of radiocarbon dating', as J. P. Mallory (1989, p. 276) calls it, in which samples of the vocabularies of languages are analysed statistically in order to estimate the ages of Indo-European branches and of PIE itself. The basic assumption of glottochronology is that as a language diverges into descendent languages, the core vocabulary will be replaced and augmented at a steady rate. Therefore the vocabularies of Indo-European languages can be assessed according to the proportion of core vocabulary that they retain, and estimates about the timelines of Indo-European divergences can be arrived at. For example, two languages whose vocabularies agree little would belong to branches which diverged long ago. This method is potentially informative, but fraught with problems, not the least being its debatable basic assumption of a steady rate of vocabulary decay and innovation.

The methods of linguistic palaeontology and glottochronology are based on theoretical assumptions about the nature of linguistic change. Also underpinning these methods is the notion of the language family, which is itself a model of linguistic change. The family-tree model is a metaphor, and metaphorical models abound in the study of linguistic change. These models can be very useful, but they have their limits. For example, the family-tree model leads us into thinking of the history of Indo-European as a process of divergence: as PIE spread out from its original homeland, carried by its speakers, it diversified into regional dialects, which gradually evolved into separate languages, whose speakers spread further, leading to new dialect regions, and so on. Noah Webster, a contemporary of William Jones, in the context of his (1789, p. 23) discussion of American and British English, described the divergence process rather poetically, predicting that the two varieties (of English) would become 'Like remote branches of a tree springing from the same stock; or rays of light, shot from the same center, and diverging from each other, in proportion to their distance from the point of separation.' The 'global village' has undercut somewhat the divergence of American and British English, by facilitating a certain convergence. In fact, throughout time, dialects and languages have been susceptible to convergence (through contact, for example) as well as to divergence, and this is not shown by the family tree. Convergence also complicates matters for glottochronologists.

The **wave model**, first developed in 1872 by Johannes Schmidt (1843–1901), encourages us to think differently about linguistic change. The wave model presents linguistic innovations as ripples or waves radiating outwards from a central region to peripheries. For example, in this model the Balto-Slavic languages are not only on the periphery of the *s*-innovation-wave of the *satem* languages, but they are also on the periphery of another wave of influences from the Germanic languages. The wave model thus can indicate convergence and divergence, but it is less explicit about the relative times of changes. And the wave hypothesis offers an answer to the anomalous position of the Anatolian and Tocharian branches of Indo-European (their belonging geographically to the broad eastern group but linguistically to the western). If we treat the *satem s*-innovation as a wave, Tocharian, located in Chinese Turkestan, would be outside its periphery. Meanwhile, the main Anatolian language, Hittite, located in the Middle East, would have become extinct before the innovation took place.

Over 200 years of endeavour on the tricky and engrossing subject of Indo-European has not prevented scholars from continuing to search for the Indo-European homeland or from attempting to decipher further the details of Indo-European family relationships. In fact the subject continues to stimulate great interest. In his extensive overview, J. P. Mallory (1989) reaches some tentative conclusions (pp. 262–5). He suggests that the homeland of Proto-Indo-European was centred in the region to the north and west of the Caspian Sea, and that PIE existed as a linguistic continuum, a collection of dialects, social as well as regional, between 4500 BC and 2500 BC (Mallory and Adams (2006) broaden the timescale, estimating from 6000 BC to 3500 BC). Expansion eastwards probably began before 3000 BC, and westwards before that, perhaps from around 4000 BC. Later, during the period 3000 to well beyond 2000 BC, a complex of Indo-European dialects existed in central Europe, out of which developed the proto-languages that head some of the European branches of the Indo-European family, including the Germanic branch.

In recent years, the study of language families in general has been given new impetus by research into the so-called **superfamilies** and by techniques from another field of inquiry, human population genetics research. Russian linguists such as Vitaly Shevoroshkin developed the idea of the **Nostratic** superfamily, out of which, it is claimed, Indo-European and several other language families evolved. Other superfamilies have been proposed. Luigi Luca Cavalli-Sforza (2000) places Indo-European in the **Eurasiatic** (roughly speaking, Nostratic under another name) superfamily, which he dates to between 20,000 and 10,000 years ago. Drawing on linguistic research and research on DNA variation, Cavalli-Sforza produces (p. 169) a tree of origin of human languages which traces all the major modern language families back through a variety of superfamilies to the original, hypothetical family placed in Africa and dated to 100,000 years ago. As for Indo-European, Cavalli-Sforza suggests (pp. 161–2) that a 'pre-Proto-Indo-European' was spoken 10,000 years ago in the area now called Turkey, and that the later expansions of Indo-European westward into Europe generated the Celtic, Italic, and Germanic branches in that order. The sound-changes that helped the pre-Germanic dialect metamorphose into Common or Proto-Germanic were likely to have been occurring around 500 BC, but the Germanic tribes had probably been in their northern Germany/southern Scandinavia homeland since at least the fifth century BC (Mallory, 1989, pp. 86–7). The division into North, East, and West Germanic is likely to have occurred during the early centuries AD, and as we know, in the fifth century AD, West Germanic began to develop a new splinter, English.

## The history of English

But we have neglected our *mouse*. *Mouse*, from Indo-European \**mūs*, via Proto-Germanic \**mūs*, was in Old English *mus*, pronounced 'moos' (that is, with a vowel like that in modern *moon*). In **phonemic** transcription it is /mu:s/ – **phoneme** is the term used by linguists to refer to the chief sound-units in the sound-system of a language. How, then, did it become *mouse*, pronounced 'maus', that is, /maus/? First its spelling changed, and then its pronunciation changed.

The spelling of *mus* changed in two stages, the first of which can be clearly linked to the Norman Conquest of England. In fact, the appearance of major changes in the English language in the century following the Conquest marks the beginning of the **Middle English** period, which lasted until the late fifteenth century. Following 1066, England was governed for over two centuries by a French-speaking elite, a phase of sustained language contact which led to thousands of French loans entering English. Also, a number of French spelling conventions infiltrated the spelling of English. One was the use of the sequence *-ou-* to represent the sound /u:/, as in Old English *mus*, which had the spelling *mous* by the time of Chaucer (late fourteenth century). D. G. Scragg reports (1974, p. 47) that, in the thirteenth century, *u* was a 'heavily overworked symbol in English', employed to represent several different sounds. The use of French *-ou-* for /u:/ in words like *mus* (another example is *hus*, which became *hous*) thus eased the pressure on the letter *u*. The second stage in the change of spelling of *mus/mous* is its acquiring a final *-e*. A small matter, but a rather long tale.

Originally the final *-e* in the spelling of English words was pronounced (as an unstressed vowel), but by the end of the Middle English period it had become silent. Its use in spelling became haphazard, but it did gradually become a device for indicating (especially in monosyllabic words) that the preceding stressed vowel of a word was long, in duration of pronunciation. For example, by the fifteenth century the *-e* in *name* had become silent but remained in the spelling; the stressed vowel in *name* at this time was a long '-aa-' vowel; a similar situation occurred in many monosyllabic words, so that silent final *-e* in spelling became associated with a preceding long vowel. The association never became absolutely regular, but final *-e* did spread to other words whose spelling already possessed an indicator of a long vowel, such as *-ee-*, *-oo-*, and *-ou-* (though it spread to such words only when they ended in certain consonant symbols, listed by Scragg (1974, p. 80)). Thus in Richard Mulcaster's *Elementarie*, a manual of 'the right writing of our English tung [tongue]', published in 1582, the recommended spelling of our word is *mouse* (and *hous* has become *house*).

However, by this time the pronunciation of *mouse* had also changed. Its vowel had become a different type of long vowel – it had become a **diphthong**, sounding very much like its present-day form in **Received Pronunciation** (**RP**), the standard accent of British English, that is, /au/ (a diphthong is a vowel phoneme consisting of two elements). The reason for this? – the **Great Vowel Shift**.

The Great Vowel Shift is the name given (by Otto Jespersen originally, in 1909) to a series of sound changes which thoroughly altered the seven long vowels of Middle English (it did not affect short vowels – a short vowel, naturally enough, is a vowel with a relatively short duration of pronunciation, like, for example, the vowels in modern *pet* and *rat*). The Shift took place during the fifteenth to seventeenth centuries, though some associated changes were still in progress in the late eighteenth century, and it is one of the factors that has led linguists to identify an **Early Modern English** period in the history of the language, which stretches from about 1500–1800. Another factor is evidence of an emerging 'standard' form of English, particularly in writing, following the arrival of printing in 1476. Also during the Early Modern period, the Renaissance and the acquisition of colonies in the Americas, Asia, and Africa stimulated a great influx of foreign vocabulary into English, and increasing anglicization of Wales, Ireland, and Scotland supported the development of Celtic varieties of English. As for the Great Vowel Shift, in addition to the /uː/ of *mouse* three more of the long vowels of Middle English were diphthongized (including the long '-aa-' in words like *name*, which eventually acquired its modern /ei/ diphthong), while the remaining three persisted as simple long vowels, but with new articulations. For example, the /uː/ that occurs in modern RP in words like *food* and *goose* dates only from the Great Vowel Shift – in Middle English such words had vowels articulated with the back of the tongue lower in the mouth than it is for the 'high' articulation of /uː/.

The completion of the Great Vowel Shift marks the beginning of the **Modern English** period, though the Shift was inconvenient for the spelling of English, in that, just as greater regularity was being achieved, a whole series of spelling conventions for representing vowels was being put out of kilter because of changes to the sounds themselves, a situation not helped by the merger of some of the vowels. The *-ea-* and *-ee-* spellings in words like *meat* and *meet* are the vestiges of the distinct vowel pronunciations that these two groups had in Middle English, a distinction erased by the later stages of the Great Vowel Shift (a few *-ea-* words, such as *break* and *great*, merged with the *name* words). But why did the Great Vowel Shift happen? The answer to this question comes in two parts.

There is the 'internal' part, which deals with the structural changes within the vowel system of English. As hinted at above, one of the ways in which vowel sounds are classified by linguists is according to their height. This refers to the relative height of the tongue during articulation – a high vowel is one where a section of the tongue is very high (or 'close') in the mouth, and a low vowel is one where the highest bit of the tongue during articulation is actually quite low (or 'open') in the mouth. When one looks at the Great Vowel Shift in terms of changes to **vowel height**, a basic pattern is apparent: each vowel became higher, with two vowels that were already very high becoming diphthongs (and at a later point two more became diphthongs). There seems to have been a chain of movements, caused either by initial changes at the top which then 'pulled' up the articulations of the lower vowels, or by initial changes at the bottom which then 'pushed' up or diphthongized the higher vowels, or even by changes in the middle which had both a push and a pull effect.

Secondly, there is the 'external' explanation for the Great Vowel Shift, which concentrates not on the structural changes within the language but on the social circumstances which produced them. Recent insight on this has come from **sociolinguistics**, a branch of linguistics in which language is studied in its social context, in connection with factors such as the sex, age, occupation, education, and social class of speakers. One of the main interests of sociolinguistics ever since it emerged in the 1960s has been the study of linguistic change. This is a central concern in the work of William Labov (born in 1927), the chief pioneer of the sociolinguistic approach. In major works on the *Principles of Linguistic Change* (1994, 2001), Labov meticulously assesses the internal and social factors involved in modern sound shifts in progress in English, particularly the **Northern Cities Shift** in the United States. He focuses on the social motivation within white urban communities in the northern United States for changes in vowels, and he identifies 'upwardly mobile female nonconforming speakers' (2001, p. 518) as leaders of what is known in sociolinguistics as '**change from below**', that is, linguistic innovation that occurs below the level of social consciousness. These speakers are 'those women who have the highest degree of social interaction on their local blocks, and the greatest proportion of their friends and contacts outside the block' (p. 501), and who also are individuals who in their youth 'adopted the linguistic symbols of nonconformity' (p. 501). In brief, these are women who are more susceptible to linguistic innovations from outside their immediate neighbourhood, and who also act as carriers or motors of change both within the local neighbourhood and throughout the larger urban speech community, owing to their involvement in social networks within and outside the neighbourhood.

The *Atlas of North American English* (*ANAE*) (Labov, Ash, and Boberg, 2006, pp. 187–215) charts the distributions and details of the Northern Cities Shift across north-eastern United States, from New York State to Wisconsin. Like the Great Vowel Shift, the Northern

Cities Shift is a **chain shift** – a set of phonological movements, but in this case affecting (six) short and long vowels. The stark questions here are why are the short vowels of English shifting for the first time in the history of the language, and why across such a grand swathe of North America? This was how Labov framed the issue at a conference in 2008 (Methods in Dialectology XIII, held at the University of Leeds). His suggestion was that the answers lie in the existence of a large and historical communal identity at work over a sustained period, that the 'mysterious uniformity' of the changes across the Inland North of the United States is 'the product of social forces larger than local identity' (2008a, p. 71). This takes the model of linguistic change onto a broader canvas than the neighbourhood-based picture mentioned above. (There is more on the Northern Cities Shift in Chapter 4.)

Sociolinguistic explanations have also been put forward for the Great Vowel Shift. The Shift was centred in London English, and the socio-linguistic view is that it began as a case of change from below. The interpretation of the details varies, but one suggestion (outlined in Fennell, 2001, pp. 160–1) is that a socially stigmatized merging of the vowels in the *meat* and *meet* groups characteristic of lower-class London-area accents eventually became the socially prestigious set of usages, which then set in train the structural adjustments in the long vowel system.

Before we leave the Great Vowel Shift, it is worth emphasizing its London roots. The prestige pronunciation that in time became Received Pronunciation emerged from London, and the Shift contributed substantially to the make-up of RP, but it affected the regional accents of British English at differing rates, as shown by the Survey of English Dialects and summarized by Leith (1983, p. 146): 'regional pronunciation today often preserves sound-patterns that characterise earlier stages of the [Great Vowel] shift, or even sounds that pre-date it entirely'.

Finally, now we reach *mouse potato* and move from change in pronunciation to change in lexis or vocabulary. There are three main ingredients in the vast vocabulary of English: its core, inherited Germanic word-stock; the huge number of loanwords from other languages, which at different times in the history of English have either trickled or flooded in; and new words, or **neologisms**, created from the existing resources of the language by a variety of processes known collectively as **word-formation**. The last hundred years or so has been rich in English neologisms, owing to swift technological and cultural change and a large increase in the number of English speakers worldwide.

The lexicographer John Ayto estimated (1999, p. iii) that the total of twentieth-century neologisms increased the vocabulary of English by about 25 per cent. But word-formation is by no means a new phenomenon in English. For example, *mouse potato* is a recent **compound**, recorded in the 1997 edition of the *Oxford Dictionary of New Words*, which dates its first use to 1994, but **compounding** is a very old type of word-formation associated with the Germanic languages. It is a major category of word-formation in present-day English, but Old English also had a great capacity for compounding (for example, two Old English compounds are *gærshoppa* 'grasshopper', and *wifman*, literally 'female person', which has evolved into modern *woman*). In compounding, independent words are joined without losing any of their parts. *Mouse potato* is a comparatively weakly joined compound – a hyphen would cement it further, and joining the two words together with no break would complete the bond. There are many types of word-formation in English. **Blending** is a variant on compounding that involves the loss of parts of the constituents (as in *brunch* from *breakfast* and *lunch*). Other major types are: **derivation**, in which new words are formed by adding prefixes (like *extra-*, *non-*, *retro-*, and so on) or suffixes (like *-able*, *-less*, and *-ster*) to an existing form; **abbreviation**, which is the shortening of a word or words (*bus* from *omnibus*, *pub* from *public house*, for example); and **back formation**, which is the reverse of derivation – a word (for example, *babysitter*) is assumed to have derived from an earlier basic form when this has not actually been the case, and a new form is created (*to babysit*).

In word-formation, then, we see change and continuity again – new words made from old constituents. But what of 'word death'? Does this happen? Yes, in that words can become archaic, then obsolescent, and then they fall out of use. For example, much of the vocabulary of Old English has not survived in use (two examples are *dryhten*, displaced by another, synonymous Old English word *hlafweard*, which became modern *lord*, and *wuldor*, pushed out by a synonymous loan from French, *glory*), and many neologisms end up having a short lifespan. Even here, however, there is the possibility of future continuity: for example, *bland*, *hostile*, and *reluctant* are just three of many words deliberately revived by the poet John Milton (1608–74) in his writing, and lexical revivalism is in no way restricted to Milton or to the seventeenth century.

But back to *mouse potato*. What is a *mouse potato*? A *mouse potato* is not the horrendous outcome of a genetic experiment, but 'a person who spends an excessive amount of time in front of a computer, especially one who uses it online' (according to the *Oxford Dictionary of New Words*, 1997). *Mouse potato* is a variation on the earlier (1970s) and similarly facetious compound *couch potato*, 'someone who spends leisure time passively or idly sitting around, especially watching television or videotapes' (Ayto, 1999, *20th Century Words*). The *mouse* in *mouse potato*, therefore, has the sense 'a small hand-held device which is moved over a flat surface to produce a corresponding movement of a cursor or arrow on a VDU' (*Oxford English Dictionary Online*, 2002). This sense, dated to the 1960s, is a **widening** or **extension** of the meaning of *mouse*, and is therefore an example of **semantic** change. The meaning of a word can also be **narrowed**, as in the case of *meat*, which in Old English meant simply 'food' (though this was a widening of an even earlier Germanic sense), and of *wife*, which in early Old English meant 'woman'. Semantic change takes other forms as well, for example, **amelioration**, in which a word with a 'negative' sense develops a 'positive' sense (as with *nice*, which in Middle English meant 'foolish'), and **deterioration**, which is the reverse of amelioration (for example, *garble*, a fifteenth-century loan from Italian, originally meant 'cleanse, sift, cull' in English).

In *mouse potato*, then, we have something old (*mouse*, from Indo-European *\*mūs*), something new (the sense 'computer peripheral' for *mouse*, the figurative use of *potato*, the compounding of *mouse* and *potato*), something borrowed (*potato* is a sixteenth-century borrowing into English from Spanish) . . . all that is missing is something blue, but maybe that is what the mouse potato spends his time online looking for. (Older readers might flinch at this joke's lack of taste, and of course its lack of wit, but I speculate that younger readers might even wonder what the joke is, owing to the possible **obsolescence** of this sense of adjectival *blue*, that is, its falling into disuse. It means here 'indecent, obscene', and (as of 2009) the *OED*'s most recent citation for it is from 1965. It also provides us with an excellent example of partial deterioration – the chief meaning of *blue* remains unaffected). Other mouse potatoes can spend their time looking up the *Oxford English Dictionary Online*, where they will find much more concerning *mouse*, including the many other compounds it has been involved in since Old English.

## Conclusion

In summary, a living language will be subjected to the effects of time, which ensure that the language changes. This is the general picture, but, as we have seen, linguistic change is not a uniform process – it has a variety of more particular causes and guises, and it can affect a language on a variety of levels, such as vocabulary, pronunciation, and spelling (the following chapter, 'Contact', looks at a major episode of change involving the grammar of English). In addition, linguistic change generally involves continuity, or as Saussure says, 'the persistence of the old substance'. Another theme implicit rather than explicit in this chapter has been the contribution to change of the essential variability of language – for example, the dialects of a language can diverge into separate languages over time. And the processes of change that affect English in general are also at work in its dialects and its slangs, and these dialects and slangs also impact on one another through intra-language borrowing – *mouse potato* began as a slang term. Will it survive in active use, or will it go the way of *mouse* in the sense of 'a muscle', now obsolete? Is it already obsolescent? Time will tell.

## Further reading

Albert C. Baugh and Thomas Cable's *A History of the English Language* (5th edn, 2002) is an authoritative and respected single-volume account, and Charles Barber's *The English Language: A Historical Introduction*, revised by Joan C. Beal and Philip A. Shaw (2nd edn, 2009), is a slimmer, highly readable overview. *A History of English: A Sociolinguistic Approach* (2001), by Barbara A. Fennell, presents a narrative informed by research in sociolinguistics. The multi-volume *Cambridge History of the English Language* (1992–2001), general editor Richard M. Hogg, charts in detail the story of English and its spread beyond the British Isles, with many contributions by leading specialists. *In Search of the Indo-Europeans: Language, Archaeology and Myth* (1989), by J. P. Mallory, is an excellent summary of the Indo-European topic, and Mallory's research is developed further in the impressive *Oxford Introduction to Proto-Indo-European and the Proto-Indo-European World* (2006), co-written with Douglas Q. Adams, which attempts a reconstruction of PIE. For even more historical context, try Nicholas Ostler's *Empires of the Word: A Language History of the World* (2005). *A History of English Spelling* (1974), by D. G. Scragg, and *A History of English Words* (2000), by Geoffrey Hughes, provide comprehensive surveys of English orthography and vocabulary respectively. See also *The Handbook of Language Variation and Change* (2003), edited by J. K. Chambers, Peter Trudgill and Natalie Schilling-Estes, for a broad introduction to the study of linguistic change from the sociolinguistic, variationist perspective. *Language Change: The Interplay of Internal, External and Extra-Linguistic Factors* (2002), edited by Mari C. Jones and Edith Esch, is a useful collection, and you can see some of William Labov's work by visiting his website, at: http://www.ling.upenn.edu/~wlabov/.

# 3 Contact
## The Case of Middle English

This chapter includes the following:
- What caused **Middle English**?
- The influence of Old Norse, French and Latin on English between AD 450–1500.
- **Inflections** and **word order** in English.
- The difference between a **synthetic** and an **analytic** language.

## Introduction

Contact is always potentially momentous because it contains the promise – or threat – of change. Our lives are full of contact, with friends, with lovers, neighbours, colleagues, teachers, bacteria, viruses, and so on. Contact can change your life. So what happens when languages come into contact with each other? This chapter looks at contact and language – specifically it looks at probably the most significant contact episode in the history of the English language, when, following the Norman Conquest of England in 1066, it appears that English changed enormously.

I say 'probably' and 'appears' because I am hedging my bets. I could simply go along here and now with Albert C. Baugh and Thomas Cable in their authoritative history of the language (2002), where they say (p. 158), 'The Middle English period (1150–1500) was marked by momentous changes in the English language, changes more extensive and fundamental than those that have taken place at any time before or since.' This they say at the start of a section headlined 'Middle English a Period of Great Change'. But if I did go along with them I would have to ignore N. J. Higham in his brief history of the Norman Conquest (1998), where he says (p. 109), 'The English language survived the Normans comparatively unaltered.' It may well be wise to be circumspect when telling the early history of the English language, by which I mean the centuries covered by the terms **Old English** and **Middle English**, that is, the fifth to early twelfth and the early twelfth to late fifteenth respectively. The documentation is comparatively sparse. The number of English texts surviving from the period up to the late fourteenth century is quite small, and important questions about a text often cannot be answered precisely: questions like, Who wrote it? When was it written? and Where was it written? Nonetheless, I feel confident in saying that Higham is wrong: English does appear to have changed enormously during the centuries following the Norman Conquest – but, appearances can be deceptive.

To clarify: it is true that English appears to change enormously in its grammar and its vocabulary, and its spelling also changes noticeably. It is the manifestation of these changes in English texts that, after all, led linguistic scholars to distinguish a new period in the language's history – Middle English. But what is uncertain is the extent to which the changes are due to the effects of the Norman Conquest. Although the changes *appear* to begin some time after 1066 – thereby marking the inauguration of the Middle English period – they may *in fact* have already begun before 1066. If this is true, then 'Middle English' actually began before the 'Middle English' period! So we have something of a conundrum. We can answer it by tackling Baugh and Cable's headline 'Middle English a Period of Great Change': is it true?

## Middle English and grammatical change

Compare the following two sentences:

(a) And se cyng syððan Þone castel æt Bures gewann 7 Þes eorles men Þærinne genam.

(b) Him com togænes Willelm eorl of Albamar, Þe Þe king adde beteht Euorwic, 7 te other æuez men mid fæu men.

The first example dates from around AD 1094 and the second from about AD 1155, and taken together they indicate significant change in the English language.

Both of the above examples are extracts from a medieval text known as the *Peterborough Chronicle*. The *Peterborough Chronicle* is one version of the *Anglo-Saxon Chronicle*, a year-by-year history of Britain and the Christian world. There are seven surviving versions of the Anglo-Saxon Chronicle, the earliest dating from the ninth century. The *Peterborough Chronicle*, written at Peterborough Abbey during the early to mid-twelfth century, falls into two main sections, each identified according to the years it chronicles. Thus the first main section is a historical record which goes from the year AD 1 up to the year AD 1121, and the second covers the years AD 1122–54. The first section was copied from another, unknown source, whereas the second section was composed at Peterborough. In other words, the first section consists of unoriginal, copied annals whereas the second consists of original continuations of the Chronicle. The first short extract above comes from the copied annals while the second comes from the final continuation. The first extract refers to the year 1094, and it was probably originally composed shortly after 1094 and copied later at Peterborough. The second extract refers to 1138, and was composed at Peterborough around 1155. The differences between the two extracts are sufficient to justify the rather bold assertion that the first extract is Old English while the second is Middle English. A more circumspect way to put it is to say that the two extracts indicate a language in transition, from the features and conventions of Old English to those of Middle English.

The copied annals of the *Peterborough Chronicle* are indeed written in Old English. More precisely, they are written in the literary West Saxon dialect that is common for Old English texts from the late tenth century onwards. The Peterborough continuations, however, increasingly show Middle English characteristics, although habits associated with Old English still persist. The extracts above illustrate the transition. To appreciate this we need two modern English translations of each extract. The first translation has to be as near to word-for-word as we can manage, as follows:

(a) And the king then the castle at Bures won and the earl's men therein captured.

(b) Him came against William Earl of Aumale, that the king had entrusted York, and the other reliable men with few men.

Also we want a translation that looks more naturally modern, as follows:

(a) And then the king won the castle at Bures and captured the earl's men inside.

(b) Earl William of Aumale (to whom the king had entrusted York) and other reliable men came to fight him with a small force.

Setting aside questions like, Where is Bures? (northern France), Who was 'the king'? (William II of England in 1094, Stephen of England in 1138, both Normans), Where is Aumale? (northern France again), and the fact that 'Him' in the second extract refers to David, king of Scotland (Earl William of Aumale, a supporter of Stephen of England, met David of Scotland in battle), *the* question is, What is it that makes the second pair of translations more naturally modern than the first pair?

The answer is to do with **word order**, primarily. Take, for example, the verbs *gewann* ('won' or 'conquered') and *genam* ('captured'). In the original of extract (a) these verbs are placed in clause-final position, after the object of the verb. Extract (a) consists of two clauses, joined by 7 'and'. (One characteristic of Old English manuscripts is the use of a large, 7-like symbol as an abbreviation for 'and'.) The object of the first clause is *þone castel æt Bures*, and the object of the second clause is *þes eorles men þærinne*. This positioning of the verb looks peculiar in modern English, as we can see from the first translation. In modern English we expect the verb to be closer to its subject – often immediately after the subject and certainly before the object. Hence, 'And the king then the castle at Bures won and the earl's men therein captured' looks peculiar, while 'And then the king won the castle at Bures and captured the earl's men inside' looks unexceptional (the subject of both clauses is 'the king'). This difference between the original of (a) and its second translation indicates a general difference between Old English and modern English. Old English can be classified as a **synthetic** language, whereas modern English is an **analytic** language. In a synthetic language, greater flexibility in word order is possible, that is, greater freedom in the order in which the parts of a sentence or of a clause occur, parts like the subject, verb, and object. In an analytic language, word order is more fixed, and in modern English the order is typically SVO: subject–verb–object. The advantage of fixed word order is that it counteracts ambiguity. In modern English we know that the noun preceding a verb (in a clause) is likely to be its subject, not its object. In the two originals above, there is only one clause with a modern SVO-type construction, *þe þe king adde beteht Euorwic*, 'that the king [S] had entrusted [V] York [O]'. Cecily Clark, in the Introduction to her edition of the *Peterborough Chronicle* (1970, p. lxxii), uses this clause to illustrate how the final continuation shows a tendency towards greater rigidity in one facet of word order: the positioning of the verb. Final placing of the verb (which we see in extract (a)) occurs less often in the final continuation than it does in the (earlier) copied annals – in other words, there is a movement under way towards the modern SVO norm and away from flexibility in positioning the verb. This is occurring, says Clark, in order to counteract ambiguity.

Two more questions now arise. Why then, in the originals above, are the non-SVO clauses not ambiguous? And how in a synthetic language, like Old English, with flexible word order, is ambiguity avoided? The two issues are connected. Taking the second question first, another characteristic of a synthetic language is its dependence on **inflections**. Inflections are usually endings attached to words (sometimes inflections change the form of a word in other ways), and they signal the different functions of words within sentences. Modern English has a few inflections; for example, verbs can be inflected, as with the -s added to *talk* when it is used in the third-person singular (*she talks*), or with the -ed inflection that indicates past tense (*talked*). Modern English nouns are inflected for number, often by adding an -s to show that a noun is plural (*girls, boys*). Old English, however, had a much more developed system of inflections. In Old English, nouns were inflected for grammatical gender (every noun was classified as either masculine, feminine, or neuter), number, and case (that is, according to whether a noun was the subject, object, or indirect object (a recipient or beneficiary of an action, rather than the direct object of an action), and there was an additional case to show whether a noun was the possessor of something – this is the genitive case, which survives in modern English as 's). In Old English, pronouns, adjectives, numbers, and the definite article (*the* in modern English) also had the four cases that nouns had. In fact, in the first clause of extract (a) we can see the subject-noun *cyng* preceded by its corresponding subject form of the definite article, *se*, and the object-noun *castel* preceded by its corresponding object form of the definite article, *þone* – thus here the functions of these nouns are indicated by the differing forms of the definite article. The endings of Old English verbs also change according to number (singular or plural), tense, and person – as they still tend to in modern English.

With such a highly developed inflectional system, word order can be more flexible, because relationships between words in a sentence can be signalled by inflections instead (though this is not to say that complete freedom in word order existed in Old English). By the time of the final continuation of the *Peterborough Chronicle*, however, such orders as we find in the earlier extract, that is, subject–object–verb (SOV), are at increased risk of ambiguity. Why?

It is because of massive loss of inflections. According to Cecily Clark, the Chronicle's continuations show a great reduction in inflections for nouns, pronouns, and adjectives. As a consequence of this loss of inflection, greater restrictions are placed on word order, and constructions like those in the extract (a), with finally located verbs, are becoming less viable. Clark notes (1970, p. lxxii) that, in the final continuation, 'The place immediately before the verb now belongs to its subject and can be taken by another noun only when the meaning is unmistakable' – either because of remaining inflections or because of the context. As a general rule, if subject-noun, object-noun, and indirect-object-noun can no longer be distinguished by inflections, one would expect them to take up fixed positions in relation to the verb, hence the element of choice in positioning the verb is reduced. Clark sees this beginning to happen in the continuations of the *Peterborough Chronicle*: 'The syntax of the Peterborough Continuations is, then, at a very revealing stage: before our eyes English is beginning to change from a synthetic language to an analytic one' (p. lxxiii).

The multiplicity of inflections characteristic of Old English was greatly simplified by the late Middle English period, and the *Peterborough Chronicle* shows us the transition. Next question: Why did it happen?

The obvious answer would be that the arrival of many French speakers in England as a result of the Norman Conquest led to significant language contact between French and English, with much bilingualism, which had the effect of simplifying the complexities in English grammar. The transition evidenced by the *Peterborough Chronicle* seems to support this: the simplification seems to take place between the end of the eleventh century and the middle of the twelfth. But while it is true that the Norman Conquest led to much French-speaking and bilingualism in England, this answer does not work. Why not?

The evidence in the *Peterborough Chronicle* is not quite what it seems. As Clark herself points out (1970, p. xliv), the language of the copied annals is archaic and demonstrates the persistence of the old West Saxon literary archetype rather than being a reflection of contemporary speech habits. The language of the copied annals is a relic. The transition that the *Peterborough Chronicle* shows is illusory, given that the language used in its copied annals was already out of date by the end of the eleventh century. Indeed Baugh and Cable note (2002, p. 159) that there is evidence of levelling of inflectional distinctions in Old English manuscripts dating from the tenth century. The Old English inflectional system depended greatly on sound-distinctions, for example, distinctions represented by the vowels *a*, *e*, *o*, and *u*. But such sound-distinctions as these are difficult to maintain in unstressed, word-final syllables, as in, for example, the masculine singular genitive *cyninges* 'king's' contrasted with the masculine plural subjective *cyningas* 'kings', or the masculine singular dative *cyninge* 'to the king' contrasted with

the masculine plural genitive *cyninga* 'kings' '. *Cyning* is put into the category of 'strong' nouns by language historians – there were also 'weak'
nouns, which had different sets of case endings from the strong nouns.
In addition, feminine nouns and neuter nouns had different sets of case
endings, for example, strong feminine nouns had inflections consisting of *-u, -e, -a*, and *-um*, and strong neuter nouns had *-es, -e, -u, -a*,
and *-um*. The full run for strong masculine nouns is *-es, -e, -as, -a*,
and *-um*. Once such sound-distinctions become blurred, inflections are
put at risk. The prolonged use of the West Saxon literary archetype
masked inflection-loss: the copied annals of the *Peterborough Chronicle*
preserved a situation that no longer obtained in speech.

The dramatic loss of inflections between copied annals and later
continuations is now explained by the continuations being more representative of the contemporary state of the language than are the copied
annals. Just to emphasize an important point about the transition overall: we are not looking at a change from a language absolutely dependent
on inflections to one absolutely dependent on rigid word order, because
there is evidence of conventions of word order in Old English, and
because inflections survive in modern English. Rather we are looking at
a movement from lots of inflections to fewer, allied with a move from
flexibility in word order to less flexibility. And the move was gradual.
The introduction of French into England on a large scale may have
intensified the process, but the simplification of Old English grammar
was already under way before 1066. Why?

Because, as I have already suggested, an inflectional system dependent on sound-distinctions between vowels in unstressed syllables is
inherently vulnerable, and also because of contact – but between
English and Norse, not English and French.

Late in the eighth century, England began to be attacked by Vikings.
These Vikings came from the territories known today as Denmark and
Norway. Vikings began to settle in England in the second half of the
ninth century, and by AD 870 most of east and northern England was
under the control of the 'Danes' (as they were called by the English),
who now threatened the west of England. After their defeat by the
Saxon King Alfred of Wessex, in AD 878 at the Battle of Edington,
the Scandinavians were confined to the 'Danelaw', that is, the eastern half of the country, from modern Northumbria to Essex. But this
did not end the Viking trouble. The early years of the eleventh century saw more invasions and in 1016 Cnut, a Viking, became king of
England. Danes ruled England for the next 25 years. Contact between
the English and the Vikings was thus rather turbulent but it was also

lengthy and extensive. From AD 850 onwards, Scandinavians settled in large numbers in the north and east of England. There was peaceful contact as well as hostile, and gradually Scandinavians and English mixed and merged; and there was, already, an ancestral kinship between the peoples.

The language of the Vikings is known as Old Norse, and is a close relative of Old English. The various dialects that made up Old English were themselves brought to the British Isles by incomers from Denmark and its nearby regions, beginning in the fifth century, and arguably there was some mutual intelligibility between Old Norse and the dialects of Old English. Baugh and Cable (2002, p. 104) say, 'in many words the English and Scandinavian languages differed chiefly in their inflectional elements. The body of the word was so nearly the same in the two languages that only the endings would put obstacles in the way of mutual understanding.' According to this view, the mixed, intermingling populations of the Danelaw spoke languages that were similar enough to facilitate and encourage linguistic mixing and intermingling, which in turn encouraged the simplification of English grammar – a process which happened at a varied pace across the country. For example, at Peterborough, which was in the Danelaw, the continuations of the Chronicle show a levelling of noun plural inflections, whereas this levelling had not yet reached western and southern dialects (Clark, 1970, pp. xlviii–xlix). David Crystal (2003a, p. 32) points out that Middle English texts show that in the matter of grammatical change the Danelaw was more progressive than the rest of the country. Change began there. The sociolinguist James Milroy (1996, pp. 177–8) agrees that contact between English and Norse led to grammatical innovation in the Danelaw, but he has a different view of the contact process. He is sceptical about the mutual intelligibility of the varieties of Norse and English spoken in the Danelaw, but suggests that the sustained contact led, by the late tenth century, to the evolution of an 'Anglo-Norse koine', a kind of amalgam-language, which 'was used for supra-local communication within England' (p. 177), and which had a marked influence on the development of Middle English.

To summarize so far: the most important difference between the grammar of Old English and that of Middle English – loss of inflection (one further consequence of which, incidentally, was the elimination of grammatical gender) – seems to have begun well before Middle English began. 'Middle English a Period of Great Change': not true? Not that simple. The *Peterborough Chronicle* has more to tell us.

# Middle English and spelling and lexical change

There are other innovations in the continuations of the *Peterborough Chronicle*, in spelling conventions and vocabulary. In spelling, for example, native English ʒ'yogh' is replaced by *g* from the Carolingian or Caroline script developed in France at the time of Charlemagne (AD 742–814), and þ 'thorn' and ð 'eth' are sometimes replaced by *th*, as in *other* in the original extract (b) above, again due to the influence of Franco-Latin conventions. Eventually yogh, thorn, and eth died out in English altogether, with the most common replacement for yogh being *gh*. The Middle English period ushered in more than a few new spelling conventions. For example, *qu* replaced *cw* in such words as *cwen* 'queen' and *cwic* 'quick', *a* began to be used in place of æ 'ash', *w* began to be used in place of p'wynn', and the letters *j*, *v*, and *z* were introduced. These changes we *can* pin on the Normans, who introduced French-trained scribes into England after the Conquest. A new spelling tradition was now imposed upon English, with the result that, by the end of the Middle English period, English spelling had become a very interesting mixture of two systems – the remnants of Old English conventions plus a liberal sprinkling of French conventions.

In vocabulary or **lexis**, the Peterborough continuations contain a significant number of new words drawn from three sources: Norse, Latin, and French.

The Norse loans, as Clark puts it, 'show intimate penetration of English by Norse grammar' (1970, p. lxix), and include, for example, the grammar-words *oc* 'but', *um* 'about, through', and *til* 'until, to'. This is a striking characteristic of the effects of contact between English and Norse during the ninth, tenth, and eleventh centuries. It is not unusual for one language to 'loan' vocabulary to another language, that is, for words belonging to one language to cross over and start another life in another language. Such words are termed **borrowings** or **loanwords**. Many everyday words crossed from Old Norse into Old English as a result of Viking settlement in England, for example, nouns such as *birth, husband, leg, skirt*, and *sky*, and verbs like *to call, die, give, nag, take*, and *thrust*. Baugh and Cable state (2002, p. 105) that the number of confirmed Scandinavian loanwords surviving in modern Standard English is about 900, but an equal number of probables could be added to these, and many more survived in the dialects of the former Danelaw, such as *beck* 'stream', *dag* 'to drizzle', and *laik* 'to play'. It is much rarer for borrowing to affect those parts of speech more closely integrated into grammar, but, for example, the pronouns *they, their*, and *them* came into English from Old Norse, as did *are*, the present plural form of the verb *to be*, and also the *-s* inflection of the third-person singular present tense of verbs. These and other 'intimate' loans can be taken as evidence either of the helpful similarity between Old English and Old Norse or of the prolonged contact between the two cultures, or, of course, as evidence of both.

The influence of Latin goes back to the very beginnings of English. The Germanic tribes who founded English had already come into contact with the Romans in continental Europe, before they (the Germanic tribes) started to settle in the British Isles. Once they were there, more Latin loans entered their language, this time borrowed from the British Celts, who had got them from the Romans. Latin was the language of the Christian church and as such it infiltrated English to a greater extent from AD 597, which marked the start of England's conversion to Christianity. Borrowing from Latin was given a new impetus at the start of the Middle English period because the practice of writing documents in Latin was at that time comparatively common among the Norman scribes. This would have encouraged the use of Latinisms in English texts. Clark notes (1970, p. lxii), for example, the new borrowings – indeed their first occurrences in English – *cardinal, concilie* 'council', and *legat* 'legate' in the *Peterborough Chronicle*.

Clark also notes a small number of new loans from French in the continuations of the Chronicle, such as *duc* 'duke' and *Pasches* 'pasch, Easter', including some which were not only new additions to English but also eventually replaced existing English words, such as *tresor* 'treasure' and *pais* 'peace', which elbowed aside *gersume* (itself a Norse loan) and *frið* respectively. Another, *iustise* 'justice', elbowed aside *rihtwisnesse*, but with a different result: *rihtwisnesse* did not exit the English language – it survives as *righteousness*. If *iustise* had not entered English, it is feasible that *righteousness* would now encompass the meanings expressed by both *justice* and *righteousness*. That is, if not for the French loan, one word might occupy the semantic space currently occupied by two.

This development – the appearance of French loans – can best be summed up by the use of a tired old cliché, a trickle that turned into a flood. By the end of the Middle English period, over 10,000 French words had been adopted. This is a very substantial number – 'unbelievably great' say Baugh and Cable (2002, p. 169) – especially given that the estimated total word-stock of Old English is 24,000 (Crystal, 2003a, p. 27). Like the *Peterborough Chronicle* examples, the French loans in general fall into two broad categories: either simply additions to the English language expressing new concepts, or additions which had a similar meaning to an existing English word. This kind of duplication would result in one of two things: either one word would be lost eventually (more frequently the English word), or a differentiation in meaning between the duplicates would develop. For example, Old English *leod* was pushed out altogether by French-derived *people*, whereas English *might* survives beside French-derived *power*, *kingly* beside *royal*, and *wish* beside *desire*. Many near-synonyms came about. Small differences in meaning can be allied with contextual or idiomatic restrictions. For example, we say *the royal family*, never *the kingly family*, and genies grant *three wishes* rather than *three desires*.

The trickle of French loans at the start of the Middle English period began an influx that has never stopped. Nevertheless over 40 per cent of all the French loans in English came in during the thirteenth and fourteenth centuries (Baugh and Cable, 2002, p. 178). How did it happen?

The obvious answer would be that just as contact with Vikings led to change in the vocabulary of the English language, so did contact with Normans lead to similar change, though on a much bigger scale. But while it is true that there was contact between Normans and English, this answer does not work. Contact was different in each case, and the sheer volume of French loans requires more explaining. Two hundred years of cheek-by-jowl proximity between Vikings and English led to intimate loans but not, it seems, to vast quantities of them. In contrast, the Norman-French in England were a ruling elite, restricted in number. For over two hundred years following the Conquest, England was governed by Frenchmen or by rulers with important French connections, but throughout this time English alone remained the language of the great majority of the population. And yet 10,000 French words were adopted. That itself is some French connection, but the historian M. T. Clanchy, in his *England and Its Rulers, 1066–1272* (2006, p. 41), says, 'It cannot even be proved that the Norman conquerors in the second and subsequent generations spoke French as their mother tongue' (though Baugh and Cable argue that French-speaking was more persistent than this).

The Normans are an odd case. They were a powerful military race, who by the end of the eleventh century held lands in northern France, England, Sicily, and southern Italy. But also, for conquerors, they had a remarkable tendency to embrace the cultures and languages of the peoples they subjugated. The Normans were in fact originally Vikings, 'Northmen'. Around AD 900 they settled in north-west France, in territory which became known as Normandy. Within a couple of generations they had shifted from speaking Norse to French, and they had become Christians. The English of the time called them Franks or French. In the century following the Conquest of England, English-speaking increased while French-speaking among the conquering classes decreased. Writing in the second half of the twelfth century, Richard Fitz Nigel comments, 'nowadays, when English and Normans live together and intermarry, the nations are so mixed that it can scarcely be decided who is English by birth and who is Norman' (1177, edition of 1950, p. 52). The fusion of the two peoples, as Baugh and Cable (2002, p. 119) put it, was rapid. Given all this, we might expect French influence on English to be shortlived and much less than it was. Once more then: why the 10,000 French loans?

First, what were they like? That is, how can we characterize the loans? Were they, for example, 'intimate'? Promiscuous? Not really. Ubiquitous? Yes. Baugh and Cable (2002, pp. 169–74), listing many examples, try to categorize the loans into governmental and adminis-trative words (like *government* and *administer*), ecclesiastical words (like *religion*, *vicar*, and *creator*), legal words (like *crime*, *judgement*, and *pun-ishment*), military words (like *army* and *navy*), words to do with fashion, food, and social life (like *button*, *mutton*, and *conversation*), words to do with art, learning, and medicine (like *painting*, *volume*, and *malady*), before they concede that the French contribution to Middle English vocabulary was 'universal' (p. 173). Some 75 per cent of the 10,000 survive in modern English.

Baugh and Cable also mention (p. 178) a small but revealing survey carried out in the early twentieth century by the linguist Otto Jes-persen, presented in his *Growth and Structure of the English Language* (first published 1905; ninth edition 1952, pp. 86–7), and showing more precisely when French words arrived in English. Taking 1000 French loans (later supplemented with further samples) and their first occurrences in English as recorded by the *Oxford English Dictionary* (first published between 1884 and 1933), Jespersen shows that very few appeared between AD 1050 and 1200. The number rises between 1200 and 1250, but the period 1250–1400 has the biggest totals. From 1400 to 1900 there is a levelling off. A follow-up survey by Baugh (1935), using a refined methodology, showed the same basic pattern. Baugh and Cable (2002, pp. 114–26) argue for a variegated bilingual situation in England during the twelfth century, with continued but declining use of French and acquisition of English in the upper classes, a little acqui-sition of French by native English speakers lower down the social scale, and greater acquisition of English by middle-class Anglo-Normans.

In the first half of the thirteenth century, French in England waned seriously, never to recover. By the beginning of the fourteenth century, English was 'once more known by everyone' (Baugh and Cable, 2002, p. 143). The period of the rising and then the greatest influx of loans coincides with the abandonment of French-speaking and adoption of English-speaking by the ruling and middle classes in England. In this context, Jespersen's survey suggests that the majority of medieval French loans into English were not so much 'borrowed' by the English as carried over by the governing classes as they gradually lost their French. (This is paralleled by the great popularity of French-derived personal names among the middle classes by the early thirteenth century, as noted by Clanchy (2006, p. 39) – this is one reason why Richard Fitz Nigel had difficulty telling Normans and English apart.) A bilingual community embodies an intense form of language contact and a transitional, temporary communal bilingualism is an excellent vehicle for the transfer of words from one language to another.

## Conclusion

Middle English a Period of Great Change? Certainly the English of AD 1500 was very different from Old English, in grammar and vocabulary especially, and great changes in the word-stock happened between 1150 and 1400, but the metamorphosis of English grammar began well before 1100. The main causes of change were the passage of time, of course, and *contact* (a word, by the way, borrowed into English in the seventeenth century, from Latin), though, as the Middle English period illustrates, the changes and processes associated with language contact are various. If we take this chapter together with the two preceding, and the two following, we can see in wider perspective the interconnection between the effects of contact, time and geographical diversity on the shaping of the English language. To sum up this chapter: placing all of the changes we have looked at here neatly into the Middle English period is something of a simplification, but there is no doubt that between the eighth and fifteenth centuries English was greatly and extraordinarily affected by contact.

## Further reading

*A History of the English Language* (5th edn, 2002), by Albert C. Baugh and Thomas Cable, includes a detailed summary of Middle English which can be usefully compared with the overview of the period provided by M. T. Clanchy in *England and Its Rulers 1066–1307* (3rd edn, 2006). There is another *A History of the English Language* (2006), this time a collection edited by Richard M. Hogg and David Denison, which includes authoritative summaries on grammar and vocabulary. Michael J. Swanton's edition of the *Anglo-Saxon Chronicle* (1996) has a comprehensive introduction to this invaluable historical document. For a clear, approachable and detailed guide to the inflectional systems of Old English, go to *Reading Old English: A Primer and First Reader* (2005), by Robert Hasenfratz and Thomas Jambeck, and its companion website, at: http://www.readingoldenglish.com/. The BBC's History web-pages have good summaries of the impact of the Vikings and Normans on England and its language, which can be accessed at: http://www.bbc.co.uk/history/trail/conquest/. Regarding the study of language contact in general, Uriel Weinreich's *Languages in Contact* (1953) is a classic and influential work, *Linguistic Change under Contact Conditions* (1995), edited by Jacek Fisiak, is a major collection, and *Language Contact: An Introduction* (2001), by Sarah G. Thomason, is a useful starting point. See also the website of the University of Manchester Working Group On Language Contact, at: http://languagecontact.humanities.manchester.ac.uk/home.html. This has a short outline of the topic of language contact and **linguistic hybridity** (the mixing of languages in individuals and societies), particularly in the present day, plus case studies and details of resources. *English and Celtic in Contact* (2008), by Markku Filppula, Juhani Klemola, and Heli Paulasto, reassesses another historical contact case. The associated website is at: http://www.joensuu.fi/fld/ecc.

# 4 'She Loves You. Yes! Yes! Yes!'

## American English Inside Out

This chapter includes the following:
- The story of English in the United States of America.
- Variety in American English.
- **Americanisms** and attitudes towards them.
- A short introduction to the work of Noah Webster.

## Introduction

If you know the original, the following sounds very odd, does it not? 'She Loves You. Yes! Yes! Yes!' Here is Paul McCartney speaking:

> We sat in there one evening, just beavering away while my dad was watching TV and smoking his Players cigarettes, and we wrote 'She Loves You'. We actually finished it there because we'd started it in the hotel room. We went into the living room – 'Dad, listen to this. What do you think?' So we played it to my dad and he said, 'That's very nice, son, but there's enough of these Americanisms around. Couldn't you sing, "She loves you. Yes! Yes! Yes!" ' At which point we collapsed in a heap and said, 'No, Dad, you don't quite get it!'.   (Paul McCartney, in Miles, 1997, p. 150)

Ian MacDonald (2005, p. 84) noted that *She Loves You* was the Beatles' biggest-selling single in Britain, and that 'the record's hottest attraction was its notorious "Yeah, yeah, yeah" refrain, from which the group became known throughout Europe as The Yeah-Yeahs'. The impact of the song's hook is summed up also by Jonathan Gould (2007, p. 158): 'The "yeah, yeah, yeahs" in the refrain of "She Loves You" were soon to become a catchphrase of the Beatles: blazoned in headlines, imprinted on promotional merchandise, and widely evoked in the press to illustrate either the innocent exuberance or the numbskulled inanity of the band.' As the song's first listener, Paul's father Jim McCartney, correctly observed, the refrain is an **Americanism**, which is the term for 'A word, phrase, or other use of language characteristic of, peculiar to, or originating from the United States', as the *Oxford English Dictionary* defines it. The *OED* also tells us that *yeah* is a colloquial form, originating in the United States, and dates its first use to the early twentieth century. It adds that it represents a 'casual pronunciation' of *yes*. It is likely that Jim McCartney thought that the *yeah, yeah, yeahs* were a bad thing because they were a lazy version of his preferred 'Yes! Yes! Yes!'. But his polite suggestion also belongs to a fine British tradition, often expressed more vehemently, of disapproval of American forms of English. Lennon and McCartney Jr's employment of *yeah*, however, belongs to another, more recent tradition of fondness for or even positive infatuation with American language and culture. This is perhaps a phenomenon so recent that it is more innovation than tradition.

Gould (2007) describes the 'Americanization' of British tastes that took place from the 1950s onwards, guided by 'the jingle and jabber of commercial television, which came on the air in the fall of 1955, feeding its viewers a steady diet of American-made or American-inspired westerns, quiz shows, and crime dramas', so that by the start of the 1960s 'three-quarters of all British households would possess a tiny window on the American Way of Life' (p. 25). At the same time, especially among youngsters in Liverpool and London, modern American popular and folk music was casting a spell. As Gould puts it (p. 25), 'To the despair of many intellectuals, this flood tide of American influence was embraced with seemingly boundless enthusiasm by the British populace.' Disapproval and captivation, 'numbskulled inanity' and 'innocent exuberance', degenerate and glamorous – this schizophrenic reaction to Americanized English is one theme of this chapter. The chapter also looks at the relationship between American English and British English, at the history of Americanisms, and at the role of popular music in promoting American language. And in the centre of all this, the chapter tells the story of American English, that is, English in the United States.

## Americanisms and Briticisms

In his autobiography (2007, pp. 19–20), the Brooklyn-born record producer, Tony Visconti, describes how his life in Britain began (in 1967) with a misunderstanding between himself and an officer of Her Majesty's Customs, over a kimono in his luggage, which the officer called a 'dressing gown'. 'What's a dressing gown?' replied the American, 'It's my bathrobe!' This is one more instance of the oft-recognized 'You say tomayto, I say tomahto' phenomenon, which we could also call the 'two countries divided by a common language' issue (an aphorism attributed to George Bernard Shaw). In private correspondence (2007), Tony Visconti provided further illustration: 'When I arrived on British shores in 1967, my Brooklyn accent was equal amounts of Italian-American and Jewish-American. My family was the former and my schoolmates were the latter. When I asked where the nearest tube (Underground) was, it sounded more like "toob" and Londoners could not understand me.' The 1937 song, *Let's Call the Whole Thing Off*, written by George and Ira Gershwin, actually goes 'You like tomayto and I like tomahto', and it is frequently mentioned in discussions about the differences (in pronunciation, vocabulary, grammar, semantics, and spelling) between American English and British English.

The phenomenon can cause minor communication problems, as it did for Tony Visconti, though he adapted quickly. On a short visit to Seattle, it took me a little while to work out what notices in cafes saying 'bus your dishes over here' were telling me to do, and a good deal longer to find out the etymology of this use of the verb *bus*. In the United States, a *busboy* is a member of staff in a restaurant, and *to bus* is a **back-formation** from *busboy*, meaning 'to clear a table of dirty dishes or to carry or remove dishes from the table'. (A back-formation is a form that is assumed to be the root-form of an existing word, but which actually post-dates the existing word, that is, it is formed from the existing word.) British viewers might be perplexed by the laughter that follows the use of the word *wiener* or *weener* in American TV sitcoms – a *wienerwurst* is a German sausage, but *wiener* and similar forms also have a US slang sense of 'penis'. The duality of the resulting double entendre may well pass the Brit by. Similarly the excellent 'Nice beaver' joke in the movie *The Naked Gun* (1988).

On the same theme, but striking quite another note, Martin Amis (2008, p. 195) observes that 'the name for what happened on September 11, 2001, is "September 11".... But the naming of September 11, that day, that event, naturally fell to America. And America came up with something pithier: "9/11".' And (p. 197), 'in Great Britain, nearly all our politicians, historians, journalists, novelists, scientists, poets, and philosophers, many of them deeply anti-American, have swallowed the blithe and lifeless Americanism, and go on doggedly and goonishly referring to September 11 as November 9.' For, whereas in America dates are given in month, day, year order, 'the British system proceeds, rather more logically, from small things to large: day, month, year' (Amis, 2008, p. 196). Martin could have referred to the advice given to all by his father, Kingsley Amis, in his *The King's English: A Guide to Modern Usage* (1997, p. 11): 'If the greater Americanisation of our speech seems undesirable, we can adopt a policy of not using an expression we recognise as an Americanism except for some particular reason.' Kingsley describes himself as 'strongly pro-American' (p. 8), and concedes that many Americanisms are so thoroughly assimilated into British English that they are no longer recognized as such (for example, *peanut, reckon, transpire*), but, well, that is also the root of his anxiety – that American English is a corrosive threat to British English, that it is an insidious force in the Americanization of Britain, and indeed the world. There is just a hint of this too in Jim McCartney's feedback to his son. There will be a hint of it in any British parent commenting on their children calling their friends *guys* or repeatedly proclaiming *cool!*

British criticism of Americanisms goes back a long way, if not quite so far back as to the first Americanism. When was the first Americanism?

It is generally agreed that the term was coined in 1781 by the Scottish clergyman, John Witherspoon, who had emigrated to America in 1768. An ally and supporter of the American colonists, he nevertheless wrote an unfavourable piece about English in America in the *Pennsylvania Journal* (9 May 1781), in which he introduced *Americanism*:

> by which I understand an use of phrases or terms, or a construction of sentences, even among persons of rank and education, different from the use of the same terms or phrases, or the construction of similar sentences, in Great Britain.

This is a narrower definition than the *OED*'s, for Witherspoon implies a straightforward equivalence between differing forms, whereas the *OED* says 'language characteristic of, peculiar to, or originating from the United States', which encompasses new and additional forms, borrowings with no existing equivalent in British English, and forms which have become archaic or obsolete in Britain but survive in the United States. In a still wider sense, the term is also applied – particularly in connection with the earliest examples – to forms originating in other parts of the 'New World', like the Caribbean.

The first record of Americanisms (in the broadest sense) goes back some 250 years prior to Witherspoon's coinage (or **neologism**). Before we deal with this, note that there is a counter-label, *Briticism*, coined by the American scholar of language and literature, Richard Grant White, in 1868 (p. 335). A *Briticism* is 'A word or phrase character-istic of the English of Great Britain but not used in the English of the United States or other countries' (*OED*). Another, more famous scholar of language in America, Henry Louis Mencken (1880–1956), devotes a section of his classic *The American Language* to 'Briticisms in the United States' (1936, pp. 264–71). Mencken's view in 1936 (p. 264) was that British English coinages were unlikely to be taken up by the major-ity of the American population, which regarded everything English as 'affected, effeminate and ridiculous'. Many of the Briticisms that he does acknowledge (for example, *maid*, *shop*, meaning 'store', and *sorry*, in place of *excuse me*), he ascribes to the social pretensions of the more elevated American classes, especially those he calls 'conscious Angloma-niacs' (p. 264). As can be gauged by the title of Mencken's book, he is keen to assert the independence of US English, and in this he belongs to a solid American tradition. He is also very aware of the British tradi-tion of disapproval. Both of these factors colour his attitude to the term *Americanism*, which is a sign of distinctness, but one invented by a crit-ical Briton. Compare with Kingsley Amis's dismissal (1997, p. 10) of the term *Briticism*, 'which word is an Americanism, and a *vox barbara* ['barbarous voice'] to boot'. One can imagine a Menckenian response, on how very English it is of Amis, in this context, to use a Latinism.

As for the earliest Americanisms, Mencken says (1936, p. 3), 'The first American colonists had perforce to invent Americanisms, if only to describe the unfamiliar landscape, weather, flora and fauna confronting them.' And if not invent, borrow. Mencken tells us of the English head-master, Alexander Gil (1565–1635), noting in his *Logonomia Anglica*, a descriptive account of English, that *maize* (originally from the Taino language of the Bahamas) and *canoe* (Haiti) were entering English. The first edition of the *Logonomia Anglica* was published in 1619, and is contemporary with the arrival in November 1620 of the *Mayflower* pilgrims at Cape Cod, on the north-eastern seaboard of America. How-ever, according to Richard W. Bailey (2004, p. 4), the accolade of first word of American origin to reach English goes to *guaiacum* (also orig-inally from Taino) in 1533. It is the name of a plant and the medicine drawn from its resin, which was used to treat another early export from the Caribbean, syphilis.

The first English speakers trying to create permanent settlements in America got there in the late sixteenth century, and, as Bailey (2004, p. 4) points out, 'they found themselves in a very diverse linguistic culture'. English speakers in America have found themselves in a diverse linguistic environment ever since, and one consequence of this is that English has acquired large numbers of new words by **borrowing** from the rich variety of languages its American branch has come into contact with. In the sixteenth century, there were over 200 Native languages in North America, belonging to about 15 language families (Ferguson and Heath, 1981, p. 112), and Native American languages were among the initial donors to English, giving scores of words (for example, *moccasin*, *moose*, *raccoon*, *tomahawk*, and *wigwam*). Words were taken from the languages of the competing European colonizers, including the Spanish (for example, *alligator*, *potato*, *tobacco*), who arrived in the Caribbean in 1492, and the French (*caribou*, *levee*, *prairie*), who had been in North America since the early sixteenth century. The Dutch also had their own colonization project, arriving in the early seventeenth century, and gifting numerous words to American English as it developed (for example, *boss* 'master', *cole-slaw*, *spook*). In the wake of the first successful settlements in the early seventeenth century came many more immigrants, including Danes, Finns, Germans, Jews, Swedes, and Swiss. The first half of the nineteenth century saw another wave of immigration from Europe, especially northern Europe, only to be surpassed by the mass migrations of the late nineteenth to early twentieth century, chiefly from southern and eastern Europe. Between the 1850s and the 1900s, big numbers of Chinese and Japanese also arrived. And so American English borrowed, for example, *yen* 'craving' (from Chinese), *lagerbeer* and *wiener* (from German), *mafia* (Italian), *lingon-berry* (Swedish), *maven* 'an expert', *schlepper* 'an insignificant person', and *schlock* 'cheap, shoddy' (from Yiddish), and many more.

There is another, large group, who arrived between the early seventeenth century and the early nineteenth, and who had a major impact on English in America. These were not settlers seeking a new life, but slaves, from West Africa. The first 20 Africans imported into the American colonies arrived in 1619, at Jamestown, Virginia, when a Dutch slave trader exchanged his cargo for food, opening an era whose consequences still course through America's nervous system. The empires of the European colonial powers were dependent on slavery. The emigrant Puritans in the colonies, seeking escape from persecution, nevertheless in general gradually embraced the trade, and they were not alone in this respect. A total of 10,000 African slaves came to the Atlantic seaboard in the seventeenth century. During the eighteenth century, some six million were brought to the New World as a whole (these statistics from Tanner et al., 1995, pp. 50–1). In America, they were put to work on the indigo, rice, tobacco, cotton, and sugar plantations of the Carolinas, Virginia, and Louisiana, as well as in the households of the north. By the start of the nineteenth century, the northern states had ceased their involvement in the trade, but even so, in 1860, according to the US census, there were approximately four million slaves in the Republic. Following the Civil War, in 1865, slavery in the United States was abolished. A century later, in July 1964, the US Congress passed the Civil Rights Act, which prohibited discrimination on the grounds of race or religion.

Tanner et al. (p. 50) say that the slaves 'came from many ethnic groups in widely separated regions of Africa, though all spoke languages of the Niger-Congo family'. Mencken (1936, p. 112) says that the slaves' native languages 'seem to have left few marks upon American'. The small number of possible loanwords that he mentions tend either not to originate in Africa or have disputed or uncertain etymologies. None is more disputed than that for *jazz*, a word for which Arabic, English, French, Irish, Native American, and Spanish, as well as African origins have been postulated. Even more surprising is the conclusion reached in 1925 by another well-known scholar of American English, George Philip Krapp (1872–1934), that 'there is very little evidence' to show that African-Americans 'have developed a special idiom of their own' (p. 162). Surprising because, to present-day linguists, the existence of **African American English (AAE)** or **African American Vernacular English (AAVE)**, as it is now called, is a given fact. It is to AAE that we must look, and to the creole Gullah, if we want to find the legacy in US English of the slave trade.

While its existence is no longer questioned in Krapp-like fashion, the status, character, and evolution of AAE continue to be debated. It has been argued (in the 'Ebonics' controversy of the late 1990s) that AAE (or Ebonics) is a language in its own right rather than a variety of English, a viewpoint which emphasizes its Niger-Congo heritage. The prevailing opinion among linguists is that AAE is a variety of English, but an exceptional one. Regarding its origins, there is the view, known as the 'Anglicist Hypothesis', that the source of AAE is the non-standard English of Britain. According to this theory, slaves speaking diverse African languages (groups with the same language were often broken up by slave traders) of necessity learned the varieties of English spoken by the colonists they were in local contact with, losing most traces of their ancestral language within a couple of generations. On the other hand, there is the 'Creolist Hypothesis', which proposes that an English-based creole language developed throughout the African diaspora, including the American South, where it led eventually to AAE. Although not a creole, AAE retains grammatical features (like absence of the linking verb *be* in phrases such as *you ugly*, and of the inflection *-s* on verbs, as in *he like music*) which it has in common with surviving creoles like Gullah and Jamaican Creole. Such features are assumed to represent AAE's African **substratum**, or underlying linguistic layer. A creole will likely take its vocabulary from the socially dominant partner in the mix of languages that gives rise to it – English in the case of Gullah and of the precursor to AAE. (There is more on creoles, and on Gullah and *its* borderline status, in Chapter 1; and more on Ebonics in Chapter 14.) Wolfram and Torbert (2006), whose summary informs mine above, conclude (p. 230) by supporting a 'Substrate Hypothesis', which argues that the origins of AAE lie in influence from non-standard British English *and* in the persistence of underlying African formations. They and John Baugh (2006) also point out that the term AAE masks internal diversity: there are, for example, at one end of the spectrum, conservative, remote enclaves of AAE in America (for example, in Hyde County, North Carolina, and in Appalachia), and at the other there is the supraregional, urban, and increasingly influential version of AAE.

Borrowings are not the only kind of Americanism, as we have already seen in this chapter. An Americanism can be a pronunciation, as in Tony Visconti's 'toob', or a grammatical construction, as in *how you doing*? (The auxiliary verb *are* is absent.) In vocabulary, as well as borrowing from other languages, Americans have indeed also been inventive. The compound *bathrobe* was first used early in the twentieth century; *busboy* too; *9/11* ... we know when that goes back to, and the similarly snappy *24/7* dates from the early 1980s; *guy* 'a man, fellow' was first used in the United States in the mid-nineteenth century; *cool* as a general term of approval was popularized by the jazz community of the 1940s. And we have slang *bodacious* 'excellent', from the 1970s, though in the dialectal sense 'complete, thorough, arrant' it dates from the 1840s; slang *mutt* 'a mongrel dog' and other senses, from around 1900, a shortening of *muttonhead*; and the idioms *don't even go there* 'don't talk about that subject', from the 1990s, and *outasight* 'excellent, extraordinary', from the 1890s – to give just a minuscule random sample. American English speakers have been ceaselessly productive coiners and compounders, whether in slang or formal language.

However, H. L. Mencken (1936, p. 3) wants us to remember 'one Francis Moore', who visited Georgia in 1735, and who subsequently (in the 1744 book about his voyage) was 'to raise the earliest alarm against this enrichment of English from the New World, and so set the tone English criticism has maintained ever since', by noting the Americanism *bluff*, 'a cliff or headland with a broad precipitous face', and calling it 'barbarous English' (1744, p. 24). Mencken adds that, by the mid-1750s, literary London was sufficiently conscious of Americanisms for there to be a suggestion that a glossary was needed, and for the 'always anti-American Samuel Johnson' (p. 4) to be calling the American dialect a corrupting influence.

Samuel Johnson (1709–84), author of the first major dictionary of English (1755), declared at dinner one evening, 'I am willing to love all mankind, *except an American*'. His biographer, James Boswell, describes the occasion (1934 edition, Volume III, p. 290; Boswell's biography was first published in 1791), on Wednesday 15 April 1778 of this sudden outburst, sadly not the first outrageous insult from Johnson aimed at the Americans. Boswell notes (1934, Volume II, p. 312) that as early as 1769, Johnson had called Americans 'a race of convicts' who 'ought to be thankful for anything we allow them short of hanging'. Rather candid, one might think, but relations between the 13 American colonies and motherland were fraught at this time, leading to the War of Independence (1775–83). And yet Johnson had several valued American friends, including Benjamin Franklin (1706–90), one of the founding fathers of the United States. Franklin was also respected by another eminent lexicographer, Noah Webster.

## Noah Webster and the American tongue

Noah Webster (1758–1843) dedicated his *Dissertations on the English Language* (1789) to Franklin, but was highly critical of Johnson. The *Dissertations* is a substantial work of philology, with a nation-building motivation, that being to promote and establish an American English, distinguished from British English, which Webster wishes to be a unifying force for the newly independent United States. He advocates a uniform pronunciation of English throughout the United States, and a reformed, American spelling of English.

Webster's *Dissertations* follows up earlier works, such as his hugely successful *American Spelling Book* (originally published in 1783), but precedes his best-known project, *An American Dictionary of the English Language* (1828), which he concentrated on from around 1800. The

*Dissertations* had been road-tested in over 20 public readings from the summer of 1785 onwards. In 'Dissertation I' (pp. 17–79), Webster speaks of the need to 'annihilate differences in speaking and preserve the purity of the American tongue', adding, 'A sameness of pronunciation is of considerable consequence in a political view' (p. 19), because such uniformity would help unite a nation comprised of disparate groups. As he says in the Appendix on spelling reform (pp. 391–410), 'a *national language* is a band of *national union*' (p. 397), and he wants his compatriots to turn away from their old attachments to their parent countries and towards a commitment to America, and to the 'American tongue' he wants to be founded. This tongue will be English, but an American English. 'Let us then seize the present moment,' he says (p. 406), 'and establish a *national language*, as well as a national government.'

The American tongue should have, Webster believed, a reformed, well-ordered, more phonetic spelling system, which would facilitate learning the language and regularize its pronunciation, and thereby 'would remove prejudice, and conciliate mutual affection and respect' (p. 397). It would reduce the number of letters in use, making books less expensive and encouraging reading. But above all 'it would make a difference between the English orthography and the American' (p. 397). This spelling reform project occupied Webster from the *Dissertations* through to his *American Dictionary*.

D. G. Scragg, in his history of English spelling (1974), notes that (p. 83) *-or* instead of *-our* was a variant that was already used by a minority of British printers before Webster, and delivers (p. 84) this verdict: 'In the sense that Webster was the first to differentiate between British and American usage, and that it was frequently he who chose the variant of two spellings in early nineteenth-century use which has subsequently been preferred in the United States, he can be said to have influenced the development of spelling. He is in a way "responsible" for such forms as *center, color* and *defense*.' In his time, Webster also supported: deletion of *-k* from words ending in *-ick*, as in *music*; substitution of *-k* for *-que*, as in *check*; use of a single *l* before a suffix, depending on the stress, as in *traveling* (stress on the first syllable) but not *excelling* (stress on the second syllable); and *mold* instead of *mould*.

In the *Dissertations*, Webster looks forward to the establishment of a distinctive language of America, spoken by all its citizens, but he is concerned also with history, and acknowledges that (p. 18), 'This language is the inheritance which the Americans have received from their British parents.' Those parents and their language had arrived in America some 200 years previously. Who were the fathers and mothers of American English? Who were the first speakers of American English?

## English arrives in America

The 'Pilgrim Fathers', as they later came to be called, in their ship, the *Mayflower*, made landfall at Cape Cod on 9 November 1620. They had been heading for the mouth of the Hudson River (at present-day New York City, but then a part of Virginia), about 200 miles to the south-west, but were thwarted by the prevailing winds. The Pilgrims explored the coastline around Cape Cod, and by December they had chosen a site known as Plymouth (named six years earlier by the English adventurer, Captain John Smith), just across the bay from Cape Cod, as their new home (see Figure 2).

The Pilgrims had sailed from another Plymouth, in south-west England, on 16 September 1620. In fact, many of their party were left behind because a second ship, the *Speedwell*, proved unseaworthy. By the time they started their new life in the New World, the Pilgrims had already endured hardship. A group of separatist Protestants, calling themselves 'Saints', and eager to leave the unsympathetic religious environment in England under James I (who ruled from 1603–25), they had been members of a community of exiles in Holland since 1607. Supported by an association of investors, the Second Plymouth Virginia Company, they obtained a charter to found an English colony at the mouth of the Hudson. On board the *Mayflower* there were no toilets or bathrooms, hardly any fresh food, mainly beer for drink, and about 130 people: 20–30 crew, 40 'Saints', and 66 'Strangers', as the Pilgrims called the other settlers foisted on them by the Company. What sort of English did they speak?

In a short article published in 1986 ('English on the *Mayflower*'), Martyn Wakelin tackles precisely this question, saying (p. 30), 'It was a linguistically very mixed group that were to lay the foundations of American English.' The majority of settlers on the *Mayflower* came from the mid- to south-east of England, although among them were individuals from other parts of England too, including the north- and south-west. In addition to this variety of regional influences, those on board ranged in age considerably (from a new-born baby to 57 years old), and there were marked differences in levels of education and in

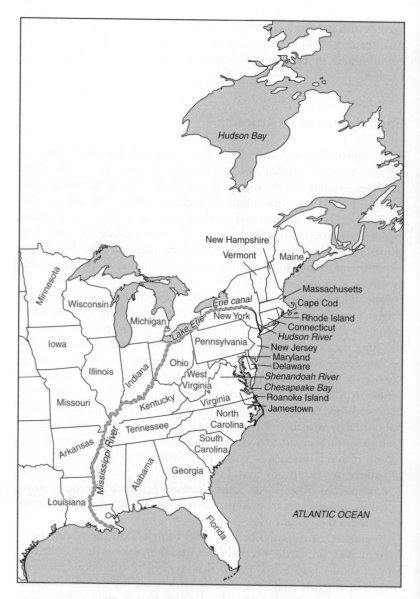

**FIGURE 2** MAP OF THE EASTERN USA

kinds of occupation. Each of these factors contributed to the linguistic mix, and increases the difficulty of making useful generalizations. Nonetheless, Wakelin does manage to conclude (p. 33) that the regional dialect of the majority, from the east of England, was the paramount factor. He also notes a few examples of the survival in the speech of 1980s New England (the region of the USA which contains the site of the Plymouth Colony) of pronunciations 'which were pretty universal [but are no longer so] in England when the pilgrims set sail' (p. 33), including 'unrounding of *o*', so that *cod* sounds like 'cahd'.

But here is a surprising fact: shortly after founding Plymouth Colony, the Pilgrims encountered English-speaking Native Americans. On 16 March 1621, Samoset (of the Wabanake tribe) walked into their settlement. He spoke some English. He knew of another Indian (as the colonists called the natives), Tisquantum (of the Patuxet tribe), who spoke better English. Tisquantum, or 'Squanto' as he was nicknamed by the English, became an interpreter for the Pilgrims, liaising between them and the local Wampanoag confederation of tribes. Samoset had picked up English from the fishermen on the vessels working the Atlantic coast of North America. English ships had been scouting the coastline since the start of the sixteenth century. Tisquantum's acquisition of English had been a little more tumultuous, for he and 23 other American Indians had been kidnapped in 1614 by Captain Thomas Hunt, a rogue English explorer, who took them to Malaga, Spain, hoping to sell them as slaves. But Hunt's plans went awry, and Tisquantum found his way to London, where he learned English. Employed as an interpreter, he eventually returned to his home in 1619, where he lived until his death in 1622.

Tisquantum was not the first Native American to have been exposed to English in its homeland. And neither was the Plymouth Colony the first English-speaking settlement in America. The Pilgrims are accorded a particular founding status because of the 'Mayflower Compact', a prototypical constitutional agreement between 'Saints' and 'Strangers', but there had been two previous settlement projects. The first, between 1584 and 1590, at Roanoke Island (over 200 miles to the south of present-day New York City), failed, though not before two Algonquin Indians, Manteo and Wanchese, had paid (willing) visits to England courtesy of the pioneers. The second, at a place the colonists christened Jamestown, some 60 miles inland from Chesapeake Bay, Virginia, a little north of Roanoke, endured. Sponsored by the Virginia Company, a group of London entrepreneurs, approximately 280 settlers arrived at Jamestown during 1607–8, to face the trials of disease, famine, and attacks by the Algonquins. The west-country-of-England origins of these settlers has been emphasized, as well as the subsequent influence on Chesapeake English of their distinctive accents, including features like **voicing** of *s*-sounds into *z*-sounds, and a **retroflex** *r*-sound (front of the tongue curled back along the roof of the mouth), and the pronunciation of *r* after vowel sounds (unlike in the standard British accent) in words like *farm* and *hair* (a trait called **rhoticity**). Some commentators talk of echoes of this west-country speech persisting in the isolated 'Tidewater' accents of the Chesapeake area, but Hazen and Fluharty (2006) scotch a myth that has grown out of this, that 'Elizabethan English' is still spoken in the region, pointing out, not unreasonably, that Elizabeth I was dead before Jamestown was founded, and, less pedantically, that major settlement in the wider Appalachian area 'did not begin until the eighteenth century' (p. 19). Furthermore, research by the Association for the Preservation of Virginia Antiquities (see the APVA Jamestown Rediscovery web pages, which I accessed in 2009) suggests that the Jamestown pioneers came from a scattering of localities across England, including the West Country. The tale of the influence of the incomers' accents and dialects on the development of American English continues in the next section.

However, to give straight answers to my questions at the end of the previous section: the fathers and mothers of American English were the settlers of Jamestown and Plymouth, and those emigrant British who followed close on their heels; the first native speakers of American English were their sons and daughters born in the New World.

## English across America

In 2006, a major event occurred in the study of American English. This was the publication of *The Atlas of North American English: Phonetics, Phonology and Sound Change* (*ANAE*), by William Labov, Sharon Ash, and Charles Boberg. Based on material collected in the 1990s by telephone interviews, and concentrating on the pronunciation of American English, *ANAE* combines the linguistic atlas approach of **dialectology** with the social science emphasis of **sociolinguistics**. Figure 3 is the *ANAE* map that shows the main dialect regions of North American English.

One of the significant findings shown by Figure 3 is the pretty close correspondence of its depiction of the main North, Midland, and South dialect areas with those presented in earlier studies by linguistic geographers, such as Craig Carver (1987), who mapped vocabulary

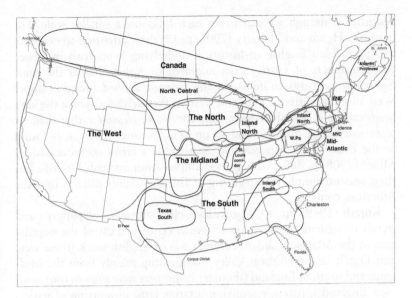

**FIGURE 3** AN OVERALL VIEW OF NORTH AMERICAN DIALECTS
(Labov et al., 2006, p. 148)

(or **lexis**) using data collected in the 1960s and 1970s for the *Dictionary of American Regional English* (*DARE*), and who in turn found the same basic dialect areas as Hans Kurath and Raven McDavid had found in the 1930s–1950s (Kurath, 1949, on lexis; Kurath and McDavid, 1961, on pronunciation). From this, we glimpse two things: the vigour and productivity of American dialectology and sociolinguistics in the twentieth century; and the persistence of the historical large American English dialect areas. As Kretzschmar observes, in his full (2004) overview, although linguistic changes have taken place and continue to take place within these regions, they (the regions) nevertheless 'have their foundations in the history of American primary settlement patterns' (p. 55). His view is that 'American English has developed a national dialect for the usually well-educated participants in a national marketplace for goods, services, and jobs' (p. 55), that is, a national, supraregional 'standard' American of the well-educated social stratum, but regional dialects remain in good health, and, what is more, there are large dialect areas whose roots can be matched to the shape of early immigrant settlement.

This does not mean that the big North, Midland, and South dialect regions can be linked straightforwardly with the Englishes spoken by the different groups of settlers of the seventeenth and eighteenth centuries – though we can make such links on a smaller scale. For example, Hazen and Fluharty (2006, p. 19) draw attention to evidence in Appalachian English of historical underlying Scots-Irish influence (large numbers of Ulster Scots migrated to Appalachia in the mid-eighteenth century), in items like the *car needs washed*, found in upper West Virginia, eastern Ohio, and western Pennsylvania, where the verb *needs* can be followed by forms like *washed* or *cleaned* rather than by *to be washed*, or *washing*, and so on. This feature, they say, is found in the British Isles, especially in Scotland – a claim corroborated by Miller (2008, p. 309), who gives examples from Scottish English. But there was no simple transplanting of British English dialects into the American context.

Kurath (1949, pp. 1–7) provides a clear summary of patterns and trends in settlement. In the seventeenth century, most of the population in the Atlantic seaboard colonies was of English stock (there were also Dutch in the Hudson Valley), originating mainly from the Midlands and south of England (though northerners were present too), with New England apparently receiving 'a rather large proportion of settlers from London and environs, from East Anglia and from Kent' (p. 3), as well as numbers from the West Country. London and the West Country were also well represented in Virginia. The colonies, isolated from each other in the seventeenth century, had become an unbroken area of settlement from Maine to Georgia by the end of the eighteenth century. In the meantime, many Ulster Scots and Germans had arrived. Kurath says that it is 'quite obvious that at first many regional varieties of English were spoken in the American colonies, which were blended into distinctively American local and regional varieties in the course of several generations' (p. 3) This is also the generally agreed view. In each colony, there was a particular mix of incomers' dialects, traces of which survive in individual features of pronunciation, vocabulary, and grammar; in time, and as new elements (including from other languages) were added to the mix, larger regional blends formed, each differing in character, a process of 'colonial levelling' (as Kretzschmar, 2004, p. 42, calls it) of a diversity of dialectal influences. Then, from the end of the eighteenth century, along rivers, wagon roads, and canals, the non-Indian population of the now-independent United States began to expand westwards, as far as the Mississippi, taking with them their American dialects. The Erie Canal, completed by 1825, connecting the Hudson River and Lake Erie, was instrumental in facilitating expansion in the North. In the South, hampered by the lack of a convenient waterway, westwards migration was slower and more uneven until the better plantation country of the Mississippi Basin was reached. In the Midlands, the National Road (now US Route 40), built in the first half of the nineteenth century between Chesapeake and Illinois, and (further south) the Shenandoah River were conduits for migration and settlement. The present-day dialect regions of the North, Midlands, and South are the result of the seaboard blends and their expansion westwards.

The foundation in 1889 of the American Dialect Society launched dialectology in the United States, a key concern of which has been the history of variety in American English. Kurath (1891–1992) believed that knowledge of colonial speech could be gained by investigating the traditional 'folk speech' of his own time, in which historical dialectal features were preserved. The *Dictionary of American Regional English* (1985–2002) lists regional words and phrases, giving their **etymologies** (origins and history), including their first recorded use and subsequent developments, supported by **citations** (quotations from authoritative sources), as well as details of where in the United States they have been used. For example, *mosquito hawk*, in the sense 'dragonfly', is first recorded in 1737, as *Muskeetoe-Hawks*, and is a term used mainly in the South of the United States, and sporadically elsewhere, according to *DARE* (1996, Volume III, p. 664). In 1949, Kurath mapped (see Figure 4) its distribution in the Eastern States alongside other regional terms for 'dragonfly'. It is the usual expression in the Virginia Tidewater, and occurs from Delaware Bay along the coast in a broadening belt to Georgia.

Of course, there are also American dialect words which originate in British English dialects, for example, *skillet* 'frying pan', recorded through the Eastern States by Kurath (1949, his Figure 68), and generally quite common in American English – it is also widespread in the dialects of the British Isles, and dated to the early fifteenth century by the *OED*. And there is general, non-dialectal American *fall* 'autumn', perceived as an Americanism in Britain, despite its long-time use in the dialects of the south of England.

One of the innovations of *ANAE* is its mapping of major sound changes, including two **sound shifts**, in progress in North American English. A sound shift happens when a sound that is common to a group of words changes or moves in pronunciation over time into a different sound, with the consequence that it forces another sound (which it has become identical with) in another group of words to change also, which in turn has the same effect on another sound in another group and so on. There are three large sound changes in progress affecting the

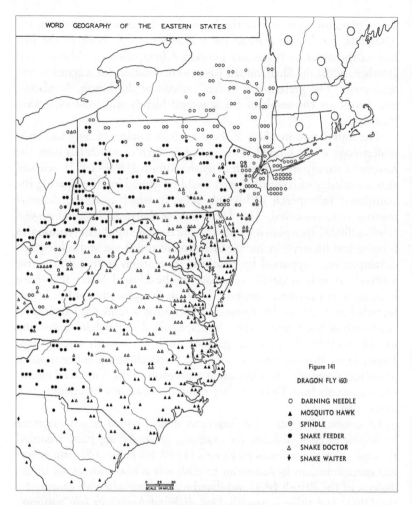

**FIGURE 4** TERMS FOR 'DRAGONFLY' IN THE EASTERN STATES (Kurath, 1949, Figure 141)

vowels of American English: **Northern Cities Shift**, **Southern Shift**, and **Low Back Merger**.

Low Back Merger involves the merging of two vowel sounds articulated with the back of the tongue comparatively low (but higher nevertheless than the front of the tongue) in the mouth, so that pairs of words such as *cot* and *caught*, *Don* and *dawn*, *hock* and *hawk*, become **homophones**, that is, they sound the same. The merged sound is often intermediate between the two earlier vowels. This merger is occurring in the West of the United States and across parts of the north-east (including East New England), and in Canada.

Southern Shift is a reasonably complex chain of movements affecting a number of front vowels (articulated with the front of the tongue higher than the back), across the South region, but extending into Philadelphia and New York City. One effect is that, to those outside this region, Southern *sit* will be heard as *see it*, and *set* as *say it* (Labov et al., 2006, p. 244).

Northern Cities Shift affects the articulation of a number of short and long vowels (that is, comparatively short or long in duration of pronunciation) in the Inland North region, so that, as Kretzschmar (2004, p. 54) summarizes it, 'each of the following words might be heard and interpreted as something else by speakers from outside the area: *Ann* as *Ian*, *bit* as *bet*, *bet* as *bat* or *but*, *lunch* as *launch*, *talk* as *tuck*, *locks* as *lax*'.

Putting the analysis of these changes into map form adds a new perspective to the classification of the dialects of American English, though again history is important. For example, Labov et al. (2006, pp. 214–15) propose that the triggering event for the Northern Cities Shift was the construction of the Erie Canal, which allowed the westward movement of diverse native-born populations and brought thousands of new immigrant learners of English into rapidly growing urban areas, leading (once more) to a levelling, coalescing, simplifying process, 'that often occurs in situations of radical dialect mixture with rapid population growth' (p. 214), resulting in a change to the vowel in *cat*-class words, which initiated the Northern Cities Shift.

## Conclusion: all speaking the same language?

In 1789, Noah Webster predicted that American English and British English would inevitably diverge (p. 23), and that 'within a century and a half, North America will be peopled with a hundred millions of men, *all speaking the same language* [English]' (p. 21). In 2009, the estimated population of the United States was over 305 million. As throughout the last four centuries, English in America is spoken alongside other languages. According to the US Census Bureau (Shin and Bruno, 2003, p. 1), at the Census of 2000 there were 47 million citizens aged 5 and over who spoke a language other than English at home (Spanish has the second-highest speaker numbers). So, not all are speaking the same language all of the time, but the United States does have more native speakers of English than any other territory – over 215 million (Crystal, 2003a, p. 109). And there are many more English speakers outside the United States who have a smattering of American.

In 1983, the British sociolinguist, Peter Trudgill, published an essay on 'pop-song pronunciation', in which he looked at the habit of 1960s British pop stars, such as Paul McCartney and Mick Jagger, of singing in what they perceived to be American accents in order to identify themselves with the American-ness of the pop genre. Later, every so often, McCartney and Jagger would flavour their vocals with phrasings more like their home accents, and there are plenty of examples of British popular singers modelling their style on British accents, but the influence of American English on British pop and rock is pervasive. Tony Visconti gives us a first-hand account:

> As I have worked with many British recording artists I couldn't help noticing how they adopted American accents for their vocals, especially the southern Black American accents (Mick Jagger). And this is not only limited to the accents, it's also the imitation of Black American phrasing and the imagined raspiness of the Black voice (Lulu, Rod Stewart, John Lennon). This is not particularly a British pop singing trait, as white American singers have often pursued the same goal (Michael Bolton). Of course the Beatles and some others imitated the accent of white southerners and Appalachia. Then there was a backlash with many British artists reverting to their regional accents – Roger Daltrey, Marc Bolan's earlier singing style, and Donovan come to mind.    (Private correspondence, 2007)

But even some of those partial to using British English nuances also show their dedication to the American turn of phrase. Marc Bolan's *Telegram Sam* (1972), for example, uses the following Americanisms: *main-man*, which the *OED* says is chiefly US African-American usage, meaning 'a favourite male friend, a "hero", the lead performer of a pop group', dating from the 1950s; *outasight*; *funk*, as a verb, but ultimately from the adjective *funky*, applied to jazz in the 1950s, meaning music that is 'down-to-earth, uncomplicated, like the blues'; *square*, as a noun, again from jazz slang, dating back to the 1940s, 'out of touch, conventional, old-fashioned' (adjectival), the opposite of *hep*. The blues, jazz, boogie-woogie, rhythm and blues, rock'n'roll, rap, hip-hop, grunge – these are not only originally American forms of popular music but also Americanisms. Great speaker numbers, the global spread of American commerce, and the post-Second World War propagation of American mass-entertainment have led to a seeding of Americanisms into English in Britain and across the world, to the extent that the overt American-ness of many Americanisms diminishes, as Kingsley Amis (1997) noted. The language of popular music provides a prime illustration of the phenomenon. The African-American jazz culture of the 1940s and 1950s was impressively prolific in its coining of new words, idioms, and senses. A slang that overtly signified difference, separation, and alienation nevertheless produced coinages and meanings that broke into the wider English-speaking consciousness. Like *bop, dude, gig, grooving, hassle, jamming, jitterbug, jive, out of this world, something else, strung out, up tight,* and the use of *bad, dirty, mean* as terms of approval and praise (these are a selection from Robert S. Gold's Introduction to his dictionary of *Jazz Talk* (1975)). H. L. Mencken once thought, like Noah Webster before him, that American would further depart from its British parent, but he had changed his mind by 1936, saying (p. vi) that Americans were 'bound to exert a dominant influence upon the course of the common language hereafter'. Perhaps Jim McCartney saw it coming too.

## Further reading

A good first port of call is *American Voices: How Dialects Differ from Coast to Coast* (2006), edited by Walt Wolfram and Ben Ward, which has a broad selection of short, accessible sketches of regional and sociocultural varieties in the United States. From there move on to *Language in the USA: Themes for the Twenty-first Century* (2004), edited by Edward Finegan and John R. Rickford, and its earlier companion, *Language in the USA* (1981), edited by Charles A. Ferguson and Shirley Brice Heath. Together these give a comprehensive introduction to American English, its history and varieties, and to other languages in the United States. *American English: Dialects and Variation* (2nd edn, 2006), by Walt Wolfram and Natalie Schilling-Estes, provides a detailed, use-ful portrait. H. L. Mencken's *The American Language* (4th edn, 1936, and Supplements, 1945, 1948) is an excellent read, as is the shorter *American English* (1958), by Albert H. Marckwardt. Use Bill Kretzschmar's 'Regional Dialects' in Finegan and Rickford (2004, pp. 39–57) to find out more about the achievements of American linguistic geography, and visit the website of the Linguistic Atlas Projects of the United States (at: http://us.english.uga.edu/), which is an impressive source of information, references, and links. You can visit the *DARE* website at: http://dare.wisc.edu/. *American Speech*, the journal of the American Dialect Society, has been a tremendous source of informa-tion and analysis since its first edition in 1925. For a handy single-volume history, see *The Penguin History of the United States of America* (2nd edn, 1999), by Hugh Brogan. *The Settling of North America: The Atlas of the Great Migrations into North America from the Ice Age to the Present* (1995), edited by Helen Hornbeck Tanner et al., is an outstanding cartographic companion.

# 5 English Across the World

## History and Varieties

---

This chapter includes the following:
- The spread of English worldwide.
- Definitions of the terms **creole continuum**, **acrolect**, **mesolect**, **basilect**, **L1**, **L2**, **EFL**, **nativization**, **contact variety** and **transported variety**.
- The three concentric circles of English.

---

## Beginning

What is the distance between Figure 5 and Figure 6?

The answer is approximately 1500 miles and 900 years.

Figure 5 is a photograph of the name of a pub on the Gower Peninsula, South Wales, in the United Kingdom. The name is unusual in that it is a translation of itself. A *pound* is a pen or enclosure for animals and *ffald* is Welsh for *pound*. The name therefore is a bilingual *chiasmus*, which is a term taken from Greek for a linguistic sequence whose second half is in some measure a mirror image of the first, as in 'ask not what your country can do for you, ask what you can do for your country' (John F. Kennedy, Inaugural Address, 20 January 1961). *Ffald* is also a Welsh borrowing of the very old English word *fold*, which has the same sense as *pound*, and *poundffald* may simply be a slight Welshifying of English *poundfold* or *pinfold*, which dates back to the late twelfth century, according to the *Oxford English Dictionary* (*OED*). But the bilingual-chiasmus interpretation is more satisfying, not only because of its linguistic balance, but because the

**FIGURE 5** *THE POUNDFFALD*

pub, The Poundffald, lies right on the historical boundary between the English and Welsh halves of the Gower Peninsula. For Gower was one of the first parts of Wales to be settled by significant numbers of English speakers, who travelled over the Bristol Channel from south-west England in the twelfth century AD or maybe even earlier. English is a language that has travelled, and Gower was among its early destinations.

Figure 6 represents English's more recent travelling. It is now a language with global reach. Figure 6 is a photograph of a road sign from the small Greek island of Paxos, which has a permanent population of no more than 3000 people and 250,000 olive trees. It also has a few Internet cafes, and many tourists in the summer, especially from elsewhere in Europe. Road signs and public notices of all kinds on Paxos are habitually translated from Greek not into Italian, or German, or French, but into English, which functions as a *lingua franca* on the island – as it does today across the world among

**FIGURE 6** ROAD SIGN FROM PAXOS

speakers of different languages, whether at international conferences or in international soccer matches or on YouTube. English is also a native and/or official language in many territories. Another way to measure the distance between what Figures 5 and 6 represent is in speaker numbers. The total population of the British Isles in the Middle Ages is hard to estimate, but in AD 1300 it was not likely to have been more than 9 million (Britnell, 2004, p. 81), and by no means all of those were English speakers. The number of speakers of English worldwide in AD 2000 is also hard to estimate, but a cautious calculation (Crystal, 2003b, p. 69) would be a total of 1.5 billion first-language, second-language, and foreign-language speakers put together. And that is a lot of speakers to put together. It is a quarter of the world's population.

This chapter follows the travels of English. It will be a bit of a whistle-stop tour. We will look at native-speaker varieties of English in the Americas, Africa, and Australasia – also known as **transported varieties**, which refers to the transportation of English from the British Isles during colonial expansion. We will consider also the global phenomenon of English as a second and foreign language, and we will look at attempts by linguists to model and describe English across the world.

## Travelling

### The British Isles

David Crystal says (2003b, p. 30) of English, 'In a sense, the language has always been on the move.' It began to spread around mainland Britain as soon as it arrived from northern Europe in the fifth century AD. At that time, Britain was peopled by Celts. The Germanic tribes who brought English were to settle in all parts except the highlands of the far north and west. The earliest known references to *Englisc* as the name of the language of these colonizers date to the first half of the eighth century. In the twelfth century, it is thought, communities of English speakers were planted in Gower and Pembroke in Wales (which to this day are known as 'Little Englands beyond Wales'), though it was not until the nineteenth century that English became the dominant language in Wales.

But it is Scotland that was the first external destination for the new language. Modern-day Scots, depending on your viewpoint, is either a variety of English or a language in its own right. It has been recognized by the European Union as a minority language, it has a rich literary tradition, and, as Paul Johnston points out (2007, p. 105), 'it is the only Germanic variety in Britain besides Standard English ever to have functioned as a full language within an independent state', that being the Kingdom of Scotland (AD 843–1707). Nevertheless, Johnston also says (p. 105) that 'Scots is, more or less, the direct descendant of the Northumbrian form of Old English', one of the original major regional dialects of English, which spread to south-eastern Scotland during the sixth century AD, from where it slowly extended further, eventually reaching Orkney and Shetland some 800 years later.

Ireland did not receive its first English-speaking settlers until the late twelfth century, led by the Anglo-Norman rulers of England. From the late sixteenth century, more waves of immigrants arrived, reinforcing the English-speaking presence – this is the colonial 'Plantation' of Ireland which saw confiscated Irish land granted to newcomers from the mainland. Large numbers of Scots speakers came to Ulster, the most northerly province of Ireland, dividing that area linguistically from the varieties of Irish English that arose in the midlands and south. Immigrants from the Midlands and south-west of England also influenced the development of Irish English.

The Celtic enclave on the Isle of Man was unaffected by English until the fourteenth century, and it was only in the nineteenth century that Manx was supplanted by English. English-speaking influence in the Norman French-speaking Channel Islands was limited until the turn of the eighteenth and nineteenth centuries, growing appreciably there after the Napoleonic wars, with English then gradually replacing Norman French.

Thus inexorably did the language of the Angles, Saxons, and other Germanic incomers progress throughout the British Isles, leading to an abundance of English dialects, those in the enduring Celtic regions exhibiting clear transfer of pronunciation, grammatical, and some vocabulary features from an array of Celtic languages. Today some of these languages survive (Scottish Gaelic, Irish, Welsh) in varying states of health, and hundreds of newer immigrant languages are also spoken in Britain (Gibson (2007, p. 264) gives an estimate of over 300 in London for the late 1990s), but English without question rules the roost. However, so far we have charted its travels on a local scale only. During the sixteenth century English took its first steps towards becoming a global language.

## The Americas and the Caribbean

If you have read Chapter 2 'Time', you will have followed the 3000-year-long story of a little word, *mouse*, from Sanskrit into modern English. There is a further, spatial dimension to this story. Take a look at the following: *mouze*, *mouser*, and *mus-mus*. What are these, and where do we find them?

The word *mus-mus*, pronounced to rhyme with *puss-puss*, is from Jamaican English, according to the *Dictionary of Jamaican English* (Cassidy and Le Page, 1980, p. 312), which records it occurring from 1868. It means 'mouse', and 'rat', and it is an iterative (it repeats itself) of an older pronunciation of *mouse* which still survived in Scottish and northern English accents in the nineteenth century. The *Dictionary* records a related form in Surinam Creole, *moisi-móisi*. England formally acquired Jamaica from Spain in 1670, having sent troops there in 1655. When the British troops arrived (some 9000 of them), most of the existing population of 6000 was Spanish or of African descent (Patrick, 2008, p. 609). Columbus had landed in 1494 on his second voyage of discovery, and the Spanish started to settle the island in 1509, importing also African slaves. By the start of the seventeenth century, only a handful of the indigenous Arawak Indians remained alive on Jamaica, and, in turn, within five years of the British occupation most of the Spanish had gone. The historical roots of Jamaican English, then, lie in the intermixture of varieties of British English with influence from the African languages brought over by slaves.

In fact, Jamaican English in the title *Dictionary of Jamaican English* refers to two entities: Standard Jamaican English (sometimes simply Jamaican English) and Jamaican Creole, popularly called 'Patwa'. However, the linguistic situation in Jamaica has been modelled as a **creole** or **post-creole continuum**, in which there are no absolutely distinct categories. (This model was put forward by David DeCamp (1971).) The continuum is an attempt to bring some analytical order to an intricately varying scenario. At one end of the continuum is the **acrolect** (literally 'highest variety'), Standard Jamaican English, more formal, associated with education, mass media, and professional life, and descended from seventeenth- and eighteenth-century British English dialects (Patrick, 2008, p. 611). At the other end, is the **basilect** ('base variety'), Jamaican Creole, which displays possible underlying African influence, especially in pronunciation and grammar, and the greatest differences from British English dialects. At all points in between is the **mesolect** ('middle variety'), 'the speech uttered by most Jamaicans, in most situations' (Patrick, p. 611). Some Jamaicans switch between lects in tune with the social context, and the mesolect itself is highly variable. As a result of emigration from the late 1940s onwards, Jamaican English has had a major role in the development of British Black English, and some of its features, like the words *natty*, 'dreadlocks' or 'a Rastafarian', and *skanking*, referring to a style of dancing, for example, are well known generally because of the international popularity of Jamaican music.

Jamaica was not the first Caribbean island to be colonized by English speakers – British settlers arrived in Barbados in 1627. In the Atlantic, about a thousand miles north-east of the Caribbean, Bermuda was colonized as early as 1612 by settlers sponsored by the London-based Virginia Company, and by the 1650s the Bahamas, between the Caribbean and the North American mainland, had been populated by English-speaking Bermudans, and became a haven for pirates before being made a crown colony in 1717. During the seventeenth century, English spread to many parts of the Caribbean, and to the Central and South American mainland flanking it, interacting subsequently with African and other European languages to produce a complex and fertile diversity of Englishes and English-based creoles – in other words, a profusion of **contact varieties**. Surinam Creole, for example, is an umbrella term for a number of English-based varieties, some closely related, spoken by several hundred thousand people in Surinam (or Suriname) and French Guiana in the north-east of South America (Smith and Haabo, 2008, p. 339). African languages, Dutch, and Portuguese have also contributed to these creoles, and present-day Surinam is a remarkably multilingual state, though Dutch is the official language. In 1667, the British let the Dutch have the then-colony in exchange for Nieuw Amsterdam, which later became New York City.

After a false start in Virginia in the 1580s, English settled in what was to become the United States of America early in the seventeenth century, and *mouser* is one small result of this. In *The American Thesaurus of Slang* (Berrey and Van den Bark, 1954), *mouser* is recorded with the senses 'cat' (p. 130), 'detective' (p. 406), and 'sodomite' (p. 461). Quite a range. The *Dictionary of American Regional English* (Volume III, Cassidy and Hall, 1996) also lists *mouser*, and *mouse*, in the sense 'a lump or swelling caused by a blow; specifically, a black eye' (p. 694). Apart from noting (i) the interesting fact that after the American Civil War (1861–5) as many as 40,000 from the defeated South left for Brazil, there to start English-speaking enclaves (Trudgill, 2002, pp. 42–3); and (ii) that present-day United States is home to nearly 70 per cent of the world's English mother-tongue speakers (Crystal, 2003b, p. 60), and is the most powerful contemporary driving force behind globalized English, that is all that I will say at this point about American English. Its story is told in the preceding chapter of this book.

Next, Newfoundland, in the North Atlantic, and *mouze*. And I have to own up: despite appearances, *mouze* is not connected to *mouse*, at least not directly. According to the *Dictionary of Newfoundland English* (Story, Kirwin and Widdowson, Online version, 1998, accessed 2009), *mouze* is a verb meaning 'to make faces'. It might be derived from *mow* 'to make grimaces', recorded in the *English Dialect Dictionary* (Wright, Volume IV, 1903, p. 183) in Scotland and northern England – an

item which we can circuitously and tentatively relate via *muscle* to earlier forms of *mouse*, if we feel the need to do so. Newfoundland has
the honour of being known as 'England's first colony', or alternatively,
'Britain's first colony', both of which titles overlook the knotty historical statuses of Ireland, Scotland, and Wales. Officially 'discovered' by
the Bristol-based John Cabot in 1497, but known to Europeans before
that, Newfoundland came under British sovereignty in 1583. Its capital,
St John's, was founded in 1504, as a base for English fishermen. Newfoundland English is the oldest variety of English in the Americas, and
throughout its history it has been very distinct in character from the
English of mainland Canada. Newfoundland island, combined with
Labrador to its north, became a province of Canada in 1949. The
island's relatively isolated position at the eastern edge of Canada fostered
the survival of dialects seeded by immigrants from south-east Ireland,
who settled in the south-east of Newfoundland, and from south-west
England, who settled most of the rest. Up until the twentieth century,
these two sources provided most of the immigrants, the major influx
taking place in the early nineteenth century (Clarke, 2008, pp. 161–3,
is my source for these details). Also, in the south-west corner of the
island, there is an area of mixed French, Irish, and Scottish lineage.

Since the mid-twentieth century, Newfoundland's links with Canada
have grown, and some of the traditional features of its English, such as
**initial fricative voicing**, as in *fan* pronounced *van*, *said* pronounced
*zaid* (Clarke, 2008, p. 176), inherited from south-west England, are
in serious decline. The *Dictionary of Newfoundland English* (first published in 1982), like a number of similar projects across the world, aims
to collect, describe, and define the distinctive vocabulary of the region's
English, giving the history of each form in the manner established in
the *OED* and Joseph Wright's *English Dialect Dictionary*. The Newfoundland dictionary includes a discussion of the disputed etymology
and first use of the word *penguin*, which provides us with a brief respite
from *mouse* tales. The balance of opinion favours Welsh *pen gwyn*, literally 'head white', as the source, and first use in the late sixteenth century
as applied to the Great Auk of Newfoundland. See too the *OED* entry
for more debate.

Canada as a whole is officially a bilingual nation, which is a legacy of
the seventeenth- and eighteenth-century contest between England and
France in North America. Newfoundland aside, English-speaking settlement in Canada got underway following the Treaty of Paris in 1763,
in which France ceded almost all of its North American possessions
to Britain. By the nineteenth century, English speakers outnumbered

French in Canada, and today Canada is generally English-speaking, with the exception of the south-east province of Quebec and neighbouring parts of Ontario and New Brunswick. In addition, in the large cities (as in the UK and USA) there are newer immigrant communities and many mother tongues: beginning from the late nineteenth century, immigrants arrived from southern, central, and eastern Europe, Asia, and Latin America (Boberg, 2008, pp. 145–8).

There were two chief stages in the English-speaking settlement of Canada. The first was the movement, particularly after the end of the American War of Independence in 1783, of tens of thousands of Americans northwards into Ontario, Quebec, New Brunswick, and Nova Scotia. Later, Americans also figured in the settlement of western Canada. The second stage was direct immigration from the British Isles, which peaked in the mid-nineteenth century.

With the exemption, again, of Newfoundland, and rural parts of the other eastern Maritime provinces of New Brunswick, Nova Scotia, and Prince Edward Island, Canadian English is unusually homogeneous. Boberg says (2008, p. 146), 'one type of English, with minor regional variations, is spoken across most of the country, and central and western Canadians are generally incapable of guessing each other's regional origins on the basis of accent or dialect'. There are two views among linguists on why this is so, which hinge on differing interpretations of the relative strengths of American and British inputs into Canadian English. One view is that a levelled US-influenced variety developed, to which gravitated the speech of the descendants of the later, larger waves of British immigration. The other view is that the chief influence on Canadian English was the regional English of the British Isles, especially of Ireland and Scotland, which produced an English similar to American English because of a similar levelling of similar (really quite heterogeneous overall) sources. For Canadian English as a whole, the majority opinion of scholars stresses the influence of American English.

So-called **Canadian Raising** is a well-known pronunciation feature in general Canadian English. The term (coined by J. K. Chambers in 1973) refers to the pronunciation of the first elements of the diphthongs in words like *price* and *house*, which are articulated with the tongue higher in the mouth than in general American English. Canadian Raising applies only when these diphthongs are followed by a voiceless consonant, so that *prizes* and *houses*, for example, in which the following consonants have voice, do not exhibit Raising. To outsiders, Canadian Raised *about* may sound like *a boat*, and the vowel of *price* may sound as if it has moved a little towards that in *choice*. Although diagnostic of the general Canadian English accent, Raising occurs less in urban areas, and in reality is to be found also in parts of north-eastern United States (Boberg, 2008, p. 153). In most other respects, the Canada–US border coincides with a sharp linguistic boundary between the pronunciation or phonological systems of Canadian English and American English, or at least it does so in the east. Across western North America, north and south of the international border, there is a lack of well-defined major dialect areas of English, 'reflecting relatively sparse and recent settlement from a mixture of sources' (Boberg, p. 157).

We move on, with just a backward glance at the Americas to remind ourselves of colonial English's modest foothold there in the sixteenth century, its widespread establishment in the seventeenth century, and its dominance as a mother tongue in North America in the twentieth century. Now we fly past

## The Falkland Islands

in the South Atlantic, some 300 miles east of the coast of Argentina, settled by British English speakers between 1765 and 1774, and again from the mid-nineteenth century onwards (though France, Spain, and Argentina have each also claimed the islands since their discovery); and past

## Tristan da Cunha

about 1750 miles west of southern Africa, in the South Atlantic, with a small population speaking a variety with an ancestry in British English dialects (the islands were annexed to Britain in 1816), but that shows signs of pidginization too (Trudgill, 2002, p. 40); and past

## St Helena

also in the South Atlantic, just over 1200 miles west of Angola, claimed by the British East India Company in 1658, and subsequently settled mainly by southern English and slaves from Africa, India, and the West Indies, and now home to a variety that ranges from a basilectal, cre-olized St Helena English or 'Saintspeak' to an acrolect close to British Standard English (Wilson, 2008, p. 225);

on our way to

## *Africa*

If you Google *mouse-hunt*, you will be led to information about the 1997 film *Mousehunt*, no doubt, which could be what you were looking for. But let me tell you about *mouse-hunt* as recorded in *A Dictionary of South African English on Historical Principles* (Dore et al., 1996), for it is not without interest. In South African English, *mouse-hunt* referred to a meerkat, a mongoose, or a weasel, though the word is now apparently obsolete. Dore et al. (p. 480) tell us that it is **calqued** on South African Dutch or Afrikaans *muishond*, that is, the grammatical components or **morphemes** of the word are each translated from the donor language into their equivalents in the borrowing language. In this case, *muis* = 'mouse', and *hond* = 'dog, hound' but in the form 'hunt'. An earlier, fifteenth-century borrowing of Dutch *muushont* occurred in the dialects of southern England, where a *mouse-hunt* was a weasel or stoat. What we also learn from this example is that English in South Africa has existed alongside a South African version of Dutch, known as Afrikaans. Each language has borrowed extensively from the other, and each has been enmeshed in the historical inter-community struggles of South Africa.

Contact between English speakers and Africa took place as early as the 1530s, as merchant adventurers from England began trading in West Africa (the Guinea Coast). But the English language did not start to entrench itself in Africa until the turn of the eighteenth and nineteenth centuries, by which time the balance of trading power had shifted from the Portuguese and Dutch to the British and French, and traffic in slaves had become the dominant business. The slave trade was abolished in the British Empire in 1807. However, Britain's colonial interest in Africa grew markedly in the nineteenth century, as did the activities of English-speaking missionaries. Formal instruction in English as a second language took place, greatly influencing the development of educated African English. But the teachers themselves came speaking a diversity of British English dialects, and they taught English to speakers of many different indigenous languages. If we add informal transmission, the presence of the languages of other European colonizers, and the development of pidgin and creole Englishes in West Africa, then we glimpse once more a complex, contact-affected English-speaking scenario.

There are over 100 million **second-language** or **L2** speakers of English in Africa (Crystal, 2003a, p. 109). English is the main language of education, administration, and business in nearly all the former colonies of Britain in Africa (Melchers and Shaw, 2003, pp. 149–50). There are significant L2 numbers in – working our way down the west coast of the continent and back up the east – Gambia, Sierra Leone, Liberia, Ghana, Nigeria, Cameroon, Namibia, Botswana, South Africa, Lesotho, Swaziland, Zimbabwe, Zambia, Malawi, Tanzania, Uganda, and Kenya. Apart from Liberia, and most of Cameroon, all of these territories were once under British control. English exists alongside other languages in each territory, often as an official language. English also has a lesser L2 presence in Rwanda, Somalia, Ethiopia, and southern Sudan.

There are some groups of native or mother-tongue or **first-language** or **L1** speakers of English in Africa. The largest of these is the community descended from British settlers in South Africa. The label 'White South African English' is used to refer to the variety spoken by this community, but as Sean Bowerman notes (2008, p. 168), this name, and 'Black South African English', and 'Indian South African English', 'are not intended to reflect the apartheid classifications', but are used because of the legacy of South Africa's history, which has resulted in considerable correlations between 'ethnic affiliation and dialect of English'. The label 'South African English' is thus now used as a cover term for all the country's varieties – as it is by *A Dictionary of South African English on Historical Principles*.

The Union of South Africa under British rule was formed in 1910. It comprised four crown colonies: the Cape in the south, Natal in the east, Orange Free State in mid-South Africa, and Transvaal in the north. The British had had an interest in the Cape since the eighteenth century, and the Napoleonic Wars led to its becoming a British colony in 1814. A settlement programme followed, in which about 4500 Britons arrived in 1820 and 1821. These '1820 Settlers' came from all over Britain, speaking many regional dialects of English, although London cockney was 'strongly influential' (Gough, 1996, p. xvii). In their new home they lived in close contact with their colonial predecessors, the Dutch, but came into conflict with indigenous peoples as the colony expanded. Within a couple of generations, a levelled 'settler English' had developed.

Tensions between the British and the Dutch in the Cape Colony increased, with the 'Boers' (*boer* is Dutch for 'countryman, peasant, farmer') at odds with the British authorities over a lack of protection in conflicts with the indigenous Xhosa People, and over the British view on the need for equality of whites and non-whites. In the 'Great Trek' of 1834–6, over 10,000 Boers left the Cape to establish the territories which eventually became Transvaal, Orange Free State, and Natal. However, after more conflict, Natal became a British crown colony in 1844, and large numbers of English-speaking settlers arrived there, though with a greater proportion of middle-to-higher-class immigrants than in the Cape, bringing along a more homogeneous and northern English (Bowerman, 2008, p. 165; Gough, 1996, p. xvii). Following the Anglo-Boer War of 1899–1902, the remaining 'Voortrekker' republics of Orange Free State and Transvaal became British crown colonies. They already had significant numbers of English speakers as a result of the gold- and diamond-rush of the 1870s, which attracted incomers from all over the world. More English L1 speakers came in the wake of British rule. By the early twentieth century, South Africa was more industrialized, urbanized, and socially stratified. The higher-class English speakers were associated, in terms of accent, with British RP (Received Pronunciation). The most socially prestigious South African variety of English, and a local norm, was that of Natal, while Cape colonial English and L2 Afrikaans English were relatively low-status varieties (Bowerman, 2008, p. 167; Gough, 1996, p. xvii). In the present day, this correlation of language and class is expressed by linguists as a categorization of White South African English into three types: **Cultivated**, associated with the upper class and RP; **General**, middle class; and **Broad**, working class, to some extent merged with Afrikaans English (Bowerman, pp. 164, 168). Clearly there is also a regional dimension impinging on this social stratification of White South African English, with the major dialect areas divided into the Cape, Natal, and Transvaal. There are also settler-based L1 varieties of English in neighbouring Namibia and Zimbabwe.

Among the characteristic features of the White South African English accent, especially in its Broad category, is the **centralized** pronunciation of the **vowel** in words like *bit*, so that to outsiders it sounds similar to *but*. This centralization does not occur in the context of a nearby **velar** or **palatal** consonant (where the tongue touches the velum or hard palate), as for example in *kit* (Bowerman, 2008, p. 170). One way in which vowel sounds are classified by phoneticians is according to which part of the tongue is highest during articulation – in White South African *bit*, the mid-tongue is high, whereas in other accents the front of the tongue is high in *bit*. It is thought (Bowerman, pp. 174–5) that this characteristic is part of a **chain shift** of **front vowels** in some speakers of White South African English, in which, for example, *bat* sounds more like *bet* to outsiders, and *bet* sounds like *bit*. With regard to this **raising** of tongue height for front vowels, White South African English can be grouped with the two other major L1 Southern Hemisphere Englishes, Australian English and New Zealand English.

*Afrikaans* is the name by which South African Dutch became known in the 1920s, and it was promoted as the premier official language of the country once the Afrikaner Nationalist Party came to power in 1948. Afrikaner nationalism was hostile to English, which, however, remained an official language. The apartheid regime sought to make Afrikaans a joint medium of instruction (with English) in black schools, which led to the Soweto uprisings of 1976, and, ironically enough, to English being perceived as the language of liberation. Since the end of apartheid in 1994, Black South African English has become more prominent and more diverse, and has begun to shift from an L2 variety to L1 use. In addition, the Indian community of South Africa (immigrants from India arrived in large numbers in the second half of the nineteenth century) has been shifting from L2 use of English to L1 since the 1960s.

South Africa now has no less than 11 official languages. In the late 1990s, the most commonly used first or home languages were Zulu and Xhosa (Kamwangamalu, 2006, p. 159), but English's prestige, its association with modernity, education, the legal system and government, and its use as a *lingua franca* ensure that it is 'highly valued in post-apartheid South Africa and enjoys far more prestige than any other official language' (Kamwangamalu, 2006, p. 163).

Liberia is another (West) African country with a significant L1 variety of English, this being 'Liberian Settler English', descended from the language of the 16,000 African-Americans who settled there, as freed slaves, in the nineteenth century (Singler, 2008, p. 102). As well as Settler English, there is a standardized English in use in Liberia, and two pidgins: Vernacular Liberian English and the waning Kru Pidgin English. There are also English-based pidgins in Ghana, Nigeria, and Cameroon, which are offshoots of Krio, spoken in Sierra Leone (Huber, 2008, p. 381); but again we must move on, eastward.

## South Asia

In an essay on 'South Asian Englishes' (2006), Ravinder Gargesh uses the following example from the *Hindustan Times* (Editorial, 4 August 2004, p. 8; Gargesh, p. 105) to illustrate **code mixing** in Indian English in informal talk and newspapers: 'After laboring hard for three days, the BJP's four day Chintan baithak has delivered a mouse.' As Gargesh explains, the *Chintan baithak* was a brainstorming session of the Bharatiya Janata Party reviewing its electoral defeat, 'and the "mouse" refers to the futility of the exercise'. Gargesh here uses the term **code** to refer to a language or a variety of a language. In a multilingual society such as India (it has over 1600 mother tongues), different codes can have different social functions, such as use at home, in work, while shopping, in the mass media, or as a *lingua franca*. The code mixing here is of a Hindi term in an English sentence, analogous to the use of Welsh *Eisteddfod* in Welsh English in an example I give in Chapter 1 of this book – except that English in India, unlike in Wales, is an L2 with chiefly non-domestic functions for the overwhelming majority of its users. Hindi has the biggest speaker totals as a home language in India, and it is an official language. The 'Indian-ness' of the example sentence above is evidenced also in the striking 'mouse'-idiom. Similarly eye-catching, to the non-Indian English speaker, is: 'The parliamentary standing committee on Railways has urged the railway ministry to lay new tracks to stop rising cases of jumbo deaths between Siliguri and Alipurduar stations. . . . It may be recalled that more than 39 elephants have been killed after being hit by trains . . .' (*The Statesman* online, Bengal, 28 December 2008, accessed 2009) – in which *jumbo* looks informal, while *It may be recalled* looks formal and slightly old-fashioned. They make an incongruous pair. Examples of such stylistic habits can be observed also on Indian satellite TV news channels which broadcast in English, like NDTV. Melchers and Shaw speculate (2003, pp. 143–4) that stylistic effect within the multilingual setting is achieved via the choice of language made, resulting in a neutralization of stylistic choice within Indian English, so that the incongruities above are not marked for the Indian English speaker.

Estimates of numbers of speakers of English in India vary considerably. Crystal (2003b, p. 63) goes with 200 million L2 and 350,000 L1 users out of a total Indian population of over 1 billion. Additionally, there are well over 22 million mainly L2 speakers in the other five countries of the region: Pakistan, Sri Lanka, Nepal, Bangladesh, and Bhutan. South Asia therefore makes an immense contribution to the character of English today. Notwithstanding its L2 status, English in South Asia has been **nativized**, that is, by means of its interaction with the region's indigenous languages and the general setting it has developed local varieties, showing local traits in phonology, vocabulary, grammar, and discourse. Attitudes towards the language are not universally positive, but overall English is seen as 'a means of economic uplift and upward social mobility' (Gargesh, 2006, p. 90), as well as the language of cultural modernity and of power.

As elsewhere in the world, the region's first contacts with English were with trading speculators, specifically the British East India Company, which received its charter in 1600, granting it a monopoly of English trade in the eastern world and Pacific. By 1612, it had established itself in Gujarat, north-west India. The Company became politically very powerful in India, controlling the territory after 1765, and fostering the growth of English bilingualism in the region. From 1858 until independence in 1947, India was under the rule of the British crown. On independence, the territory was partitioned into Pakistan and India, and in 1971 East Pakistan seceded from its union with West Pakistan, and was renamed Bangladesh. By 1947, English had become well established as a medium of education and administration. It is an associate official language in present-day India and Pakistan, has prestigious functions throughout South Asia (Gargesh, p. 92), and is used as a *lingua franca* as well. English also has a substantial presence in the mass-media output of South Asia, especially in India.

Under other circumstances, we would spend more time in

## South-East Asia

than we are going to. For there are, in each of Malaysia, Singapore, the Philippines, and Hong Kong, significant numbers of L1 and L2 speakers of English. Setting aside the Philippines, all these territories have British colonial pasts, and, as in South Asia, English is a prestige language, associated with education, technology, and professional society. Most of its speakers here are L2, but in Singapore a colloquial variety, 'Singlish', has emerged, which shows input from other local languages, such as Hokkien, Cantonese, Malay, and Tamil (Wee, 2008, p. 260). In the Philippines, not far under 50 per cent of the population of 96 million (in 2008) has English as an L2, and it is an English with a definite American influence, as the country was under US control in the early twentieth century.

Furthermore, in South-East Asia, in Thailand, Vietnam, and Indonesia, and in

## East Asia

in China, Taiwan, Japan, and Korea, English is accruing huge numbers of speakers who are learning it as a **foreign language**. Although labelled as an international language in these circumstances in these countries, rather than as territory-specific or *intra*national, it seems that (as Honna, 2006, p. 114, suggests) national varieties are emerging in East Asia.

## Oceania and the Pacific

Papua New Guinea is located at the far south-east edges of Asia, but is a part of Australasia, which is a part of Oceania, in the South Pacific. The word *mausgras* in Tok Pisin, the *de facto* national language of Papua New Guinea, means, obviously, 'moustache', or literally 'mouth-grass'. The Tok Pisin term for 'mouse' is actually *liklik rat*, literally 'small rat'. Another word for a type of coarse grass in Tok Pisin is *kunai*, and another word for 'little' is *smolpela*. The suffix *–pela*, or *–pla*, is derived from the English word *fellow*, and it is used in Tok Pisin to mark monosyllabic adjectives, as in *smolpela*, and to indicate the plural of pronouns, so that *yu* = 'you' singular, *yutupela* = 'both of you', and *yupela* = 'you' plural (more than two). The origins of Tok Pisin (literally 'Talk Pidgin') were in a Pacific Pidgin English that developed in the early nineteenth century as a result of maritime trade involving contact between English speakers and speakers of other languages, including indigenous languages. Tok Pisin is related to two other pidgins in the South Pacific: Pijin, spoken in the Solomon Islands, and Bislama, in Vanuatu. Together, this group is called Melanesian Pidgin English. Most of the vocabulary of Tok Pisin derives from English, though some comes from indigenous sources, including *kunai* (G. P. Smith, 2008, p. 192). There has been some German influence too, as Germany held part of Papua New Guinea in the late nineteenth century.

There are other contact varieties of English scattered through Oceania and the Pacific: on the far-apart (over 3500 miles) Norfolk Island and Pitcairn Island, Englishes originating with the Bounty mutineers in 1792, now with fewer than a 1000 speakers; and in Fiji, and Hawai'i. Each of these varieties, including the Melanesian Pidgins, exists within the kind of creole continuum that we saw in Jamaica, with a local version of Standard English constituting the acrolect. Contact varieties occur also in New Zealand and Australia. These are Maori English and Aboriginal Australian English respectively, and they exist in conjunction with the final **transplanted** Englishes that we visit in this chapter.

## Australia and New Zealand

It so happened that I was once interviewed, over the telephone, on a New Zealand radio station. I was introduced by the presenter as 'dippidy hid' of my section of the university that employs me. And it is true, I was *deputy head* of my school at the time. This is an example of the **raising of front vowels** in New Zealand and Australia mentioned earlier. The raising in *bat-* and *bet*-type words is higher in New Zealand English than in Australian, and New Zealand *bit* can sound like *but* to outsiders (that is, the vowel is centralized), whereas in Australian English *bit* can sound like *beat* (the vowel is raised), especially in the Melbourne dialect of the south-east (Bradley, 2008, p. 118).

New Zealand English and Australian English are similar in many ways, especially in pronunciation (including the intonation pattern known as **High Rising Terminal** or **Tone (HRT)**, which makes statements sound like questions), and in grammar, but there are differences too. One, in vocabulary, is the conspicuous Australian penchant for **hypocoristics** or pet-names, such as *coldie, journo*, and *ump*, for 'a cold beer', 'journalist', and 'umpire' (Simpson, 2008, pp. 400–1). The contact setting is different in each country, resulting in loanwords from Maori in New Zealand English and from Aboriginal languages in Australia, particularly for referring to indigenous flora and fauna. And, as mentioned above, there are additional and different contact varieties in each country, including two major English-based creoles in Australia: Kriol, spoken in the north and west; and Cape York Creole, in the north-east.

Although there is a consensus among linguists that, compared with the United Kingdom and even the United States, the general national varieties of New Zealand and Australia are pretty homogeneous, there is some regional and social diversity. In Australia, bearing in mind that most of the population lives in coastal areas, dialect areas have been identified in the west, the central south, the south-east, and north-east (Kiesling, 2006, p. 82). In New Zealand, the Southland dialect, in the south of the South Island, still has a **rhoticity** (pronunciation of *r* after a vowel and before a consonant, or finally in a word, as in *bird* and *burr*, for example) which is otherwise mostly absent in New Zealand English. This may be due to the strong Scottish presence in the nineteenth-century settling of the area. Gordon and Mclagan report (2008, pp. 66–7) strongly held views in

New Zealand that there are notable regional variations in the country's English, but they add that the differences are minor compared with other varieties. Following Mitchell and Delbridge (1965a, 1965b), it became customary to categorize Australian English pronunciation in terms of the three social-prestige-related types, **Cultivated**, **General**, and **Broad**, and this categorization is also used for New Zealand English, even if not all specialists agree that the differentiation is so clear-cut.

These Antipodean Englishes are also relatively recent varieties. James Cook claimed New Zealand for the British crown in 1769, though the official colony was not established until 1840, and it was between 1850 and 1890 that large-scale immigration from the British Isles, Europe, and Australia took place. The vast majority of immigrants came from Ireland, Scotland, and, most of all, from southern England (Baxter et al., 2008, p. 4; 2009, p. 260). There were concentrations of southern Englanders in the North Island, and of Scots in the far north of the North Island and in Otago in the South Island. After the discovery of gold, Otago and the West Coast of the South Island received many immigrants from Australia between 1860 and 1870. (These details are from Bauer and Warren, 2008, pp. 39–40.) By the time of the second generation of native-born New Zealanders, at the end of the nineteenth century, a levelled, relatively stable and distinctive New Zealand English had emerged (Baxter et al., 2008, p. 4; 2009, p. 261; Trudgill, 2004, pp. 24–5, 113).

Although Europeans had begun exploring Australia in the seventeenth century, the first territorial claim was made in 1770 by Cook on behalf of the British crown. From 1788, Britain established a penal colony in Sydney, and a preponderance of early settlers came from the south-east of England (Kiesling, 2006, pp. 75–6). 'Free settlers' did not arrive in numbers until the mid-nineteenth century, with English speakers coming from all of the countries of the British Isles. Again a blending or levelling seems to have occurred which led to a new national variety. In addition, since the 1950s, immigrants have come from northern, eastern, and southern Europe, and from Asia, and consequently an ethnically based and 'hyper-broad' version of Broad Australian English has developed (Kiesling, 2006, pp. 81–2).

Our tour stops here, but not before I tell you that, according to the *Australian National Dictionary: A Dictionary of Australianisms on Historical Principles* (Ramson, 1988, p. 405), a *mouser* is a slang term from the Australian shearing industry, meaning a money-grabbing and disruptive shearer.

# Modelling

We have seen the key role of English/British colonialism in the spread of English across the world between the sixteenth and the nineteenth centuries. In the twentieth century, the expansion of American economic and cultural influence, and the internationalization of media communications, fuelled further growth in English speaker numbers. Despite the great range of new circumstances in which the language found itself, linguists have attempted to identify a common process at work in the many re-rootings of English. For example, Edgar W. Schneider (2003) describes 'a fundamentally uniform developmental process' (p. 233) consisting of five consecutive stages: foundation, exonormative stabilization (in which foreign, mainly British, linguistic patterns hold sway), nativization, endonormative stabilization (the gradual adoption of a new, indigenous set of norms), and differentiation (the new national variety itself diversifies, developing its own dialects). S. S. Mufwene put forward (for example, in 1996) the 'Founder Principle', which stresses the critical effect that the make-up of the first generation of a new variety has on its subsequent character. In their research on New Zealand English, which builds on work by Peter Trudgill (2004), and draws on evolution theory and mathematics, and which has relevance for other Englishes too, Baxter et al. (2008, 2009) propose that the persistent replication of the more prevalent linguistic variants in social interaction was at the heart of the 'levelling' that created New Zealand English. The decisive period in this levelling, they argue, occurred when immigration had tailed off and the national infrastructure had improved sufficiently to enable larger social networks to come into being, at the end of the nineteenth century.

Linguists have also devised models which, as McArthur (1998, p. 95) puts it, seek 'to make sense of the present-day diversity within the English language complex'. These include Peter Strevens's (1980) global family tree of Englishes, Manfred Görlach's (1990) circle of International English, with a supranational variety at its centre, and McArthur's (1987) own circle of World English, with World Standard English as its hub, encircled by regional varieties. However, the most influential model is that of the **three concentric circles of English**, first advocated by the Indian-American linguist Braj B. Kachru in 1985. The **Inner Circle** refers to the traditional bases of English, to the major L1 or **ENL** (English as a native language) territories: the United Kingdom, the United States, Canada, Australia, New Zealand. The **Outer Circle** is the L2 or **ESL** (English as a second language) group, which includes, for example, Nigeria, India, Malaysia, and the Philippines. Since 1985, the final **Expanding Circle** has lived up to its name, and now refers pretty much to the rest of the world, where English is seen as an important foreign or international language, that is, the **EFL** (English as a foreign language) territories. Some countries, like South Africa, do not fit exclusively into just the one category; and just as a group of L2 speakers can shift over time into L1 use, so too can there be a change in a region's status, for example, from EFL to ESL. But Kachru's model has become widely used as a tool for analysing the ongoing progress of worldwide English.

## Concluding

David Crystal (2003b, p. 69) encourages us to remember that, if one quarter of the world's population is able to use English, that means that three-quarters are not. He adds, 'Populist claims about the universal spread of English thus need to be kept firmly in perspective.' Nevertheless, if English is not all-pervasive, it is at least very pervasive indeed. The status of English as the world's leading international language is indicated by the increasing number of EFL-territory-based TV networks that broadcast channels via satellite, cable, or the Internet in English, such as CCTV (China), Press TV (Iran), NHK (Japan), Al Jazeera (Qatar), and RT (Russia). Back in Europe, outside the British Isles English is the first foreign language among students, is taking over in a growing number of social domains, and its use as a *lingua franca* has led to an emergent EFL variety – 'Euro-English' (Modiano, 2006, pp. 223, 230–1). Figure 7 serves as a final symbolic illustration.

This is a postcard-sized advert that I picked up on a visit to Paris. The franchise it promotes began in Paris. This chapter started with a bilingual place-name, but here is something more unusual, a bilingual pun, in which English *first* is inserted into French *coiffure*, with the number *1* inserted into *first* for good measure. The pun assumes that its target audience, presumably originally mainly French-speaking, has a competence in English. It is a bold piece of branding in a country renowned for its official determination to repel English linguistic intrusions, and it brings into play English's association with modernity and internationalism. Very pervasive, very global – English has come a long way.

**FIGURE 7**    *COIFF1RST*

## Further reading

There are two major twenty-first-century collections on varieties of English worldwide: the four-volume *Varieties of English* (2008), edited by Bernd Kortmann et al., which is a superb guide and resource, containing concise histories and structural descriptions of L1 and L2 varieties written by leading specialists; and *The Handbook of World Englishes* (2006), edited by Braj B. Kachru et al., which is more discursive, setting description in the context of discussion of ideology and identity. These differing approaches are paralleled in the output of two of the foremost academic journals in the field: *English World-Wide*, and *World Englishes*. For something slimmer and more synoptic, go to *An Introduction to International Varieties of English* (2002), by Laurie Bauer, and for an accessible run-through of varieties and issues use David Crystal's *English as a Global Language* (2nd edn, 2003b). I also recommend *World Englishes* (2003), by Gunnel Melchers and Philip Shaw, and *English: One Tongue, Many Voices* (2006), by Jan Svartvik and Geoffrey Leech. Tom McArthur's *The Oxford Guide to World English* (2002) and *The Oxford Companion to the English Language* (1992) are exceptional works of reference, as is David Crystal's *The Cambridge Encyclopedia of the English Language* (2nd edn, 2003a). Online, Raymond Hickey's *Studying Varieties of English*, at: http://www.uni-due.de/SVE/, is excellent, as is its companion *Studying the History of*

*English*, at: http://www.uni-due.de/SHE/. In addition to the national dictionaries mentioned in the chapter above, there is also: the *Dictionary of Caribbean English Usage* (1996), edited by R. Allsopp; *A Dictionary of Canadianisms on Historical Principles* (1967), edited by W. S. Avis et al.; the *Dictionary of New Zealand English: A Dictionary of New Zealandisms on Historical Principles* (1997), edited by H. W. Orsman; and the *Macquarie Dictionary* (of Australian English, 4th edn, 2005), edited by A. Delbridge. The last three of these have associated websites. Some other useful works are: *Focus on South Africa* (1996), edited by V. de Klerk; *World Englishes in Asian Contexts* (2006), by Y. Kachru and C. L. Nelson; *New Zealand English: Its Origin and Evolution* (2004), by E. Gordon et al.; and *English in Australia* (2001), edited by D. Blair and P. Collins.

# 6  Signs
## The Semiotic View of Language

This chapter includes the following:
- An introduction to Ferdinand de Saussure's theory of the **linguistic sign**.
- C. S. Peirce's classification of semiotic signs: **icon**, **index**, and **symbol**.
- A guide to types of sign in writing systems.
- Explanation of the term **hyperreality**.

## Introduction

What have signs got to do with language? Everything, and this chapter is about why. It introduces the **semiotic** theory of language and explains key properties of the English language from this point of view. It looks especially at the **linguistic sign**, but does so in the context of a discussion of signs in general and their influence on our lives. I will begin with a broad definition of what a sign is before progressively refining this definition. **Signs** are, broadly speaking, representations which express a meaning.

## Signs, iconicity, and convention

Some signs quite clearly simulate objects, and with surprisingly powerful consequences. For example, in the film *Falling Down* (1992), the character played by Michael Douglas, D-Fens, becomes violently upset in a fast-food restaurant because the sorry, miserable, squashed hamburger he has just been served does not live up to the promise offered by the bright neon-picture of a hamburger above the restaurant's bar. This is a peculiar but not totally unusual event. It is not unusual in that we often find ourselves in situations where reality does not live up to the glossy pictures of advertisements, though admittedly the response of D-Fens is extreme. On television a loaf of bread looks warm, springy, and full of natural goodness, but on your plate a slice of it has the texture of ropy cardboard. Your holiday hotel might, in so many ways, fail to live up to the images in the brochure. That futuristic mini hi-fi may turn out to be made of tacky plastic. What is peculiar is that these advertising pictures are copies which become more real to us than the objects they represent.

The surrealist painter René Magritte (1898–1967) says in his picture of a pipe (*The Treachery of Images*, 1928/29), '*Ceci n'est pas une pipe*' ('This is not a pipe'). His point is, a picture of an object is not the object itself (a point he made again with his 1964 painting of an apple). Similarly, a picture of a hamburger is not a hamburger, it is a picture. It is a representation of a hamburger. It has a relation with a hamburger, it stands for a hamburger, but as an object it is not a hamburger. The glossy hamburgers that we see in advertisements simulate hamburgers. What is peculiar about D-Fens's response to the object-hamburger he is served is that he judges the object against its simulation: 'Can anyone tell me what's wrong with this picture?' he yells, referring to his miserable (object-)burger. His judgement inverts the original–copy relationship. He treats the simulation of the hamburger as more authentic than the hamburger itself, and while this is peculiar it also exemplifies a common symptom of modern global capitalist–consumerism.

This power that signs have to affect our judgement (in the case above, signs that simulate objects) is a theme that I shall return to, but let us move on quickly now to my second example, a pair of ubiquitous modern signs. What the psychoanalyst Jacques Lacan described as Western Man's need 'by which his public life is subjected to the laws of urinary segregation' (1957, p. 151) is often symbolized by simple pictures such as Figures 8 and 9.

A picture such as Figure 8 can be found on a door in a public place like an airport, a shopping mall, or a workplace, often though not invariably in proximity to another door with a picture such as Figure 9

**FIGURE 8**

**FIGURE 9**

on it, and both figures (like Magritte's picture of a pipe) are found in association with a short text, in this case the abbreviation 'WC'. In such public contexts, the message conveyed by Figures 8 and 9 is obvious and universal. Why? Because, one might answer, these symbols look like what they stand for. Not so, not if by 'stand for' we mean their meaning. What these symbols mean is 'Here, behind this door, is the gentlemen's/ladies' public convenience.' Figures 8 and 9 do not look like this message. Figure 8 resembles in rather geometric fashion the human form, with head, two arms and two legs discernible, and Figure 9 is more geometric, with head, two arms, and three triangular shapes discernible. The meaning of each symbol is in fact not immediately obvious. A visiting alien from, say, the Tau Boo solar system could not be expected to understand their significance, although if he/she/it had seen the SETI (Search for Extraterrestrial Intelligence) plaque (see Figure 10) designed especially for him/her/it and placed on board the Pioneer 10 and 11 space probes, then he/she/it would have a fighting chance of deducing that Figures 8 and 9 are stylized representations of male and female humans, respectively, in stereotypical attire.

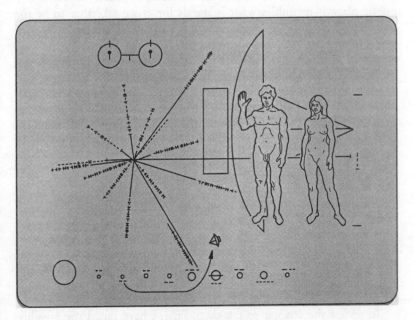

**FIGURE 10**  SETI PLAQUE

It would take sensitive observation and further time for the alien from Tau Boo to work out the full meaning of Figures 8 and 9, but having travelled 55 light years he/she/it is more likely to be looking urgently for a door marked with Figure 11.

**FIGURE 11**

Figures 8 and 9 are, of course, signs, and well-known signs at that. They can be called **iconic** signs, in that they *resemble* the objects they represent, though they do not resemble in straightforward fashion what they stand for, not if we take that to be the meaning 'Here, behind this door, is the gentlemen's/ladies' public convenience.' Their meaning is in fact established through a mixture of **iconicity** and **convention**. Iconicity is important in our use of signs, and convention is crucial.

Let us consider a couple more examples. The sign ♥ is iconic, in a stylized way, of an organ of the body, the heart. It is used, however, in graffiti, on greetings cards, and in trademarked slogans similar to 'I ♥ a great metropolis on the east coast of the USA' and 'I ♥ some famous pop group or other' in reference to matters of the heart, that is, as a substitute for the word *love*. ☎ seems to be a very iconic sign, because it looks like the object it represents, a telephone, and if displayed in a public place it resembles what it stands for, if we take that to be the meaning 'Here is a telephone.' It is also a **pictorial** sign (as is ♥), and it is a **logogram**, that is, a sign that can represent a word, in this case *telephone*, as it does exactly when marking a telephone number. ♥ also qualifies as a logogram, when used as a substitute for the word *love*. A less exotic logogram is & (*and*). Figures 8 and 9 just about qualify as logograms if we accept a terser interpretation of their meaning, such as 'toilets'. However, a flaw in the categorization of ☎ as iconic is that there are proportionally far fewer telephones that actually look like ☎ than there used to be. No self-respecting modern capitalist–consumerist teenager, for example, carries around a 'phone that looks like ☎. So what will happen to ☎ as an iconic logogram? It could fall out of use, swept aside by new-fangled, blobby representations, such as ( or, arguably, ▤, or the like, or it could survive as an increasingly conventional and decreasingly iconic sign. Not only can a sign depend on a mixture of iconicity and convention, but the balance between the two can shift over time. (Another threat to the continued use of ☎, and (, and maybe even ▤, would be the gradual, painful extinction of public telephones.)

To review the chapter so far, then. First, I have raised the possibility that a picture of something, that is, a simulation of something, a representation of something, can be treated as more real or authentic than the something itself. This is an idea that I will be working my way back towards during the remainder of this chapter, in order to suggest that a **linguistic sign** can be involved in the same effect, though before that I will explain what a linguistic sign is. Up till now in this chapter I have used the term **sign** pretty much in its everyday sense, that is, a symbol or representation which conveys a meaning or a message, and we have seen that signs have a role to play in human communication. In fact, they have an indispensable role to play in human communication, for in addition to our use of signs of the kinds discussed so far, speech and writing involve the use of signs. We could define **speech** and **writing**, or **language**, as the use of signs. I am not now thinking of sign language, that is, a means of communication using gestures, I am thinking of language as the use of **linguistic signs**.

Also in the chapter so far, we have looked at a few examples of signs – using the term in its everyday sense – mainly to illustrate signs' dependence on iconicity and/or convention, and I will return to closer scrutiny of these terms shortly. Before that it will be useful to survey several categories of sign (everyday sense) that occur in writing systems.

## Categories of sign in writing systems

The letters of the Roman alphabet – currently in use in this sentence – are signs. They are **phonograms**. A phonogram is a sign which represents an individual sound, or more precisely speaking a group of closely related sounds, for example, the letter *r* represents quite a variety of *r*-sounds scattered across different languages and dialects. Phonograms or letters are the signs used in modern alphabets, for example, the Greek, Cyrillic, Hebrew, Arabic, and Roman alphabets. Another similar category of signs is **syllabograms**, as used for instance in the Japanese *kana* scripts. A syllabogram represents an individual syllable. Phonograms and syllabograms are the two types of **sound-based signs** used in writing systems. Sound-based signs represent sounds, and they form one of the two major categories of written sign in the everyday sense of the term (**sign**). The other major category is the **pictorial** or **picture-based sign**, of which we have already seen examples.

Pictorial signs are very common in modern life, in computer software, at the sides of roads, in shopping malls, at work, in manuals telling you how to operate audio and video equipment, even in my shoes telling me what they are made of (Figure 12), and so on.

Adrian Frutiger comments, in his mammoth survey of *Signs and Symbols* (1998, p. 226), 'pictorial signs are becoming ever more indispensable for human communication', as more humans travel internationally (✈) more often. And perhaps, one could add, as more (young) people IM or 'instant message' more often ☺. But pictorial

**FIGURE 12**   SIGNS FROM INSIDE THE AUTHOR'S SHOE

signs, including pictorial signs of mammoths, are also probably the oldest written signs. It is generally thought that, in the evolution of writing systems, pictorial signs came first and sound-based signs were a later development. (The earliest writing system is usually dated to around 3000 BC, and the first sound-based alphabet is the North Semitic, dating from around 1700 BC.) The pictorial signs of writing systems can be divided into three types: logograms, which we have already defined, **pictograms**, and **ideograms**. Of these, pictograms are thought to be the earliest. A pictogram is a picture which looks like the object it represents. For example, dating from the fourth millennium BC from Sumer in the Middle East, we find pictograms such as ⫸ 'fish' and ♡ 'heart' (Frutiger, 1998, p. 121). An ideogram is also a picture, but one which represents an idea rather than an object. Again, in evolutionary terms, ideographic writing is seen as a later development of pictographic writing. An ideogram may result when a pictogram becomes stylized and the object it represents is less recognizable, and/or the pictogram's meaning extends to cover a concept which cannot be represented directly in pictorial form. In early Sumerian writing, for example, represented ⫦ 'walk' (Frutiger, p. 121). The evolutionary drift then in general seems to be from the iconic to the conventional.

The term **iconic** has been utilized a fair bit in this chapter so far and I should now further clarify my use of it. Set aside thoughts of icons on a VDU, or of religious images and fashionable celebrities, and focus on the notion of resemblance. In linguistics and semiotics, an iconic sign is one which has some kind of resemblance either to the object it represents or depicts, or to its meaning, or to both of these. Note that I have differentiated throughout this chapter between the object represented by an iconic sign and the meaning of a sign, because, as we have seen, these will not necessarily amount to the same thing. Note also that I have deliberately equated a sign's meaning and what a sign stands for, for reasons that I will discuss very soon. And note furthermore that while the general evolutionary drift of written signs may have been from the iconic to the **conventional** (that is, a culturally agreed meaning that has to be learned rather than being simply obvious), iconic pictorial signs are still very much with us, and even among the prehistoric cave art of 10,000–30,000 years ago we find abundant so-called 'abstract', that is, conventionalized signs. And remember in addition that, notwithstanding the impression given by the survey above, a sign may belong to more than one category; for example, ♥, which arguably is a pictogram, an ideogram, and a logogram. And one more thing: most of the examples we have looked at so far have a large measure of iconicity, but many of them also depend for their meaning on a degree of convention. However, of the two major categories of written signs, pictorial signs seem to show greater iconicity, while sound-based signs have systematic correspondences, established by convention, with sounds.

## Semiotics and C. S. Peirce

In the paragraph above I mentioned semiotics. **Semiotics** is the study of signs and the systems that they form. Semioticians work with a different, perhaps more all-encompassing definition of the term **sign**, a definition which we find in the work of Charles Sanders Peirce (1839–1914). Peirce said (1893–1910, p. 99), 'A sign, or *representamen*, is something which stands to somebody for something in some respect or capacity.' According to this definition, a sign can be a sign in the everyday sense of the term, but it can also be, for example, a facial expression, such as a raised eyebrow, or it can be a cough, which signifies that the cougher is unwell or nervous or impatient, or it can be a pair of branded running shoes, which signify that their wearer wishes to convey an air of moneyed, casual youthfulness. In Peirce's definition, interpretation of the sign is important: for a sign to be a sign it must *stand to somebody* for something. Peirce calls the something that a sign stands for its **object**, but he uses this term nebulously – the object can be a physical entity, or a concept, or an action or event. For Peirce, a sign stands for its object by means of an idea or mental impression of the object, so that the sign itself is already an interpretation of an object.

Peirce was a prolific philosopher, one of the founders of modern semiotics, who devoted much energy to categorizing types of sign, in the semiotician's sense of the term. One of Peirce's sets of categories has been particularly influential. This set divides signs into three categories: **iconic**, **indexical**, and **symbolic**. Peirce's definition of an iconic sign enlarges upon the notion of resemblance: anything can be an icon of anything 'in so far as it is like that thing and used as a sign of it' (Peirce, 1893–1910, p. 102). Thus a photograph is an icon, and if I surmise that zebras are likely to be obstinate animals it is because I am treating donkeys as icons of zebras. An indexical sign stands for its object not by means of similarity but because it is in a dynamic connection with the object. For example, Peirce says (p. 108), 'I see a man with a rolling gait. This is a probable indication that he is a sailor.' The man's rolling gait is taken as an index of something else (the man's occupation) with which it has an effect-and-cause relation. Similarly, smoke is an index of fire, a sundial is an index of the time of day, mud on the carpet is an index of someone walking through the house in dirty footwear. A symbolic sign, however, 'refers to the Object that it denotes by virtue of a law, usually an association of general ideas, which operates to cause the Symbol to be interpreted as referring to that Object' (p. 102). Accordingly, 'All words, sentences, books and other conventional signs are Symbols' (p. 112). This is to use the term **symbol** in contrast with **icon** and **index**, that is, a symbol is a sign that operates not through resemblance or through cause and effect but through convention.

The use of the terms **stands for** and **refers to** in Peirce's definitions requires comment, but we can best do this while considering the additional, vital use of the term **sign** in the phrase **linguistic sign**. This is where we come to the work of another founding figure in semiotics, and in modern linguistics, and in the school of thought known as structuralism, that is, the linguist Ferdinand de Saussure (1857–1913).

## The linguistic sign and Ferdinand de Saussure

Saussure's reputation is based on one text, *Cours de linguistique générale*, published in French in 1916. Two English translations eventually appeared, in 1960 and 1983 – in this book, I quote from the 1960 translation. Between 1906 and 1911, Saussure gave three courses of lectures on 'general linguistics' at the University of Geneva, and following his death in 1913 the *Cours* was put together by some of his colleagues, who had to rely mainly on the lecture notes of his students. The *Course in General Linguistics* is among the most influential books of the twentieth century. It outlines a beautifully simple theory of language, though not all of its analyses or its ramifications are fully worked through within the text, which is not surprising given the manner of the *Course*'s composition. (In 1996, further material by Saussure came to light, which was published in 2002 as *Écrits de linguistique générale*,

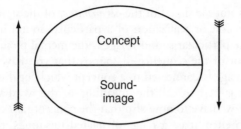

**FIGURE 13**  THE LINGUISTIC SIGN (from Saussure, 1916, p. 66)

and in English in 2006 as *Writings in General Linguistics*. These *Writings* put some additional flesh on the bones of the *Course*.) Aspects of Saussure's theory are discussed in several chapters of this book, and for the rest of this chapter we will discuss the meat of Saussure's notion of the linguistic sign, and – I am reminded – hamburgers.

According to the *Course*, a language is structured on linguistic signs – the linguistic signs form a system, and this system is the underlying structure of the language. Each linguistic sign is comprised of two halves: the **concept** and the **sound-image**. At this point, here are two important things to remember about the linguistic sign: the linguistic sign is **arbitrary**, and the linguistic sign is a psychological entity. And two important things to remember about Saussure's theory of language: Saussure wished to redirect linguistics away from the study of written texts and towards the study of speech (which he considered the primary medium of language), but more exactly his theory is about the psychological underpinnings of speech.

Within the sign there is nothing but the concept and sound-image, which are 'intimately united', each recalling the other (Saussure, 1916, p. 66), as indicated by the arrows in Figure 13. Concept and sound-image are distinguishable but indispensable, that is to say, the linguistic sign vanishes if either the concept or sound-image is missing. A linguistic sign is an associative bond between a concept and a sound-image, so that the concept will always call to mind its partner sound-image, and the sound-image will always conjure up the concept. Neither exists independently outside the boundary of their sign. Moreover, both the concept and the sound-image are abstract and mental in character, which is why the linguistic sign is a psychological entity.

For example, take a word, any word on this page. Say it. 'It'. You have just performed a linguistic sign. The sequence of sounds you have just uttered is not *the* sign, but the *performance* of the sign. The sounds are the expression or realization of a particular sound-image in your mind, and the particular sound-image is the mental picture or psychological imprint of the sequence of sounds that you have just uttered. The sound-image is connected to a concept which, at this point in the discussion, it is best to call the 'meaning' of the word you have just uttered. Here we have to note also that the concept part of a sign must be allowed to encompass a range of related meanings, though this is not an issue confronted by the *Course*. It is better to understand it not as a single, concise thought but as a slice of thought. The word 'it' is not an especially helpful illustration of this, but as this chapter has amply demonstrated, the word 'sign' *is* – the linguistic sign *sign* comprises a sound-image united with a concept which encompasses a range of related meanings.

There is more to say about the psychological nature of the linguistic sign, but first I will explain its **arbitrariness**. Saussure says (1916, p. 67) that the bond between concept and sound-image is arbitrary, and therefore the linguistic sign is arbitrary. For example, take the linguistic signs *dog* and *cat*, as does one of the characters in David Lodge's satirical novel *Small World* (1984, p. 22): 'There's no absolute reason why the combined phonemes *d-o-g* should signify a quadruped that goes "woof woof" rather than one that goes "miaou". It's a purely arbitrary relationship, and there's no reason why English speakers shouldn't decide that from tomorrow, *d-o-g* would signify "cat" and *c-a-t*, "dog".' And this is just about true. The sound-image of the sign *dog* (the term **phoneme**, if used strictly in accordance with structuralist thinking, refers to an abstract unit underlying a speech sound) is in a conventional relationship with its concept, 'dog' – a relationship based not on resemblance or cause and effect but on communal agreement, the community being speakers of English. The relationship is like a generally accepted law. It does not depend on any intrinsic, natural link. It is arbitrary. It is entirely possible for a different sound-image to be connected to this concept, as supported by the evidence of other languages, for example, French *chien*, German *Hund*, Spanish *perro*, and so forth. And it is possible that English speakers could decide tomorrow on a completely different sound-image for the concept 'dog', but it is highly unlikely, because it would require all English speakers to agree to the change. Such a sudden turnabout would be very unusual. The beauty of arbitrary signs is that they are free from the restrictions of iconicity (that is, they do not have to resemble what they represent), and a system of arbitrary signs therefore has immense potential. The linguistic signs *walk*, *heart*, *fish*, *telephone*, *love*, *toilets*, and *hamburger* belong to one such system, the English language, a system far more versatile than one dependent on iconicity and signs such as ☎ and ♥. On the other hand, a system based on convention needs a measure of stability and fixity, which militates against sudden, wholesale change, and (by definition) it has to be learned, whereas the meanings of many iconic signs are more transparent.

However, not all linguistic signs are completely arbitrary. Some are to an extent **motivated**, to use Saussure's terminology. For example, new words built out of old elements are motivated, that is, we can discover a logic in their construction, as in the case of *telephone*, from Greek *tēle-* + *phōnē* 'far off voice'. And despite the fact that hamburgers are actually (or allegedly) made from beef, there is a logic in *hamburger*, which derives from Hamburg, Germany. While the whole system of a language is based on what Saussure calls (1916, p. 133) 'the irrational principle of the arbitrariness of the sign', motivation brings a measure of logic to the system. A few linguistic signs even exhibit some iconicity: for example, some, when we perform them in speech, *sound* like what they stand for. 'Woof', for instance. Such signs are onomatopoeic.

Words, then, are the most obvious manifestations of linguistic signs. A linguistic sign is a strange union of structured thought with a mental image of structured sound. For reasons of terminological neatness, Saussure called the concept part of the linguistic sign the **signified**, and the sound-image the **signifier**. In Saussure's theory, the meaning of a word is bound up with what goes on *inside* its underlying linguistic sign, and also with the place that sign occupies in the language system. The relationship between signifier and signified is crucial, the signifier providing a route for the expression of the signified. This is the relationship that I have had in the back of my mind when I have used the term 'stand for' in this chapter, equating it (the relationship) with the meaning of a sign, and remembering that meaning is generated *within* the system of signs. In semiotics, as we have seen, this term is not necessarily used in this specific way. In semiotics, a sign as a whole can be said to stand for something. This is a different matter. This is **reference**. Reference concerns the relationship that we perceive between a sign and the real-world object (here using the term **object** rather vaguely) or **referent** that it appears to represent. In Saussure's theory of the linguistic sign, however, we find something quite different and shocking.

The linguistic sign is a psychological entity, and a language system is structured on these entities. Linguistic meaning happens within the sign and the system, with the result that language draws reality into it. Saussure says (1916, p. 112) that the role of language 'is not to create a material phonic means for expressing ideas but to serve as a link between thought and sound, under conditions that of necessity bring about the reciprocal delimitations of units'. That is to say, linguistic signs (the units of language) structure thought (and sound), and thought thus structured does not pre-exist language. In Saussure's theory, language is not a nomenclature, a list of names corresponding to things. In his personal notes (in Rudolf Engler's critical edition of the *Cours*, 1968, p. 148), Saussure acknowledges that some words, for example, *horse* and *sun*, may appear simply to name real-world things, but he claims that this is the result of accident. In other words, it is an effect of language rather than an explanation of it. An illusion is created: that language acts to translate ready-made things and ideas into words. Although Saussure himself does not explicitly state it, his theory implies that what language actually does is produce another reality, a psychological, linguistic reality, a virtual reality of signs. René Magritte (in 'Words and Images', 1929, p. 32) put it more starkly, 'A word can take the place of an object in reality.'

The theorist Jean Baudrillard used the term **hyperreality** to describe the collapse of the real into its simulation and vice versa. This is the condition of the modern capitalist–consumerist world. 'In this vertigo of serial signs', says Baudrillard (1976, p. 150), 'who can say where the reality of what they simulate resides?' The hyperreal is tabloid newsstories about soap-opera actors and characters, TV docu-soaps about ordinary people who then are TV personalities, 'reality' TV, media news coverage, it is confessional theatre, it is you in a home-movie, in a photograph, and so on. It is not simply a blurring of boundaries, it is a collapsing of boundaries. Which hamburger is real? The photograph of the hamburger is a simulation, a representation, and a sign, an iconic sign. It reflects back on its referent and affects our perception of it. The linguistic sign *hamburger*, though not a simulation, nevertheless produces the same effects, as all linguistic signs do. How? Next chapter ☺. 📖 Read on ☞.

## Further reading

Of the two English translations of Saussure's *Cours de linguistique générale* (1916), the 1960 version by Wade Baskin is more readable, while the 1983 by Roy Harris is more technically consistent in its translation of key terms. There is also an excellent critical edition of the original French text, prepared by Tullio de Mauro (first published in 1972). For a concise book-length introduction to Saussure's work and influence, see Jonathan Culler's *Saussure* (1986). The collected *Writings in General Linguistics* (2002), edited by S. Bouquet, R. Engler and A. Weil, sheds fresh light on how advanced Saussure was in his thinking, and the volume includes an extensive bibliography of work on Saussure. The 2nd edn of *Saussure and his Interpreters* (2003), by Roy Harris, assesses Saussure's legacy, his interpretation and misinterpretation by other scholars, and takes account of the rediscovered material in the *Writings* volume. *The Essential Peirce: Selected Philosophical Writings*, Volumes 1 and 2 (1992, 1998), edited by Nathan Houser, Christian Kloesel and the Peirce Edition Project, is a comprehensive but comparatively convenient selection of C. S. Peirce's essays, Volume 2 dealing with his work on signs. The Peirce Edition Project has an informative website, at: http://www.iupui.edu/~peirce/. In addition, *A General Introduction to the Semeiotic of Charles Sanders Peirce* (1996), by J. J. Liszka, is a methodical introductory commentary. For Baudrillard, begin with *Jean Baudrillard: Selected Writings* (2nd edn, 2001), edited by Mark Poster. *The Gulf War Did Not Take Place* (1991) is Baudrillard's most infamous text on mediated reality. Jacques Lacan's 'The Agency of the Letter in the Unconscious or Reason Since Freud' (1957; in *Écrits: A Selection*, 1977, translated by Alan Sheridan), quoted from briefly in this chapter, is one of his key reworkings of Saussure, and is best read alongside the clear account of it given by Samuel Weber in Chapters 4 and 5 of his *Return to Freud: Jacques Lacan's Dislocation of Psychoanalysis* (1991).

# 7 Strange Orchestras
## The Underlying Symbolic Structure of Languages

---

This chapter includes the following:
- Saussure's theory of linguistic structure or **langue**.
- Explanation of other key terms from Saussure: **parole**, **langage**, and **linguistic value**.
- The relationship between **langue** and the 'real world'.

---

## Linguistic structure and Saussure

In his first colour animation, *The Band Concert* (1935), Mickey Mouse conducts an outdoor performance of Rossini's *William Tell* in the face of disruptions from Donald Duck and a tornado. The tornado whisks Mickey and his orchestra up into the sky as they play. The orchestra plays, whirling round and round, nothing but air below and above, as if held up by the sound of its own music, bound together like a noisy flying wobbly jigsaw. Like a language, in fact. A language is held together by its own internal structure, each part locked into place, but also moving, jostling, while still holding together, as if without external support. Picture it as a strange orchestra, like Mickey Mouse's.

This is the Saussurean, structuralist, semiotic view of language. As mentioned in the preceding chapter, Ferdinand de Saussure's *Course in General Linguistics*, originally published in French in 1916, outlines a vastly influential theory of language. According to Saussure, any language is structured on **linguistic signs**, which are psychological entities each comprised of a **signifier** (or sound-image) and a **signified** (or concept). Together the linguistic signs form the underlying (mental) symbolic structure of a language. Saussure calls this structure *langue* (in the original French). *Langue* is the self-contained, relational system of mental units (linguistic signs) which holds a language together, instituted by the strange force of communal agreement and 'the irrational principle of the arbitrariness of the sign' (Saussure, 1916, p. 133). According to this view, a language is not a piece-by-piece straightforward translation of the real world of objects into a linguistic world of names. Rather a language is a social, communal interpretation of the real world which produces another virtual, symbolic reality which then impinges upon and affects our perceptions of the 'real' world in mesmerizing fashion. This chapter explains *langue* and its effects in relation to English.

In the *Course in General Linguistics*, *langue* is contrasted with two other terms: ***parole*** and ***langage***. *Langage* is the 'total phenomenon' (Saussure, 1916, p. 77) of language – it is language in general. *Parole* is the performance or execution of a language by individuals – it is the act of speaking (and of writing, though for Saussure writing is of secondary importance compared with speech). *Langue* is *langage* minus *parole* – it is 'the whole set of linguistic habits which allow an individual to understand and to be understood' (p. 77), and it is 'both a social product of the faculty of speech [*langage*] and a collection of necessary conventions that have been adopted by a social body to permit individuals to exercise that faculty' (p. 9). *Langue* is also the ensemble of linguistic signs of a language – it is, very strangely, a mental *and* a social symbolic system.

To clarify: linguistic signs, as we know, are psychological entities. As such, they belong to *langue*. Linguistic signs are manifested or performed in *parole* as words, idioms, grammatical units and the like, that is, as individual segments of meaning. We can only perform speech because it is underpinned by the ensemble of linguistic signs, each sign constituted by the arbitrary bonding of a signifier with a signified. For example, the bond between the signifier *mouse* (that is, the mental sound-image of the word 'mouse') and the signified 'mouse' (the concept of 'mouseness') is arbitrary because there appears to be no logical reason why the sequence *m-o-u-s-e* should represent the concept of 'mouseness'. Theoretically, any sequence would do, even *d-u-c-k*. The arbitrary bond is established through convention, through an implicit law to which speakers of English assent, and by a habit which speakers of English follow. *Langue* could be described as the sum of necessary conventions agreed by the community of speakers of a particular language, that is, the sum of all the linguistic signs in a language, except that *sum* is not the best word to use here, for *langue* is a structure, an integral, relational system. This is a central point of Saussure's explanation of language.

If you have already read the preceding chapter in this book, 'Signs', you will know that I said there, cautiously, with reference to the linguistic sign, that 'The sound-image [signifier] is connected to a concept [signified] which, at this point in the discussion, it is best to call the "meaning" of the word.' Now I can add to that statement, for it does not tell the full story. Because linguistic signs belong to *langue*, forming a system, the meaning of a sign (and of the word that is its manifestation) is generated by the bond between its signifier and signified *and* by the sign's relationships with all the other linguistic signs in a particular language system. For example, take the linguistic sign *dog*, as indeed does the cunning servant Baldrick in the television comedy *Blackadder the Third* (1987), on being charged with the task of rewriting Samuel Johnson's Dictionary in a single night (having inadvertently burnt the manuscript to a cinder). Baldrick says, 'I'm quite pleased with "dog".' Blackadder says, 'Yes. And the definition of "dog" is . . .?' Baldrick: ' "Not a cat." ' Baldrick's is a highly Saussurean perspective. It is much like the familiar view on life in general that 'everything is relative', that, for example, we cannot appreciate sunshine without a little rain in our lives, or good times without bad times. The Saussurean perspective on *dog* is not that we cannot appreciate dogs without the existence of cats in the world, but that we cannot understand the linguistic sign *dog* in the way that we do without the existence of the linguistic sign *cat*. The meaning of the linguistic sign *dog* is generated not only by the bond between its signifier (*dog*) and its signified ('dogness'), but also by its not being the meaning of other linguistic signs in the English language, *cat*, for example, not to mention *duck*, *mouse*, *shrew*, *cow*, *horse*, and so on. Imagine that the English language did not categorize domesticated and farm animals but instead had only one word to cover all of them and that the word was *dog* – its meaning would of course be quite different, though even in this hypothetical realm we would still use it to refer to the animal we currently call *dog*. It is the Saussurean view that, in this hypothetical realm, the meaning of the sign *dog* would be different because it would stand in contrast to fewer other signs. According to this view, then, the system of linguistic signs or *langue* is a self-regulating structure, each part held in place by its distinct function, which in turn is determined by the distinct functions of every other part. In the *langue*, linguistic signs are held together in a formation of mutual dependence. Each sign is distinct but gains its distinctness through the opposition or contrast between it and other signs. Saussure says (1916, p. 120), 'in language [*langue*] there are only differences *without positive terms*'. That is to say, in *langue* there are no absolutes, everything is relative.

This leaves us with some intriguing questions. Such as, how does *langue* come into being? And, what exactly is the relationship between the 'real world' of objects and *langue*?

## How does *langue* (linguistic structure) come into being?

Saussure does not provide a total answer to this question. As I have already mentioned, communal agreement and arbitrariness are factors. In addition, Saussure says (1916, p. 112), 'language [*langue*] works out its units while taking shape between two shapeless masses'. The shapeless masses are thought and sound, the units are linguistic signs. It is tempting to see *langue* as a bridge between thought and sound, except that *bridge* is not the best word to use, for it suggests merely a link, whereas *langue* makes new use of thought and sound, changing shapeless thought and sound into structured thought and sound by means of psychological units (linguistic signs). This structuring process, if it can be called a process, Saussure acknowledges as 'mysterious' (p. 112). The neuroscientist Susan Greenfield, in a passage on humankind's linguistic capacity in her 2008 book, *ID: The Quest for Identity in the 21st Century*, says (p. 164), 'Language doesn't just enable us to communicate more efficiently – it gives order, in both senses of the word, to thought itself.' This too is a Saussurean perspective.

Let us picture it with the help of another animation, the Oscar-winning *A Close Shave* (1995), starring Wallace and Gromit. At one stage the pair participate in a climactic chase-sequence, in which Wallace rides a motorcycle at high speed with a dozen or so sheep as passengers. The sheep find themselves disorganizedly clinging on to the bike in a precarious and confused pile, something of a shapeless mass. Then quite mysteriously, for it takes place off-camera, the sheep order themselves into the kind of inverted pyramid used by motorcycle display teams (Figure 14). Imagine that each sheep has its own individual identity. This distinctness of each sheep is apparent in the pyramid, but not in the previous amorphous, shapeless woolly mass. The Saussurean view would be that in the amorphous woolly mass the sheep do not actually exist as individual sheep, only as a mass. However, in their ordered pyramid, what matters is not only their distinct identities but also the place and role of each sheep in the overall structure. We could even say that their very being depends upon the integrity of the structure.

**FIGURE 14** FROM AARDMAN'S *A CLOSE SHAVE* FEATURING WALLACE AND GROMIT (©AARDMAN/W&G LTD AND BBC WORLDWIDE LTD 1995)

The pyramid is like the underlying structure or *langue* of a language, and the sheep in the pyramid are like linguistic signs. In *langue* and in the pyramid of sheep, the overall structure and each of its parts are mutually dependent. If one sheep tragically were to fall off, the pyramid would not necessarily collapse but could be maintained if the remaining sheep rearranged themselves, though it now would be a changed pyramid. The overall structure would have changed and the load carried or function performed by each sheep would have changed. *Langue* also needs stability, fixity, but change in a language does occur. When it does it affects individual signs and the structure as a whole, that is, in principle all the linguistic signs in a language, though the effect on most would be imperceptible. For example, if the sign *sheep* were to fall out of English, this might have a considerable effect on the signs *ram* and *ewe* (one of these might even take over the functions of *sheep*), but less of an impact on *dog*, and presumably no noticeable impact on *grape*.

What keeps the sheep-pyramid going, and what would keep any subsequent changed structure going, that is, what would keep it going as a
structure, is the sheep and the connections between them. What keeps
*langue* going is linguistic signs and the connections between them, and
in *langue* the connections are connections of contrast. Saussure says
(1916, p. 121), 'In language [*langue*], as in any semiological system,
whatever distinguishes one sign from the others constitutes it.' What
is in a sign is determined by what is not in it but is elsewhere in
the system, in other signs. Therefore the linguistic sign *sheep* means
what it does ultimately not because it names a certain kind of fleecy
quadrupedal mammal but because of the position it occupies in the
*langue* of English, because of its differences from other linguistic signs,
its distinctness from them. From the Saussurean point of view, the
appearance of naming is just that – an appearance, not an explanation of language. This is not to say that signs or words appear as if by
magic, with no 'input' from the 'real world'. For example, the community of speakers of English has decided that sheep exist and that a word
is needed so that we can speak of sheep (in English). But once a word
or sign is in the system, in *langue*, *langue* takes over – the sign's meaning
is determined by the system. The result, then, is that the relationship
between a linguistic sign and the real-world object it appears to name
is indirect. There is not a straight line connecting *sheep* and the certain
fleecy mammal. Rather the connection is mediated via the whole system of signs, via the *langue* of English. Here we are now beginning to
answer the second question above: What is the relationship between the
'real world' of objects and *langue*?

### *Langue* and the 'real world'

Although it may be in poor taste, we now have to discuss *mutton*.
Saussure compares (1916, pp. 115–16) English *sheep* and *mutton* with
French *mouton*. The French term refers to the animal and also to its
meat, so that it has what Saussure calls a different **value** from either
of the English terms. 'The difference in value between *sheep* and *mouton* is due to the fact that *sheep* has beside it a second term while the
French word does not' (p. 116). In Saussure's view, each language brings
about its own *langue*, its own structuring of thought within its own
system of linguistic signs, and the interplay of signs within each *langue*
ensures that the value of each sign is determined by its environment and
place in the system, and this militates against exact equivalence between

terms from different languages. It follows from this that each language interprets and classifies the real world through its *langue*, which is a self-regulating, relational system in which meaning (which includes value) is determined ultimately by the relations *within* the system. Like Mickey Mouse's orchestra, *langue* is affected by the real world (more specifically, *langue* is affected by communal opinion of or indoctrinated beliefs about the real world), but it also hangs together, keeps going, because of what is happening within itself.

Hence, for example, English has *sheep* and *mutton* where French has only *mouton* (*sheep* therefore is not equivalent to *mouton*), English has *wife* and *woman* where French has *femme*, English has *grape* and *raisin* where French has *raisin* ('grape') and *raisin sec* (literally 'grape dry'), English has *do* and *make* where Spanish has *hacer*, English has *learn* and *teach* where Welsh has *dysgu* (which can translate as 'learn' and as 'teach' – the English terms suggest oppositeness, while the Welsh suggests unity), and English has *he* and *she* where Finnish has only *hän* (neither 'he' nor 'she', nor 'it', but a third-person singular pronoun which does not specify the sex of the individual it refers to – it can refer to a male or to a female). Even in terms for animals, an area of vocabulary where, you would think, there will be identical correspondences between words and things across different languages, different languages can nevertheless arrive at different conceptual classes. For example, Umberto Eco (1985, p. 165) points out that Latin has only one sign, *mus*, where English has *mouse* and *rat*, and that furthermore, 'In Italian, we have two names, "topo" and "ratto", but many Italians today confuse the terms, using "topo" for both animals.' Again, some speakers of Welsh use the one term *llyffant* where English speakers have two, *toad* and *frog*. In all of these examples we find, as Saussure puts it (1916, p. 117), '*values* emanating from the system'. What Saussure does not spell out is that a newly fashioned, symbolic reality also emanates from the system (*langue*), equipped with a capacity to affect our perceptions of the 'real world'.

Saussure is concerned to demonstrate that language is not simply a naming-process, by showing that each language is structured on a system of linguistic signs, but beyond that he has nothing to add on language and reality – this is, however, a subject that has occupied semioticians who have followed Saussure. For example, Eco comments (1985, p. 165) on the not unimportant effects of Italians' use of *topo* for both mice and rats, that is, that it 'deters them from paying attention to the morphological differences between a "little mouse" and a "big one" – an attitude that can produce a number of sanitary and social consequences'. The Welsh speakers (and they were lifelong, native, first-language speakers of Welsh) that I have met who used *llyffant* for toads and frogs had difficulty in appreciating that it might be possible to differentiate two such animals. The central topic of Eco's essay is the notion that different languages divide up the colour spectrum differently. He says (p. 171), 'The different ways in which cultures make the continuum of colours pertinent, thereby categorizing and identifying hues or chromatic units, correspond to different content systems.' Eco's viewpoint (a highly Saussurean viewpoint) is that cultures analyse real-world phenomena (such as colours and rodents) and thereby produce 'cultural units' which are expressed by linguistic terms, and that these units and their terms operate within a structured system which will be different from culture to culture. So the 'semantic space' concerning rodents is structured differently in English and Latin, according to Eco, as is the semantic space concerning colour (where English has seven terms – *red, orange, yellow, green, blue, indigo,* and *violet* – Latin has four – *fulvus, flavus, glaucus,* and *caerullus*). Thus real-world phenomena affect our linguistic system, and our cultural, communal perceptions of real-world phenomena affect our linguistic system even more; but ultimately meaning issues from the system.

Of course, nobody could argue that Finns cannot distinguish between male and female because they say *hän* when English speakers say either *he* or *she*, though this does mean that Finns have available to them a ready-made non-sexist generic third-person singular pronoun, whereas English speakers have to make do with clumsy formulations like *he or she*, as in 'Please could each reader ensure that he or she reads this sentence all the way to its end no matter how long it takes'. And, of course, one can quite reasonably point out that mice and rats look similar-ish, and toads and frogs more so, and therefore that it is not surprising that people confuse them (mice with rats, toads with frogs, not mice with toads, or . . . *et cetera*) or that a language fails to distinguish them. But a distinction, once established and maintained in a language, then has a higher profile in one way or another for the speakers of that language. You could not argue that Welsh speakers will find it impossible to distinguish between a toad and a frog, or indeed that an English speaker will always find it easy to tell apart the two animals. The argument is rather that if habitually you are required by your language to make a lexical and semantic distinction, then you will be more aware of the corresponding real-world distinction than if your language did not make the division. Eco (p. 171) puts the case more firmly: 'This semiotic phenomenon is not independent of perception and discrimination ability; it interacts with these phenomena and frequently overwhelms them.' That is to say, the language we use has the capacity to condition our perceptions or even overpower our senses. It interacts with and acts on the 'real world' somewhat like the way a software program such as Photoshop interacts with and acts on an image.

Similarly, once a thing or a phenomenon has been recognized by a language, that is, once it has a 'name', the thing or phenomenon becomes more 'real' for that language's speaking community. Take the particular perspiration experience that occurs after a sauna. If you are an English speaker you are probably asking: what particular perspiration experience? If you are a Finnish speaker, you will know, because the Finns have a word for it, and the word is *jälkihiki*, literally 'after-sweat'. No doubt thanks to their long-standing and detailed knowledge of *sauna*, Finns have noticed that, after *sauna* is over, after your final shower, you will continue to sweat for a while. Having given this phenomenon a name, an identity, Finns are better equipped to take appropriate measures to deal with it: specifically, do not dress, but sit down, rest for a few minutes, and maybe sip a beer. We English speakers, in the dark regarding 'aftersweat', tend to get dressed while 'aftersweating' and this really is neither advisable nor comfortable.

This example suggests that the local cultural and physical environment will lead different cultures to differing awarenesses of the world and that their different languages will reflect this – Finns have noticed 'aftersweat' and named it, English speakers (less versed in the niceties of the sauna) have not. This may be true, but it is not the main point. There are in fact two main points here: first, that 'naming' a thing and then speaking of it is a process also of constituting the thing; and secondly, that this process is dependent on meaning as it emerges from the interplay of parts in a language system, in a *langue*. For example, to the modern eye the terms *teenager* and *homosexual* refer to identities that are entirely natural, that is, natural in the sense that they have always existed. The words, it seems, merely describe natural categories. It is surprising to learn, therefore, that both words are recent additions to the English language (as is *sauna*). The first use of *homosexual* as recorded by the *Oxford English Dictionary* (*OED*) dates from 1892, while *teenager* is even newer, dating from 1941. Does this mean that homosexuals did not exist before the late nineteenth century, and that teenagers did not exist before the Second World War? In a sense, no they did not. That is, these modern identities are social constructs that have emerged out of and through discourses that named and spoke of them, and the places that the names themselves occupy in the language system – that is, the relational roles of the linguistic signs – are crucial in the construction of these identities.

According to the historian Michel Foucault in *The History of Sexuality: An Introduction* (1976), the modern notion of homosexuality was inaugurated in the late nineteenth century. Foucault was not arguing that love or sex between individuals of the same sex did not happen before this time. That would be an absurd thing to say. Rather Foucault argued that homosexuality as an identity, as a defining quality of an individual's very being, was constituted from this time on. Previously, 'As defined by the ancient civil or canonical codes, sodomy was a category of forbidden acts; their perpetrator was nothing more than the juridical subject of them' (Foucault, 1976, p. 43). But, 'The nineteenth-century homosexual became a personage, a past, a case history, and a childhood, in addition to being a type of life, a life form, and a morphology, with an indiscreet anatomy and possibly a mysterious physiology' (p. 43). A new category of individual was defined, in medical and other discourses, a type whose whole being was seen as determined by a sexuality. 'The sodomite had been a temporary aberration; the homosexual was now a species' (p. 43). The history of the term *homosexual* in English corroborates Foucault's argument. According to the *OED*, the first recorded use of *homosexual* is as an adjective in an English translation of a German work, Richard von Krafft-Ebing's *Psychopathia Sexualis*, in 1892. But especially pertinent as far as we are concerned is the fact that from the same translation (by C. G. Chaddock) comes the first record of the word *heterosexual*, also as an adjective. From the very start then, in English, the meaning of *homosexual* was dependent on its opposition with another word in the 'semantic space' of human sexuality. Being *homosexual* entails not being *heterosexual*, and vice versa. It took a little time for these mutually defining identities to become consolidated in English by the use of the terms as nouns, according to the evidence of the *OED*. First use of *homosexual* as a noun dates from 1912, and first use of *heterosexual* as a noun from 1920.

But perhaps even more revealing is the history of the term *bisexual* in English. The *OED* records this as pre-dating the two other terms. First use is from 1824, in the sense, 'Of two sexes; specifically having both sexes in the same individual.' First record of its more familiar and modern sense, 'Sexually attracted to individuals of both sexes', is 1914. This is its adjectival use in this sense – noun status followed in 1922. The evidence suggests that this shift in the meaning of *bisexual* was prompted by the fixing of identity brought about by the terms *homosexual* and *heterosexual* and by the discourses employing them. What was now needed was an additional term to fix the identity of individuals who did not appear to have a fixed sexual identity in keeping with the parameters set by *homosexual* and *heterosexual*. A new way of perceiving things was marked by the introduction of *homosexual* and *heterosexual*, and, it can be argued, individuals began to adjust themselves towards this new way. However, the first use in 1914 of *bisexual* in its modern sense, in the *American Medical Association Journal*, itself indicates that the other two terms mark cultural rather than natural categories. That first use states, 'By nature all human beings are psychically *bisexual* – capable of loving a person of either sex.'

   The first record of *teenager* is from *Popular Science Monthly* in 1941: 'I never knew teen-agers could be so serious.' The semiotician Marcel Danesi discusses (1994, pp. 135–9) the term *teenager*, noting that it signalled the emergence of a new category of person 'belonging to a new recognizable subculture', this following a rising interest among psychologists in the puberty-to-adulthood phase of individuals' development. Once named, the cultural unit *teenager* is the centre of a discourse which progressively and further constitutes it (the unit). Danesi notes the impact of teenagers' 'own music', 'rock 'n' roll', in this process, from, let us say, Chuck Berry's *Sweet Little Sixteen* (1958) to The Who's *My Generation* (1965) to David Bowie's *All the Young Dudes* (1972) to The Ramones' *Blitzkreig Bop* (1976) to Nirvana's *Smells Like Teen Spirit* (1991) to Eminem's *Marshall Mathers* (2000) to Plain White T's *Hey There Delilah* (2005). Developing in tandem with the 'subculture', feeding off it, catering for it, helping delineate it are large sections of what Danesi calls the 'current economic structure' (p. 136) – industries selling or sectors providing music, film, television, magazines, fast food, drugs, computer games, holidays, education, and so on (and capitalist–consumerism has become aware of a *homosexual* or *gay* or *pink* market as well). In his 'prehistory of the Teenager' (2007, p. xiii), Jon Savage notes that the word was a marketing term from the outset, and he ends his book with the comment (p. 465), 'The future would be Teenage.' Vast chunks of our cultural reality have developed around a word, which itself marks a unit of cultural reality. The process is one of crystallization, centred around a word. And the word, as a linguistic sign, operates in the context of a system (*langue*). 'There can be no units without a system,' says Eco (1985, p. 171). And the meaning of the word ultimately emanates from the system. *Teenager* is constituted by its distinctness from older terms such as *child* and *adult*. *Homosexual* is constituted by its distinctness from *heterosexual* and *bisexual* (we should note also that the term *homosexual* initially was persecutive, but like one of its many later slang synonyms, *queer*, it was in time commandeered by the community it identified). Once such categories are constituted, individuals locate themselves in relation to them and are judged accordingly. Teenagers, as we all know, are notoriously moody and self-centred. This is what we expect of them and what they expect of themselves as teenagers. Even though, if we think about it, there are plenty of toddlers and adults who are little different in these respects, moodiness and self-centredness are defining characteristics of the *teenager*.

## Conclusion

In the chapter before this, 'Signs', I used the example of shiny advertising pictures of hamburgers to illustrate how a representation of a thing can affect our view of the thing, and even seem more 'real' to us than the thing itself. In this chapter, we have seen how words can produce similar if not more radical consequences by their involvement in the constituting of things. For example, people whose age ends in *-teen* are perceived according to the criteria associated with a word which 'names' them. There are 'external' (to the language) reasons for the categories *teenager* and *homosexual* in English, and for the category *jälkihiki* in Finnish, that is, they were not magicked into existence by language alone. Nevertheless, once in the language, in the system – *langue*, the strange orchestra, 'where elements hold each other in equilibrium' (Saussure, 1916, p. 110) – a linguistic sign is swept up, determined by the structure of which it is a part. The language itself, underpinned by *langue*, becomes a powerful determiner of meaning and of our perception of reality.

## Further reading

For further explanatory discussion of Saussure's *Course*, see Chapter 2 of *Linguistic Theory: The Discourse of Fundamental Works* (1991), by Robert de Beaugrande (available to download free at: http://www.beaugrande.com/), and for discussion of its place in the development of structuralism, see *Structuralism* (2nd edition, 2003), by John Sturrock. Rather trickier readings are given by Samuel Weber in Chapter 3 of his *Return to Freud* (1991), and by Paul Thibault in *Re-reading Saussure: The Dynamics of Signs in Social Life* (1996). As well as the editions of the *Course* mentioned at the end of the preceding chapter, there is the impressive and illuminating two-volume version prepared by Rudolf Engler (*Cours de linguistique générale*, 1968 and 1974), which places the original published French text alongside first the students' notes from which it was constructed and secondly Saussure's notes. Umberto Eco's essay 'How Culture Conditions the Colours We See' is in the excellent collection *On Signs* (1985), edited by Marshall Blonsky, which includes contributions by many major figures in semiotics. A later, very useful collection is *The Routledge Companion to Semiotics and Linguistics* (2001), edited by Paul Cobley. Marcel Danesi's discussion of *teenager* is in his *Messages and Meanings: An Introduction to Semiotics* (1994), and also worth investigating are the same author's *Of Cigarettes, High Heels, and Other Interesting Things: An Introduction to Semiotics* (1999), and his collaboration with Thomas A. Sebeok, *The Forms of Meaning: Modeling Systems Theory and Semiotic Analysis* (2000).

# 8 Myth
## Language and Reality

This chapter includes the following:
- A discussion of the **'Sapir–Whorf Hypothesis'**.
- The term **myth** as used in the semiotic work of Roland Barthes.
- Jacques Lacan's **symbolic order**.
- A brief introduction to Steven Pinker on **conceptual semantics**.
- Dale Spender on the word *God*.

## Introduction

'We're not experiencing the ultimate reality: the "real" is hiding all through life,' said the film director David Lynch, 'but we don't see it' (Rodley, 1997, pp. 243–4). Lynch is saying that something which we do not experience and which we do not see nevertheless not only exists but is the ultimate existence, and everything that we do experience in life is not really (in the ultimate sense) real. This may seem a weird thing to say, but actually it is not unusual, given the great religions of the world, all of which propose a really real reality beyond the reality we experience. But what is it that makes us doubt the realness of the reality we experience? Could it be *language*?

This chapter is about language and reality. More specifically, it is about the view that language and other 'sign systems' provide us with an experience of reality which may be the only one accessible to us as linguistic beings. This view allows for the possibility that reality of the 'ultimate' kind lies somewhere beyond language, and is inaccessible to us because of language, because we are *linguistic* beings. The preceding chapters ('Signs' and 'Strange Orchestras') looked at Ferdinand de Saussure's theory of language as a **semiological** or **semiotic** phenomenon, that is, the view that each language is based on a structure or system of symbolic signs: linguistic signs. Saussure's theory also implies a certain view of reality summed up as follows by Jonathan Bignell (2002, p. 6):

> It is usual to assume that words and other kinds of sign are secondary to our perception and understanding of reality. It seems that reality is out there all around us, and language usefully names real things and the relationships between them . . . . Saussure proposed that our perception and understanding of reality is constructed by the words and other signs which we use.

According to this view, then, words are not simply labels attached to things, but elements in a symbol system which constitutes our perception of reality, that is, which builds our working model of reality.

Let us look at this, taking David Lynch's words as our cue. Let us assume that there are two categories of reality: 'reality', which is what we experience here in our (linguistic) lives on this Earth; and 'ultimate reality', which is currently denied to us. And as for language, imagine for a moment that language is an enveloping suit completely wrapping your body, like a space-suit. But rather than simply acting as a barrier, the language-suit is a filter, filtering 'out-space', the truth out there, the objective physical world, so that out-space reaches you and your 'in-space' filtered, altered. And once you put on the language-suit you live your life in that altered state. This is the first category above – 'reality'. Our reality is linguistic, a language-mediated reality.

This chapter also explains the 'Sapir–Whorf Hypothesis' and examines some influential work of a pioneer of semiotics (or semiology), Roland Barthes (1915–80), each of these subjects taking our discussion of language and reality into new areas. The word which connects all the parts of this chapter is **myth**. 'Myth', says Barthes (1970, p. 109), 'is a type of speech' and 'a system of communication'. We shall look at what he means by this. As we shall see, his use of the term is specialized, but it also acknowledges its traditional usage. Barthes applies the term **myth** to the connotations of signs and his work is a semiological analysis of 'the language of so-called mass-culture' (Barthes, 1970, p. 9) – we shall see what this means also – but the word **myth** in its traditional usage provides us here with a more general analogy for language. Myths are stories that attempt to explain the universe as we know it, and languages are like myths in that they interpret our universe for us. A language categorizes, it glosses, it makes known to us the world we live in – in the Saussurean view, it thereby *provides* us with the world we live in, hands it to us on a plate, as it were. Each language is like an old, traditional story, passed down and evolving through the generations. In addition, of course, the word **myth** is used for a story that we do not now believe to be entirely truthful or accurate. Are languages truthful and accurate? Is English truthful and accurate? We would not expect each 'story' that a language tells to be completely without foundation, but how can we know? It could be in parts without foundation. How *can* we know? If each language, as well as being myth-like, were also space-suit-like, how would we, suit-wearers, know the truth? Only via language. So we seem to be in a catch-22 situation.

If language affects our perception of reality, our perception of reality is, at least in some measure, dependent on language. Let us put it no more strongly than that at this point. If we want to test the realness of this reality, how can we? By stepping outside language? Is that possible? Once we become linguistic beings, consciously reverting to a non-linguistic state looks impossible. But putting some distance between ourselves and our *native* language seems highly achievable – it happens whenever we learn something of another language. This might give us some perspective. Contrariwise, if language does *not* affect our perception of reality, everything becomes much simpler. No enveloping language-suit, none of these reality problems. We are alright, on firm ground, unless we are deceived into thinking that language does not affect our perception of reality, by language! Here we might do well to turn to a higher authority: *God*. That is, the word *God*, in English, looked at from the point of view of the feminist linguist Dale Spender.

## The English language and sexist reality

Words or linguistic signs, to use the terminology of Saussure, sometimes **refer** to actual things, to physical objects and entities. For example, the English noun *chair* refers to a type of physical object, and it can refer to an individual physical object, such as the object that I am sitting on as I write. The word *chair* has an observable **referent** (the thing to which it refers). Words or linguistic signs do not always have observable referents. For example, the word *unicorn* does not ('the unicorn', says Umberto Eco (1999, p. 6) resignedly, 'like bachelors, can never be absent from any reflections on language' – for corroboration, regarding bachelors, see Chapter 15, 'Slippage'), and neither does the word *God*. God would not be God if He were observable in the way that my chair is. Even if He appeared unto me, I would be reluctant to class his observability as equivalent to that of my chair. And yet the word *God* implies observability – it implies substance – in the same way that the word *chair* does. Both are **nouns** (naming words), and having a noun for something suggests that that something *is* a something, and in the case of *God*, the Something is Male.

In her book *Man Made Language* (1985), Dale Spender argues that the masculinity of the Almighty is a fabrication, a fabrication aided by the word *God*. Spender says (1985, pp. 165–71) that the word *God* incorporates a deliberate act of biased naming by a patriarchal or male-dominated society. God was made male by men, a process supported by the masculine reference of the noun *God*, establishing 'one of the primary categories of our world as a male category' (pp. 166–7), and casting 'females into a negative position which can be further exploited' (p. 167). The noun *God* puts a particular and powerful slant on reality. Spender says (p. 166), 'we think male when we use *God*', and we are more likely, as a result, to see maleness as superior to femaleness. Put bluntly, the word *God* and the word *man* are bedfellows.

From the Christian point of view, the Bible is the word of God. This has not prevented the Biblical text from being the subject of dispute and negotiation among Christians for two millennia. Drawing on feminist biblical scholarship, Spender points out how accounts in which God was androgynous or female were gradually edited out of the Biblical anthology as it took shape during the early centuries of Christianity. The outcome was not only a God made in the image of man, but (in the case of English) the word *God* made in the image of the word *man* – which also throws a positive light on *man*. Beverley Clack and Brian R. Clack, in their book on the philosophy of religion (1998), sum up the situation as follows: 'Replace the word "God" with the word "man" and one is left with the stereotypical picture of what constitutes masculinity in a patriarchal society' (p. 121). In other words, the concept 'God' incarnated in the word *God* is an idealized version of masculinity.

Spender's aim was to reform the English language from a feminist perspective, an essential project for her because of her belief that English is prejudiced in favour of males and also that a language constructs a reality, a process which involves (as far as Spender is concerned) *naming*. 'Names are essential for the construction of reality for without a name it is difficult to accept the existence of an object, an event, a feeling' (1985, p. 163). For Spender, naming orders and structures our existence, and *God* is an example (perhaps The Example) of an especially powerful name.

Spender's book made a considerable impact in the fight against the perceived sexism of English (I look at further examples from it in

Chapter 10, 'The Tyranny of Language', and the topic of sexism also features in Chapter 9, 'Sex'), but her belief in the reality-constructing nature of language is based on a logic she finds in the (not noticeably feminist) work of two anthropologists and linguists active in the United States in the early decades of the twentieth century, Edward Sapir (1884–1939) and Benjamin Lee Whorf (1897–1941).

## The 'Sapir–Whorf Hypothesis'

The key work of Sapir and Whorf is often referred to under the label 'Sapir–Whorf Hypothesis', a convenient though somewhat misleading name, because it suggests that here is something which is a single proposition. Actually the label 'Sapir–Whorf Hypothesis' summarizes a variable body of work contained in a series of publications, written through the 1910s to the 1930s, in which Edward Sapir and Benjamin Lee Whorf (separately) explored the connections between language, culture, behaviour, thought, and reality. I would summarize the principal ideas of Sapir and Whorf as follows: a language and the culture or society that uses it interlock, and a language incorporates the prevalent ways of thinking of a culture and substantiates those ways of thinking. According to this view, the ways of thinking and the language will be interpretive of reality, and the behaviour and thought of speakers will be guided or even governed by their language. Dale Spender developed this view by arguing that a language will incorporate the ways of thinking of the dominant groups of a culture. If a culture is patriarchal, so too will its language be. Her reform project is thus not only an attempt to eradicate the patriarchal ways of the English language, but an attempt to adjust the impression of reality experienced by its speakers. Her belief was that English could be made to classify the world more accurately (1985, p. 190), even though she also claimed, in David-Lynch-like fashion, that linguistic beings are incapable of 'grasping things as they really are' (p. 139).

The 'Sapir–Whorf Hypothesis', then, implies that each language is loaded, in the 'biased' and 'weighted' senses of the word, and that the speakers of each language are also loaded, in the 'drugged' sense of the word, under the influence of a language. Sapir says, 'Language is a guide to "social reality"' (1929, p. 162). He continues:

> It is quite an illusion to imagine that one adjusts to reality essentially without the use of language and that language is merely an incidental means

> of solving specific problems of communication or reflection. The fact of the matter is that the 'real world' is to a large extent unconsciously built up on the language habits of the group. No two languages are ever sufficiently similar to be considered as representing the same social reality. The worlds in which different societies live are distinct worlds, not merely the same world with different labels attached.

Sapir concludes with, 'We see and hear and otherwise experience very largely as we do because the language habits of our community predispose certain choices of interpretation.' So even what we think of as our sensory experiences are guided by our native language, and those of us on the English language-drug will experience things differently from those on, say, the Finnish language-drug, or the French, or Spanish, and so on. The experiences of different language communities, according to Sapir, will be sufficiently dissimilar to count as separate communal realities.

This famous passage by Sapir is also quoted by Whorf (a pupil of Sapir) at the start of his 'The Relation of Habitual Thought and Behavior to Language' (1941). In this key essay, Whorf illustrates how the analyses of 'real-world' phenomena that languages carry out influence personal and cultural behaviour. For example, the phrase 'empty gasoline drums' encourages careless behaviour around containers which *are* empty of gasoline, but nevertheless full of explosive vapour (Whorf, 1941, p. 135). The linguistic analysis follows a regular analogy in the use of the adjective *empty*, but gives a false impression of the situation, at least with regard to explosive vapour. (It is a bit like the way that the physicality associated with nouns such as *chair* gets carried over into the noun *God*.) This choice of example, plus another six involving fire hazards that Whorf gives, might seem eccentric, but for 22 years, in addition to his academic pursuits, Whorf worked for a fire insurance company. He aims to show that everyday language is as persuasive as the manipulative expressions of politicians. In fact, it is much more persuasive because its persuasiveness generally goes unrecognized.

Rather more metaphysically, Whorf goes on to compare the perception of time in different languages. Both he and Sapir undertook studies of Native American languages, and Whorf was struck by what he saw as significant differences between the conceptualization of time in the language of the Hopi tribe of the south-western United States and in that of European languages like English, French, and German. For example, European languages like these, says Whorf (1941, p. 139), analogically apply 'objective' plurals to 'non-objects'. The phrase 'ten men' can apply to something which can be objectively perceived (a group of ten men), but when it comes to time, all that we can objectively perceive, possibly, is a single moment. A phrase like 'ten days', therefore, is an imaginary, metaphorical plural. We cannot point and say, 'Look at those ten days.' 'Ten days' depends on an analogy with phrases like 'ten men', and it objectifies time. The process of time is expressed in terms of quantities of countable units, and these 'Standard Average European' (**SAE**) languages, as Whorf calls them, present us with the illusion of time-objects. Hopi, according to Whorf (p. 140), has no imaginary plurals, but instead has 'ordinals used with singulars.' He says that the European 'ten days is greater than nine days' would be expressed in Hopi as 'the tenth day is later than the ninth'. Instead of the SAE 'linguistically promoted objectification' which 'cloaks' our subjective experience of time, Hopi allows that subjective experience of 'becoming later' a clearer expression.

This is just one of the ways in which, according to Whorf, these European languages and Hopi differ in their treatment of time, both in their vocabularies and in their grammars. SAE and Hopi represent different ways of thinking about time and, in turn, they help shape different experiences of time for the speakers of SAE and Hopi. Behaviour is matched with the analyses carried out by a language. SAE speakers are used to categorizing time in a manner also used for the categorization of space, and time thus objectified is essential to the kind of record-keeping and, indeed, time-keeping which underpins 'western' culture. For the Hopi, time is a 'getting later' of everything, a continuity, and their cultural behaviour emphasizes preparation for what time will bring.

For Whorf, as for Sapir, cultural features and behavioural patterns can be linguistically conditioned. Whorf pursued the argument to greater lengths than Sapir, which is why the 'Sapir–Whorf Hypothesis' is sometimes relabelled the 'Whorfian Hypothesis'. Whorf says (1940, pp. 213–14) that each language presents us with its own categorization of the universe, and in using our native language, we are obliged to go along with this categorization. That is, a language is based on convention, on communal agreement, and none of us has the power, individually, to change its conventions. As Whorf says (pp. 213–14), emphatically, 'ITS TERMS ARE ABSOLUTELY OBLIGATORY.' This is no different from the Saussurean, and (C. S.) Peircean, observation that a symbolic system is like a generally accepted set of laws. Whorf goes on, by way of example, to remark that English 'gives us a bipolar division of nature' (1940, p. 215) in its use of nouns and verbs, 'But nature herself is not thus polarized.' Whorf asks (p. 215) why *lightning, pulsation,* and *flame* are nouns in English while Hopi analyses these phenomena as verbs. (A similar question is asked in Dale Spender's discussion of *God* – why is *God* not a verb?)

Sapir's and Whorf's theories have been much disputed. An argument made against the 'Sapir–Whorf Hypothesis' is that, if it were correct, then translations between languages would not be possible. As an argument, this is a red herring. To make another analogy, it is perfectly possible to translate between the metric system of measurement and the imperial system. Eight kilometres, for example, equals approximately five miles. The process is one of conversion. The terms of one system, when converted, are expressed in the terms of the other, and each system, quite literally, structures the world differently. Or, to put it more cautiously, each system applies its own structure to the world. Similarly, we can translate between languages, but this does not disprove the claim that different languages structure the world differently (or apply differing analyses to the world). It is more useful to focus on the pitfalls of translation. Idiomatic expressions, like 'As an argument, this is a red herring', and metaphorical expressions, like 'I see what you mean', are eminently mis-translatable. If English speakers were a small Amazonian tribe instead of an immense global community, imagine the excited response of a foreign scholar to literal translations of these expressions. Whorf has been accused of using excessively literal translations in his analyses of Hopi. Subsequent research on the Hopi and their language, by Ekkehart Malotki (1983) and by the Hopi Dictionary Project (1997), indicated that, while their culture is not characterized by western time-keeping ('not every culture has developed an obsession with time ("time is money") as ours nowadays', Malotki, 2001, private correspondence), their linguistic analysis of time is not as different from that of SAE languages as Whorf believed. While this calls into question some of Whorf's conclusions about Hopi, it does not invalidate his view of the universe-categorizing nature of languages. Translation is difficult. One would expect it to be if languages are different in the way that Sapir and Whorf say they are.

A prominent and firm opponent of the 'Sapir–Whorf Hypothesis' is the linguist Steven Pinker. In *The Language Instinct* (1994), he says, 'But it is wrong, all wrong' (p. 57), and you cannot get much firmer than that. He continues, 'The idea that thought is the same thing as language is an example of what can be called a conventional absurdity: a statement that goes against all common sense but that everyone believes because they dimly recall having heard it somewhere and because it is so pregnant with implications.' There is a problem here, nonetheless. In Sapir's and Whorf's writings one can certainly find turns of phrase that offer opponents the opportunity to accuse them of going too far in their claims, but one also finds (in their writings) much qualifying and precision. For Sapir and Whorf, language essentially guides our thoughts. They say that different languages will channel our thoughts differently. Language patterns and cultural norms will 'have grown up together, constantly influencing each other', but in this partnership it is the language which 'rigidifies channels of development' (Whorf, 1941, p. 156). Language habits solidify ways of thinking, and ways of perceiving reality. But they do not argue that language is *the same thing* as thought.

In *The Stuff of Thought* (2007), Pinker devotes over 25 pages (pp. 124–50) to the case against **Linguistic Determinism**, which he equates with the 'Sapir–Whorf Hypothesis', and which he defines as 'The idea that the language people speak controls how they think' (p. 124). This is perhaps less of an overstatement of the 'Hypothesis', though the verbs 'guide' or 'channel' might be fairer (to the 'Hypothesis') than 'control'. (If we believe that a language, as the outlet of a cultural evaluation of the world, has the capacity in certain ways to influence behaviour and thought, and to fortify that cultural evaluation, can we then also say that a language *controls* thought?) The term Linguistic Determinism often comes up in discussions of Sapir and Whorf, as does the term **Linguistic Relativity**. Generally, the former is used as a label for belief in the thought-determining quality of language, and the latter for belief in the social-reality-forming power of any given language. But these terms are comparatively blunt instruments. Better to base discussion on a reading of Sapir and Whorf in the original.

Pinker (2007) puts forward his own take on language and reality, called **conceptual semantics**. For Pinker, language as a whole does indeed provide us with 'a distinctively human model of reality' (p. vii). In this model, 'There is a theory of space and time' and 'a theory of matter and a theory of causality, too'. It is, in fact, pretty hard to distinguish Pinker's thesis from the view that, as linguistic beings, we live in a language-mediated reality. But Pinker argues that language as we use it does not determine our thoughts. Quite the reverse. Language is the expression of a deeper and universal template that underlies all individual languages, a basic set of concepts (notions of being, connection and distinction, space, time, causation, possession, and goals (pp. 81, 83), which 'shape our understanding of the physical and social worlds' (p. 82)), a way of understanding that is essentially human, that he calls 'a language of thought'. In this view, individual languages merely express – with much diverting variety – underlying semantic, mental universals. (This theory parallels that on grammar put forward by Noam Chomsky, discussed in Chapter 17.)

To return to Sapir and Whorf: following on from their work, many scholars from the 1950s onwards have attempted to construct experiments that test the 'Hypothesis'. This is an arena that is dogged by dispute. In the opposing corner to Pinker is a research group at the Max Planck Institute for Psycholinguistics in the Netherlands. Steven Levinson and colleagues have carried out a series of studies into the relationship between language and cognition, including work on how different languages structure the 'spatial domain' (Levinson, 2003; Levinson and Wilkins, 2006), arguing that our native language can influence how we think about spatial relations and directions, and that the great variety of ways in which languages structure space throws into doubt the extent to which the semantic categories of language are innate. Pinker, an innatist, is unconvinced (2007, pp. 141–8) by such 'neo-Whorfianism'.

Some experiments on the perception of colour categories by English speakers compared with speakers of isolated languages (for example, Brown and Lenneberg, 1954; Davidoff, Davies and Roberson, 1999; and Kay and Kempton, 1984) seem to provide support for the 'Sapir–Whorf Hypothesis'. The categories embedded in the different languages seem to influence speakers' perceptions. Yet maybe it is fair to say that, up to a point, the 'Hypothesis' is a statement of the obvious. It is obvious that different languages refer to the world using different classifications, to the extent that there are some words that are 'untranslatable'. Howard Rheingold's *They Have a Word for It* (1988) is a dictionary of such words compiled from the English-speaker's point of view, including Japanese *wabi* (p. 95), 'a flawed detail [for example, in an object] that creates an elegant whole' (like, I suppose, the cracked fingers of Michelangelo's *David*), and German *Schadenfreude* (p. 162), 'joy that one feels as a result of someone else's misfortune'. We need also to remember that languages change. The classifications that a language carries out by means of its vocabulary, for example, can shift. After all, much of the vocabulary of present-day English is comprised of **loanwords** – words taken into English from other languages which may extend the range and subtlety of reference of the language (at other times a loanword may simply oust an existing English word). *Schadenfreude* above is a **foreignism**, an item not yet fully naturalized into English, and is used by English speakers to fill a conceptual gap in their language. A foreignism can become a naturalized loanword, and loanwords by definition begin their lives as foreignisms. There may be no end of such conceptual gaps, if we believe Douglas Adams and John Lloyd, who 'compiled' *The Meaning of Liff* (1983), a mock dictionary of words for things for which English has no words, like *ely* (p. 47), 'the first, tiniest inkling you get that something, somewhere, has gone terribly wrong', and *liff* (p. 83), 'a book, the contents of which are totally belied by its cover'.

## Language and the 'symbolic order'

The view that different languages correlate with different communal or societal realities (**linguistic relativity**) is particularly associated with Sapir and Whorf, but there is no shortage of scholars willing to affirm the reality-constructing nature of language in general. For example, the psychoanalyst and theorist Jacques Lacan (1901–81) argued that when we acquire language as infants we enter a different register, a different, symbolic register. After this point our existence is negotiated via a symbolic system – language. Our understanding of the universe, of relationships, and of identity happens via language. Lacan calls this different register the '**symbolic order**'. He says (1956, p. 65), more starkly than Sapir and Whorf, 'It is the world of words that creates the world of things', and, 'Man speaks, then, but it is because the symbol has made him man.' In other words, our experience of reality, including our sense of self, is different once we enter language. Reality becomes a language-mediated existence. The neuroscientist and anthropologist Terrence Deacon, in his substantial book on the origins of language (1997), calls this existence a 'virtual world'.

Lacan's writings from the early 1950s onwards were influenced by the model of language provided by Saussure's *Course in General Linguistics* (1916). According to Saussure (and as discussed in Chapters 6 and 7 of this book), a language is structured on an underlying system of linguistic signs, in which meaning arises largely out of the relationships between the signs. A language is a sign system, and words are linguistic signs, or, putting it more strictly in keeping with Saussure's thinking, a word is the expression of an underlying linguistic sign – the linguistic sign being an abstract and theoretical construct. Whatever the object or thing that a word refers to, a large part of the word's meaning will be generated by its being unavoidably caught up in a network of contrasts with other words in the same language. This is

Deacon's 'virtual world' – the network of symbol-to-symbol relationships. When we acquire language, we enter this virtual world. According to Saussure, linguistic signs are psychological units which bring together sound and thought, and which then appear to name things. Different languages arise because different communities have made different choices in forming linguistic signs. A language, therefore, is a vast network of symbolic, communally agreed categorizations of the world.

Although Saussure did not develop his theory along 'Sapir–Whorfian' lines, his model of the structure of languages is in keeping with the famous 'Hypothesis'. Once a community's categorizations are enshrined in a language they take on a guiding, reinforcing role, and they are themselves reinforced by being in language. This can be seen even in apparently straightforward object-categorizations. For example, although an office chair and a deckchair are different from each other in some ways, and similar to each other in other ways, the word *chair* encourages us to see them as variants of the same thing. However, we are encouraged to see a 'three-seated chair' as a distinct entity rather than a variant, because of the word *sofa*. A report by David Concar in *New Scientist* (12 December 1998, p. 10) provides support for this: a study of an autistic girl's abilities at an age when she knew almost no language indicated that she was inclined to be oblivious to such linguistically conditioned links and distinctions between objects.

Saussure's work had a founding role to play in the branch of study now known as **semiotics**: the study of the life of signs and sign systems in society. Language is a sign system, but semiotics shows that it is only the most important sign system. Semiotics, or **semiology**, as it has also been known, shows that sign systems abound in the human world, and, as Jonathan Bignell (2002, p. 7) puts it, 'consciousness and experience are built out of language and the other sign systems circulating in society that have existed before we take them up and use them'. That is to say, sign systems provide us with ready-made interpretations of the universe. From this point of view, reality is conditioned by language and other sign systems. In language, words are the most obvious signs. In sign systems generally, a **sign** is simply something which carries a meaning. Semioticians deal with all kinds of signs or potential signs, from birdsong to medical symptoms to fashion styles to the usages of cinema, but it is symbolic signs – signs whose meaning is established through communal agreement or convention – that will invariably belong to systems. The work of Roland Barthes provides us with examples of non-linguistic sign systems (for example, clothing, food), though one of his main points is that these systems operate like language.

## Roland Barthes, semiotics, and myth

In the mid-1950s, Barthes read Saussure and decided to apply the notion of the sign system to the study of mass culture in France. He showed that cultural and social activity consists of the use of signs. For example, in an essay called 'The Romans in Films', Barthes says that a hairstyle is a sign (1970, p. 26). He notes that, in the 1953 film *Julius Caesar*, 'all the characters are wearing fringes' (p. 26). In this context, the fringe carries a meaning: 'Roman-ness'. Historical accuracy in this matter is not important. As Barthes points out, although there were plenty of bald Romans, none are allowed in the film. We could say that the hairstyle is shorthand for 'Roman-ness' – Barthes says the fringe is a 'little flag' on the foreheads of the actors, for here in this film 'Romans are Romans thanks to the most legible of signs: hair on the forehead' (p. 26). In the vocabulary of semiotics, the fringe is a sign whose connotation is 'Roman-ness'.

But exactly how can a hairstyle be a sign, and how can a sign connote? The sign, in semiotics, is an analytical tool. Barthes's use of it follows Saussure's basic model, that of the linguistic sign. A linguistic sign consists of two parts: a mental picture (that is, our/your/my mental picture) of its form, say, of the sequence of sounds *f-r-i-n-ge*, and this mental picture Saussure calls the **signifier**; and a mental concept, say 'fringeness' ('fringiness'?), termed the **signified**. These two halves are united in a linguistic sign, which Saussure insists is a psychological entity, distinguished from its actual performance in speech or writing. The (mental) sign underpins the actual performance, and the signifier connects the signified with its expression. If we apply this model closely to the fringe in *Julius Caesar* – a pictorial, not a linguistic sign – we can say that the signifier is expressed as the visual image on the screen, which calls to mind a signified, the concept of a fringe. It is not untoward, however, in the case of such pictorial signs, to find semioticians skipping over the distinction between the signifier and its expression, and rather equating the two – so we could say that the signifier of the fringe sign *is* the visual image on the screen. Either way, this sign so far has a direct or literal meaning, that is, a **denotation**: it **denotes** a fringe. It is a (moving) pictorial image of a fringe hairstyle, and as such (so far) it is an iconic sign, so termed because it resembles what it denotes.

(Words, however, are not usually iconic.) But one of Barthes's particular achievements was to demonstrate the importance of signs' additional or **connotational** meanings. A sign during its life can gather around itself associations. The fringed-hairstyle sign has acquired an association with the Romans, and in *Julius Caesar* this association is brought into play. It **connotes** 'Roman-ness'. This aspect of the sign's meaning is more cultural or conventional than iconic – our association of a fringe with Roman-ness is a collective, learned bond. Compare it, for example, with the connotations of the black moustache in Western films.

'The Romans in Films' is one of 28 short essays by Barthes in a collection called *Mythologies*, first published in French in 1957. In *Mythologies*, Barthes applies his semiotic technique to a variety of subjects (and sign systems), including wrestling, French toys, steak and chips in France, and the advertising of soap-powders and detergents. He uses the term **myth** as a label for what happens when a sign is combined with connotation in shaping a message.

It is in the long 29th essay of *Mythologies*, 'Myth Today', that Barthes sums up the workings of myth. The central example in 'Myth Today' is a photograph that Barthes saw on the cover of an edition of the magazine *Paris Match* from 1955 (Figure 15). The photograph shows a black youth in French military uniform, saluting, with his eyes uplifted. Barthes treats the photograph as a sign. Its signifier is (expressed as) the photographic image, its signified can be glossed as 'a black soldier is giving the French salute'. This is the photograph's denotation, but it also has connotations. Barthes argues that the connotational meaning of the photograph belongs to a 'second-order semiological system' which builds on an already-existing semiological or sign system. This second-order system is **myth**. **Myth** takes hold of the photographic sign, whose meaning is 'a black soldier is giving the French salute', and uses it as a new signifier. It attaches to it a new signified – the concept that French imperial rule is egalitarian. The **mythical** message of this 'second-order' sign is that the French Empire is great and good and fair. There is no better answer to its critics than the zeal shown by the black soldier.

Myth, for Barthes, is another 'language' which works like language itself, and which uses language and other sign systems as raw material. This is why he says 'Myth is a type of speech' and 'a system of communication'. In his use of the term, he is recognizing its usual sense of a traditional story and adding to it another meaning. In its Barthesian usage, **myth** refers to ways in which the humdrum messages of everyday and mass-media life are ideological, ideology here meaning culturally determined ways of thinking and of perceiving and

**FIGURE 15**   COVER OF *PARIS MATCH*, NO. 326 (25 JUNE–2 JULY 1955)

presenting reality. Myth has the effect of making the ideological seem natural and matter-of-fact: the photograph of the black soldier presents a contentious point of view in the guise of a neutral statement of fact. Similarly, the fringes in *Julius Caesar* project authenticity while concealing their conventionalized character.

Barthes's work in *Mythologies* was not only an important contribution to European, Saussurean semiotics, but also a major influence on the development of a popular, journalistic semiotics in the mass media itself, and in the long run even on advertising. For example, the London-based market research company Semiotic Solutions, founded in 1988, used its version of semiotic analysis to develop marketing strategies for its clients, among them Glaxo, who wanted to overcome the trivialization of migraine as a 'women's complaint' in order to promote a drug for the condition. Semiotic Solutions recommended creating, through an ad campaign, a 'fundamental cultural paradigm shift by hiving off migraine from the "headache", thus giving it the serious consideration the pain and distress of the condition merits – possibly, eventually, renaming it' (Semiotic Solutions website, accessed 2001). Semiotic Solutions looks at the cultural context that 'surrounds and informs' consumers, because 'consumers are products of the popular culture in which they live' (website, 2001). It later concentrated on providing training in semiotic 'techniques' for market researchers, including 'how to find the coded cultural assumptions hidden in patterns of communication' (website, accessed 2009).

Back in late-1950s France, Barthes wanted to demonstrate how dominant, established ways of thinking and systems of belief are able, with the help of myth, to present themselves as self-evident and commonsensical. In *Mythologies*, he pays attention mainly to non-linguistic signs, but myth takes hold of linguistic signs too. Think of the linguistic sign *man*. Think of its association with 'strength'. Think of its association, by means of its masculine reference, with All-Powerful Strength, with *God*. The **mythical** meaning of *man*, so often invoked, is 'primacy'.

## Conclusion

To sum up: a language is like a myth, in that it interprets, it tells a story of the world, and **myth**, as Barthes uses the term, is like a language. In addition, the analyses provided by Barthes, semiotics, Lacan, Sapir and Whorf, and others show up the reality-affecting, mind-bending capabilities of sign systems in general, including language. Our native language is our language-suit, enveloping us, between us and the world. If we are bilingual or multilingual, then we have a useful wardrobe of suits, which broadens our perspective. But once the language-suit is donned, there is no return to nakedness, not in this analogy.

And finally, what about 'ultimate reality'? 'Ultimate reality', as David Lynch described it, or '**the Real**', as it is termed in the work of Jacques Lacan, does not appear to be accessible to us, cocooned as we are by the symbolic order. Even Steven Pinker says (2007, p. 158) that, 'since we grasp the world only through the structures of our minds', 'we can never directly know the world', and everyone seems to agree that there is a umbilical relationship between our mind and language. The universe appears to us in mediated form, mediated especially, that is, by language. Via language, it becomes our known universe, the speakable, 'reality'. The outside of language, the unspeakable, appears not to be 'directly' knowable. What lies out there is not knowable except trammelled by language. The feeling that there is something beyond, before or after, something which we cannot express, could even be an effect of language. David Lynch said 'the "real" is hiding all through life'. Is it hiding in language or outside it?

## Further reading

Barthes's *Mythologies* (2nd edn, 1970) is an entertaining and essential read. Jonathan Bignell's *Media Semiotics* (2nd edn, 2002) is an excellent, clear introduction to semiotic analysis of the mass media since Barthes, and the *Encyclopedic Dictionary of Semiotics, Media, and Communications* (2000), edited by Marcel Danesi, is a convenient reference guide. *Semiotics: The Basics* (2nd edn, 2007), by Daniel Chandler, is a superb introduction. For a concise and readable introduction to the work of Jacques Lacan, see Malcolm Bowie's *Lacan* (1991). For an initiation into the work of Whorf, see *Language, Thought, and Reality: Selected Writings of Benjamin Lee Whorf* (1956), edited by John B. Carroll, and for Sapir, see *Selected Writings of Edward Sapir in Language, Culture, and Personality* (1949), edited by David G. Mandelbaum. The 'Sapir–Whorf Hypothesis' has its supporters and its detractors, and discussions can veer distressingly away from what Sapir and Whorf actually wrote – so sampling their writings first-hand is strongly recommended. Then you will be better equipped to tackle the variety of studies and altercations that follow on from the 'Hypothesis'. Pinker's writings on the topic are lively, and *The Stuff of Thought* (2007) is also a useful source of references to other work. Ekkehart Malotki's *Hopi Time: A Linguistic Analysis of the Temporal Concepts in the Hopi Language* (1983) is a substantial, thorough piece. The web-pages of the Max Planck Institute for Psycholinguistics can be accessed at: http://www.mpi.nl/. There you will find details of projects and publications. Begin with *Space in Language and Cognition: Explorations in Cognitive Diversity* (2003), by Stephen C. Levinson. For lighter reads, have a look at the title essay of Geoffrey K. Pullum's *The Great Eskimo Vocabulary Hoax and Other Irreverent Essays on the Study of Language* (1991), and browse *The Meaning of Tingo* (2005) and *Toujours Tingo* (2007), by Adam Jacot de Boinod, which follow in the footsteps of Howard Rheingold's *They Have a Word for It* (1988). There is also a website, at: http://themeaningoftingo.blogspot.com/.

# 9 Sex
## Language and Gender

This chapter includes the following:
- Why is gender an issue when discussing language?
- Linguistic behaviour of men and women.
- Linguistic treatment of men and women.
- Definitions of the terms **sex** and **gender**.
- **Performing** gender identity.

## Introduction

This chapter is about sex and language. More specifically, it is about sex and the English language. Why is sex an issue in discussions about language? There are two main reasons:

1. The widely held belief that the linguistic behaviours of women and men differ significantly, perhaps to the extent that (metaphorically speaking) women and men speak different languages, even when they are (literally) speaking the same language.
2. The contentious view that individual languages treat women and men differently, even to the detriment of women.

This chapter will consider both of these issues, giving a historical overview of research, and concentrating especially on the linguistic behaviours of women and men.

The relationship between sex and language is intricate, and scholars investigating it have found it useful to distinguish between **sex** and **gender**. The distinction highlighted by the terms is a key one in, for example, feminist analysis, critical, cultural, and literary theory, and sociolinguistics. **Sex** refers to the biological categories of humankind: female and male. **Gender** refers to feminine and masculine behaviour, to ways of acting and being which are constructed socially and culturally, and which vary across cultures and historical periods. **Sex** refers to biology, **gender** to culture. The terms **female** and **male** apply to sex, the terms **feminine** and **masculine** to gender. Key though this distinction is, we should be alert to the fact that it is not always observed in the literature on sex, gender, and language. This chapter, then, is also about connections and correlations between language behaviour and gender.

However, the distinction between sex and gender cannot be absolute. There are differences between female biology and male biology, triggered by genes on the Y, or male, chromosome, but the distinction 'man/woman' is a conceptual, cultural one as well as a biological one, because much gender-stereotyping is imposed onto these biological differences. It is a very powerful conceptual distinction, and it strongly reinforces the biological distinction. The conceptual distinction encourages us to see differences between women and men, and discourages us from seeing differences among women, and differences among men. In fact, not absolutely everyone is born either female or male. A surprising number of babies (about 1 in 30,000) are born **intersexed**, a condition which in Western societies is adjusted by medical intervention. In these cases, sex is socially constructed in keeping with the man/woman conceptual distinction.

The issue of language and gender, therefore, involves the following snag: any analysis of the construction of gender identity may fall prey to the construction of gender identity itself simply by analysing it. In other words, to analyse gender identity is, from the start, to go along with the conceptual distinction 'man/woman', which itself is a part of the construction of gender identity. Does this mean that discussions of language and gender are always intrinsically compromised? Not necessarily always, but please read on.

## Women and men speaking differently

As a *Cosmopolitan* feature entitled 'How to Talk to a Man So He Really Understands You' put it, 'the styles of communication between the two sexes vary so dramatically, we might as well come from different planets' (British *Cosmopolitan*, March 1998, p. 103). Here is a notion familiar to most heterosexual couples – women and men just do not understand each other. It seems that the use of language by the one sex just does not match up with the use of language by the other. In the 1990s, this was the subject of the best-selling books *You Just Don't Understand* by Deborah Tannen (1990) and *Men are from Mars, Women are from Venus* by John Gray (1992; Gray's book is the inspiration behind the *Cosmopolitan* piece). But the story of modern scholarly investigation of the issue goes back to 1973 and an essay by Robin Lakoff called 'Language and Woman's Place'. (The essay was reprinted in 1975, as the first half of a short book also called *Language and Woman's Place*.)

Lakoff tells us what the following items have in common:

*Mauve, beige, ecru, aquamarine, lavender.*

*Adorable, charming, sweet, lovely, divine.*

*Oh dear, you've put the peanut butter in the refrigerator again.*

*The war in Vietnam is terrible, isn't it?*

Each word or sentence, according to Lakoff, is typical of women's speech and untypical of men's speech. Lakoff is not concerned with communication difficulties between the sexes. She is concerned with the ways in which women's speech is different from men's speech. Her thesis is that, compared with men's speech, women's speech is more polite, more hesitant, and less confident, and she argues that this is due to women's subordinate status in society. It also contributes to women's subordinate status. She argues that women are conditioned into performing language in this way. 'Little girls are indeed taught to talk like little ladies,' she says (1973, p. 57).

Lakoff's essay is located in a specific historical and social context, that is, early-1970s, English-speaking, educated America. Nevertheless, it struck a chord across the English-speaking world. According to Lakoff (p. 49), certain words are associated with women's vocabulary rather than men's. Some of these, like the colour words *mauve, beige, ecru, aquamarine*, and *lavender*, are relegated to women's vocabulary because they refer to comparatively trivial matters, like the fine discrimination of colours. Lakoff contends that if a man were to say 'The wall is mauve', we might conclude that 'he was imitating a woman sarcastically or was a homosexual or an interior decorator', which need not be taken to imply that these are mutually exclusive categories, of course. The gist of Lakoff's argument is that these are women's words because society is dominated by masculine values, and therefore the finer points of colour discrimination are considered unimportant and of interest to women rather than men.

Similarly, adjectives like *adorable, charming, sweet, lovely*, and *divine* are associated with women because they typically are applied to 'unimportant' (p. 52) things, according to Lakoff. She says (p. 53) that such words are not basically 'feminine', rather, they are connected with lack of power, and 'women are the "uninvolved", "out of power" group *par excellence*' (p. 53).

Lakoff argues that men are allowed, by society, 'stronger means of expression' (p. 51), which reinforces their dominant position. Weaker expletives, like *Oh dear*, are associated with women, stronger expletives, like *Shit*, with men. Because swearing is considered unfeminine, women's ability to express strong emotions is restricted – but it could be that in this area women have subsequently made great advances. In his book on swearing in English, Geoffrey Hughes says (1991, p. 212) that there is 'plenty of evidence that women are swearing to a greater extent than previously', and personal, unscientific observation is likely to coincide with this viewpoint, though Hughes's examples are from literature and the mass media. There has been some research on the matter in sociolinguistics (see, for example, Limbrick, 1991; de Klerk, 1992; S. E. Hughes, 1992; Sutton, 1995; Stapleton, 2003), but even if it could be proved conclusively that women swear more than they used to, this is not the same thing as proving that swearing is no longer considered unfeminine behaviour, which leads us into a number of fascinating questions. How much are attitudes connected with actual behaviour? Is 'feminine' behaviour judged to be 'feminine' because that is the way women actually behave? Or is feminine behaviour society's opinion about how women *should* behave? And if women then *do* behave as society thinks they should, will it not seem as if feminine behaviour is feminine because that is the way that women actually behave?

For Lakoff, the situation is uncomplicated. She contends that society is dominated by men, and that this leads to women being conditioned to 'talk like ladies', which leads to women actually 'talking like ladies', which helps sustain the dominant position of men. This is a circular process, but Lakoff emphasizes the straight line of cause and effect, in which 'linguistic imbalances' are *symptoms* of 'real-world imbalances' (p. 73).

Other feminist scholars have argued differently. Dale Spender, for example, in *Man Made Language* (1985), argues that the English language itself has been constructed from a male perspective. For Spender, the language itself is biased and has a crucial role in *determining* real-world imbalances. (**Determinism** like this is evident in much feminist linguistics.) As for differences in the linguistic behaviour of women and men, Spender is critical of previous research, including Lakoff's. She sees Lakoff's essay as an example of what has become known as the **deficit approach** to studying women's language, that is, an approach which presents women's language behaviour as deficient in comparison with men's, and which implies that men's language behaviour is a norm from which women's deviates. Spender (1985, pp. 7–11) sees this approach as an effect of a male-dominated world. For Spender, Lakoff's work is flawed because it is imbued with a masculine perspective.

But the last example from Lakoff – *The war in Vietnam is terrible, isn't it?* – will help us get to the bottom of the whole issue. Dated though it is, it is too an example of a feature which 'has really got into the bones of the debate on language and sex', as Cameron et al. (1989, p. 80) put it.

*The war in Vietnam is terrible, isn't it?* contains a **tag question**. A **tag** is a word or phrase added to the end of an utterance, and a **tag question** is a tag in question form, like *isn't it?* A tag question appears to turn a statement, like *The war in Vietnam is terrible*, into a question. Lakoff (1973, p. 54) describes a tag question as being intermediate between a straight statement and a straight question. She identifies three kinds of tag question (1973, p. 55).

1. Tag questions which seek information, as in 'I had my glasses off. He was out at third, wasn't he?'
2. Tag questions which try to elicit conversation from the person being addressed, as in 'Sure is hot here, isn't it?'
3. Tag questions which seek corroboration for a personal opinion being put forward by the speaker, as in 'The war in Vietnam is terrible, isn't it?' (Or as in 'The way prices are rising is horrendous, isn't it?' This example was substituted for the already-dated Vietnam tag in the 1975 reprint of Lakoff's essay.)

It is the third type which interests Lakoff. She says that putting forward an opinion in this way is a strategy for avoiding conflict with an addressee. Unlike the war in Vietnam, it is non-aggressive. But in so doing the speaker may appear unconfident and tentative. Lakoff suggests that this kind of tag question is more likely to be used by women than by men, and that this might be because women are conditioned into using it.

This view of tag questions has been tested within the field of inquiry known as **sociolinguistics** (briefly mentioned above). Since Lakoff, sociolinguists just have not been able to leave tag questions alone. Tags have seemed more suited to their investigative methods than Lakoff's other examples. Sociolinguistic research typically involves the collection and statistical analysis of quantities of linguistic data culled from interviews with or exchanges between speakers. Its aim is to correlate this data with social variables like class, age, and sex, as well as with region. Although Lakoff's essay was first published in one of the leading journals of sociolinguistic research, *Language in Society*, her methods were not typically sociolinguistic. Her examples were not taken from an extensive sample or corpus of actual speech, but were designed to illustrate her argument, which was based on intuition and personal observation. This partly explains the disparity between her suggestions and the findings of subsequent sociolinguistic research.

For example, Dubois and Crouch (1975) found that, in one 'genuine social context' (an academic conference in the USA), men did and women did not use tag questions. They conclude that the claim that tag questions indicate avoidance of commitment, thereby creating an impression of hesitancy, is 'open to serious doubt' (p. 294). Spender suggests (1985, pp. 9–10) that such a finding ought to have led to the conclusion that men 'lack confidence in their language'. If only things were that simple, as they are in *Cosmopolitan* magazine. The logic of Dubois and Crouch, and of Spender, stems from Lakoff's initial claim. In drawing attention to the possibility of a correlation between sex and the degree of use of tag questions, Lakoff set an agenda which invited researchers to overlook other factors.

Janet Holmes (1984) attempted to compensate by developing Lakoff's summary of the different functions of different types of tag question. Holmes argues that tag questions must be studied within the context of discourse, **discourse** here meaning a linguistic interaction between two or more people. Holmes gauges the meanings of tag questions by assessing their functions within discourses, and by assessing the relationships between participants in discourses. For Holmes (1984, p. 53), tag questions elicit responses from addressees and dilute the strength of utterances.

Using a speech-corpus of 43,000 words (from New Zealand, though this is not explicitly stated), Holmes divides tag questions into two main groups, according to their more specific functions.

1. There are tags which express a **modal meaning**, that is, they indicate how certain the speaker is about a proposition, as in 'She's coming around noon, isn't she?' (p. 53). Holmes says that modal tags are 'speaker-oriented' (p. 54).
2. And there are tags which express **affective meaning**, the most common of which oil the wheels of conversation, that is, they

**facilitate** contributions to an interaction, as in 'Still working hard at your office, are you?' (p. 55). **Facilitative tags** are supportive of addressees, encouraging them to take up their turn in the conversation. Affective tags generally are 'addressee-oriented' (p. 54).

According to Holmes, the tag question is associated more with affective than with modal meaning. In some interactions a speaker will have a leadership or facilitating role, like, for example, a teacher in a classroom, a host entertaining guests, or an interviewer in radio and television programmes. In her corpus, Holmes found that the use of tag questions was much more associated with leaders/facilitators than with participants in non-leadership roles. Most of the tags used by facilitators were facilitative, but some were modal. This raises the possibility that modal tag questions also might, when used by facilitators, have a facilitating function. Feigning uncertainty, after all, is one way to oil the wheels of conversation. This is a complication that Holmes did not discuss in 1984.

What did Holmes discover about women and men using tag questions? In her sample, she found that women used more facilitative tags than men, that female facilitators used more tags than male facilitators, that women used more facilitative tags than modal tags. She found that men used more modal tags than women, and that men used more modal tags than facilitative tags. Phew. Her conclusions? That tag questions can be perceived primarily as 'conversational support structures' (p. 59) and that her findings strengthen the view that women 'tend to adopt a supportive role in interactions' (p. 57).

This places Holmes's study into a body of research which argues that women contribute more than men to the maintenance of interaction in English. An article by Pamela Fishman (1978) is the most renowned early example of this research. It is an analysis of tape-recorded conversations between three American heterosexual couples. Fishman is interested in the acting out of power relations between the sexes, and she believes that interactional discourse is a part of the process of *making* power.

Her finding that women work harder to keep mixed-sex conversations going is, for Fishman, confirmation of women's subordinate position in society. For example, according to Fishman, women ask more questions than men, they have to work harder to gain men's attention in interaction, and they are more supportive of men's contributions, as shown by women's particular skill, as addressees or listeners, at inserting

**minimal responses** into the brief pauses of a speaker's performance. These minimal responses, such as 'yeah', 'mhm', and 'oh', when used in this way, are signals from the addressee that she is attentive to and interested in what is being said. 'Women are the "shitworkers" of routine interaction,' Fishman concludes (p. 405), 'and the "goods" being made are not only interactions, but, through them, realities.' That is to say, what counts as real or important is determined according to values associated with men rather than with women, but nevertheless, in their interactions with men, women actively (in a passive kind of way) help to perpetuate these values.

The studies by Holmes and Fishman exemplify two trends in sociolinguistic research on language, sex, and gender after Lakoff.

1. The trend which focused on interactional discourse and which investigated the functions of linguistic features.
2. The trend which restyled women's language as cooperative and supportive rather than hesitant and unconfident. The conviction that men occupy a dominant position in society remained, but women's speech, while still subject to male power, was cast in a positive light.

The new view of women's language, and of men's language, which emerged by the mid-1990s was summed up in Jennifer Coates's *Women, Men and Language* (1993). For Coates, sociolinguistic research suggests that women and men use distinct styles of speech. The data suggests that women are more likely to use supportive minimal responses, that women use more politeness features, and use more **hedges** (uncertainty indicators like 'I think' or 'you know' or 'sort of'). These features are traits of a style of interaction which expresses 'mutual support and solidarity' (Coates, 1993, p. 140). Men, however, in this view, dominate mixed-sex conversations by the use of interruptions, by becoming silent at strategic moments, and by controlling the choice of topics. Contrary to popular belief, it seems that men talk more than women. Men's interactive style seems to be domineering rather than cooperative. But this view does not tell the whole story. There is research, summarized in Mary M. Talbot (1998, p. 97), that indicates that men's speech can equally express solidarity, but differently – it can involve sparring and mock abuse. Think of the dialogue at the end of the film *Butch Cassidy and the Sundance Kid* (1969). Wounded and about to be shot to pieces, do Butch and Sundance bond by telling each other directly how they feel? No, they bond by insulting each other and by joking about starting a new life in Australia.

Coates says that 'women and men pursue different interactive styles' (p. 139) and that 'women and men may constitute distinct speech communities' (p. 140). This is the line of thought pursued by Deborah Tannen in a number of publications. Tannen analyses talk between women and men as 'cross-cultural communication'. Her position is that women and men belong to 'essentially different cultures' (1990, p. 18), this use of the word *culture* being, arguably, metaphorical. The framework it provides Tannen with is a response to the insufficiency of the **dominance approach** to language and gender. The dominance approach interprets language and language behaviours as effects of male dominance (as in the work of Dale Spender, and of Pamela Fishman, for example). Instead, Tannen employs a **difference approach**, which interprets behaviours in the context of the different 'cultures' that women and men inhabit. As with any cross-cultural communication, misunderstandings arise easily. For example, men who adopt a competitive approach to conversation may interpret women's supportive responses as interruptions (Tannen, 1990, p. 215).

Although there has been some conflict between 'dominance-ists' and 'difference-ists', the two approaches are not incompatible. Behaviour can be dominant *and* different. Nevertheless, the two approaches represent two stages in the evolution of Anglo-American feminist linguistics, with the difference approach supplementing and to some extent superseding the dominance approach. Tannen's *You Just Don't Understand* (1990) marks an unusual cross-over. As Cameron (1996) shows, popular women's magazines have regularly raided sociolinguistic research for 'self-improvement' articles like 'How to Talk to a Man So He Really Understands You'. Tannen's book, however, is both sociolinguistics and self-improvement. As Neil Armstrong did not say, it's one small step from the different-cultures analogy to the different-planets metaphor.

Before finishing the tag-question saga we shall take a short but not uninteresting diversion.

## Her master's voice: language treating women and men differently

It would be unfair to call Robin Lakoff the 'mother of political correctness'. I can think of three reasons why.

1. *Political correctness* is a negative, derogatory label, used to refer to all kinds of real and imagined attempts at reforming traditional practices, but especially used to refer to real and imagined attempts at reforming linguistic usages.
2. Lakoff was wary of attempts to reform linguistic usages, arguing that 'social change creates language change, not the reverse' (1973, p. 76), and that many proposals for linguistic reform 'are founded on misunderstanding and create well-deserved ridicule' (p. 75), with the result that justifiable suggestions suffer guilt by association.
3. The phrase 'mother of political correctness' itself is troublesome. One does not hear 'mother of' phrases used to describe pioneering figures in the way that 'father of' phrases are, as in 'father of modern linguistics'. If we live in a male-dominated world, we can expect founding fathers to be more numerous than founding mothers. But 'mother' in 'mother of political correctness' calls to mind other usages, such as *mother of invention*, as in 'Necessity is the mother of invention', or *mother of all battles*, or *Mother of Presidents* (the State of Virginia), or terms like *mother-ship* or *mother-tongue* or *Mother Earth* or even *mother-fucker*. It appears that figurative use has eroded the oppositional equivalence of *mother* and *father*. 'Mother of political correctness', therefore, does not work quite as one would hope.

Nevertheless, there is an evolutionary line connecting Lakoff's 'Language and Woman's Place' with 'political correctness'. The second part of Lakoff's essay, subtitled 'Talking about women' (pp. 57–73), discusses the treatment of women in the English language. Lakoff argues that the language treats women and men unequally. She says that the personal identity of women is 'linguistically submerged' (p. 45). Lakoff's essay discusses two kinds of 'linguistic submergence'.

1. In English, says Lakoff, women are identified by their relationship to men, while men are not identified by their relationship to women. For example, the title *Mr* makes no reference to a man's marital status, while the titles *Miss* and *Mrs* tell us whether or not a woman is married. The proposal that *Ms* should replace both *Miss* and *Mrs* seemed fairly new in 1973 (although, astonishingly, *Ms* is first recorded in 1901, in the USA, according to the *Oxford English Dictionary*), and Lakoff was pessimistic about its chances of success. In the event, *Ms* has tended to become a third option rather than a replacement.

2. The language has difficulty coping with the sexual identity of women. Lakoff says that the use of the word *lady* is euphemistic, a way of avoiding the direct reference to sexual identity inherent in the word *woman*. The terms *gentleman* and *gent*, says Lakoff, are not used frequently enough to function in the same way, as euphemisms for *man*. Lakoff also points out the imbalance in some pairs of words which might at first appear to show a simple male/female opposition. For example, *master* and *mistress* are not equivalent opposites. *Mistress* has an overtly sexual content, and refers to a woman according to her relationship to a man, while *master* indicates power over something. If Robert Plant had sung 'Let the music be your mistress' instead of 'Let the music be your master', on Led Zeppelin's *Houses of the Holy* (1975), he would not simply have swapped a feminine word for a masculine word. He would have chosen to sing about sex (as a recreation not as a biological category) rather than power. These examples illustrate what Geoffrey Hughes calls (1991, p. 212) the 'angel/whore dichotomy'. This is the tendency in English for terms for women to divide into two extreme categories: elevatory words which treat women as praiseworthy objects and which cover up women's sexual identity, and derogatory words which castigate women for their sexuality.

All of this suggests that the English language reflects men's perspective more than it reflects women's. Lakoff's essay drew attention to this idea, and Dale Spender's book *Man Made Language* (1980, and 1985) developed the theme considerably. Spender argues that the English language is the product of a **patriarchy**, that is, a society in which much social and cultural practice is organized around the belief that the male is the superior sex. A patriarchy is a society in which the male is the dominant sex, and in which males have the power to exclude females from the production of cultural forms, including language. This means, says Spender (1985, p. 52), 'that the language has been made by men and that they have used it for their own purposes'. The English language is 'man made', not 'woman made'. This is an unnerving thought. For example, it would mean that whenever any of us, woman or man, expresses anything in English – even when we are discussing language, gender, and sex – we are compelled to express ourselves according to a slanted male mindset, which seems tyrannical. Spender is one of many scholars and writers who have perceived kinds of tyranny at work when we use language. The view that language is tyrannical is evaluated further in the next chapter of this book.

# Conclusion

As the writer James Thurber (1894–1961) observed, in 'My Own Ten Rules for a Happy Marriage' (1953, p. 51), 'The wife who keeps saying, "Isn't that just like a man?" and the husband who keeps saying, "Oh, well, you know how women are," are likely to grow farther and farther apart through the years. These famous generalizations have the effect of reducing an individual to the anonymous status of a mere unit in a mass.' And yet each of us is, barring some exceptions, either a woman or a man. This makes us all highly susceptible to mere-unit reduction, for the categories female and male provide a classification system that is hard to resist.

Allan and Barbara Pease's *Why Men Don't Listen & Women Can't Read Maps* (2001), which makes use of research 'collected from studies in scientific, medical, psychological and sociological studies' (p. 5), goes for mere-unit reduction in a big way. It includes a lengthy chapter on 'Talking and Listening', which adds linguistic studies to the list above to produce an impressive mélange of generalization (for example, 'men aren't much good at talking', p. 75, 'A man's sentences are shorter than a woman's and are more structured', p. 88) and self-improvement advice ('The first rule of talking to a man: Keep it simple! Give him only one thing at a time to think about', p. 88). While the Peases' book is aimed at the same market as *Men are from Mars, Women are from Venus* (indeed, something of a Mars/Venus genre has developed), it is also eerily redolent of a well-known chapter on the language of women and men in *Language: Its Nature, Development and Origin*, by the linguist Otto Jespersen, published in 1922. Jespersen's chapter, called 'The Woman', has come to be seen as something of a black mark in an otherwise rightly respected published output, and is summed up by Talbot (1998, p. 36) as 'based on little more than speculation', which 'simply reiterates the stereotypes and prejudices of the period'. The Peases' present their book as a debunking of political correctness, but what it does mostly, and simply, is follow the man/woman conceptual classification. This is not, however, to deny the relevance of modern scientific research which, according to Doreen Kimura, in *Scientific American Presents* (Summer 1999, p. 27), 'suggests that the effects of sex hormones on brain organization occur so early in life that from the start the environment is acting on differently wired brains in boys and girls'. Susan Pinker (2008, p. 37) argues that the differing linguistic abilities of boys and girls (girls, on average, perform better) must be to an extent biologically determined. Kimura's article summarizes research that, to varying degrees, provides evidence for biological bases of sex differences in behaviour, including linguistic behaviour, but she adds (p. 28) a significant rider: 'On the whole, variation between men and women [that is, in cognitive tasks] tends to be smaller than deviations within each sex.' We can also draw in here the linguist, and supporter of the biological view, Steven Pinker (Susan's brother), who warns (2007, p. 86) against over-interpretation of statistical tests which show differing *average* results for men and women: 'It's as if people heard the statistic that women outlive men on average and concluded that every woman outlives every man.'

Sociolinguistic research seems to have identified patterns of different behaviour that correlate with gender, but the famous generalizations that James Thurber referred to are not unknown even in sociolinguistics. Sociolinguistic research on language, gender, and sex has itself been over-influenced by the female/male classification system.

Take, once again, but in a closing kind of way, tag questions. When Cameron, McAlinden and O'Leary (1989) applied the gender categorization and Janet Holmes's modal/affective categorization to tag questions in two corpora of British English speech, they found a lack of fit. Cameron et al. could not fit their tag questions consistently into either one or the other functional category, and they could not correlate patterns of use easily with the sexes. Cameron et al. particularly wanted to consider additional factors affecting the use of tag questions. Their findings confirm the view that a linguistic feature, such as a tag question, can be **multifunctional**. Not only can a tag have different functions in different contexts, but it can have more than one function in a single context. They point out (p. 84) that in 'You were missing last week, weren't you', the tag is modal (it indicates uncertainty), but it also softens an accusation, and could be considered affective (showing concern for the addressee). In addition, factors like the role that participants take in particular interactions, the objectives of particular interactions, and the social status of participants relative to each other have a bearing on patterns of use of linguistic features. In 'It's become notorious, has it' (p. 90), a comparatively powerful participant, a medical doctor on a radio phone-in programme, uses a modal tag to summarize and cut off a caller's narrative. This is an assertive use of a supposedly 'uncertain' form. Similarly, politeness features, sometimes described as supportive and characteristic of women's speech, can in hierarchical situations be used to exert power over addressees. As Talbot (1998, p. 93) says, 'It is possible to interpret a compliment as a patronizing "put-down".'

Later, Deborah Cameron dedicated a whole book (2007) to arguing against 'The idea that men and women metaphorically "speak different languages" – that they use language in very different ways and for very different reasons' (p. 163), which she calls 'one of the great myths of our time'. She concludes (p. 163) that overall the research shows that both sexes engage in both cooperative and competitive talk, and that there is 'no good evidence' that men and women systematically misunderstand each other. She does, however, go along moderately with one linguistic gender divide, saying 'research suggests that it is commoner for men to talk more [than women]'. Earlier, Cameron et al. (1989) concluded their piece by placing inverted commas around the term 'women', saying that 'women' are not a 'homogeneous social group' (p. 91). James Thurber, after much less effort, arrived at a similar conclusion 40 years earlier. Women are different. That is to say, women are different from women. Men are different from men. Moreover, a woman is different from herself, a man is different from himself. While there has been an explosion of work (and teaching) in all manner of 'gender studies' since the 1970s (several branches of linguistics besides sociolinguistics have taken an interest, including discourse analysis, pragmatics, and stylistics), some strands in gender-analysis destabilize the very notion of gender identity.

Gender can be understood as a series of roles rather than as an identity. Jennifer Coates's *Women Talk* (1996) looks at women **performing** 'woman-hood', or rather a variety of 'woman-hoods', in and through conversation, while Cameron's 'Performing Gender Identity' (1997), taking its cues from the work in philosophy of J. L. Austin and of Judith Butler, looks at masculine **performativity** in speech. **Performativity** here refers to gender as an effect of behaviours, as something which is continually constructed through performance (as opposed to gender being seen as the root of behaviours). Bing and Bergvall (1996, p. 24) describe the question 'How do women and men speak differently?' as a 'tired and repressive old dichotomy', adding that 'every time we seek and find differences, we also strengthen gender polarization'. Furthermore, there is a strand of feminist analysis (exemplified by the work of Julia Kristeva) which argues that identity is, as Bennett and Royle (2009, p. 185) put it, 'fissured, haunted, at odds with itself'. Like tag questions, each of us is more than one thing. Each of us is more than one self. We all are, to use David Bowie's phrase, 'cracked actors'. This position, influenced by psychoanalytic thought, argues against **essentialism**.

**Essentialism** can be defined here as the view that the biological differences between the sexes are echoed by essentially female and male ways of behaving. The Mars/Venus view. But if the scientific research described by Kimura (1999) in *Scientific American* represents an essentialist view, then it is an essentialism that talks of trends and patterns, and which is also compatible with the ideas above, of role-play and the fractured self – which probably makes it not essentialism at all. It is difficult to identify with certainty *essentially* female and male ways of behaving, not without descending into James Thurber's 'famous generalizations'. Life, it appears, is not that simple.

## Further reading

Two useful collections are *The Handbook of Language and Gender* (2003), edited by Janet Holmes and Miriam Meyerhoff, and *The Feminist Critique of Language: A Reader* (2nd edn, 1998), edited by Deborah Cameron, which together provide a wide-ranging introduction to approaches and key work. *Language and Gender* (2003), by Penelope Eckert and Sally McConnell-Ginet, is a handy guide to themes in language use and gender. Mary M. Talbot's *Language and Gender: An Introduction* (1998) is an excellent and astute survey of research, and the third edition of Jennifer Coates's *Women, Men and Language: A Sociolinguistic Account of Gender Differences in Language* (2004) updates a detailed appraisal of the achievements of sociolinguists on language, gender, and sex, by one of the field's leading practitioners. *Language and Sex: Difference and Dominance* (1975), edited by Barrie Thorne and Nancy Henley, was an important early overview, and *Rethinking Language and Gender Research: Theory and Practice* (1996), edited by Victoria L. Bergvall, Janet M. Bing and Alice F. Freed, is a collection which took a questioning stance towards orthodox approaches. For a discussion of the interrelationship of feminism and linguistics in initial work, see Deborah Cameron's *Feminism and Linguistic Theory* (2nd edn, 1992). *Language and Masculinity* (1997), edited by Sally Johnson and Ulrike Hanna Meinhof, is an influential collection that marked a natural but in some ways belated expansion, and *Language and Sexuality* (2003), by Deborah Cameron and Don Kulick, on the relationship between language use and the construction of sexuality, signifies another development in the fertile domain of contemporary language-and-gender studies.

# 10 The Tyranny of Language
## Some Daring and Ingenious Escapes

---

This chapter includes the following:
- The ideas of Alfred Korzybski and **General Semantics**.
- Roland Barthes on the 'fascism' of language.
- William S. Burroughs on the 'word virus'.
- **Cut-up**.
- Literature as a revolutionary activity.
- Feminist escapes from the tyranny of language.

---

## Introduction

In the preceding chapter, 'Sex', mention was made of 'political correctness', a label applied to what is perceived to be a body of liberal opinion, dating from the 1970s, which aims among other things to rid the English language of discriminatory, oppressive usages. The present chapter places 'political correctness' in the wider context. Its main title echoes that of a 1938 book, *The Tyranny of Words*, by Stuart Chase, a follower of the **General Semantics** movement inspired by the writings of the scientist and philosopher Alfred Korzybski. This chapter deals with the view that language is tyrannical.

It is not an uncommon view; in fact, it is quite a phenomenon. This phenomenon provides us with distinctive and sometimes radical ways of looking at language. Many people have, like Korzybski, argued that language is oppressive, and have proposed ways of either fighting or escaping this oppression. Their theories are quite disparate, but nearly all have one thing in common: the belief that the tyranny of language can be countered by changing or subverting language and its use. This frequently involves play, that is, wordplay in the most general sense, and frequently (though less entertainingly) it involves some kind of reform movement. This chapter, then, surveys the variations on the tyranny-of-words theme and assesses the assorted escapeful and revolutionary measures proposed. All of the people whose views I consider here have something to say about the tyranny of language in general and of individual languages in particular – almost all, including Korzybski and Chase, are concerned with the English language. Korzybski sets the scene for us.

## 'Statements are verbal; they are never *it*'

This is Korzybski writing in 1946 (p. 240). In the same paragraph, he also says, 'we may state correctly that whatever we *say* something *is*, it *is not*'. The paragraph concludes, 'in our socio-cultural environment, we unfortunately still believe and train our children in the poisonous dogma that "in the beginning was the word" '. Korzybski (1879–1950), a Pole who became a naturalized American, argued that we tend to confuse words with the things they refer to. Just as René Magritte states in his 1964 painting '*Ceci n'est pas une pomme*' ('This [the pictorial representation of an apple] is not an apple [that is, an actual apple]'), so Korzybski says that the word *apple* is not the thing, apple. The word and the thing do not have the same identity – they have a relation. But we tend to see an identity instead of a relation, to such an extent that words impress themselves upon things. Words have assumed a primacy, according to Korzybski. They have even assumed a primacy over what Korzybski calls the 'silent levels' of experience – happenings and feelings. The 'verbal levels' of experience (language) are powerful. They provide a (remarkable) means of transmitting the accumulated knowledge of generations of people, but if this knowledge is not 'properly verbalized', then the verbal levels 'may seriously twist or even arrest human development' (Korzybski, 1946, p. 240).

The proposition that language affects our perception of the world is most often associated with the work of Edward Sapir and Benjamin Lee Whorf (discussed in Chapter 8, 'Myth'). Korzybski, by a different route, identifies language's sway over the human world. However, he goes further than Sapir and Whorf by suggesting that this power in language can be dangerous and oppressive, and by suggesting a way of combating the problem – by becoming aware of the non-identity of the silent and the verbal levels of experience.

The **General Semantics** movement dedicated itself to pursuing Korzybski's project – I discuss General Semantics in more detail later in this chapter, in the section on William Burroughs, but Korzybski's views provide a theme and a comparative reference point for the chapter as a whole.

## Language is quite simply fascist

This is the view of Roland Barthes in his 'Inaugural Lecture' (1978) as professor of literary semiology at the Collège de France, Paris. What he actually says is, 'language – the performance of a language system – is neither reactionary nor progressive; it is quite simply fascist' (p. 461).

Obviously, what Barthes is *not* talking about here is the language of fascism, as expressed by, say, Adolf Hitler or Benito Mussolini. Barthes *is* saying that language involves compulsion. Acquiring a language involves being compelled to speak only in certain rule-governed ways. We cannot just invent our own language and then be understood by others. Barthes's point is that the (amazing) capability that language gives us – to communicate and express ourselves – happens within confines over which we have no control.

Barthes works with the Saussurean model of language (discussed in more detail in Chapters 6 and 7), in which each language is structured on an underlying system, or *langue*, to use Saussure's term. *Langue* arises out of communal agreement. For example, a word means what it means because a community of speakers agrees that that is what it means. A language is based on a system of such conventions. No doubt Saussure would not have described language as fascist if the term had existed when he delivered the lectures that led to his *Course in General Linguistics* (1916), but even he said 'language furnishes the best proof that a law accepted by a community is a thing that is tolerated and not a rule to which all freely consent' (p. 71). Any speaker of a language is powerless to do anything but use the system that he or she has inherited. Thus Barthes, using French, is compelled to indicate his relation to another individual in their presence 'by resorting to either *tu* [informal 'you'] or *vous* [formal 'you']' (Barthes, 1978, p. 460). It is a choice over which he has no choice, because he *must* choose. Also he 'must always choose between masculine and feminine' (p. 460), because French classifies its words according to grammatical gender. The performance of a language system is fascist because the system compels us to speak in certain ways, according to inherited conventions.

We can only say what a language allows us to say, in ways permitted by the language. At the same time, as linguistic beings, we *must* use language.

What, then, can be done? According to Barthes (1978), the best strategy is cheating, trickery and evasion, in other words, **literature**, which elsewhere (1968, p. 147) Barthes describes as a 'truly revolutionary' activity. By **literature** Barthes means not a particular body or canon of work but the outcome of the practice of writing. For Barthes, literature is where the conventions of language can be played with and made to work against themselves. It is in literature that language can be twisted and stretched. By way of quick example, we can do no better than to mention the supreme wordsmith of English, William Shakespeare, who was an exceptionally productive creator of puns and of new words and idioms.

## 'We see that "victory" always comes down to the same thing: things get hierarchical'

This is the writer and literary theorist Hélène Cixous, in her essay 'Sorties: Out and Out: Attacks/Ways Out/Forays' (1975, p. 64). She is talking about the symbolic systems of the human world, language being chief among these systems. The psychoanalyst Jacques Lacan, whose work Cixous draws upon, calls these systems the 'symbolic order'. Cixous uses the term **logocentrism**. The Greek term for 'word' is *logos*, and **logocentrism** refers to ways of thinking which put linguistic meaning at the centre of things (that is, as Alfred Korzybski (1946, p. 240) put it, the 'poisonous dogma that "in the beginning was the word" '). For Cixous, logocentrism is the product and the pillar of **patriarchy** – a world based on the notion of the superiority of the male. Logocentrism interprets and orders the world, but this ordering is inherently biased and oppressive. For example,

> Activity/Passivity
> Sun/Moon
> Culture/Nature
> Day/Night
> Father/Mother
> Head/Heart
> Intelligible/Palpable
> Logos/Pathos
> (Cixous, 1975, p. 63)

each of these couples being related to a basic pair,

Man
___
W*oman*

Cixous is suggesting that logocentrism organizes concepts into pairs of opposites, that it relates these pairs to a basic, underlying opposition, between male and female, and that the opposites are not equal. There is a hierarchy which privileges the male over the female, and women are silenced because the language that they are obliged to use is designed to suppress and obscure the female perspective. Instead it presents the female from the male perspective.

What can be done? Like Barthes, Cixous sees the practice of writing as the arena in which oppression can be countered. Unlike Barthes, Cixous argues that women can free themselves by *writing their bodies*. Certainly, Cixous is *not* here referring to some kind of tattooing habit. Cixous *is* imagining a 'feminine writing' (*écriture féminine* in the original French) which escapes the silencing effects of the male logocentric order. She says (1975, p. 95), 'Woman must write her body, must make up the unimpeded tongue that bursts partitions, classes, and rhetorics, orders and codes, must inundate, run through, go beyond the discourse with its last reserves.' According to Cixous, logocentrism has stifled the diffuse sexuality of each individual. Patriarchal logocentrism has imposed a reductive sexual categorization on individuals. The logocentric order is dominated by the **phallus**, that is, the symbolic significance of the penis, with the result that some aspects of human physicality are privileged while others are ignored or neglected. Women, says Cixous, 'have turned away' from their bodies (1975, p. 94), coerced into doing so by logocentrism, and feminine writing would be the practice in which women turn back towards their bodies, using language to express their physicality while freeing their physicality from the oppression of language. Cixous appeals to the (Lacanian) notion of an existence beyond language which has been obscured by language, but which she believes can be reclaimed by feminine writing. 'If woman has always functioned "within" man's discourse', Cixous says (1975, pp. 95–6), 'now it is time for her to displace this "within", explode it, overturn it, grab it, make it hers, take it in, take it into her woman's mouth, bite its tongue with her woman's teeth, make up her own tongue to get inside of it.'

Cixous's views can be grouped with those of Luce Irigaray and Julia Kristeva, and illustrate a French strand of feminist thought on language, inspired in particular by the work of Lacan. The feminine writing that Cixous imagines cannot be comfortably, easily defined because it is a practice which seeks to escape the confines of traditional language. It is a practice which Cixous has pursued in her writing and performances. It can be called poetic, intuitive, passionate, but these are familiar words, and Cixous wants to de-familiarize language by bringing it into contact with that which it has disregarded.

## 'The Word is literally a virus'

This is the writer William Burroughs in his essay 'Ten Years and a Billion Dollars' (1986a). It goes, 'My general theory since 1971 has been that the Word is literally a virus, and that it has not been recognized as such because it has achieved a state of relatively stable symbiosis with its human host' (p. 47).

Surely what Burroughs meant to say was 'the word is *metaphorically* a virus'. Surely he is making a *comparison* between language and a virus. Can he be misusing the word *literally*? The word *literally*, when used emphatically, is supposed to drive home the sense 'actually', but it is often misused, as when, on a radio phone-in programme about health-care that I once heard, a doctor said, 'We are literally juggling beds.' If Burroughs is misusing the word *literally*, then he is wilfully, deliberately misusing it. He wants us to understand fully the hold that language has on us. He wants us to believe that the Word really is in us, in our bodies, occupying us, living off us:

> The word may once have been a healthy neural cell. It is now a parasitic organism that invades and damages the central nervous system. Modern man has lost the option of silence. Try halting your sub-vocal speech. Try to achieve even ten seconds of inner silence. You will encounter a resisting organism that *forces you to talk*. That organism is the word. (Burroughs, 1967, pp. 49–50)

To describe him after the style of the glossy pop-culture magazines where his name is regularly mentioned, William Seward Burroughs (1914–97) is: author, junkie, wife-killer (an accidental shooting), spokesman for the beat generation of the late 1950s, mascot for the American punk generations of the late 1970s and late 1980s, all-time winner of the title Coolest Name To Drop, and dead person. He coined the following names: *heavy metal* (in *The Naked Lunch*, 1959), *The Soft*

*Machine* (from *The Soft Machine*, 1961, a metaphor for the human body), *Steely Dan* (the name of a dildo in *The Naked Lunch*), and *Blade Runner* (from *Blade Runner: A Movie*, 1979). Of his first meeting with Kurt Cobain (1967–94), Burroughs said, 'There were no drugs. I never showed him my gun collection' (Sandford, 1995, p. 219).

Burroughs had a good deal more to say about the English language. For example, in 'On Coincidence' (1986b, p. 105) he says, 'In the beginning was the word and the word *was* God. And what does that make us? Ventriloquist dummies. Time to leave the Word-God behind. "He atrophied and fell off me like horrible old gills" a survivor reported. "And I feel ever so much better." ' In 'Last Words' at the start of *Nova Express* (1964, p. 4) he says, 'What scared you all into time? Into body? Into shit? I will tell you: "*the word.*" Alien Word "*the.*" "*The*" *word* of Alien Enemy imprisons "*thee*" in Time. In Body. In Shit. Prisoner, come out. The great skies are open. I Hassan i Sabbah *rub out the word forever.*'

For Burroughs, language is an affliction, an alien organism in the human body, an occupying force in the human mind, controlling the perceptions of its host, who is largely unaware of his/her subjugation.

Burroughs's views on language were influenced by Alfred Korzybski, whose seminars he attended in 1939, at the University of Chicago. Korzybski's *Science and Sanity* (1933) inspired **General Semantics** – not a military person nor a car manufacturer but a reform movement in the United States, whose proponents perceive a dangerous lack of objectivity in language, coupled with a harmful lack of precision in our use of language. For example, Stuart Chase, in *The Tyranny of Words* (1938), reports that when he asked a hundred people to tell him what they understood by the word *fascism*, the responses were disturbingly varied. He says (p. 133), 'Multiply the sample by ten million and picture if you can the aggregate mental chaos.' Chase's main concern, following Korzybski, is with the effects of words' lack of correspondence with things, combined with our blind faith in words' efficiency, combined with our tendency to privilege words over things. What is required, according to General Semanticists, is a corrective realignment of words with things. Burroughs, following Chase, following Korzybski, says of *fascism*: 'we have so many different phenomena lumped under this word that the use of the word can only lead to confusion. So we can drop the word altogether and simply describe the various and quite different political phenomena' ('Technology of Writing', 1986c, p. 35).

Burroughs's writing is a fitting resting place for the General Semantics programme, though, unlike Burroughs, General Semantics is alive and well. The Institute of General Semantics has an impressive website, which highlights its strong leanings towards 'self-improvement'. The programme, suggested in the very title of Korzybski's *Science and Sanity*, imagines that a language can be redesigned scientifically, regimented, thereby ensuring that its users see the world clearly. General Semanticists argue that language interferes with language users' ability to experience the world directly, and their solution is to make language a neutral, transparent link between the human and the world. This, however, would be to work against the grain of language itself. Similarly William Burroughs's statements about language typically work against the grain of accepted knowledge. They are deadpan serious and ridiculously, sometimes monstrously comic, as in *The Place of Dead Roads* (1984). Here language is a sexually transmitted virus which originated in a species of red monkey, 'larynx fuckers', some of whom survive, 'throwbacks in remote valleys who still use the larynx as a sexual organ . . . rather like those horrid kissing fish' (1984, p. 242). Infected humans are addicted to automatic speech habits. Americans 'will swarm out of a derelict building and yack in the faces of pedestrians: "We love New York!" or stick their heads into car windows and yack out: "Have a good day!" ' (p. 258); ' "THE YACKS! THE YACKS! THE YACKS!" ' (p. 258).

Why does the General Semantics solution go against the grain of language? Because each language is a symbolic system, a system of symbols, in which the symbols or **linguistic signs** – for example, words – are bound together in relationships with each other. A word *appears* to refer directly to a thing, but any word is immersed in relationships of contrast with other words in the same language, theoretically with *all* other words in the same language. Words are thus defined by each other. They are mutually dependent. There is no direct line of connection between a word and a thing, but rather the line from the word travels around the symbolic system before reaching the thing, and then the thing ends up being specified by the workings of the system rather than by the individual word. This again is the Saussurean model of language – each language structured on a system of symbols or signs. General Semantics treats the symbolic system (a language) as if it is not a system but a list of correspondences in need of correction. Furthermore, as Saussure says (1916, p. 73), language 'is at every moment everybody's concern; spread throughout society and manipulated by it, language is something used daily by all'. Seen in this light, the kind of revolution proposed by General Semantics looks unfeasible.

What then can be done? Says Burroughs (1986a, p. 47), 'give me ten years and a billion dollars for research, and I'll get some *answers* to the question of Word'. In the meantime, his wish is to *rub out the Word* and regain the option of silence that the language virus denies us. For linguistic beings, however, there appears to be no going back to a non-linguistic state, except possibly as dead persons. But William Burroughs had a few tricks up his sleeve, notably **cut-up** and **fold-in**. These are creative techniques that Burroughs used in his writings. He described the two methods in a BBC broadcast in 1964 (quoted in Mottram, 1971, p. 25). Cut-up: 'Brion Gysin, an American painter living in Paris, has used what he calls the cut-up method to place at the disposal of writers the collage used in painting for fifty years. Pages of text are cut and rearranged to form new combinations of word and image, that is, the page is actually cut with scissors, usually into four sections, and the order rearranged.' Fold-in: 'A page of text, my own or someone else's, is folded down the middle and placed on another page, the composite text is then read across, half one text and half the other. The fold-in method extends to writing the flashback used in films.' David Bowie, an admirer of Burroughs, used cut-up in the lyrics of one of the most peculiar pop-music chart-toppers, *Diamond Dogs* (1974), an album about apocalypse, freaks, and alienation. Bowie was much taken with the meaning-fracturing effects of cut-up. Burroughs himself was interested particularly in what he saw as the capacity of cut-up/fold-in to counteract the oppressive linearity that language imposed upon the writer. His biographer Barry Miles (1992, p. 131) says cut-ups provide 'a way of thinking in association blocks', and indeed cut-up does at times seem hooked into the associative powers of language. For example, ' " 'The Priest' they called him ... used to be me, Mister" shabby quarters of a forgotten city ... tin can flash fare ... smell of ashes ... wind stirs a lock of hair ... "Know who I am? hock shop kid like mother used to make ... Wind and Dust is my name" ' (all *sic*, from *Nova Express*, 1964, p. 98). The very act of disruption calls attention to the associative binding of language.

Cut-up is a particularly audacious form of the trickery, evasion, and revolt that Roland Barthes saw as characterizing literature. For Burroughs, cut-up/fold-in produces writing that is in keeping with the modern world. Television, said Burroughs (1965, p. 42), 'That's a *real* cut-up.' Thus a television documentary will comprise an interview cut-up and then spliced together with other interviews, each shot separately with different interviewees, and joined in a new sequence. A wildlife programme will show footage of a stalking lion intercut with footage of grazing antelope, shot elsewhere and/or at a different time, in order to suggest that *this* lion is stalking *these* antelope at *this* moment. (In an episode of *Life in Cold Blood* (2008), Sir David Attenborough and a local naturalist are seen trying to locate a rare breed of frog by imitating its call. Cut to film of one such frog, apparently responding to the call. Cut back to Attenborough and companion, hearing the response. Plainly, the frog must have been filmed after Sir David and his crew had located it, not while they were trying to find it. But they and we are willing to accept this cut-up pretence in the cause of narrative. For more on narrative, see the next chapter.) Movies are cut-up. Martin Scorsese's *Goodfellas* (1990), for example, is very cut-up. Moving visual images are edited into sequences, while one pop song after another is segued into a continuous background soundtrack, while a voice-over provides a commentary while the actors deliver dialogue. Every day you can watch cheaply made TV magazine programmes using cut-up. Anything made out of recordings on tape or film will be a cut-up. You can do cut-up with your television remote control, and with your computer's mouse. Digital media are a boon for cutter-uppers. I have visited Burroughs websites on the Internet that do cut-up, such as the 'cutup machine', into which you could type text and have it spliced into elements of Burroughs's *The Naked Lunch*. You click 'Rub Out' to have words removed at random. If William Burroughs were not a dead person he would point out that the Internet is a cut-up. Cut-up is anti-linear. Many years before the Internet, Burroughs told his readers 'You can cut into *The Naked Lunch* at any intersection point' (1959, p. 222). Cut-up also reconstitutes existing materials – 'the whole sublime concept of total theft is implicit in cut-ups and montage' ('Les Voleurs', 1986d, p. 20). Your word processor can cut, copy, and paste. Your software can cut-up writing, speech, music, photos, and video. It turns out that this escape route is being followed every day, all over the place.

Above all, in using the cut-up and fold-in methods, Burroughs was attempting to return the written word to an earlier existence and to bring it into line with human perception – or at least with his understanding of these things. He says ('The Fall of Art', 1986e, p. 61), 'Consciousness *is* a cut-up; life is a cut-up. Every time you walk down the street or look out the window, your stream of consciousness is cut by random factors.' For Burroughs, the written word's earliest existence was as non-linear images on the walls of caves. Cut-up/fold-in does not rub out the word forever – it attacks our lines of communication. Burroughs wanted to fragment the linearity of writing, and cut-up arguably achieves this to a degree, but it also highlights a fundamental property of language, that is, that it is structured on relations, on associations. It is a curious fact that Ferdinand de Saussure – in whose theory of language associative relations are important – was also, one might say, something of a cut-up obsessive. Between 1906 and 1909, Saussure filled over a hundred notebooks with his thoughts on 'anagrams' of proper names, which he believed Latin poets had deliberately hidden in their poetry. For example, the line '*Taurasia Cisauna Samnio cepit*' is, says Saussure, 'an anagrammatic line containing the entire name of *Scipio* (in the syllables *ci* + *pi* + *io*, in addition to the *S* of *Samnio cepit*, which is the first letter of a group in which almost the entire word *Scipio* appears – correction of – *cepi* – by the – *ci* of *Cisauna*)' (translation (Emmet, 1979, p. 16) of a passage reproduced in Starobinski, 1971, p. 29). In a way, Saussure was engaged in a process that was the reverse of Burroughs's – Saussure was disentangling (what he believed to be) a cut-up text. He thought that the anagrams were a conscious (though secret) device of Latin poetry, but it is perhaps easier to accept them as evidence of the cross-connections of written words.

William Burroughs's strivings are also extravagantly emblematic of two threads running through American literary culture: first, a desire to return the English language to a basic or even primeval state (as exemplified by Ezra Pound's interest in Chinese ideograms) while at the same time reinvigorating it, perhaps with a nationalistic impulse (see Noah Webster's *An American Dictionary of the English Language*, 1828, or Walt Whitman's *An American Primer*, 1904); and secondly, what the critic Tony Tanner (1971, p. 429) calls a 'deep dread' and 'prevalent feeling' in mid-twentieth-century American fiction 'that all sorts of invisible "organizations" and "systems" are manipulating the minds and lives of their unaware puppets', there being no more pervasive manipulator than language.

## An analog world

In order to help sum up the chapter so far, then, let us use a similar view to that of Korzybski which is put forward by the psychologist Julian Jaynes (1990), who says that human consciousness inhabits an 'analog world' constructed on and by language. Each language analogizes the world of things, and a language is a world that is analogous to the world of things. The two worlds are related but not identical. Although their analyses are each different, Burroughs, Cixous, and Barthes all see that there is no easy escape from this 'analog world'. Their revolutionary measures attack language on its own terms. They make use of characteristics inherent in language. For example, our performance of language – in writing or in speech – may be linear, but Saussure's model (in his *Course in General Linguistics*) shows us that, in our minds, a language is a network of relations. The 'association blocks' that cut-up brings to the surface are already there in language. Language use abounds with 'slippage' – slips of the tongue, puns, wordplay – because each language system is chock-a-block-hock-shop-kid-like-mother-used-to-make-full of word and meaning associations. Wordplay seems like trickery, it can appear to be subversive, but it is also simply characteristic of language use. Language already has the mechanisms to permit the disruptive measures that Cixous and Barthes advocate, which, when you think about it, is highly counter-revolutionary.

So far we have concentrated on literary escapes from language tyranny. Next we look at the exotic case of Aldous Huxley, before dealing for the remainder of the chapter with feminist measures (not forgetting that Cixous comes into this last category as well).

## The universe of reduced awareness

In his long essay *The Doors of Perception* (1954), the writer Aldous Huxley (1894–1963) argues that language is both beneficial and oppressive (p. 12). Beneficial in that a language gives an individual access to the accumulated knowledge of a community, and oppressive in that languages formulate and express the 'reduced awareness' that humans have developed as a survival mechanism. To protect us from being overwhelmed by information provided by our senses, we have evolved this reduced awareness, argues Huxley (1954, p. 12), and 'That which, in the language of religion, is called "this world" is the universe of reduced awareness, expressed and, as it were, petrified by language.'

What did Huxley do to break free from his reduced awareness? Like William Burroughs, he tried drugs. Now there is no scarcity in the history of English literature of writers known for their use of intoxicants. Thomas de Quincey (1785–1859) advocated the use of opium, arguing that 'whereas wine disorders the mental faculties, opium, on the contrary (if taken in a proper manner), introduces amongst them the most exquisite order, legislation, and harmony' (*Confessions of an English Opium Eater*, 1821, p. 73). Burroughs sometimes took drugs with the aim of widening his consciousness, and as James Grauerholz says, referring to the group of writers and artists around Burroughs in the early 1960s, 'everyone was now taking a potpourri of psychedelic drugs in the name of spiritual discovery' (*Burroughs Reader*, 1998, p. 180). But Huxley's intention was more specific. He took a particular hallucinogenic drug, mescalin, in order to escape from language-petrified awareness. Ironically enough, he wrote about his experience, in *The Doors of Perception*. For example (pp. 15–16), 'A rose is a rose is a rose. But these chair legs were chair legs were St Michael and all angels.' But *a rose* is not a rose, as Korzybski would put it. *These chair legs* never were the legs of the chair that Huxley sat on. Statements are verbal; they are never *it*. A language is an analog reality. It may well be a reality of reduced awareness, but one could equally claim that it is a reality of heightened, honed, focused awareness. Language is itself an altered state, and the expression of a *familiar*, *conventionalized* awareness.

## 'The Virtue of Laughing Out Loud'

In her *Webster's First New Intergalactic Wickedary of the English Language* (1987), the theologian and philosopher Mary Daly defines the *Virtue of Laughing Out Loud* as 'Lusty habit of boisterous Be-Laughing women: habit of cracking the hypocritical hierarchs' houses of mirrors, defusing their power of deluding Others; cackling that cracks the man-made universe, creating a crack through which cacklers can slip into the Realms of the Wild' (pp. 142–3). So, *dick-tionary* is 'any patriarchal dictionary' (p. 194), *logorrhea* is 'diarrhea of the mouth: communicable disease transmitted by paternal politicians and propagandists' (p. 208), and *male-function* is 'characteristically unreliable performance of phallic equipment. *Example:* the explosion of the space shuttle *Challenger*' (p. 209).

The *Wickedary*, I have been told, is funny. Like Cixous, Mary Daly wants a way out of patriarchy, which she sees as the current state of oppression that women find themselves in. Nonetheless, Daly's work belongs more in the tradition of rights-based Anglo-American feminism than it does in psychoanalytical French feminism, and it has not been without influence. One can speculate that her style might be patriarchally inspired by Lewis Carroll or James Joyce or William Burroughs or the Marx Brothers (they really were funny). In the *Wickedary*, she perverts and appropriates a chief enforcer of patriarchy, in her view – language. The *Wickedary* is a dictionary (but not a 'dick-tionary') of English whose aim is to rescue the English language from patriarchy, and to do so un-po-facedly, if such a thing is possible. In it Daly draws heavily on certain images of female power: a woman can be a *Crone* ('Survivor of the perpetual witchcraze of patriarchy', p. 114), a *Hag* ('a Witch, Fury, Harpy who haunts the Hedges/Boundaries of patriarchy', p. 137), and a *Spinster* ('one who has chosen her Self, who defines her Self by choice neither in relation to children nor to men', p. 167), for example. And she, Daly, revels in relentless, grinding, wordy wordplay.

## Strangers in a strange land

This phrase (originally 'stranger in a strange land', from the Bible, Exodus 2:22) encapsulates the central charge in *Man Made Language*, an influential book by Dale Spender (1985, first edition 1980). The 'strangers' are women, and the 'strange land' is the English language. English is patriarchal, says Spender. From a female perspective, it is the oppressor's language (Spender, 1985, p. 183). For Spender, English is an especially powerful instrument of oppression because she believes (following Sapir and Whorf) that language conditions our perception of reality.

Spender's approach is influenced by Anglo-American descriptive linguistics. Her analysis, therefore, dwells on specific examples, such as the effects of the masculinity of the word *God* (discussed in Chapter 8 of this book, 'Myth'), the use of the words *he* and *man* in certain expressions to include reference to females (Spender, 1985, pp. 146–62), and the biased account of sex and sexuality in the English language (pp. 171–82): for example, *virile* suggests healthy sexual power in a male but is not applied to females, for whom there is no equivalent term.

What is to be done? Spender's revolutionary measures are less insidious than Cixous's and less ostentatious than Daly's (and not a million miles away from those of General Semantics). Sexist usages, such as woman-encompassing *he* and *man*, have to be identified, censured, and avoided; new terms have to be coined, like *sexist* (first used in 1961, and in a different sense before that in 1949, according to the *Oxford English Dictionary* (*OED*), *sexual harassment* (1975), and *womb envy* (Spender's own suggestion, p. 181); and other words can be 'invested with new woman-centred meanings' (p. 186), something which has already happened to *patriarchal*, for example.

## 'I'll tell you what it means: it's almost an evil, satanic plot!'

This is the film director David Lynch, talking about 'political correctness'. He continues (Rodley, 1997, p. 153), 'To be politically correct is to be so sort of lukewarm, and in this weird little spot where there's no offence committed. It's like hiding.' But let us be clear about this. *Political correctness* is not political correctness. The term is not the thing. But what is the thing?

It is not a good thing, whatever it is. The term is used disparagingly – most people assume that it refers to an extremist movement dedicated particularly to the removal of all offensive and even potentially offensive expressions from the English language. People assume that it is an assault on their freedom of expression, and that the day will soon come when we all are forced into not uttering words like *short* or *fat* or *old*. In fact, it's already come. Political correctness gone mad!

People assume also that political correctness was started by feminists, like Dale Spender, for instance. Deborah Cameron points out (1994, p. 18) that the adjectival phrase *politically correct* was first used in the early 1970s self-mockingly by 'the countercultural movements of the American new left'. The noun phrase *political correctness* is an appropriation and perversion of the prior, ironic term. (Evidence from the *OED* is in line with this account.) It is, in the words of Richard Gott (1993; quoted in Alibhai-Brown, 1994, p. 60), 'a notional construct put together by the Right to create a non-existent monster on the Left that it can then attack'. As a movement it is fictional. As a thing, it is not. (Dare I wonder, has anyone anywhere ever said, 'I belong to the political correctness movement'?) As a term, nevertheless, it *implies* a thing. (Evidence from the *OED* is in line with this too, of course.) The term allows serious arguments for reform (Spender's, for example) to be grouped with ludicrous, fabricated, and tongue-in-cheek suggestions – the like of which can be found in Beard and Cerf's *The Official Politically Correct Dictionary and Handbook* (1994), such as '*h'orsh'it*: An artful contraction of "he or she or it"' (p. 32), '*msterbation*: Female auto-eroticism' (p. 46), and '*pedal sizism*: The oppression of those whose feet are larger than the norm' (p. 54).

## Conclusion

The term *political correctness* provides us with an excellent concluding example, as it illustrates both the reactionary and the revolutionary
powers in language. It hints also at the measure of escapefulness from
language inherent in language itself. On the one hand, the term labelled
a thing – a movement – which did not even exist, but because, as
Korzybski says (1946, p. 239), 'we usually objectify words and react
correspondingly', it has been easy for us to be persuaded by the term
that the movement does exist. This is a symptom of our 'semantic disease', as Korzybski calls it (p. 240), a description intensified in Stuart
Chase's tyranny label and William Burroughs's 'virus' imagery. On the
other hand, terms like *political correctness, sexual harassment*, and *sexism* show that the English language is open to the kind of innovation
that entails new forms and meanings being created by reconstituting
old materials. Language is a cut-up!

But proposals for discrete reforms involving individual expressions
always face an unpredictable future. **Neologisms** (new words and new
senses of words, discussed also near the end of Chapter 2, 'Time') and
new usages in English are continually occurring, but one can never
be certain of their long-term (or even short-term) fate. Of the numerous alternative formulations for woman-encompassing *he* and *man*, for
example, some are used by some people, but not everybody on all occasions will use *he or she*, say, instead of woman-encompassing *he*. And
*womb envy*? Where did that go? *The Handbook of Non-Sexist Writing*
(Miller and Swift, first published in 1981) and similar guides can influence the usage of some groups, state legislation can affect language
use in public situations, but each individual proposal for reform is up
against the conservative power of the language *as a system*, a network of
mutually supportive symbols.

Literature, if we agree with Barthes and Cixous, is the arena where
language can be turned against itself, by means of itself. Poetry, for
example, argued the English Romantic writer Percy Bysshe Shelley
(1792–1822), 'creates anew the universe, after it has been annihilated in our minds by the recurrence of impressions blunted by
reiteration' (1840, p. 105), a statement which, if put in Korzybski's terms, seems to claim that the 'verbal levels' of experience can
be revolutionized in poetry in a way that reawakens the 'silent levels' of feelings. Indeed, the common notion expressed by the collection of scholars and writers encountered in this chapter (with
the possible exception of Huxley) is the paradoxical idea that the

only possible release from the tyranny of language is through using language.

## Further reading

You can cut into the work of William Burroughs at almost any point and find him making some kind of statement about language. However, *Word Virus: The William Burroughs Reader* (1998), edited by James Grauerholz and Ira Silverberg, is the best place to start, and after that *The Adding Machine: Selected Essays* (1986f), while *The Soft Machine* (1961, 1966 and 1968), *The Ticket that Exploded* (1962 and 1967), and *Nova Express* (1964) form a famous trilogy of cut-up novels. A very useful feature on Alfred Korzybski's theories can be found in the journal *Synthese* (Volume V, Numbers 4 and 5, 1946), and his 'The Role of Language in the Perceptual Processes' (1951) is also a helpful summary. The Institute of General Semantics has published *Alfred Korzybski: Collected Writings, 1920–1950* (1990), compiled by M. Kendig. See also the Institute's website at: http://www.generalsemantics.org/. For further Barthes, see *A Barthes Reader* (1982), edited by Susan Sontag, and for more Cixous, see *The Hélène Cixous Reader* (1994), edited by Susan Sellers. Dale Spender's *Man Made Language* (1985) is a classic work of polemical linguistics. For a comprehensive discussion of 'political correctness', see *The War of the Words: The Political Correctness Debate* (1994), edited by Sarah Dunant.

# 11　Telling Stories

## The Structure of Discourse in English

---

This chapter includes the following:
- A guide to the term **discourse**.
- An introduction to **discourse analysis**.
- An introduction to **speech-act theory** and **conversational maxims**.
- Definitions of the terms **genre** and **medium/media**.
- Summaries of **critical discourse analysis (CDA)** and **systemic linguistics**.

---

## Preamble

Stories and story-like structures are everywhere in language use. This chapter is about the interrelation of language use, stories, and story-like structures. It looks at the templates and conditions that mould stories and language in use. This chapter is also about **discourse**. It examines the underpinning patterns and conventions that predetermine the shape and content of everyday and media discourse in English.

## A beginning

*In which we are introduced to the scene-setting example of this chapter*

I will begin by talking about a movie sequel. Later I will draw parallels between the structural characteristics of movie-sequel narratives and the structural characteristics of everyday discourse. I will also be looking for evidence of the *self-reflexivity* of movie sequels and of everyday discourse.

Shortly after arriving on Isla Sorna, Jeff Goldblum's character in the film *The Lost World: Jurassic Park* (1997), Dr Ian Malcolm, commenting on his companions' reaction to the sight of a herd of stegosaurus, says, 'That's how it always starts – the "oos", the "ahs" – but later there's running and screaming.' Dr Malcolm has had previous tension-packed experience of dinosaurs on the nearby Isla Nubar, site of the theme resort Jurassic Park. Just as important, Jeff Goldblum starred previously in the motion picture *Jurassic Park* (1993), to which *The Lost World* is the first sequel. As well as being a part of the narrative of the film, Malcolm/Goldblum's comments are about *The Lost World* as a story.

Motion-picture sequels are many. It is the original movie that lures audiences to the sequel. They expect to enjoy again what they enjoyed in the first movie. The sequel-watcher wants a viewing experience that recaptures a previous viewing experience, except that the freshness of the previous experience will be diminished or missing. Hence the sequel-watcher feels a little cheated. But if the sequel is not like the original, the sequel-watcher feels more than a little cheated.

Thus the basic plot of *The Lost World* is the same as that of *Jurassic Park*. A company of well-groomed people, consisting of an interesting mix of men and one woman, adults and minors, the unsuspecting and the sceptical, is marooned among prehistoric wildlife, endures a variety of close encounters with an assortment of startling special effects (during which one member of the group – fortunately not one of the central characters – is eaten alive by a tyrannosaurus rex), and ends up a company of unkempt but wiser individuals. Other character types appear in both films. For example, the macho white-hunter type, of *Jurassic Park*, is replayed in *The Lost World* as a macho and slightly sinister white-hunter type; the naive Jurassic Park founder is replayed as his naive and slightly sinister nephew. Sequences are replayed. The buggy-being-pushed-over-a-precipice-by-a-tyrannosaurus-rex episode is replayed as a trailer-being-pushed-over-a-precipice-by-a-tyrannosaurus-rex episode; the frantic chased-by-velociraptors sequence is replayed as a . . . frantic chased-by-velociraptors sequence. The two films are not identical, but many basic components occur in both. *The Lost World: Jurassic Park* aims to satisfy the contradictory desires of its audience, in that it aims to be the same as and different from its predecessor.

*The Lost World* also comments upon its condition, upon its 'sequelness'. For example, at one stage in the original movie the approach of a tyrannosaurus rex is signalled by the vibrations of water in a glass tumbler. In the second film, this image becomes a recurrent motif – water vibrates in glasses and pools on several occasions, each time warning the audience of a nearby monster. The device becomes an in-joke shared by film-makers and audience: we've seen this before, we know what it means, we know what's coming next. The image has become a certain **indexical sign**, to use a term from semiotics, that is, it has a meaning generated by cause and effect – we know now what causes the water to vibrate, and the image of water vibrating now incorporates the meaning 'a big dinosaur approaches'. On our first encounter with the image, as audience, in *Jurassic Park*, we are uncertain momentarily as to its significance, but it is a memorable and chilling image, sufficiently so for it to be parodied in *Wayne's World 2* (1993). When we encounter it again in *The Lost World*, we know its meaning immediately, and repetition reactivates and reinforces the previous connection.

In addition, *The Lost World* comments upon its condition as a 'monster movie' and upon its very 'movie-ness'. Its title echoes that of the book by Sir Arthur Conan Doyle (1912), itself twice made into a movie (1924 and 1960). Its closing passages – where a tyrannosaurus rex runs amok in San Diego – refer to the closing passages of the most famous monster movie, *King Kong* (1933). As a review in *Sight and Sound* (July 1997, pp. 44–6) pointed out, there are references to a variety of cinematic moments, from, for example, *Hatari!* (1962), in the dinosaur hunt using jeeps; *Bambi* (1942), in the sequences of the crying baby T-rex; and *E.T.: The Extra-Terrestrial* (1982) and *Poltergeist* (1982), 'in a jokey reprise of the uncannily invaded suburbia' (p. 45). *The Lost World* is a movie about itself as a sequel, as a monster movie, and as a movie. It says, 'Look, I'm a sequel, I'm a monster movie, I'm a movie.' Its self-awareness and its largely predetermined narrative are bolstered by its allusions to other films. Some of these allusions are examples of **intertextuality** (a term from literary theory), that is, they amount to citations from other films, as in the vibrating-water image.

When Ian Malcolm/Jeff Goldblum says 'That's how it always starts', we know what he means, because we, as audience, have seen it all before as well. His comments betoken a movie drawing attention to its own condition, just like, for example, Ripley/Sigourney Weaver's 'I can see where this is going' in *Aliens* (1986, another sequel) and O'Connell/Brendan Fraser's response to the question 'So what's the challenge then?' in *The Mummy* (1999, not a sequel in the strict sense, but such a self-aware movie): 'To rescue the damsel in distress, kill the bad guy, and save the world.' And also like the basic pitch of *Scream* (1996) and its sequels: 'The sleepy little town of Woodsboro just woke up screaming. There's a killer in their midst who's seen a few too many scary movies' (*Scream* official website, accessed in 2000). These are examples of **self-reflexivity** (to use another term found in literary theory, where it describes a piece of writing referring to or reflecting upon itself as a piece of writing): here are films reflecting upon themselves as sequels, as movies, as stories. Like any story *The Lost World* has familiar elements, and like any story it is in some measure a story about being a story.

To sum up so far: I have focused on one narrative event, one example of a story – a movie sequel. We have seen that it comments on itself as a type of story. I have been less concerned with the temporal ordering of its narrative (though chronology and progression in stories is a major interest of narrative theory) than with the factors which predetermine its shape and content. The next part of this chapter gives a fuller picture of these factors and explains how they affect all types of story. This discussion then leads as seamlessly as I can manage into consideration of the predetermined nature of **discourse**.

# A middle

*In which we meet the term **discourse** and its three main usages*

The movie sequel could be described as an example of a particular **genre** of film. The term **genre** refers to a kind or style of creative work, examples of which are seen to have significant characteristics in common. As Jonathan Bignell (2002, pp. 199–200) points out, placing a film in a particular genre involves recognizing the **signs** associated with that genre, such as type of setting, characteristic camera shots, style of title graphics, not to mention story structure. Some widely recognized genres of film would be the Western, science-fiction, horror, action, *film noir*, the war movie, and the thriller. Within these we can distinguish sub-genres, such as classic *noir* and neo-*noir*. The Vietnam movie could be considered a sub-genre of the war movie. In literature, the genres poetry, drama, and novel can be subdivided into, for example, lyric poetry, epic poetry, tragedy, comedy, romantic novel, murder mystery, and so on. In television, we find the sitcom, soap opera, the cop/police drama, the hospital drama, the wildlife documentary, and so on. A particularly interesting wildlife documentary series is the BBC's *Walking with Beasts* (2001), which has prehistoric animals as its subject. Ostensibly, wildlife documentaries present scenes from the natural world filmed as they happen. Obviously *Walking with Beasts* cannot do this, but it can follow the narrative template of the wildlife documentary by telling the story of a beast from birth to maturity or through the seasonal cycle of a year. In doing so, and because of its 'virtual' nature, *Walking with Beasts* highlights the predetermined character of its narrative. The series even has some self-reflective (and self-mocking) moments where virtual beasts splash water and mud over the camera lens or charge at it.

Any creative work is likely to belong to at least one genre or sub-genre. *The Lost World: Jurassic Park* is an action/monster/science-fiction movie with elements of horror; *The Mummy* is an action/horror movie with comic elements. Membership of a genre involves use of the conventions or 'rules' of that genre, but the conventions do not have to be followed slavishly. They can be mixed with the conventions of another genre, they can be played with or subverted, but they cannot be escaped. For example, the film *The Wild Bunch* (1969) expanded the style of the Western genre, while *Unforgiven* (1992) exposed some of the Western's myths, but both films introduced something new to the genre by working with and against its existing conventions. The conventions of a genre become most visible when the genre is parodied, as in films like *Hot Shots! Part Deux* (1993), which pokes fun at *Rambo* (1985) and a host of other films, and at the titles of sequels. On television, the Monty Python team parodied *The Wild Bunch* by transferring its blood-spurting brutality to the setting of an English countryside picnic, in their sketch of 'Sam Peckinpah's *Salad Days*' (1972). Technological advance can affect genre. The advent of computer-generated imagery (CGI) invigorated the production of science-fiction movies, revived the dormant epic genre (*Gladiator* (2000), *Troy* (2004), *Kingdom of Heaven* (2005)) and pirate-action movie sub-genre (the *Pirates of the Caribbean* series (2003, 2006, 2007)), and transformed the animation genre (the *Toy Story* (1995, 1999) and *Shrek* (2001, 2004, 2007) series, for example). One could even argue that the CGI-movie is another genre in itself, distinguished by, say, action spectacle on a large and colourful and intricate scale, often at the expense of character and plot development.

**Genre**, then, helps determine a story. As we shall see shortly, the term has also been taken up in the branch of linguistics known as **discourse analysis** to describe kinds of speech event, even that kind which we would expect to be least predetermined and most spontaneous, that is, everyday conversation.

In the case of *The Lost World*, another predetermining factor is its 'movie-ness'. Cinema is an example of a particular **medium** of communication. A medium is anything which acts as or uses a channel for communicating something. The **mass media** include newspapers, television, cinema, radio, and the Internet, but as Bignell says (2002, p. 1), 'a large part of our experience of the world involves interactions with media'. In this sense, **media** would include such things as shop signs, traffic lights, clothes, and hairstyles. Any particular medium both opens up and shuts down possibilities in comparison with other media. For example, unlike a film, a printed book cannot use music or moving visual images, but it can use descriptive prose passages. Then again, new media emerge, and interact with older media: video computer games influence cinema, and an *electronic* book *can* use moving images. Language itself has two chief media: speech, which uses an oral–aural channel of communication; and writing, which uses a visual channel. (See Chapter 16 for more on channels of communication.)

Another factor is the 'who' (and 'whom') of storytelling. Every story is told by someone to someone. A story is a communicative event that requires at least one storyteller and an audience, and the identity of storyteller and audience affects the story. A father reading a bedtime story to his daughter will be reading a certain kind of story in a certain way, depending on the age of the daughter, how much she joins in, and the father's feelings about the gender-stereotyping of many fairy tales, for example. *The Lost World* was made by a vast array of creative and technical staff (*Sight and Sound* lists 400), constrained by commercial considerations and the necessity to identify and reach the film's target audience.

A story is affected also by when and where it is told, factors which are interlinked with medium and genre. For example, we can identify six broad categories of time-slot in television scheduling – breakfast, day-time, tea-time, early evening, late evening, and night-time – each of which will be matched with types of story deemed appropriate to that slot.

The who, when, and where of a story, interlinked with medium and genre, together provide a context in which the story is performed, and this context affects how the story is performed, and its structure and its content. It is at this point that we turn to the term **discourse**. The term can refer to the structure and content of stories. It is also sometimes used as a synonym for *story* itself, sometimes to refer to storytelling, and sometimes as a label for language in use generally. It is used in other ways as well. As Sara Mills explains in her book *Discourse* (2004, p. 1), the term is widely used in several disciplines, including critical theory, sociology, linguistics, philosophy, and social psychology. It is a key and ubiquitous term, but it is used very variously. It is possible, however, to identify the three main usages of **discourse**.

The first main usage of the term is where **discourse** is language in use. This is a general summary of the ways in which the term is employed. **Discourse** here is language in action, language when it is used by people, between people. This is an everyday usage, but it also interconnects with the more specific and theoretical usages of the term.

The second main usage of the term is where **discourse** is a stretch of language larger than a sentence. This summarizes the ways that the term is employed in linguistics, where **discourse** usually refers to extended stretches of speech, and the term is often contrasted with **text**, which refers to extended stretches of writing. (Occasionally, however, in linguistics, the term **discourse** is used to refer to extended stretches of speech and writing, *and* moreover the term **text** is sometimes used in this way also.)

In the first half of the twentieth century, work in American and European linguistics concentrated on analysis of the sentence and its components. From the 1950s onwards, there developed a growing interest in the view that there are, in language use, units larger than the sentence, and that these units possess components and structures. **Discourse** and **text**, therefore, in linguistics, refer to structured wholes and not merely to haphazard stretches of language. Indeed, the suggestion is that no stretch of speech or writing is haphazard. A new sub-discipline within linguistics, **discourse analysis**, emerged during the 1960s. The term **discourse analysis** usually refers to the analysis of extended stretches of speech, and is often contrasted with **text analysis** or **text linguistics**, terms which usually refer to the analysis of extended stretches of writing.

Discourse analysis has shown, for example, that everyday conversations can be considered to be manifestations of a genre, that is to say, a conversation is conditioned by its belonging to a type of event underpinned by certain expectations and characteristics. **Conversational analysis**, a strand of discourse analysis, has shown that conversations are highly structured activities: a conversation has a beginning, a middle, and an end, and within this framework participants tacitly abide by a number of basic conventions and rituals. A conversation in English usually begins with a formulaic exchange of **greetings**. The main topic of a conversation tends to be introduced by the initiator of the conversation. A conversation progresses through an exchange of **turn-taking**: a speaker can signal that he or she is about to conclude an utterance by such means as explicitly saying so, or by lowering the pitch, loudness, or speed of their speech, and a listener may lean forward or breathe in audibly to indicate that he or she wishes to access the speaking floor. There is an elaborate procedure involved in bringing a conversation to an end, with participants rounding off a topic, implicitly or explicitly agreeing that there is nothing more to say, and then moving from this **pre-closing** sequence into the formulaic farewells of the **closing** sequence.

In a way then, every conversation is like a movie sequel. We expect a conversation to be different from previous conversations, but at the same time we expect it to be the same in some essentials. We expect a conversation to conform to certain genre conventions, even though we may only be dimly aware of these conventions. We are most aware of these conventions when they are contravened, for example, when a conversation ends abruptly, or when it seems to us as if it is never going to end.

The theory of **conversational maxims**, proposed by the philosopher H. P. Grice (1913–88) in a paper published in 1975, is an account of some *sub*structural conventions of conversation. Grice argues that conversations depend on an underlying **cooperative principle**, which is to do with the implicit collaboration between interlocutors that smoothes interaction. The cooperative principle is based on four conversational maxims: the maxim of Quantity (do not say too little or too much), the maxim of Quality (be truthful), the maxim of Relation (be relevant), and the maxim of Manner (avoid obscurity and ambiguity, be brief and orderly). It is unlikely that a conversation will live up to these maxims, but they are not descriptive statements, and neither are they rules of etiquette. They are about our assumptions regarding conversations, our expectations of conversations. In fact, we rely often on flouting the maxims for making meaning. For example, a parent infers that an utterance made by a teenage son such as 'I thank you very much indeed for reminding me that it's now 11 o'clock and I must still revise tonight for my exam tomorrow' is sarcastic because it plays around with the maxim of Quality. Its sarcasm is based on the assumption that the sentiments expressed by an utterance will be sincere.

These yardsticks enable listeners to infer a great deal about utterances. They help listeners work out whether an utterance is sarcastic, untruthful, long-winded, cryptic, and so forth. Grice's maxims help explain how listeners can work out the **implicatures** of utterances, that is, 'extra' information that exceeds what is actually said. Let us take our imaginary parent and teenage son again and an exchange that occurred some hours before the utterance quoted in the preceding paragraph:

*Parent*:  I've seen your exam timetable and I see you've got Geography tomorrow.

*Son*:  I'm going up to my friend's house to practise the guitar this evening at six o'clock.

Using the maxim of Relation, the parent, and any third party listening, will infer that the son has no intention of doing any revision that evening.

A study by the English Language Research unit at the University of Birmingham (Sinclair et al., 1972; Sinclair and Coulthard, 1975), of classroom interaction, suggested that a 'grammar' of discourse would have to take into account inferences made by listeners. These inferences depend not only on expectations about conversations but upon expectations about conversationalists and about the situation in which a conversation occurs. In other words, the who, when, and where of a conversation will affect its content, and how the content is interpreted. Pupils expect teachers to behave in certain ways, and vice versa, and this affects interaction. Children expect parents to behave in certain ways. Such expectations affect inferencing. This is most clearly seen when mis-communication occurs. For example:

| | |
|---|---|
| *Parent*: | Are you going to eat this toast? |
| *Younger son*: | I didn't know it was there. |
| *Parent*: | Yes, but are you going to eat it? |
| *Younger son*: | I didn't know it was there! It's cold. I didn't know Mum had put it there! |
| *Parent*: | Yes, but . . . no, I'm not telling you off – if you don't want to eat it, I will. I'm hungry. |

The son's responses were based not only on what the parent actually said, but on the assumption that, if the parent was asking him if he was going to eat the food in front of him, then the parent must be scolding him for not eating it. It's what parents do.

Discourse analysis in general, including the Birmingham study of teacher–pupil interaction, owes much to an influential idea first set out in book form in 1962 by the philosopher J. L. Austin (1911–60). The idea is not primarily about the structural conventions of types of discourse, and it is not about the assumptions underlying discourse: it is about what words do in discourse. The idea is that words *do*, that language in use is social *action*. The idea amounts to a radical theory of communication which has become known as **speech-act theory**.

In *How to Do Things with Words* (1975; first edition 1962), Austin begins by using the term **performative** for utterances which under appropriate conditions perform an action, such as 'I name this ship the *Queen Elizabeth*' (when smashing the bottle against the bow) and 'I give and bequeath my watch to my brother' (as in a will). In such cases, says Austin (1975, p. 6), to utter is not to describe an action or to state that an action is being done – here to utter is to do. *Saying* 'I promise to revise for two hours every evening from now on' is also the *act* of promising, though not the act of keeping a promise.

Austin distinguishes performatives from **constatives**, that is, utterances which describe or report something, such as 'I revised for two hours last night.' Constatives can be judged to be true or false, performatives cannot. A performative can only be successful or unsuccessful, or, to use Austin's terms, **happy** or **unhappy**.

However, having made this distinction, Austin proceeds to unravel it. Some constatives cannot be judged to be true or false. The statement 'John's children are all bald' is neither true nor false if John has no children – 'void' or unhappy would describe it better (Austin, 1975, pp. 50–1). Furthermore, an utterance which begins 'I state that . . .' is the act of making a statement, and such an utterance could therefore be both performative and constative. In fact, any utterance can be analysed as an abbreviation of a longer 'I state that . . .' version.

Austin then makes a fresh start. He acknowledges that saying is always, in a sense, doing. He now distinguishes (p. 109) three different kinds of acts that we perform when we say something. The **locutionary act** is the act of saying, of uttering an utterance, the act of making a statement. The **illocutionary act** is the 'force' of an utterance, such as informing, naming, or promising. (In my earlier example, 'Are you going to eat this toast?' has the illocutionary force of a question.) The **perlocutionary act** is what is brought about or achieved by an utterance, such as convincing, persuading, or surprising, that is, the effect of an utterance on a listener. The effect may or may not correspond with the speaker's intention. (The perlocutionary effect of 'Are you going to eat this toast?' on the son is of some sort of command.)

Austin's theory has been taken up by many scholars in linguistics and other fields, most famously by the philosopher John R. Searle. The notion of the performative has been influential also in literary studies. The title of a literary work, indeed any title, can be considered a promise, a performative. If, for example, *The Lost World: Jurassic Park* were retitled *Death in the Jungle*, then we would expect a different viewing experience.

So we have seen that discourse (to employ the term in its second main sense) includes genres of language use, such as conversation (other examples are lecture, sermon, and newsreading). As a genre, conversation possesses conventions of structure and style, and underlying expectations that are obeyed or disobeyed (but not escaped), and that are continually reflected upon or monitored by interlocutors, sometimes explicitly so (as in 'Stop interrupting!' and 'Please get to the point'). A conversation, precisely because it has conventions which can be followed or abused, will always in part be about the process of having a conversation. It will be self-reflexive. And meaning in a conversation is bound up with inferencing as well as with speaking. Variants of such an analysis could also be applied to other genres of language use.

The third and final main usage of the term **discourse** is where **discourse** is made up of **discourses**, which are regulated genres of expression. This summarizes the ways that the term is employed in critical and cultural theory. One of the main influences on the development of this usage was the work, during the 1960s and 1970s, of the historian of knowledge Michel Foucault (1926–84). In *The Archaeology of Knowledge* (1969, p. 22), Foucault describes discourses as 'groups of statements'. He says that discourses 'are not, as one might expect, a mere intersection of words and things' (p. 48), but are 'practices that systematically form the objects of which they speak' (p. 49). In 'The Order of Discourse' (1971, p. 67), he says that we must conceive discourse 'as a violence which we do to things, or in any case a practice which we impose on them'. In the Foucauldian usage, a discourse is a story, an account, an explanation of a phenomenon or phenomena. It is a mode of interpretation, a way of speaking about phenomena. A discourse is regulated, so some ideas, beliefs, and modes of expression are permitted (within the discourse), some things are considered, while others are excluded (from the discourse). A discourse reflects back on the phenomena it deals with – indeed, in dealing with phenomena a discourse actively forms the phenomena. Because they are everywhere, the practices of discourse are difficult to escape. They provide templates for understanding things, and it is difficult to think or act outside them. Discourses, in this usage, are stories which we tell and they are stories which tell us.

According to this usage, then, most aspects of our lives are connected with discourse and its effects. To take a trivial phenomenon, that is, my bad back. My back hurts, but my back does not tell me why it hurts. Foucault says (1971, p. 67), 'we must not imagine that the world turns towards us a legible face which we would have only to decipher; the world is not the accomplice of our knowledge'. Over the years, my bad back has become the object of a number of discourses: the discourse of conventional Western medicine, the discourse of psychoanalysis, the discourse of acupuncture, the discourse of shiatsu ... and this is not an exhaustive list. Each of these discourses is a body of knowledge and a mode of interpretation. Each body of knowledge is affected by the mode of interpretation. My bad back is explained differently by each discourse – my local doctor identifies a posture problem and prescribes painkillers, an acupuncturist sticks needles in my meridians, friends and acquaintances politely suggest a psychosomatic complaint, and so on. Ultimately, what is explained is not simply my back, but my back as understood by, as objectified in, each discourse. (Needless to say, it still hurts, but I have a better idea why, thanks to X-rays and an MRI scan, which are the outcomes of technological advance, which has a connection with the discourse of science.)

The discourses pertaining to my bad back are not necessarily contradictory, but they are in a state of struggle with one another, just as, for example, the discourse of Marxism exists in a state of struggle with the discourse of capitalism, or the discourses of Christianity and Islam with the discourse of science (and the discourse of Christianity with that of Islam). In her discussion of Foucauldian discourse, Sara Mills (2004, pp. 14–24) points out that discourses are bound up with power and power struggles, with the result that all knowledge is an effect of power struggles (p. 19). Any discourse is ideological – any discourse is a way of thinking. At any one time, or in any one age, discourse in general is made up of discourses in states of struggle. Discourse or knowledge in general will change as discourses adapt and shift – for example, the discourse of Christianity has changed substantially in response to developments in the discourse of science. There are discourses of masculinity and femininity, which set out criteria for masculine and feminine behaviour in a given culture at a given time. Over time these criteria may change. In the second half of the twentieth century, the criteria for masculinity and femininity shifted continually, thanks to, for example, the after-effects of world war, developments in pop culture, and the discourse of feminism.

Foucault's exploration of discourse was a deliberate questioning and broadening of Ferdinand de Saussure's theory of language, itself a formative influence on the discourse of modern linguistics. Saussure saw languages as symbolic systems, each system constituted from **linguistic signs** and the relations between them. For Foucault a discourse was the outcome of signs in action, not merely a group of signs but a practice. Foucault's work has influenced cultural studies, critical theory, and modern literary theory. Curiously, it has had comparatively little impact on linguistics. One of the effects of the discourse of linguistics has been to endow linguistics with a scientific, 'objective' quality. This quality sits uneasily with the examination of power, ideology, and struggle provoked by Foucauldian discourse theory. However, **critical linguistics** or **critical discourse analysis (CDA)**, which emerged during the 1980s, is an attempt to bring together linguistics and Foucauldian discourse theory. It amalgamates Foucault's definition of discourse with descriptive procedures derived from discourse analysis.

One of the best-known practitioners of CDA is Norman Fairclough, whose work includes examination of struggles between dominating and dominated groups in British and American society by analysing the discourse of everyday interactions, such as doctor–patient exchanges and police interviews (1989), and the discourse of the mass media (1989, 1995). He has also explored the role of language in political and economic globalization (2006). Fairclough draws on speech-act theory and **systemic linguistics**, an approach most associated with the work of M. A. K. Halliday. Systemic linguistics foregrounds the purposes or **functions** of language in use, such as the **ideational**, **textual**, and **interpersonal** functions. The **ideational** function conveys information about our experience of the world: 'With this component,' says Halliday (1975, p. 17), 'the speaker expresses his experience of the phenomena of the external world, and of the internal world of his own consciousness'. The **textual** function is to do with how linguistic elements combine to form a text. And the **interpersonal** function is to do with how language influences social relations: 'it expresses the speaker's role in the speech situation, his personal commitment and his inter-action with others' (Halliday, 1972, p. 99). (These quotations from Halliday are taken from de Joia and Stenton, 1980, pp. 35, 40.) The systemic approach pays attention to the systems of alternatives available to speakers and writers with regard to these functions of language. Fairclough (1995) uses Halliday in his attempt to describe representations, identities, and social relations in media discourse. His analysis (1995, pp. 139–42) of an *Oprah Winfrey Show* broadcast in 1992, for example, shows how interactions between participants on the show obey and reinforce a hierarchy in which the voices of 'ordinary' people are subordinated to those of 'experts'. This hierarchy characterizes the discourse of *Oprah Winfrey* and the discourse affirms the hierarchy. It is a hierarchy which is echoed in genres of television programme other than the confessional talk show – in the relationships between 'stars' and contestants on game shows, for example, or between 'personalities' and ordinary people on make-over shows, or judges and competitors on talent shows. It is underlined by the parallel existence of 'ordinary' and 'celebrity' versions of game and reality shows.

Teun A. van Dijk is another major figure in CDA, or **critical discourse studies** (**CDS**), as he prefers to call it. He is perhaps most recognized for his work on racism and discourse, which, as his website explains, began in 1981 with an investigation into 'the role of the Dutch media in the reproduction of racism', and which grew into a project which has looked at the discourse of racism elsewhere in Europe and in the United States and Latin America. The reason he prefers the term *critical discourse studies* is because of his wish to distinguish not a method of analysis but 'a movement of socially and politically concerned scholars in the field of discourse studies and related fields' (van Dijk's *Discourse in Society* website, accessed in 2009). Again, and as van Dijk is aware, this troubles those scholars who see linguistics as a discipline which aims for neutrality and objectivity. (Similar tensions surround feminist linguistics, a movement discussed further in Chapters 9 and 10.)

## And an end

*In which we go to the Ball, and return in a concluding way to our opening example*

In summary, discourse – however we define it – is structured for us in advance. Wherever we look at language in use we find ready-made ways of speaking, and the story-like characteristics of discourse go hand in hand with language in use. Stories are everywhere, and old stories reappear in new guises. *Cinderella*, for example.

Cinderella is a neglected, downtrodden beauty whose Fairy Godmother provides her with the wherewithal to attend a Ball at the Palace, which leads to her marrying a Prince. They live happily ever after. *Cinderella* is replayed in every example of the television makeover show, in which 'ordinary' people undergo happy transformations. The make-over can involve an ordinary person being given a new and glamorous hairstyle, or a new and glamorous wardrobe of clothes, a new and glamorous living-room or garden or home or even a new and immobile surgically enhanced face, and so on. TV make-over 'personalities' combine the authority of the 'expert' with the transformative capabilities of the fairy godmother, and the happy ending is signified by an emotional response from the recipient (and their loved ones) on being presented with the make-over (the 'reveal'). Ostensibly, make-over shows set out to bridge the gap between the world of television and the world of ordinary people, bringing the two together and placing ordinary people in centre-stage, but the passive role of ordinary people in relation to personalities in these programmes accentuates the rift between television-world and ordinary-world, and shows up this rift as a televisual construct. The rift is a part of the discourse (in the CDA sense) of television.

*Cinderella* has also provided a template for news-reporting, for example, in coverage during the 1980s and 1990s of the life of Princess Diana. And *The Lost World: Jurassic Park* is but one expression of an old and familiar story, found also in, for example, Mary Shelley's *Frankenstein* (1818), Isaac Asimov's 'Three Laws of Robotics' (1942), and at least several episodes of *Star Trek*. It reappears in the discourse of news in the coverage of cloning, stem cell research, and the genetic modification of foodstuffs. The story warns of the consequences of men usurping the role of God as creator of life. Each example is like a sequel, containing something new and something so familiar that we almost don't notice it is there, though maybe we notice it sufficiently to find ourselves thinking something like 'That's how it always starts . . .'. It is the same in everyday conversational discourse: we almost don't notice the rules, structures, and limits we abide by.

## Further reading

For an accessible extended discussion of the uses of the term **discourse**, see *Discourse* (2nd edn, 2004), by Sara Mills. Urszula Clark's *Studying Language: English in Action* (2007) has a handy and practical introduction to studying discourse. Malcolm Coulthard's *An Introduction to Discourse Analysis* (2nd edn, 1985) is a standard work on the study of speech beyond the sentence, and *Conversation Analysis: Principles, Practices and Applications* (1998), by Ian Hutchby and Robin Wooffitt, provides a good grounding in the theory and methods of its subject. *The Discourse Reader* (2nd edn, 2006), edited by Adam Jaworski and Nikolas Coupland, has a wide selection of key writings. *The Handbook of Discourse Analysis* (2001), edited by Deborah Tannen and Heidi E. Hamilton, is also a helpful and informative collection. For an overview of the study of media discourse, see *Approaches to Media Discourse* (1998), edited by Allan Bell and Peter Garrett, and follow that with *Media Discourse: Representation and Interaction* (2007), by Mary Talbot. In addition, *Television Discourse: Analysing Language in the Media* (2008), by Nuria Lorenzo-Dus, is a clear and perceptive introduction to the practice of media discourse analysis. Norman Fairclough's *Media Discourse* (1995) is a valuable example of the CDA approach, while *Methods of Critical Discourse Analysis* (2001), edited by Ruth Wodak and Michael Meyer, gives a very useful introductory insight into the history and development of CDA. *Critical Discourse Analysis: Theory* *and Interdisciplinarity* (2007), edited by Gilbert Weiss and Ruth Wodak, provides a later progress report. Teun A. van Dijk's excellent *Discourse in Society* website, which makes available downloads of articles and books, and has information on journals and projects, can be accessed at: http://www.discourses.org/. A good place to start with Foucault's theory of discourse is his 'The Order of Discourse' (1971), in *Untying the Text: A Post-Structuralist Reader* (1981), edited by Robert Young. For M. A. K. Halliday, start with his *An Introduction to Functional Grammar* (3rd edn, 2004, co-written with Christian Matthiessen). This chapter has focused on discourse rather than theories of narrative, but for a fuller introduction to narrative theory, see *Narrative and Genre: Key Concepts in Media Studies* (2000), by Nick Lacey.

# 12 What's in a Norm?
## The Nature of Standard English

This chapter includes the following:
- What is **Standard English**?
- What are its origins and history?
- Is there more than one Standard English?
- What is **Received Pronunciation**?

Standard English is a bit of an enigma, attended by muddle, with a rather clouded history. As a standard, it ought to be stable, but change continually affects living languages. As a standard, it ought to represent ideal behaviour, but the term **Standard English** is frequently perceived to have an association with normal behaviour. As a 'norm', Standard English is judged to be normal, neutral English *and* ideal English. And, as Tom McArthur puts it in *The Oxford Companion to the English Language* (1992, p. 982), **Standard English** is 'A widely used term that resists easy definition but is used as if most educated people nonetheless know precisely what it refers to.'

But I have thrown down the gauntlet to myself and in this chapter I aim to make it clear what Standard English is. What I have done is assemble a small number of key assertions about Standard English which summarize views that I have come across among scholars and lay people, and I will subject each of these assertions to a 'true or false' test.

1. True or false? Standard English is the 'best' kind of English.

    Answer: true, and false.

The majority view in the discipline of linguistics is that it makes no more sense to claim that any one variety of a language is superior linguistically than it does to say that any one language is superior. The orthodox view (in linguistics) is that any variety or dialect (that is, a sub-type) of a language will be suited to the needs of its users and will possess (linguistic) rules and conventions that have evolved through time. To say that one variety, Standard English, is better than all the others is to make a value judgement that arises out of opinions about the speakers of Standard English rather than out of consideration of the linguistic data. It arises also out of opinions about the speakers of so-called **non-standard** varieties of English. The perception that Standard English is superior to non-standard English arises because Standard English is closely associated with a cultural elite. Its perceived superiority, therefore, is a social fact but not a linguistic fact.

In truth, the belief in a 'best' kind of English is deep-seated. It goes back a long way, to well before the name **Standard English** was first used, in 1836 (according to the *Oxford English Dictionary*). Compare the following passages.

> Now the whole language of the Northumbrians, and most particularly at York, is so uncouth and strident, that we southerners can understand none of it. This comes about because of their proximity to barbarous peoples, and because of their remoteness from the kings, who were once English but are now Norman, whom we know to be more inclined to the south than to the north.

> Some features of American English, however, deserve to be resisted by anyone concerned for intelligibility and clear communication. One of these is the American treatment of the '*t*' sound, which suffers a variable fate depending on where it comes in a word. In most cases it is pronounced in the expected way, but if it appears between vowels, as in le*t*ter and ci*t*y, it becomes almost a '*d*', making it difficult to distinguish between *writer* and *rider*, *bidden* and *bitten*. When a CNN reporter says, 'At the UN, delegates are added again', it turns out he means *at it again*.

The sentiments of the two passages are strikingly similar considering that nearly 900 years separate them. Both passages criticize the speech habits of certain groups of speakers. In the first extract, it is the English spoken by north Englanders that is under attack, because it is unpleasant to hear and incomprehensible. In the second, the habits of American speakers of English are associated with incomprehensibility. Presumably, neither twelfth-century north Englanders nor twentieth-century Americans would consider their own English incomprehensible. The two passages are written by outsiders. In the first extract the perspective is that of the south Englander, in the second it is that of the speaker of British Standard English. Despite the distance of nearly 900 years, there is a direct line connecting the two perspectives.

Both passages are from scholarly works. The first is from a historical chronicle written by the Benedictine monk William of Malmesbury
(*Deeds of the English Pontiffs*, edited by N. E. S. A. Hamilton, 1870,
p. 209). It dates from around AD 1125. The original was written in
Latin; the above is a modern translation (see Bibliography for more
details). The second passage is from John Honey's book *Language is
Power: The Story of Standard English and its Enemies* (pp. 248–9), published in 1997. In between there is a substantial body of writing that
advocates and gradually establishes one kind of southern English, originally a very localized, educated London English, as the 'best' English
(see Chapter 14 for examples from this body of writing). Gradually
all the regions of Britain became familiar with the notion of a best
English, and this London English evolved into Standard English. North
Englanders, midland Englanders, west Englanders, and so on all got
used to the idea that their Englishes were somehow inferior in comparison with Standard English. In the end, Standard English became
a yardstick against which the merits of all varieties of English were
measured. But how and why did this happen?

Both the above passages are dealing, in highly biased fashion, with
one of the fundamental characteristics of any language: it will vary. Different groups of English speakers, for example, in different parts of the
world, will speak English differently. To the members of a group their
own English seems 'normal'. When they encounter the English of a
different group, that English will seem different, even strange. It is not
uncommon for the members of a group to denigrate the language habits
of other groups and extol the virtues of their own. They may even come
to see others' language habits not only as strange but also as abnormal
and improper. Or, as Noah Webster (1789, pp. 19–20) put it, 'All men
have local attachments, which lead them to believe their own practice
to be the least exceptionable. Pride and prejudice incline men to treat
the practice of their neighbors with some contempt.' The charge that a
group's dialect is less than fully intelligible is related to the outsider perspective of the person making the charge. John Honey's anxiety about
the clarity of American *t*s occurs because they (Americans and their *t*s)
do not follow the patterns most familiar to and most valued by Honey.
He does not mention the possible reasons for American *t*s. According to
the linguist J. C. Wells (1982, p. 250), this **T Voicing** might well be an
American innovation, or it might have travelled over the Atlantic with
settlers from the south-western counties of England or from the north
of Ireland. Neither does Honey mention that **homophones** (words with
the same pronunciation but different meanings) occur in all varieties of

English, and in the standard accent, and moreover that it is possible for standard homophones to have distinct pronunciations in non-standard English (*road* has a different vowel sound from *rowed* for some speakers of Welsh English, for example, and, as Nagy and Roberts (2008, p. 59) report, eastern New Englanders 'traditionally made a distinction between pairs like *for* and *four*, or *horse* and *hoarse*, which is not heard in most of the rest of the U.S.').

For the sake of clarity, which is after all a stated aim of this chapter, I should here say '**Received Pronunciation** or **RP** homophones' rather than 'standard homophones', though I risk a measure of un-clarity by introducing this term before addressing some other basics. Honey is here concerned with pronunciation, and the standard accent (or pronunciation model) of British English is called Received Pronunciation (RP), and, as we will see shortly, it is best in the present day to distinguish or even to separate out RP (pronunciation) from Standard English (vocabulary, grammar), while still remembering that both refer to standard ways of speaking British English. Accordingly, we are here discussing Honey's RP-influenced perspective. Even so, it is also true that, in the historical overview, (i) the full emergence of a distinct pronunciation model (RP) occurs comparatively late in the story, and (ii) the full separating out by linguists of RP from the definition of Standard English occurs recently. I will return to these points.

To conclude the present section first: over time it is possible that the language habits associated with the most powerful group in a society will become the most extolled. In Britain, it was the dialect of governing circles that became, gradually, Standard English. During the nineteenth and twentieth centuries, Standard English was promoted by the education system and by the mass media in Britain. No group in Britain can now be said to have a completely 'outside' perspective on Standard English, because everyone encounters it often. Standard English is far less localized than, say, Liverpool English or West Country English or even Irish, Scottish or Welsh English. It is now a **supraregional** dialect, which means, literally, that it exists above any regional level – it is super-imposed over many regions. Nevertheless, it remains the *native* dialect of a minority of British English speakers. But once a dialect acquires the label *standard*, it will be perceived differently. The comments of John Honey above gain an additional force compared with those of William of Malmesbury because Honey is not simply measuring one dialect against another – like against like – he is measuring American speech against an accent, RP, and more generally in his book against a dialect, British Standard English, which he believes to be linguistic touchstones.

2. True or false? Standard English is a dialect of English like any other dialect of English.

   True, and false.

This assertion is a bolder restatement of the view in linguistics, mentioned above, that no one dialect or variety (whether standard or not) of a language is linguistically superior to any other, so I have already dealt with it to some extent – but it is worth emphasizing a couple of points here, which also lead into true-or-false number 3, below. Historically speaking, Standard English originated out of a regional and social dialect. Hypothetically speaking, Standard English could have been based on the dialect of, say, Hampshire or Cheshire, rather than on the dialect of educated circles in London – any dialect of English could have adapted to fill the linguistic requirements of a standard. Realistically speaking, however, it was the social context that rendered educated London English suitable as a standard. London, by the end of the fourteenth century, was the established administrative centre of England, as well as its major economic and cultural centre. The basis of Standard English seems to have been in the language, written and spoken, of government and court circles at this time. Judged purely on its linguistic make-up, Standard English remains a fairly unexceptional dialect, but its exceptional social prestige elevated it above all other varieties of English in England and eventually, arguably, the world.

3. True or false? Standard English was originally a dialect which emerged as a 'standard' variety early in the fifteenth century.

   True, up to a point, and as far as we can tell.

This assertion summarizes the findings of scholarly detective work on the origins of Standard English, which suggest that one dialect of English was beginning to gain a certain kind of prestige in early-fifteenth-century England. The emergence of this prestigious dialect is one of the factors that has led language scholars to identify the fifteenth century as the boundary between the end of the Middle English period and the start of the Early Modern English period in the history of English. The *beginning* of the Middle English period follows upon the Norman Conquest of England in 1066, after which major changes in the vocabulary, grammar, and spelling of English become apparent. For some two-and-a-half centuries after the Norman Conquest, French was the 'official' language of the state in England, being used, along with Latin, for the conduct of governmental business. During the course of the fourteenth century, English began to replace French and Latin in this arena, and there was now a demand for an official written English. In 1476, printing arrived in England, leading subsequently to a demand for a uniform, printed English.

No one dialect in the Middle English period possessed more prestige than the others, though William of Malmesbury's comments in 1125 indicate a superior southern attitude towards northern speech. It was another language, French, which possessed most prestige during this period. The decline of French, and Latin, in England left the way open for the development of a prestigious variety of English. By the time William Caxton had set up his printing press in Westminster, it seems that this variety had already begun to emerge. It is called **Chancery Standard**, a name coined by the language historian M. L. Samuels in 1963.

Chancery writing was, as J. H. Fisher (1977, p. 891) points out, under the control of 'a handful of men'. Chancery Standard is not Standard English, but modern *written* Standard English evolved out of Chancery Standard. Chancery Standard is the earliest identifiable precursor to *written* Standard English. It is not a precursor, at least not in any straightforward way, to modern *spoken* Standard English. The term **Chancery Standard** refers to the early-fifteenth-century writing conventions of the clerks of Chancery in Westminster, who prepared the royal documents. Chancery English was the emergent official written standard that filled the gap left by the decline of French and Latin. By 1430, the clerks of Chancery had developed a relatively consistent form of written English – consistent in handwriting, spelling, and grammar. Its official nature, plus the large number of documents produced using it, meant that Chancery English exerted considerable influence on the development of written English generally during the fifteenth century. During the Middle English period, scribes produced documents that exhibited clear regional characteristics, that is to say, written English was expressed solely in regional dialect. After Chancery Standard, things began to change. According to Manfred Görlach (1990, p. 23), by as early as 1450 there was a significant accumulation of writing in English that 'had generally become impossible to date or localize'. The consistent written English developed in Chancery had spread outwards into London and beyond. Although written English would continue to be decidedly variable for the following two centuries, a homogeneous written variety had begun to spread by 1450. And although it was the advent of printing that provided the greatest impetus for the development towards a uniform written standard, printers in England 'found the way for a supraregional literary language fairly well paved' (Görlach 1990, p. 24). To use a term from Benedict Anderson's *Imagined Communities* (1991), Chancery English was one of a number of 'administrative vernaculars' in late medieval western Europe which provided ready models for the printing trade. The interplay of printing and administrative vernaculars produced 'print-languages' (Anderson's term) – early written standards exhibiting greater linguistic uniformity and fixity than had been possible before print.

The relationship between printed English and Standard English has been a symbiotic one. Print required a uniform written English, and the written standard gained more prestige and authority through being a vehicle for the earliest form of the mass media. The rise of the dictionary and the prescriptive grammar in the eighteenth century further standardized written English, and these also continually aimed thereafter to delimit the vocabulary and grammatical constructions of Standard English – to lay down the forms considered standard. In the case of vocabulary, this process reached a culmination in the mid-to-late nineteenth century with two enormous and parallel projects, the *New English Dictionary* (which became the *Oxford English Dictionary*, 1884–1933), which detailed the standard lexis, and Joseph Wright's *English Dialect Dictionary* (1898–1905). The *OED* remains the first (vast) port of call for anyone wanting to check up on the standard vocabulary of English. As for grammar, the second half of the eighteenth century saw a significant increase in **prescriptivism** in this area. A **prescriptive grammar** stipulates which usages are correct and which are incorrect. A **descriptive grammar**, on the other hand, describes objectively the usages that occur in the variety under observation. First stop for a thorough but manageable and modern, descriptive account of the grammar of Standard English would be the *Oxford English Grammar* (1996), by Sidney Greenbaum. But now I stray into **Further reading** territory.

To resume my brief history: Standard English became closely associated with written English in general. Literary renderings of non-standard dialects are not that easy to pull off, if only because the spelling conventions of English became closely tied to Standard English. With the exception of Scots, no non-standard dialect of British English has had a sustained literary tradition since the start of the Early Modern

English period, and in the case of Scots, it is significant that there is a long-standing debate over whether it should be considered a dialect of English or a separate language.

Regarding the influences that contributed to Chancery Standard, it has been shown that early Chancery included features connected in particular with the Central Midlands written dialect of the Middle English period. This can be explained by the considerable immigration from that area into London during the second half of the fourteenth century. In later Chancery English, more London features become apparent. None of this is especially helpful in our search for the origins of *spoken* Standard English. It is reasonable to assume that educated London speech was prestigious in the fifteenth century, though there is little indication of an emerging spoken standard at this time. It seems that educated spoken London English did become increasingly influential as a prestige variety from the sixteenth century onwards. But the whole concept of a spoken standard did not really take hold until the late nineteenth century, when the idea of a standard *pronunciation* (not vocabulary or grammar) crystallized around the model subsequently named **Received Pronunciation** or **RP**, which was promoted in and by the public school system.

In the present day, we are able to identify a standard spoken variety, but spoken Standard English is not 'standard' in the way written Standard English has been. Written English as a whole became homogenized, conforming in general usage to a standard model. Spoken English as a whole remains far from homogenized. Much if not most present-day spoken English does not conform to the traditional standard model. Thus spoken Standard English is a 'norm' mainly in the sense of being a model to aspire to. In Britain, *native* Standard English speakers are a minority; in the world, they are more so. This takes us to the next true-or-false.

4. True or false? There is more than one Standard English.

   True.

In the historical long run, there is one Standard English. This is the Standard English of which I have been speaking so far in this chapter, although I have underscored its Britishness. This is the Standard English which arose in England, and which gradually assumed a primacy among varieties of British English and, arguably, as I have already indicated, among varieties of World English. However, this British

Standard English can no longer be said to be the only Standard English. Ironically, in present-day global English there is not only a great diversity of non-standard English but also there are many regional varieties of Standard English.

Right from its beginning as a collection of dialects spoken by the various Germanic tribes who arrived in fifth-century Britain, English has been a diverse language. It became more and more diverse as it radiated outwards in tandem with English expansionism, first into the Celtic areas of the British Isles and eventually to North America, Africa, Australasia, and south and south-east Asia. At the end of the twentieth century, Tom McArthur stated (1998, p. 36) that English was 'routinely used' in 112 out of a world total of 232 internationally recognized territories. Its nearest rival as an international language, French, was used in 54 territories. He estimated (p. 30) that English was used as a 'mother tongue or other tongue' by over a billion people. In 2003, David Crystal (2003b, p. 69) calculated the figure at about 1.5 billion. The population of England by 2001 was not greatly above 49 million. British Standard English began in England, and its authority is strongest in England and Wales. Although, at the start of the twenty-first century, the United Kingdom has the second-highest (after the USA) number (about 58 million) of native English speakers, the English language now belongs to the world. British Standard English has authority internationally, but its status as a contemporary world standard is questionable.

The enormous expansion in the use of English has led to new standardizing pressures, but in a diverse kind of way. The use of English worldwide has led to the development of new local varieties, the use of English by peoples other than the English has entailed the language becoming bound up with issues of national identity, and the combination of new varieties of English and national needs has led to the development of 'local' standards. Manfred Görlach (1990) describes the evolution of standard Englishes in Scotland, the United States of America, Canada, Australia, New Zealand, South Africa, the Caribbean, Nigeria, and India. McArthur adds (1998, p. 6) Singapore and Malaysia to this list.

However, some of these standards are less evolved than others. Even in the United States, where standardizing pressures have a comparatively long history, Standard American English remains a rather fuzzy entity. Noah Webster's view in 1789 (p. 27) was that a national standard should be based on 'the *rules of the language itself*, and the *general practice of the nation*' (italics in the original). The philological works of

Webster (1758–1843), including *An American Dictionary of the English Language* (1828), helped to set up an American English model to rival British Standard English, especially in matters of spelling, while in 1947 Eric Partridge (*Usage and Abusage*, p. 304) proposed the term **Standard American** to refer to 'the speech of the educated classes' in the United States, but scholars have had some difficulty in pinning down a close definition of this entity. G. P. Krapp (1925) introduced the term **General American** to describe a purported supraregional accent, but although the term became popular, **Network Standard** is preferred by some on the grounds that American English pronunciation has proved to be less homogeneous than once thought. Network Standard refers to the variety of pronunciation purportedly used by radio and television announcers on national networks in the United States, but this also is less homogeneous than the term implies. Nevertheless, the term **General American** is used for a model of pronunciation taught to foreign learners, and in this way it is in direct competition with RP. William Kretzschmar, Jr (2008) tries to resolve the matter by delineating a **Standard American English** pronunciation used by 'educated speakers in formal settings' which also allows for variation, 'because speakers from different circumstances in and different parts of the United States commonly employ regional and social features to some extent even in formal situations' (p. 38).

Fuzzier still, or as McArthur (1998, p. 212) puts it, 'nebulous yet nonetheless real', is the entity called **International Standard English**. As if to emphasize its indistinctness, it is also known as **Standard International English**, **World Standard English**, and **Standard World English**. This construct is an attempt to explain what is happening now that English is the worldwide language of business, commerce, and international communication. Manfred Görlach (1990, p. 42) calls it **International English**, saying that it is 'not itself standardized', but could be regarded as 'the area of intersection of the great national varieties of English'.

5. True or false? The term **Standard English** refers to written English and to the vocabulary, grammar, and pronunciation of a variety of spoken English.

No, not really, not anymore. That is, false.

First, let us set aside the issue of multiple Standard Englishes. Here we are back again with that historical entity (or enigma), British Standard English.

Unquestionably the term refers to a kind of written English. As for the prestigious variety of spoken English, the traditional, older view of **Standard English** (British Standard English) is that the term refers to the following kinds of linguistic features: vocabulary, grammatical constructions, and pronunciation. In addition, the last of these was given its own name, **Received Pronunciation** or **RP**, mentioned previously. The term dates from 1818, according to the *OED*, although it was the philologist A. J. Ellis who first used it in 1869 (p. 13) in something close to its current sense, in the phrase 'the theoretically received pronunciation of literary English'. It gained capital initials in the 1920s, when Daniel Jones began using it (in 1926) in his *English Pronouncing Dictionary* for the catalogue of pronunciations he had previously labelled 'Public School Pronunciation'. Traditionally, then, RP is the accent part of Standard English. As recently as 1992 we find Tom McArthur (p. 983) saying, 'Use of the term [Standard English] to include, and specifically identify, an accent (and most commonly the accent known as *Received Pronunciation*) has long been common and continues in use'.

However, during the 1980s and 1990s another view attracted much attention. According to this more recent definition, RP is *not* included as a part of Standard English. In this definition, the term **Standard English** refers only to vocabulary and grammar in speech, and to writing and print. It does not refer to pronunciation. The influential linguists Peter Strevens and Peter Trudgill were among those who strongly advocated excluding RP from the definition of Standard English – Strevens as early as 1981 (see p. 8 especially), Trudgill reiterating the argument in 1999 (pp. 118–19). This development was connected with the heated public debate over the role of Standard English in primary and secondary education in Britain, especially in England and Wales. Some linguists argued that, although Standard English was the model promoted in schools, it is unreasonable to expect non-standard speakers to acquire a new standard *accent* easily during their school life, and failure to acquire this new accent (RP) stigmatizes even further their already-stigmatized non-standard accents. Better to take RP out of the school model altogether. The 1995 document describing the National Curriculum specifications for English in schools therefore included the following statement: 'spoken standard English is not the same as Received Pronunciation and can be expressed in a variety of accents' (Department for Education and Welsh Office Education Department, 1995, p. 3).

Clarity on this is a matter of being aware that there are differences of definition at liberty, and of knowing which definition you are following at any given time. In the first edition of *Studying the English Language*, I followed the traditional view, that RP is one aspect of (British) Standard English. In this edition, the text is revised so that it is in keeping with the more recent view, that RP (in the present day) is not a part of (British) Standard English. To do otherwise feels like swimming against the tide. There's clarity for you.

6.  True or false? Standard English is 'correct' English.

    False, and true.

Now then, bear with me. If any of my children when young had said something like 'Them books over there are mine', as a professional linguist and teacher I should have sat them down quietly and said, 'Now then, listen. When you say something like "them books", you are using a form that is common across Britain. You are using **demonstrative** "them" to describe the **plural noun** "books". It is quite acceptable generally in spoken, non-standard English. But I should point out that this grammatical construction is not acceptable in Standard English. In Standard English, you would have to say "*Those* books over there are mine."'

If any of my children had said 'My friend got into big trouble for mitching off class', I should have said, 'Whilst the **verb** "mitch", meaning "to play truant", is attested in many historical dialects of Britain, and is of course perfectly legitimate as a dialectal form, it is not an acceptable word in Standard English.'

If any of my children had said 'I drawed a good picture today', I ought to have said: 'Now that is very interesting. You have observed that the **past tense** in English is often signalled by adding an *-ed* to the basic or **root** form of the verb. But unfortunately *draw* is one of many **irregular verbs** in English. Its past tense form is in fact *drew*.' If anyone was still left in the room by this time I would have been obliged to add, ' "Drawed" is not acceptable in Standard English. In fact, to the best of my considerable knowledge, this is neither a slang nor a dialectal form – I am afraid this is best considered simply to be incorrect English.'

However, what has frequently happened in Britain is that *any* feature not perceived to be Standard English is classified as 'incorrect'. Dialectal forms, slang forms, and errors are all grouped together as incorrect or bad English. Why? Standard English is the most prestigious kind of English in Britain, so prestigious that it has often been referred to as 'the King's English' or 'the Queen's English'. It is the only variety of

British English to have been the subject of prescriptive manuals. These factors led to its being viewed as equivalent to the English language itself, rather than being a variety *of* English. Therefore anything not acceptable in Standard English is in danger of being labelled 'incorrect' or 'sloppy' or 'bad' English, and Standard English is erroneously equated with 'correct' English.

7. True or false? Standard English is controversial.

True.

Standard English has often been surrounded by controversy. Historically, Standard English has been associated with a cultural elite, and because of its prestige and its adoption as a norm by the education system, Standard English has come to be associated with educatedness and even with high intelligence. Speakers of British Englishes therefore have found their intellectual and professional capabilities being measured in part according to how standard their English is. This has disadvantaged non-standard speakers. Educationalists and linguists have been divided about how to tackle the issue, a debate which reached a climax in 1980s and 1990s Britain. Some – John Honey, for example – argued that individuals will be empowered if they are instructed in the use of Standard English. Others – Peter Trudgill, for example – argued that this will only further disadvantage many native speakers of non-standard Englishes. Changing one's dialect is not as simple as changing the colour of one's hair, or even as simple as learning another language, for that matter. It can involve unlearning or abandoning ingrained habits, and the consequence of failure to acquire the Standard in a system which privileges it further will be greater exclusion. The position adopted in the National Curriculum for England and Wales (Department for Education and Welsh Office Education Department, 1995) was that pupils' non-standard dialects should not be deprecated, while at the same time pupils should become proficient in Standard English – an uneasy compromise. (There is further discussion of this in Chapter 14.)

8. True or false? The English language has always had a standard variety.

False.

A common view among specialists is that the Middle English period represents a bit of a blip in the progress of standardizing tendencies in the English language. At the end of the Middle English period, Standard English began to evolve. Before Middle English, they suggest, in the tenth century (the late Old English period), the written dialect of the kingdom of Wessex, West Saxon, was emerging as a literary standard. But we must treat this view with caution. Comparatively little written Old English has survived, and much from outside Wessex was destroyed by the Vikings. The majority of surviving texts are in late West Saxon. What survives is not representative of the diversity of written Old English, and the impression of a developing standard is based on fairly meagre evidence. Better perhaps to call late literary West Saxon an archetype, or a model, rather than a standard, a term which invites a misleading association with modern Standard English (of which the first glimmers occur in the fifteenth century).

9. True or false? Standard English is a myth.

   True.

Standard English is attended by mythical elements. Here I am using the term *mythical* in line with the work of Roland Barthes (as described in Chapter 8), meaning to have ideological, culturally determined associations. The perception that the linguistic features of Standard English are correct while all others are incorrect, and the perception that Standard English is a centre of normal usage surrounded by deviant non-standard Englishes, are opinions based in societal attitudes and beliefs, not in objective analysis.

10. True or false? Standard English is out of date.

   Maybe.

As well as leading to a diversity of Standard Englishes, the spread of English worldwide has loosened the symbiotic bond between print and Standard English. Some English-related **pidgins** and **creoles** have established their own (non-standard) written forms, though in such cases there is debate over whether these are varieties of English or languages in their own right. Tok Pisin ('Talk Pidgin'), for example, is recognized as an official language of Papua New Guinea. Added to this, the unconstrained opportunities offered by the Internet, by instant and text messaging, open up the possibility that print English, and written English generally, has entered a period of *de*-standardization.

Standard English and RP may also be out of date – may have passed their period of greatest use – in that it has become more acceptable in Britain for the dialects and particularly the accents of non-standard British Englishes to be heard in contexts, for example on television and radio, where previously only standard forms were deemed appropriate (for more on this, see the next chapter 'Language with Attitude'). And we can include in this trend the non-British-English accents of some newsreaders and announcers on the BBC World Service.

And they may be out of date because there tends to be resistance to modernizing the linguistic features of Standard English and RP – though it may also be that in this instance, resistance is futile. No variety or accent of a living language is immune to the effects of time. Contact with other languages, and technological and social change, have led to a persistent influx of new words into modern English, and many new words become quite acceptable quite rapidly in Standard English. But sometimes innovations attract attention and antagonism. At the 1998 British Association science festival, J. C. Wells detailed some of the late-twentieth-century changes in RP (reported in the *Guardian*, 10 September 1998, p. 11). One example was the tendency to use a **glottal stop** at the ends of words instead of a *t* sound – where a *t* occurs in the spelling – so that *Quite nice, it seems* is pronounced as 'Qui' nice, i' seems'. This was thought to be an innovation that spread from so-called 'Estuary English', a variety influenced by London Cockney English (the estuary is that of the River Thames) and described by the *Sunday Times* (14 March 1993, p. 1), as 'the classless dialect sweeping southern Britain'. John Honey speaks of his 'deep unease' (1997, p. 168) at the 'invasion' (p. 167) of this 't-dropping' into RP. The conservative-RP-speaker and art critic Brian Sewell, responding to J. C. Wells's findings, said, 'One could never make love to a woman with a glottal stop.' He was echoing, colourfully, the sentiments of another response to the invasion of the glottal stops: ' "God forbid that it becomes standard English," said Anne Shelley, chairman of the Queen's English Society, "Are standards not meant to be upheld?" ' (*Sunday Times*, 14 March 1993, p. 24). (Note that, for her, Standard English includes matters of pronunciation.)

People expect Standard English to be stable and may be affronted if it moves with the times. People do not especially want this of standards. As the Headmaster in Alan Bennett's 1969 play *Forty Years On* says, in reply to the charge that his standards are out of date: 'Of course they're out of date. Standards are always out of date. That is what makes them standards' (p. 80). Linguists – J. C. Wells, Peter Trudgill, for example – have regularly attempted to update descriptions of Standard English, and especially of Received Pronunciation (there is a scholarly tendency to subdivide RP into a conservative and a modern style), in order to bring them into line with current usages or judgements. Many people regularly object to this, perhaps because they too believe that being out of date is what makes a standard a standard.

## Further reading

Manfred Görlach's 'The Development of Standard Englishes', in his *Studies in the History of the English Language* (1990), is an excellent survey of the history of standardization in English. The collection *Standard English: The Widening Debate* (1999), edited by Tony Bex and Richard J. Watts, provides a range of perspectives on the history and nature of Standard English. Michael A. K. Halliday's essay, 'Written Language, Standard Language, Global Language' (2006) considers English's standardization (and diversification) in the global context. Peter Trudgill's *Accent, Dialect and the School* (1975) was an important contribution to the debate on education and non-standard and Standard English in Britain. Chapter 1 of Richard W. Bailey's *Images of English: A Cultural History of the Language* (1991) charts the earliest (medieval) commentaries on the notion of a 'best' kind of English, and my collaboration with Adrian Willmott, 'Dialect/"England's Dreaming" ', in *Debating Dialect: Essays on the Philosophy of Dialect Study* (2000, edited by Penhallurick), looks closely at the genesis of Standard English. The same collection contains a discussion of the character of Received Pronunciation by Clive Upton, 'Maintaining the Standard'. See also Peter Roach's sketch in 'British English: Received Pronunciation' (2004). If you require an operator's manual – for RP use *Gimson's Pronunciation of English* (7th edn, 2008), by A. C. Gimson, revised by Alan Cruttenden, and *The Oxford Dictionary of Pronunciation for Current English* (2003), by Clive Upton, Bill Kretzschmar Jr and Rafal Konopka; and for written British Standard English, see *The New Fowler's Modern English Usage* (3rd edn, 1996; revised, 1998), edited by R. W. Burchfield.

# 13 Language with Attitude
## Dialect, Accent, and Identity

This chapter includes the following:
- The relationship between dialect, accent, and regional identity in Britain.
- The power of offensive language.
- Jacques Lacan on identity-bearing words or **master-signifiers**.
- Explanations of the terms **dialectology**, **sociolinguistics**, and **covert prestige**.

## Introduction

As far as the majority of the British public was concerned, punk rock really got going when Steve Jones of the Sex Pistols used the 'f-word' live on tea-time television, on 1 December 1976:

*'Say something outrageous.'*
'You dirty bastard.'
*'Go on, again.'*
'You dirty fucker!'
*'What a clever boy!'*
'You fucking rotter!'

Following this, the interviewer Bill Grundy got suspended from his job, while the Sex Pistols topped the music charts. Steve Jones said later, 'From that day on, it was different. Before then, it was just music: the next day, it was the media' (Jon Savage, 1991, p. 260). This probably is not altogether accurate, but the point is that the Sex Pistols' impact was relatively restricted until Steve Jones cursed so impressively on air. No matter how revolutionary their music was, it did not compare with the stir created by their bad language. As Andersson and Trudgill, in *Bad Language* (1990, p. 60), point out, slightly hesitantly, 'Perhaps one of the most interesting and colourful words in the English language today is *fuck*.' It is a word, they add, that has many uses. Steven Pinker (2007, p. 359) notes that *fuck* and its variant forms are among the most commonly used expletives in English, despite their 'nonsensical semantics and syntax', that is, in phrases like 'Shut the fucking door!' and 'What the fuck?!' Steve Jones's use of the word was aggressive, but coupling it with the rather charming *rotter* suggests that it was also mocking. On the evidence of the uproar that followed Bill Grundy's interview of the Sex Pistols, it looks as if Andersson and Trudgill are right – *fuck* is a very interesting and colourful word. But is that why there was such an uproar? Not entirely. And what is the connection between the following three things: Steve Jones's *fucking rotter*, terms such as *nigger* and *cockney*, and dialect? The short answer is: language and attitude. In this chapter, we look at the power of offensive words and names, at the relationship between names (including offensive names) and personal identity, and at the connection between dialect, identity, and names, with an emphasis on these in British society.

## Master-signifiers and offensive language

*Fuck* is a swear word and a taboo word. Andersson and Trudgill (1990, p. 57) observe, 'We expect swearing to be related to the areas which are taboo or significant in a particular culture.' Talking about a taboo area (such as death, sexual matters, bodily functions, some religious figures) can be either prohibited or restricted, depending on which taboo area one is talking (or not talking) about, and in addition swear words themselves can form a taboo area, that is, their use can be subject to social restrictions. Andersson and Trudgill note (p. 66) that 'swearing is more frequent in informal situations than in formal ones'. Thus, and no matter how severe the provocation, we do not expect the President of the United States at a press conference to say, 'What the hell kinda fucking question is that? Get your ass outta here!' This explains why Steve Jones's f-words in December 1976 led to such a commotion. It was not simply because he used a powerful swear word – it is true, *fuck* is, after all, a word of common occurrence, generally speaking – it was also because he used it in a particularly socially inappropriate context. In 1970s Britain, *fuck* was not to be heard on television, and even today it would be highly irregular, to say the least, on tea-time television. The Sex Pistols and Bill Grundy imported the colloquial antagonism between youths and adults into the highly formalized and public arena of early evening prime-time TV, and it was shocking. What viewers saw in explicit form was the sullen, sarcastic, and hilarious posturing of the teenager in a context where they did not expect to see it. The Pistols showed *attitude*, in the slang sense of the word ('antagonistically insolent manner, posture, and especially style and tone of speech, lip', *Chambers Dictionary*). For many thereafter this was the quintessential 'punk' moment. To identify yourself as a *punk* was to identify yourself with the Sex Pistols as they were in that interview.

In fact, the word *punk* is an example of a 'master-signifier'. A **master-signifier** is an identity-bearing word. The term comes from the work of the psychoanalyst and theorist Jacques Lacan, and is found in his *Seminars* (especially Seminar XVII, published in French in 1991), many of which remain unpublished in English. The term used by Lacan in French is *signifiant-maître*. For the reader of English, Bracher (1993) provides an extensive discussion of master-signifiers.

Lacan began his influential synthesis of the work of Sigmund Freud with that of the linguist Ferdinand de Saussure in the 1950s, in an attempt to make language a central concern of psychoanalysis. Saussure (1916) saw language as being formed on structured systems of **linguistic signs**, each sign comprising a **signified** or concept and a **signifier**, that is, the mental image of the linguistic expression of a concept. In short, a signifier is the mental picture that we have of a word or similar unit of meaning. For Saussure, the linguistic sign and the relationships between signs in a language system (or *langue*, as he called it – *langue* is the network or structured system of linguistic signs that underpins each language) were the focus of interest (Saussure's theory is discussed more fully in Chapters 6 and 7 of this book). Lacan, however, chose to draw attention to the signifier, and his special use of Saussurean terminology has to be distinguished from Saussure's own use of it. For Saussure, the linguistic sign as a whole is the crucial unit. For Lacan, the signifier (one half of the sign and psychological in character, from Saussure's point of view) is crucial, worthy of more attention than the signified, and indeed the driving force of meaning. For Lacan, the process of acquiring language is a process of entering into a different order of things, a **symbolic order** in which our understanding of ourselves and our world is negotiated via and constituted by language, and in which we become the subjects of signifiers. In the Lacanian view, a human **subject** 'is no longer a substance endowed with qualities, or a fixed shape possessing dimensions, or a container awaiting the multifarious contents that experience provides: it is a series of events within language' (Bowie, 1991, p. 76, describing Lacan's work). In other words, although we may think of ourselves as individuals, as 'I's with singular, autonomous identities, the Lacanian view is that we are divided subjects (determined at least in part by our unconscious minds) who are also the subjects of language. We are subject to forces inside and outside us which call into question our singular, independent 'I'-ness.

In this view, **master-signifiers** are important because, in short, they are identity-bearing words, but more than that, they are also identity-constituting words. As Bracher (1993, pp. 23–4) puts it, master-signifiers arise from the urge 'to have an identity in which I can recognize myself and be encountered and recognized by others'. It is master-signifiers in particular which furnish us with the comforting illusion of 'I'-ness. We seek out master-signifiers which create a positive identity for us. *Being* such a signifier 'allows subjects to feel good about themselves and also provides the sense of temporal continuity and coherence essential to identity, since the signifier can be reproduced and communicated' (Bracher, 1993, p. 24).

Once a punk, for example, always a punk. That is, even if I have stopped being a punk and have become a soberly dressed, politely spoken, middle-aged lecturer, *saying* that I once was a punk gives me access to an established, defined, and reiterable identity. It gives me a purchase on myself, if I choose to describe myself as a punk or ex-punk, but that purchase comes from language. (When I say 'choose', it would help, of course, if my description of myself as a punk were backed up by real-life evidence, such as having seen The Ramones play live several times, well over two decades before every teenager and his father started to wear a Ramones t-shirt.) If I chose to say 'I am a lecturer' this would provide me with another such identity. Bracher says (p. 26) that all subjects are motivated by a desire to have 'these identity-bearing signifiers repeated', and that attempts at repetition operate continuously in our discourse and behaviour, for example, when we behave in ways that embody master-signifiers like *masculine* or *feminine* or *honest* or *tough*, or when we ally ourselves with religious terms like *God* and *heaven*, or political terms like *freedom* and *democracy*. 'Such signifiers,' he says (p. 26), 'as well as our proper name, give us a sense of substance, significance, and well-being when we manage to ally ourselves with them'. Master-signifiers provide us with definition, continuity, and stability, because these are characteristics (up to a point) of words.

As well as allying ourselves with certain master-signifiers (say, *God*, if you are a *Christian*), we also oppose ourselves to certain other master-signifiers (maybe *Darwin*, for our Christian). Bracher states (p. 24) that a master-signifier can be any signifier that a subject identifies with or against – either way the subject is investing his or her identity in a word.

Moreover, *being* a certain signifier (such as *man* or *Welsh* or *punk*) may involve *not being* certain other signifiers (such as *woman* or *English* or *hippie* respectively). Taking this logic of master-signifiers further entails thinking of any kinds of encounter with other human subjects as events in which we are represented by 'our' signifiers, and in which 'our' signifiers communicate with the signifiers of others, which means that 'what happens to our sense of being or identity is determined to a large degree by what happens to those signifiers that represent us' (Bracher, p. 25). It follows then that we can be greatly affected by any discourse which is permeated by prejudice, because it will be prejudiced in favour of certain signifiers and against certain other signifiers. For example, a patriarchal or masculine-centred language will encourage patriarchal discourse, which will privilege male and masculine signifiers at the expense of female and feminine signifiers. A racist discourse will harbour master-signifiers which promote racial discrimination. Whereas discourses in which 'our' master-signifiers are dominant give us a sense of security, 'Discourses that fail to provide a reassuring encounter with our representatives [master-signifiers] tend, in contrast, to evoke feelings of alienation and anxiety and responses of aggression – including rejection of the discourse, or indifference toward it' (Bracher, p. 26). Such troublesome discourses could include encounters in which our master-signifiers seem to be chosen for us or imposed on us, like it or not. In this light, some of the enterprises rather unthinkingly characterized under the umbrella term 'political correctness' can be seen as attempts to abolish or replace or taboo harmful master-signifiers.

Another response to negative, imposed master-signifiers is to seize them, accept them but turn them positive. We can find both responses (tabooing and turning) at work regarding the word *nigger*. For example, on their release the films *Jackie Brown* (1997) and *Pulp Fiction* (1994) met with controversy because of their scripts' frequent use of the term. This word, because of its offensive, racist usage, had become taboo in many public and social spheres, but in these movies, written and directed by a white man, Quentin Tarantino, it is used approvingly by black characters. Following *Pulp Fiction*, Tarantino said, 'The minute any word has that much power, everyone on the planet should scream it' (1995, in the *Cassell Dictionary of Contemporary Quotations*, 1996, p. 524), and following *Jackie Brown*: 'There's a segment of black society in America that says the word constantly and uses it in a zillion different ways' (interview in *Radio Times* magazine, 14–20 March 1998, p. 48). Pam Grier, one of the black stars of *Jackie Brown*, said, 'the African American community has embraced a word that was originally created to be hurtful, and it has been turned into a positive word. It can be used in different contexts – you can use it as a slur for black man to black man. You can use it as an endearment from black man to black man. Just last week I saw it used as an endearment from a black man to a white man!' (interview in *Uncut* magazine, April 1998, p. 48). This positive use of the word was marked by a new spelling, *nigga*, plural *niggaz*, dating from the 1980s. As in Jay-Z's *99 Problems* (2003), 'I'm from rags to riches, niggaz, I ain't dumb', and, perfectly, in the name of the seminal hip hop group, Niggaz With Attitude, known for living up to their name with tracks like *Fuck Tha Police* (1988). The spelling (actually a resurgence of an earlier variant) signifies that this form is treated as a separate, positive word. Conversely, a white contestant on the 2007 British run of the television 'reality' show, *Big Brother*, was removed from the programme by its makers for saying 'Are you pushing it out, you nigger?' to a black housemate, while they were dancing (BBC News Online: Entertainment, 7 June 2007, accessed 2008). (And in 2002, an academic book about the word by Randall Kennedy was published, using the original spelling in its title, thereby causing controversy.)

Similarly *queer*, as a derogatory term for a (usually male) homosexual, dating from the early twentieth century, was adopted as a term of pride by homosexuals, reversing its polarity and opening up new possibilities for the affirmation of homosexual identity. For example, a feature on the London Gay and Lesbian Film Festival of 1998 mentioned 'The American singer and "dykon" Sophie B. Hawkins' and 'the US "queercore" culture of dyke rock-bands and underground fanzines' (*The Independent*: 'Eye on Tuesday', 10 March 1998, p. 5) – here are celebratory wordplays using two reappropriated terms, *queer* and *dyke*.

In these examples we see master-signifiers which have been imposed on individuals and their communities, and which label them from a hostile, outsider's viewpoint. This, as Bracher implies, has a damaging effect on the subjects thus named, who have reacted by accepting but refashioning the name in keeping with their own wishes. The result is that one word can have a consistent **denotation** but different **connotations** across different communities and contexts. The denotative or primary or literal sense of *nigger* is 'a black or dark-skinned person', but a white racist uses it as a term of abuse, the people referred to by Pam Grier use it as a term of pride, and to many others it is a taboo term. The word itself has become a site of contest and its connotative or additional or associative sense – and the attitude that it conveys – has been augmented and transformed.

Something comparable can be unearthed in the following remark: 'I'm every bourgeois's nightmare – a cockney with intelligence and a million dollars.' This was attributed to the actor Michael Caine (*The Times*: 'Analysis', 28 March 2000, p. 7). The term *cockney* is another example of a master-signifier, and of one that was originally a derogatory term. In fact, *cockney* originally was Middle English *coken* 'of cocks' + *ey* 'egg', that is, 'cocks' egg', and evolved, according to the *Oxford English Dictionary*, from a term for a molly-coddled child into 'A derisive appellation for a townsman, as the type of effeminacy, in contrast to the hardier inhabitants of the country', before being used (from 1600) for a person born within the city of London and 'particularly used to connote the characteristics in which the born Londoner is supposed to be inferior to other Englishmen' (*OED*). Michael Caine's remark tells us that (he thinks that) the name *cockney* is derogatory, because it connotes ignorance and poverty, but also that it is a term of pride, because he (as a cockney) uses it to underpin his own character and achievement. Curiously then, *cockney* is not only an insulting term of low prestige but also a term of high 'reverse' prestige.

There is a whole raft of similar terms (master-signifiers all) which are applied to the regional and national communities of the British Isles.

## Master-signifiers and cultural stereotypes

We can get an impression of what these terms are and what they do from a controversial review by the TV critic A. A. Gill (*Sunday Times*: 'News Review', 28 September 1997, p. 6). He began with *Paddies* or *Micks* (Irish people), concluding that 'overall they come across as lovable idiots savants'. He moved on. *Brummies*: 'A report last week confirmed that the rest of us hate and distrust Birmingham accents. We are all more likely to think Brummies guilty of crimes than normal people.' *Scousers* (people from Liverpool): 'serial adulterers and the sexually incontinent who only cease pelvic jigging to sign on and add to the black economy'. Surprisingly he overlooked the term *Geordies*, contenting himself with *people from Newcastle*(-on-Tyne): 'We all know that people from Newcastle are drunk, violent, obsessed with football and are chippy inverted snobs', and 'few outside the northeast can understand a word they say'. Gill did not use colloquial names for people from Yorkshire or Lancashire, but was nevertheless able to identify *Yorkshiremen* as 'stoical, hard-working bigots' and *Lancastrians* as 'those miserable souls west of the Pennines'. Gill could have referred to *Jocks* but chose the more polite *Scots*, who are either 'feck-less junkies with battering ram heads' or 'selfish bunny huggers with oatmeal in our [Gill described himself as "an expatriate Scot"] hair and second sight'. He could have referred to *Taffs* but chose the neutral *Welsh*: 'We all know they are loquacious dissemblers, immoral liars, stunted, bigoted, dark, ugly, pugnacious little trolls.' It is not possible 'for the Welsh to say "honest" without the rest of us laughing cynically', he said.

The reported reaction to Gill's column in at least one part of Britain (Wales) was outrage. In the opinion of local politicians, according to newspaper accounts, Gill had to be reported to the Commission for Racial Equality. But if the accounts were true, then the politicians had missed the point. Gill was writing about the use made by British tele-vision drama of regional stereotypes. His article was provocative, but deliberately and fairly carefully so. Each of his little caricatures of a regional type was preceded by a qualifying remark, like 'We all know that . . .' or 'as we all know . . .', and he described his theme variously as 'creative bigotry' and 'cultural stereotyping' and 'regional prejudice' and 'a national shorthand wisdom'. In other words, he was writing about the historical stereotypes of the regional communities of the British Isles and of how they provide television with a quick route to easy character-ization. ('Television uses regional prejudice as a shorthand for character. If you have only got a couple of lines to fill in a cameo, the easiest way is to give it a regional accent and let the audience thrash it out with their collective assumptions.') Admittedly he added the odd twist and gloss of his own for comic or shock effect, but his piece also indicated how the mere mention of certain names for these stereotypes brings into play traditional attitudes towards communities, or rather to communities as constituted by these names.

This kind of stereotyping works on other groups as well: the British have access to a similar range of ready-made attitudes regarding for-eigners. The journalist Harry Pearson, in an article inspired by the behaviour of the Grand Prix driver Michael Schumacher (*Guardian*: 'Sport', 3 November 1997, p. 7), wrote, 'national sporting stereo-types have dark and lengthy roots. South Americans have flair which inevitably means they are temperamentally unstable; Germans are effi-cient and therefore calculating. What in [Ayrton] Senna would have been seen as hot-headed, in Schumacher is ruthless.' (In the journal *Discourse and Society*, O'Donnell (1994) also looks at such sporting stereotypes.) Frequently foreigner-types are matched with a colloquial or offensive or racist name, such as *kraut*, *dago*, or *frog*. Similar kinds of names have been applied to the modern immigrant communities of Britain.

Even an apparently neutral name may turn out to be less than objective in its origins. It is ironic, for example, that the incoming Angles and Saxons applied the name *Welsh* (or, to be more accurate, *wealisc*) to the longer standing Celtic inhabitants of Britain. *Welsh* derives from Old English *wealh*, the basic meaning of which is 'foreign', although at a really basic level the term means 'different from us'. Nevertheless, what we see in all these names for communities is the outsider's perspective. A. A. Gill began his article with a quotation from Robert Burns (1759–96): 'O wad some Pow'r the giftie gie us/To see oursels as others see us!' (That is, 'O would some Power the gift give us/To see ourselves as others see us!' from the poem 'To a Louse', 1786.) And that is what these names do – they provide those thus named with the 'gift', if gift it be, of an identity assembled from a perspective that is external (to the community thus named). The identity and its name may well be derogatory, prejudiced, and will have been constructed over a period, or as Gill put it, 'Prejudice is the distillation of years of experience.' In some cases, the name and identity will be deeply historical, the 'distillation' of centuries of attitude-constructing. For example, in his description of the Welsh, Gill said nothing particularly new – in part at least he said something very old. In AD 1215, the churchman Gerald of Wales (1145–1223) said, 'The Welsh people rarely keep their promises .... They have no respect for their plighted word, and truth means nothing to them' (Thorpe, 1978, p. 256). I should declare an interest at this point. I am *Welsh*. I have a personal interest in the fate of *Welsh* as a master-signifier. However, my discussion of the term here is entirely objective and professional. Honest.

## Cultural stereotypes, dialect, and accent

Such stereotyping is closely allied to dialect, and to accent. A brief definition of the term **dialect** would be: a regional or social variety of a language, a sub-type of a language. The term **accent**, in this context, refers to regionally based or social-class-based pronunciation. (See Chapter 1, 'Space', for more on these definitions.) There is a (regional) dialect of English known as Welsh English. Being Welsh, I spoke it, and to a degree I still speak it, although my Welsh English has been modified in the direction of another (social) dialect, British Standard English. My Welsh-English accent too has moved towards the standard accent of British English, Received Pronunciation or RP. Years and years ago, when I was a young speaker of unadulterated Welsh English, I was struck and perplexed by the speech of two Welsh characters in a children's story, *The Mountain of Adventure* (1949), by Enid Blyton. So struck that I remember it still. For example, ' "This iss Effans, my husband," said the plump woman. "We hope you will be very happy with us, whateffer!" ' (p. 10), and ' "A parrot, look you!" cried Mrs Evans to her husband' (p. 11). I remember thinking, who are these peculiar people and why do they speak in this strange way? I know now that Enid Blyton's portrayal of Welsh English was not entirely inaccurate. There is a tendency, particularly in North Wales, for speakers to **unvoice** consonants that are **voiced** in RP, a tendency caused by the influence of the Welsh language. Thus the z-sound that occurs in the RP version of the word *is* would be an s-sound for these speakers. The *-ff-* in 'Effans' and 'whateffer', however, is an exaggeration of this unvoicing, and as for 'look you', I have never heard a Welsh person or *Taff* say this, any more than I have heard an Irishman or *Paddy* say 'bejabers', a Londoner or *cockney* say 'gorblimey luvaduck', or a German or *kraut* shout 'achtung!' This is not to claim that no Taff, Paddy, cockney, or kraut has ever uttered these phrases. Rather, it is to propose that these are just a few examples of dialect or language features that are cultural stereotypes, just as the names Taff, Paddy, cockney, and kraut are. Enid Blyton's characterization of Welsh English is more likely to be drawn from a traditional, stereotypical model than it is from studious, direct observation, and there is an early version of this model in Shakespeare's *Henry V*, first performed in 1599, in the speech of Captain Fluellen.

Nonetheless, it is of course possible to distinguish regional types of a language, that is, not stereotypes but groupings of lexical, grammatical, and pronunciation features that can be assigned to a regional community. The branch of linguistics known as **dialectology** is based on the premise that such groupings exist, and, starting from the late nineteenth century, dialectologists have produced a vast body of data, published in atlases and dictionaries, especially (but by no means exclusively) in Europe and North America, charting the intricacies of dialect areas large and small. See, for example, the publications of the Survey of English Dialects, and of the Linguistic Atlas Projects of the United States (go to **Further reading** at the end of this chapter for some suggestions, and to Chapters 4 and 5 for more on such atlases and dictionaries). However, the systematic, scholarly study of English dialects is a recent development compared with a certain cultural awareness of the language's regional diversity that contains within it prejudiced attitudes.

The first record of significant comment on diversity in English dates from around AD 1125, in the work of the monk and chronicler William of Malmesbury, who made disparaging remarks about northern English (reproduced in the preceding chapter, 'What's in a Norm?'). The dialects and accents of English in the British Isles are important constituents of regional and national identity. To speak one is to show that one belongs (like it or not) to a given community, and to show that one is allied (like it or not) with one or more master-signifiers that name this community, possibly disparagingly. To speak one is also to open oneself to traditional attitudes towards one's community and its speech.

In A. A. Gill's 1997 article there are throwaway remarks that indicate the relevance of dialect and accent to regional identity in Britain. For example, 'few outside the northeast can understand a word they [Geordies] say', and, 'A report last week confirmed that the rest of us hate and distrust Birmingham accents.' I found two news items from 1997 on such surveys. One went, 'People with strong regional accents are often discriminated against at work or when applying for jobs.... Consultants singled out the Liverpool, Glasgow and Birmingham accents as being seen as "negative" by some employers' (*Financial Times*, 2 January 1997, p. 6). The other went, 'Regional accents still influence candidates' chances of getting a job.... Those taking part [in the survey] rated which accents were an advantage or a liability. Irish, Scottish and Home Counties' accents scored top marks; bottom were Birmingham and Liverpool' (*Financial Times*, 31 July 1997, p. 18). As linguists have pointed out, no one dialect or accent (or language for that matter) is intrinsically superior to any other. But these surveys tell us that some accents are judged to be superior to others. These judgements are social, and culturally ingrained. Hence the first news item quotes a recruitment consultant as saying that an accent 'communicates background, education and birthplace, and frankly, some backgrounds are more marketable than others'.

The regional dialects of British English – some of which have the same name as their associated regional stereotype, such as *cockney*, *brummie*, *geordie* – are classified as non-standard Englishes, in contrast with Standard English. Historically, Standard English is the dialect, and Received Pronunciation the accent, with the highest social prestige in Britain. Possession of both has been seen as an aid to career advancement. Historically, all non-standard dialects and accents of British English have tended to be judged against the 'norm' of Standard English and RP, a comparison which has added to the perceived peculiarity and even comicality of regional varieties. For example, the thing that is odd and funny about the Welsh characters of Enid Blyton and William Shakespeare is their Welshness as articulated through their Welsh English. But there is a reverse movement in this matter of prestige, as noted in his way by A. A. Gill: 'anyone with my sort of middle-class accent' will be 'deemed by the rest of you to be vapid, superficial, snobbish and insincere'. There is thus a reverse stereotype. In addition, there is a reverse prestige attached to regional and non-standard dialects and accents.

**Sociolinguistics** is another branch of linguistics concerned with studying regional varieties of language, focusing on the relationships between linguistic variation and social factors such as class, age, and sex. Sociolinguists also look at the **style** (sometimes called **register**) of language, that is, its degree of formality in different contexts. There is a correlation between formality and the social prestige of a dialect, in that Standard English is associated with formality, and non-standard with informality. In a conference paper delivered in 1964, the leading sociolinguist William Labov gave a name to the 'reverse' prestige attached to openly stigmatized (non-standard) varieties. He called it **covert prestige** (Labov, 1971, p. 108). While a standard dialect or accent will have an openly acknowledged, overt prestige, typically supported by the education system and national media, and while this bestows low status on non-standard dialects and accents and their speakers, nevertheless those very speakers will attach a less publicly acknowledged, covert prestige to their own speech. Their non-standard speech is a sign of their belonging to their community and incorporates a counter-attitude, connoting friendliness, warmth and solidarity, even trustworthiness and honesty. In local interactions it will more than likely be desirable to speak the local dialect.

But again the situation is not static. The covert prestige of an overtly stigmatized dialect or accent, or of features of these, can transmute into overt prestige. For example, Mark Newbrook, in his study of the English of West Wirral, Merseyside (1999, pp. 90–106, based on data from 1980), found that, 'In a number of instances, informants appeared to attach overt prestige to certain local variants (Liverpool, Cheshire or shared), to the point of identifying them as "correct" or "good" usage in preference to the RP equivalents' (p. 101). The main instance of this was the vowel sound in words like *bath*, where the local, short 'a'-sound was preferred to the RP, long 'ah'-type. Furthermore, in the introduction to the volume in which Newbrook's study appeared, Foulkes and Docherty (1999, p. 3) noted how the upsurge in telephone sales and call centres in Britain led to commercial interest in attitudes towards regional accents: 'Telesales companies have apparently taken great care to locate their call centres in regions where their workers' accents will be favourably perceived. The south of Scotland, the north-east of England, Yorkshire, south Wales, Derby and Merseyside have all recently reaped the benefit of this new line of industry.' (Cost, including workers' wages, inevitably is also a factor affecting the location of call centres, one which can offset the accent factor. An article by Claire Cowie (2007) looks at 'accent training' for major call centres in Bangalore, South India.)

A similar development is the use of some non-standard British English accents in TV advertising campaigns because of their posi-tive, covert connotations. Supermarket chains have shown preferences for down-to-earth, no-nonsense northern accents and friendly Celtic accents in their voice-overs. In 2008, an ad by Anchor Butter used a northern England accent, speaking over *South Park*-influenced ani-mation and bluegrass-style music – quite a combination, suggesting contemporary, ironic and yet unaffected, traditional values. A case of having your butter and eating it, perhaps. Some media person-alities with non-standard accents, such as Bob Hoskins (cockney), Rob Brydon (Welsh), and Julie Walters (West Midlands), have voiced several campaigns. Distressingly, for former punks, the most unforget-table TV ad of 2008 featured the Sex Pistol, Johnny Rotten (John Lydon), promoting Country Life butter. Non-standard accents also appear in TV programmes aimed at the youth audience, in their voice-over narrations (*Big Brother*'s 'Geordie Voice' (actor Marcus Bentley), for example) and out of the mouths of their hosts. Overall, there is plenty of evidence of the exploitation of the informality – the matey-ness, humour, trustworthiness, sturdiness, the old-fashionedness *and* up-to-the-minute-ness – of non-standard accents.

There is no doubting that the overt prestige of standard dialects and accents still has relevance, but can we continue to call the pres-tige of non-standard speech 'covert', or should we come up with a different description of the 'opposing' attitudes at work? As William Labov himself put it (2008b, private correspondence), 'How would you make something that was covert into something overt?' He sug-gests that much can depend on your perspective: the covert prestige of given non-standard forms may be recognized only patchily across dif-ferent communities and classes. However, the media examples above indicate that there *is* a general, public acknowledgement in Britain of the positive connotations of non-standard dialects and accents. Rather than *overt* and *covert prestige*, maybe we should say 'competing value systems' (Labov, 2008b, private correspondence).

# Conclusion

In this chapter, we have looked at names, dialect, and accent, particularly among the British. 'What's in a name?' says Juliet in *Romeo and Juliet* (Act 2, Scene 2, line 43), beseeching Romeo to 'doff [remove] thy name ... which is no part of thee' (lines 47–8), a plea which both struggles against and acknowledges the power of names. The question ('What's in a name?') was used to headline an article on job titles in the *Guardian* ('G2', 19 April 2000, pp. 10–11), which quoted a marketing consultant as follows: 'By the time you are a "chairman", for instance, your title says that you are good at running meetings. That's nonsense. The point of language is to energize, not to put a label and a limit on things.' Well, titles and names probably do both (limit and energize), and names for regional stereotypes are in addition bolstered by opinion about regional dialects and accents. A negative label can be turned into a badge of pride, and the low status of a dialect can embrace positive associations, but either way we are our names and we are how we speak.

# Further reading

Mark Bracher's *Lacan, Discourse, and Social Change: A Psychoanalytic Cultural Criticism* (1993) is a valuable guide to the master-signifier in Lacan. For a history of attitude-building in relation to dialects and accents of English, see *Images of English: A Cultural History of the Language* (1991), by Richard W. Bailey, and *'Talking Proper': The Rise of Accent as Social Symbol* (2nd edn, 2003), by Lynda Mugglestone. Also, Chapter 3 of Martyn F. Wakelin's *English Dialects: An Introduction* (2nd edn, 1977) offers an excellent, concise survey in its discussion of dialect study. Currently, the best basic guide to dialectology is still *Dialectology: An Introduction* (1983), by W. Nelson Francis, though *Dialectology* (2nd edn, 1998) by J. K. Chambers and Peter Trudgill is more recent. For an introduction to 'perceptual dialectology', an approach which assesses folk-attitudes towards and folk-perceptions of language varieties, go to the *Handbook of Perceptual Dialectology*, Volume 1 (1999), edited by Dennis R. Preston, and Volume 2 (2002), edited by Daniel Long and Preston. And for a thorough and accessible overview of sociolinguistics, Ronald Wardhaugh's *An Introduction to Sociolinguistics* (5th edn, 2006; 6th edn, 2009) is hard to beat. If you want an introductory sampling of dialects and accents of British English, use *English Accents and Dialects: An Introduction to Social and Regional Varieties of English in the British Isles* (4th edn, 2005), with its accompanying CD, by Arthur Hughes, Peter Trudgill, and Dominic Watt, and the book and CD of series 3 of BBC Radio 4's *The Routes of English* (2000), by Simon Elmes. There is also a *Routes of English* website at: http://www.bbc.co.uk/radio4/routesofenglish/, and a large, expertly annotated selection from the British Library's archival sound recordings of English accents and dialects, available at: http://sounds.bl.uk/maps/Accents-and-dialects.html. Start your journey into the world of dialect surveys and linguistic atlases by looking at *An Atlas of English Dialects* (2nd edn, 2006), by Clive Upton and John Widdowson,

*The Linguistic Atlas of Scotland: Scots Section*, Volume 1 (1975) edited by J. Y. Mather and H. H. Speitel, and *A Word Geography of the Eastern United States* (1949), by Hans Kurath. *Studies in Linguistic Geography: The Dialects of English in Britain and Ireland* (1985), edited by John Kirk, Stewart Sanderson and John Widdowson, serves as an introduction to this field. Scholarly and unavoidably entertaining analyses of swearing and taboo language can be found in *An Encyclopedia of Swearing: The Social History of Oaths, Profanity, Foul Language, and Ethnic Slurs in the English-Speaking World* (2006), by Geoffrey Hughes, and in Chapter 7 of Steven Pinker's *The Stuff of Thought: Language as a Window into Human Nature* (2007).

# 14 Fixing
## Language Planning and Regulation

---

This chapter includes the following:
- A guide to **language planning**.
- Language planning in present-day English.
- A history of attempts to regulate English.
- The **Ebonics** controversy.

---

## Introduction

Compare and contrast the following selections. The first is John Major, speaking as Prime Minister of Great Britain to the Conservative Party Conference of 1993.

> I saw a letter recently from over 500 university teachers of English and they say that it is disastrous and harmful to teach standard English, great literature and Shakespeare in our schools! ... What claptrap! Well I'll answer them in words perhaps they might approve of. *Me and my party aint gonna take wot them on the Left ses is OK? Right?*

The second is the comedian Sacha Baron Cohen, as his character Ali G, interviewing a former headmaster and Conservative Member of Parliament, Rhodes Boyson, in 1999.

| | |
|---|---|
| *Ali G:* | Do you believe kids should be caned? |
| *Rhodes Boyson:* | I do. |
| *Ali G:* | You do? *Wicked* man! You believe kids should be caned?! Even in school?! |
| *Rhodes Boyson:* | Even in school. |

Each extract illustrates the central subject of this chapter, that is, the tension between chaos and order in language use. This chapter is about the perception that language use has a tendency towards the chaotic, and it is about the subsequent desire to bring order to it. The chapter will look at the history of anxiety about this perceived chaotic tendency in English language use, at the history of attempts to regulate the language, and at the debates that have surrounded these attempts.

The joke in Ali G's interview, should it need explaining, is that *caned*, in addition to referring to the infliction of corporal punishment on wayward school-children, has a modern (dating from the 1980s) slang sense of 'stoned', 'extremely intoxicated by a drug, usually cannabis' (Green, 1998, p. 195), and that the former headmaster and MP is blissfully unaware of this slang use of the term. The humour, if that is the right word, in John Major's speech is in his impression of the sloppy English that would result if his party's policies on education were not followed. It is likely that John Major wanted to evoke fond memories of the traditional prescriptive grammar once taught in British schools, and of rules such as *never split an infinitive* (one should say 'to go boldly' not 'to boldly go') and *never end a sentence with a preposition* (say 'I'll answer them in words of which perhaps they might approve' not 'I'll answer them in words perhaps they might approve of'). What underpins John Major's declaration is the belief that without proper guidance (from his party) the use of English among young people will become unruly. Ali G therefore is John Major's bad dream come true, a comic character who gets the better of an authority figure by means of 'improper', non-standard, modern English. Creative, playful too, even *fresh* ('new, exciting, fashionable, excellent', dating from the 1970s, *Oxford English Dictionary*). Ali G's language is a mock version of street slang, and his exchange with Rhodes Boyson reverses a conventional power relationship by playing on Boyson's ignorance of this talk. In this encounter, Ali G becomes the authority figure. The exchange demonstrates the potency of unregulated English – of innovative English, of non-standard English. However, from the point of view of would-be language regulators, what Ali G's English needs is fixing. You can just imagine it: 'You think I need a fix?! *Wicked*!'

The idea that language can be fixed is not new. In 1755, Samuel Johnson (1709–84) wrote, 'Those who have been persuaded to think well of my design, require that it should fix our language, and put a stop to those alterations which time and chance have hitherto been suffered to make in it without opposition.' This is from the Preface to Johnson's *A Dictionary of the English Language*, the first major dictionary of English. Johnson is here referring to the view that a dictionary should bring stability to the language, for example, by setting down for all time the meanings and spellings of English words, and by ruling on which words should be included in and which should be excluded from the language – the dictionary should bring a permanent order to the language. This is curious. In 1755, the English language was approximately 1300 years old. Why, suddenly, did it need 'fixing', that is, stabilizing? Why, suddenly, did it need a dictionary? And did Johnson's Dictionary fix English?

'If it ain't broke, don't fix it' is a maxim attributed to Bert Lance, a government official in the United States in the late 1970s (according to the *Oxford Dictionary of Quotations*, 1996, p. 407). In Samuel Johnson's use of the word, *fixing* means 'stabilizing', but I am here also suggesting that inherent in attempts at language regulation is the desire to *fix* in the sense of to 'repair', as if the language and its use have in some way become faulty, as if something has gone a bit *Pete Tong*, or, wrong. The case of Johnson's Dictionary sets the scene. Before reaching an answer to the questions above, we will consider the language fixing (stabilizing and repairing) issue in the wider perspective, for it is a common as well as a historical trend. For the sake of good order, I have decided to arrange the following illustrations alphabetically, by language name.

## Language regulation: examples

### French

'Under a law passed in 1994, the French campus of an American university, Georgia Tech, has been prosecuted for posting a website in English' (*Guardian*, 17 November 1997, p. 5). The fixing of French is particularly associated with the *Académie française*, founded in 1635, its role being to regulate and codify the language. The *Académie* and the French state have taken a purist and vigorous line on the upkeep of French, seeking by law, for example, to repel influences from the English language, which represent, as the *Académie*'s own website puts it, 'une réelle menace pour le français'. From the early 1970s, official action was taken to counter the influx of English loanwords into French, for example, 'On ne dit plus *tie-break* mais *jeu décisif, baladeur* remplace *walkman*, *logiciel* se substitue à *software*, etc.' (*Académie* website, accessed 2009). From 1975, by law, unadulterated French was made obligatory in many public domains, and as the above news snippet indicates, this law was enlarged upon in another, passed in 1994.

The *Académie* has also had a long-standing interest in the reform of French spelling. In 1998, it found itself in conflict with an opposing group of language fixers who agitated for 'feminized' titles for women's jobs in the teaching profession (*Guardian*, 1 July 1998, p. 15). In some cases this meant that titles previously prefaced only with the masculine article *le* (which precedes nouns which are masculine in **grammatical gender**) would take the feminine *la* when referring to a woman (even though the masculine grammatical gender of the noun remained). Against the *Académie*'s wishes, in 1998 the French Education Ministry ordered the use of feminized titles such as *la professeur* and *la proviseur*. In July of 2003, the *Académie* announced that it had chosen the Québécois word *courriel* as the official translation of *email*, for the reason that the terms commonly used in France (*email, mail, mèl*) were too close to the intruding English word (Laura K. Lawless at About.Com: French Language, blog of 12 July 2003, accessed 2008). Subsequently, the French Culture Ministry banned the use of the word *email* in government documents, despite objections. The *Guardian* (*Guardian Online*, 21 July 2003, accessed 2008) quoted Marie-Christine Levet, the president of a French Internet service provider, as saying: '*Email* has sunk into our values. Protecting the language is normal, but *email* is so assimilated now that no-one thinks of it as American. *Courriel* would just be a new word to launch.' (The first academy to deal with language regulation was the *Accademia della Crusca* of Florence, founded in 1572. The *Real Academia Española*, founded in 1713, is another early academy with linguistic interests.)

## German

'The Constitutional Court in Germany has begun hearings into challenges to controversial proposals to simplify the German language. The spelling reform, which involves halving the number of spelling rules and eliminating more than 40 instances of where to place commas, has caused anger and division since it was put forward two years ago' (BBC News Online: 'Despatches', 12 May 1998, accessed 2008). Here we have spelling reform again and, of all things, punctuation reform, sponsored by government and put forward (in July 1996) with the aim of modernizing and simplifying written German, but meeting with a very divided response: 'The whole reform threatens to descend into chaos with some regional courts ruling in its favour and some against' (BBC News Online: 'Despatches', 12 May 1998). In July 2000, the sense of disorder was underscored when one of Germany's leading newspapers, the *Frankfurter Allgemeine Zeitung*, announced it would no longer follow the new rules. In August 2004, *Der Spiegel* declared that it would return to the old spelling rules, and in February 2006, in response to the extensive criticism, the *Kultusministerkonferenz* ('Conference of German Education Ministers') produced a 'reform of the reforms', which was met with criticism ('The History of German Spelling Reform' at About.Com: German Language, accessed 2008.) According to a report in the *Daily Telegraph* (12 February 2001, p. 12), Germans are also divided over 'the corruption of everyday German into "Denglisch"', with some politicians calling for legislation against the use of English words in advertising and the media, while the then Minister for Culture, Julian Nida-Ruemelin, said, 'We don't need a language protection law, nor a language police. The state should not interfere in a process to which a living language is always subject.' The online guide, german.about.com (accessed 2008), reported that 'very few German-speakers seem to perceive the invasion of English as a threat to their own language', seeing English terms as cool, or, in Denglisch, *cool*. More soberly, Busse and Görlach (2002, pp. 31–2) suggest that 'the number of English loanwords [in German] considered dictionary-worthy will pass the mark of 5,000 in the next century', still only a fraction of those from French, or Greek and Latin.

## Icelandic

'But now, say Iceland's linguistic patriots, Microsoft stands poised to lay waste to all they hold dear, by refusing to translate its Windows programme into Icelandic' (*Guardian*, 1 July 1998, p. 15). Here English again poses a threat to another language – because English is now a global language of international communication, and more particularly in this instance because it is the first language of Microsoft computer software. But the situation in Iceland is not identical to that in France and Germany. Icelandic has comparatively few speakers (300,000), and it is a language which has changed remarkably little since the Middle Ages, with its speaking community apparently determined to resist foreign loanwords. The director of the Icelandic Language Institute said, 'It seems to us to be a very practical thing, not to absorb foreign words for new objects, but to make new [Icelandic] words for things as they come up' (Ari Páll Kristinsson, quoted in the *Guardian*,

1 July 1998, p. 15). The particular problem facing Icelandic is that, in global terms, it is very much a minority language, and major companies targeting a global market can have relatively small incentive to cater for minority languages. In addition, in Iceland every school-pupil learns English. The Icelandic government's response to the situation was to ask Microsoft to translate its Windows 95 program into Icelandic. Microsoft did not, though it did undertake to review the situation with regard to future editions.

What then did Microsoft do? In September 2008, Ari Páll Kristinsson himself provided me with the details (private correspondence). Following the publicity of 1998, Microsoft entered into an agreement with the government of Iceland to market Windows 98 in an Icelandic translation. This experienced teething problems, but the Icelandic version of Windows XP (2004) became widely used, and the Icelandic government announced it would give preference in public tenders to Icelandic-localized software. In 2008, Windows Vista in Icelandic became available.

## Japanese

'Some are calling it an issue of national "aidentitii" (identity), and others a failure of bureaucratic "akauntabiritii" (accountability), but there is no escaping the growing bewilderment in Japan at the flood of English loan words into the language' (*Guardian*, 6 May 1999, p. 15). This is another example of the global influence of modern English, but in Japan the adoption of English words is accepted, up to a point. The *Guardian* quoted Yasuyuki Suzuki, a professor of linguistics, as saying, 'It sometimes feels like the situation has got out of hand and there are definitely occasions when we adopt language unnecessarily, but this is a positive step toward the internationalisation of Japan.' The *Guardian* reported that a survey by the Japanese government had shown that a majority of the population did not understand the English adoptions in official documents. As a fixing strategy, the response of the government at the time, judging by the reported comments of its spokesperson, was unusually muted: 'this is something that needs to be debated by the research community' (*Guardian*, 6 May 1999, p. 15). In 2002, the National Institute for Japanese Language convened a panel which had the task of coming up with native words to replace English loanwords. The Institute's guide (2007, p. 10) states that 'A great number of [English] loanwords are continually introduced into Japanese and their popularity is growing rapidly', but excessive use of loanwords 'may interfere with accurate communication in Japanese among people with diverse backgrounds'. Between 2003 and 2007, the Institute published lists of *gairaigo* (as these loanwords are known in Japanese) deemed beyond comprehension, the worst offender being *rodo puraishingu*. In an article on the phenomenon in the *Japan Times Online* (23 September 2007, accessed 2008), staff writer Tomoko Otake pointed out that the *gairaigo* are conventionally written in the simplified *katakana* Japanese script rather than the more sophisticated *kanji* script, and that *katakana* relies on 'Japanized pronunciations' which 'often bear little resemblance to those of the English originals'. This is detrimental to comprehension, as can be gauged from *rodo puraishingu* (here in the Roman alphabet), which is 'Japanized' *road pricing*. Curiously, then, the anxiety in this case is not so much about the English loans in themselves, as about their 'Japanization'-induced incomprehensibility. The National Institute for Japanese Language politely offers its solution, which is to provide 'tables of loanwords that may not be understood easily and correctly, with suggested paraphrases in native and/or Sino-Japanese words' (2007, p. 10). (One could mention here that some recent additions to the English language have come from Japan, such as *anime*, *manga*, and *walkman*... however, you will notice the flaw in that last example; and Japanese *anime* is a twentieth-century borrowing of French *animé*, as in *dessin animé* 'animation'. *Manga* has been in Japanese since at least the eighteenth century – ultimately it is a borrowing from Chinese.)

These illustrations suggest that national identity is bound up with language. In each case above we see an association between a single language and a single nation state, and we see evidence of a desire to preserve the integrity of the national language – absolutely in the case of French and Icelandic, moderately in the case of Japanese, undecidedly in the German case, and of course these are not the only languages affected by influence from modern English. (Chapter 5 also looks at the worldwide impact of English, which itself has a vocabulary substantially comprised of loanwords.) We also see that the national language can be the site of contestation between different groups within its speaking community. These are definite pointers towards understanding why the English language has been subjected to attempts at fixing, and towards understanding the controversies surrounding such attempts.

The cases above illustrate several language-fixing scenarios. However, there is another, technical, more proper term used to label the efforts of the various governments, bodies, and groups mentioned above, that is, **language planning**.

## Language planning

A succinct definition of **language planning** would be, 'Official intentions and policies affecting language use in a country' (Crystal, 1997, p. 431). A slightly less succinct but useful definition is, 'a government authorised, long term sustained and conscious effort to alter a language itself or to change a language's functions in a society for the purpose of solving communication problems' (Weinstein, 1980, p. 55, as quoted by Cooper, 1989, pp. 30–1). A further, more technical definition is, 'Language planning refers to deliberate efforts to influence the behavior of others with respect to the acquisition, structure, or functional allocation of their language codes' (Cooper, 1989, p. 45). To put it bluntly, 'Language planning is an attempt to interfere deliberately with a language or one of its varieties' (Wardhaugh, 2006, p. 357). I will say a little more about these definitions very shortly.

There are three main types of language planning. **Corpus planning**, as the name suggests, applies to the body or make-up or structure of a language, or of a variety or dialect of a language. Spelling reform, punctuation reform, vocabulary regulation and reform are all examples of corpus planning. 'It refers, in short, to the creation of new forms, the modification of old ones, or the selection from alternative forms in a spoken or written code' (Cooper, 1989, p. 31). Another example, in addition to those above, is the revival in Palestine and then Israel of the ancient language of Hebrew, which included corpus planning because of the elaboration of vocabulary that its modern everyday use necessitated.

**Status planning** affects the relative prestige of a language or a variety of a language, and typically involves promoting the role or function of a language or variety in relation to other languages or varieties. Making a language an official language of a territory is status planning, as, for example, when French was made the official language of Quebec, Canada, in 1974; action which was supplemented by further status planning in 1977, in the adoption of the *Charter of the French Language*. These measures promoted and protected the use of French in professional and public life in Quebec. It is not unusual for status planning to be accompanied by corpus planning, and vice versa. Efforts to advance the functions of a language or variety may well go hand in hand with efforts to ensure its upkeep. The revival of Hebrew, obviously, involved status planning as well as corpus planning.

**Acquisition planning** refers to efforts to enable individuals or groups to learn a language, either as a first or as a second or a foreign language. The teaching and learning of English in Iceland's schools is an instance of acquisition planning. Clearly again acquisition planning can occur with status and corpus planning – immigrants to Israel, for example, have access to a comprehensive range of Hebrew-learning opportunities, designed to facilitate their 'absorption' into Israeli society. (In April 2008, it was reported (BBC News Online: Middle East, 7 April 2008, accessed 2008) that members of the Knesset (MKs), the Israeli parliament, were being encouraged by Oved Yehezkel, Cabinet Secretary, to set an example to the country by improving their own proficiency in Hebrew. Worried about the intrusion of English and Arabic words into Hebrew, he ordered the Academy of the Hebrew Language to design a programme of instruction for MKs, saying: 'Believe me, I know how to create motivation in the parliament.')

As for definitions of **language planning**, I gave four above. Cooper (1989, pp. 30–1, 45) lists 11 others, which makes 15 altogether. Some commentators have wished to confine the use of the term to government-sponsored programmes, but others have felt that this excludes similar enterprises by other bodies (such as the *Académie française*), or groups (such as those opposing sexist usage), or even individuals (such as Samuel Johnson). So we have another term, **language policy**, and 'The commonly accepted definition of language policy is that it is language planning by governments' (Tollefson, 1991, p. 16). I have not dared to mention the alternative terms to 'language planning' that Cooper (1989, p. 29) lists, that is, in chronological order, **language engineering**, **glottopolitics**, **language development**, **language regulation**, and **language management** (and neither have I added that both Cooper and Tollefson give further definitions for **language policy**). In this chapter, however, I use **language planning**, in its wider, more inclusive sense, and, when being less technical, **fixing**.

Language planning is very widespread in the modern world. It is, as Ronald Wardhaugh (2006, p. 356) puts it, 'part of modern nation-building because a noticeable trend in the modern world is to make language and nation synonymous', and at the same time, 'a demand for "language rights" is often one of the first demands made by a discontented minority almost anywhere in the world'. There is an implicit and sometimes an explicit recognition in all language planning that identity (national identity, group identity, personal identity) is connected with language and its use. Language planning can be controversial, different groupings of language fixers can be in conflict with each other – those who wish to unify a nation versus those who want recognition for 'minorities', for example – but the bond between language and identity is ever-present. We see it in the history of attempts to fix English. In the following sections are some examples, modern and antique.

## Language planning and English: the present day

One would suppose that a global, international language would be impossible to regulate, but nevertheless modern English is subject to much language planning, a lot of it precisely because it *is* a global language. English is a target for acquisition planning across the world. It is also the subject of status planning because it is frequently used alongside other languages, and its status in relation to these languages is likely to be of some importance to national governments. Throughout the world, English is either a native or a second or a significant foreign language, and as a result in many countries English is a declared official language. McArthur (1998, pp. 38–42, 44) categorizes the various circumstances in which English operates as an official language, such as: (1) in the form of a standard variety co-occurring with non-standard (non-official) varieties of English and with other languages, as in parts of the Caribbean; (2) in territories where it is a second but colonial or postcolonial language, as in Nigeria and some other African countries; (3) as a colonial/postcolonial language alongside other official languages, as in India; (4) as a mother tongue alongside other official languages, as in Australia, Canada, New Zealand, and South Africa; and (5) as a second language alongside other official languages which are themselves (arguably) varieties of English, as in Papua New Guinea, where the English-based creole, Tok Pisin, is also an official language. In its original home, in the United Kingdom, English is not a declared official language. In its leading modern base, the United States of America, it is not at present an official language at federal level. English is an important modern language which may be seen as threatening or as desirable or as both by speakers of other languages, and its legal status anywhere will therefore be potentially contentious.

There are two kinds of English that have been designated official: (1) what we can call, in a summarizing kind of way, a local variety of English, such as Australian English, Canadian English, or South African English; and (2) what we can call, broadly speaking, a more standard variety of English, something nearer to an international standard English, as in territories where English is a second language. However, the boundary between (1) and (2) here is not hard and fast – in category (1) varieties there may be standardizing tendencies, and in category (2) varieties there may be local features. Throughout its history, English has been a diverse language, a language of dialects or varieties. Since the fifteenth century, there have been pressures in the English-speaking community in favour of the standardization of the language, first in Britain, then in other territories, and then globally in favour of an international standard English. The tension between the diversity of English and the pressures in favour of standardization has been one of the fundamental themes in the fixing of English. There has been status planning of English because of its diversity, because of the perceived need to regulate relationships between its varieties, and especially between its standard and non-standard varieties. Here are two modern examples.

First, Ebonics. The term **Ebonics** is a blend of *ebony* and *phonics*, and is another name for **Black English** or **American Black English** or **African-American Vernacular English** (**AAVE**) or **African American English** (**AAE**), to mention just four alternative labels for a category based on the view that there is a comparatively homogeneous variety of English spoken by Americans of African ancestry. Ebonics became a news story in 1996 when the local school board of the city of Oakland, California, passed a resolution, on 18 December, which declared: 'The validated and persuasive linguistic evidence is that African-Americans (1) have retained a West and Niger-Congo African linguistic structure in the substratum of their speech and (2) by this criteria are not native speakers of black dialect or any other dialect of English' ('Original Oakland Resolution on Ebonics', from *The Linguist List* website, accessed 2008). From this we learn, first, that the Oakland School Board apparently erroneously used *criteria* instead of the correct singular form, *criterion*, and secondly, that in the opinion of the Oakland School Board, Ebonics or AAVE is a language in its own right, not a variety of English. What prompted the Oakland resolution was the apparent relative failure of black/African-American pupils to acquire (American) Standard English, which affected their educational performance generally. In a testimony to a Senate committee, the sociolinguist William Labov, a pioneer in the study of AAVE, described the Oakland position as supporting the view 'that children learn most rapidly in their home language, and that they can benefit in both motivation and achievement by getting a head start in learning to read and write in this way' ('Testimony', 23 January 1997, from William Labov's website, accessed 2008). The Oakland School Board believed that black pupils' acquisition of Standard English would be facilitated by 'imparting instruction' to them 'in their primary language', that is, Ebonics; and designating Ebonics a language (not a dialect) was intended to enable this. But the resolution provoked controversy, mainly because it was interpreted as a scheme to teach children Ebonics rather than Standard English.

In its 'Resolution on the Oakland "Ebonics" Issue', the Linguistic Society of America (LSA) commented, 'There is evidence from Sweden, the US, and other countries that speakers of other varieties can be aided in their learning of the standard variety by pedagogical approaches which recognize the legitimacy of the other varieties of a language' (January 1997, LSA website, accessed 2008). John Baugh (2006, p. 219) calls the Oakland Ebonics controversy 'one of the most contentious linguistic episodes ever to jolt America', connecting as it does with the legacy of the African slave trade. Baugh reminds us that AAVE has a unique linguistic heritage, beginning with the slave traders' practice of separating captives who spoke the same language, 'a crude form of language planning' (p. 218) which was designed to disrupt communication among slaves. Baugh's view is that AAVE is a dialect of English, but one that the educational system should try to accommodate, because of the 'historical linguistic dislocation born of slavery that has made it far more difficult for slave descendants to blend into the melting pot' (p. 219). The episode points us towards the essential dilemma for language-fixers dealing with a standard variety of a language. If one's language has a standard variety or dialect, this will be the variety with the highest public prestige. One may want to look after the condition of this standard through corpus planning, and one may want to promote it through status and acquisition planning. But this will be to favour the standard and disadvantage the non-standard varieties, and therefore to disadvantage those who are native speakers of nonstandard varieties (this issue has been a theme in sociolinguistics and sociology, in the work, for example, of Labov, Peter Trudgill, and Basil Bernstein).

For John Major and other politicians and for some academic commentators in Britain in the 1980s and early 1990s, there was no dilemma – for their own sake, all school-children should be equipped with British Standard English. The academic John Honey went so far as to say that this should happen 'even at the expense of their development in their original non-standard variety', and further, 'Even at the expense, I am tempted to add, of their self-esteem' (1983, p. 31, quoted in Crowley, 1989, p. 266). This is the opposite of the Oakland strategy. The dilemma occurs only for those fixers who agree that acquisition

of the standard variety benefits pupils, and who believe that an educational policy should be formulated with this in mind, but who also wish
to avoid denigrating non-standard varieties. With regard to the teaching of British Standard English, the National Curriculum – which is
a British government policy statement on primary and secondary education, the first version of which came into force in 1988, and which
is also my second modern example of status planning of varieties of
English – sought to appease all fixing factions and to resolve this essential dilemma. The National Curriculum's basic formula is as follows:
'The aim is to add Standard English to the repertoire [of pupils], not to
replace the other dialects or languages' ('The Cox Report', 1989, section
4.43, as quoted in Moon, 1994, pp. 52–3). Some would argue that this
is rather like saying, 'The aim is to paint all school buildings white,
not to replace the original colours or finishes', on the grounds that one's
native dialect is eroded (admittedly perhaps not blotted out completely)
by the difficult process of acquiring another dialect. When the National
Curriculum was relaunched in September 2008, its aims with regard to
Standard English remained broadly the same. It emphasized the acquisition in speaking and writing of Standard English, but placed alongside
this the promotion of a kind of **bidialectalism** – proficiency in the
use of standard *and* non-standard codes, according to situation and
purpose. In addition, it included a more developed emphasis on knowledge of how the English language varies. (My summary here is distilled
from information found in the fertile web-pages of the Standards Site,
Department for Children, Schools and Families, during 2008–09.)

The Oakland Resolution and the implementation of the National
Curriculum's aim are two recent episodes in a long-running saga. The
main characters in the saga are, in alphabetical order: dialects (that
is, regional dialects or varieties of English, or more precisely attitudes
towards them), dictionaries, linguistic change (the effects of time on
English, or more precisely anxiety about the effects of time), nationalism and purism, and Standard English (and before the term, or indeed
the thing, was invented, the idea of a standard or best English). I will
wrap up and round off this chapter by taking these one at a time.

## Fixing English: the historical background

Taking dialects first. On 4 March 1999, the *Guardian* (p. 9) reported
that the novelist Beryl Bainbridge had called for 'the eradication of
Scouse along with the rest of Britain's "uneducated regional accents"'.

Referring to a television soap opera set in Liverpool, she said, according to the report, 'Have you ever listened to the kids on *Brookside*? They don't speak the English language.' Negative, derogatory comments about the regional dialects of English in Britain have a long history – though it seems that Bainbridge here is talking of the *pronunciation* of dialects, that is, accent. An earlier novelist, Daniel Defoe (1660–1731), described the dialect of Somerset as 'boorish country speech' and complained that in Somerset, as 'in many parts of England besides', 'the country way of expressing themselves is not easily understood' (Defoe, 1724–6, p. 218, in the edition of 1974). Inherent in these negative comments is a comparison with a better kind of speech, indeed a best English. The first clear demarcation of this best English is in *The Arte of English Poesie* (1589), believed to have been written by George Puttenham, which advises writers in their works to 'take the vsuall speach of the Court, and that of London and the shires lying about London within 10 myles' as their model (edition of 1936, p. 145). Critical commentary on non-south-eastern varieties of British English can be traced back to medieval times, but by the late sixteenth century, as Richard W. Bailey notes (1991, p. 32), some writers 'saw linguistic differences as a source of social discord and thought it necessary to select a perfected English that would fix the language for eternity'. Here then is a basic theme which recurs, in differing contexts and with differing outcomes, in debates about regulating the English language from the sixteenth century to the present day. The theme is based on anxiety about the diversity of English geographically and socially (to regional dialects we can add slang), and about the changeability of English through time.

What is advocated by would-be fixers is the delimitation, codification, and then the promulgation of a 'perfected' English which would have a unifying effect on a (linguistically) diverse nation. Ideally, as far as the fixers are concerned, this perfected English should be free of both provincial and foreign influence. Behind this idea of a perfected English, then, is a nationalism which seeks to override diversity and a purism which wants to keep out words from other languages. For example, regarding pronunciation, in 1764, the elocutionist James Buchanan wrote, 'it would turn greatly to the advantage of the British youth, especially of our young nobility and gentry . . . were a Standard Pronunciation to be taught in all our public schools' (1766 edition, pp. viii–ix; reproduced in Crowley, 1991, p. 78). This Standard Pronunciation, said Buchanan, 'would soon exclude all local dialects' (1766, p. ix) and would assist in unifying the nation, adding a linguistic dimension to the political union of England and Scotland, formally established in 1707. But Buchanan's notion of unity applied chiefly to noble gentlemen, and his Standard Pronunciation was based on that of the English court, 'and therefore becomes more of a marker of political and national difference than a means to overcome it' (Crowley, 1991, p. 74). This is a familiar tension – how can inclusiveness be achieved by the imposition of an exclusive variety of English? By the early twentieth century, the idea of a standard pronunciation had solidified into 'Received Pronunciation' or RP, but it did not unite the nation, as Beryl Bainbridge's comments illustrate.

Next, dictionaries. In 1712, Jonathan Swift (1667–1745) wrote, 'our Language is extremely imperfect', adding 'its daily Improvements are by no means in proportion to its daily Corruptions' (p. 8; reproduced in Crowley, 1991, p. 31). During the eighteenth century, anxiety about the chaotic tendencies of the English language came to something of a head. There was awareness that since its earliest times English had changed immensely, transformed, for example, by French influence after the Norman Conquest, and by the influx of many loanwords from many other languages during and following the Renaissance (approximately 1400–1650), which included a period of great worldwide exploration. There was now a feeling that the language was changing too rapidly, that it was degenerating, and Swift's *A Proposal for Correcting, Improving and Ascertaining the English Tongue* (1712; extracts in Crowley, 1991, pp. 30–41) contributed to the clamour for a remedy. Swift attacked what he saw as the abundance of new words in the language; he attacked poets' and other writers' habit of abbreviating syllables (for example, *drudg'd, rebuk't*), 'as to form such harsh unharmonious Sounds, that none but a *Northern* Ear could endure' (p. 21; Crowley, p. 35); he attacked spelling reform, which was 'a foolish Opinion . . . that we ought to spell exactly as we speak' (p. 23; Crowley, p. 35) – all in all, he was against change in language, except, that is, for the changes which he himself recommended. He believed that if English 'were once refined to a certain Standard, perhaps there might be Ways found out to fix [stabilize] it for ever' (p. 15; Crowley, p. 33), and he advocated setting up an academy to do the job (after the example of the *Académie française*). Despite some support for an academy, it never happened. What did happen was the English dictionary.

To an extent, dictionaries have done the job of regulating and codifying English. Samuel Johnson's was not the first dictionary of English (this was Robert Cawdrey's *Table Alphabeticall* of 1604), but it was a significant departure because of its scope and methods (definitions of around 40,000 words, supported by quotations from those whom Johnson considered to be 'the best authors'), and because of its aims. In his *Plan* (1747) for the Dictionary, Johnson says, 'The chief intent of it is to preserve the purity and ascertain the meaning of our English idiom' (in Crowley, 1991, p. 46). It would be 'a dictionary by which the pronunciation of our language may be fixed [stabilized]; by which its [the language's] purity may be preserved, its use ascertained, and its duration lengthened' (p. 60). Johnson adjudicated on what counted as English, for example, on which words of foreign origin ought to be allowed in the language. As such, the Dictionary is an example of corpus and status planning, the first major step in delimiting a standard variety of the language, a process aided by the flowering of prescriptive grammars of English that occurred in the second half of the eighteenth century, and later comprehensively carried forward by the compilation of the first edition of the monumental *Oxford English Dictionary* between 1858 and 1933.

As for linguistic change, nationalism and purism, and Standard English, well, the best-laid plans of mice and men often go awry, and it turns out that the points I wanted to make about these here in this chapter I have already covered under 'dialects' and 'dictionaries' above. However, there is more on linguistic change and on Standard English in Chapters 2 and 12 respectively.

There is also more in Chapters 9 and 10 on a mode of language-fixing here touched on without being named – that mode which can be seen as 'conforming to a body of liberal or radical opinion, especially on social matters, usually characterized by the advocacy of approved causes or views, and often by the rejection of language, behaviour, etc., considered discriminatory or offensive', as the *OED* puts it (*OED Online*, accessed 2009), that is, the *politically correct* mode. It is a disparaging and ticklish label, but we can, in a shorthand kind of way, associate this mode on occasion with some examples of government-sponsored language planning, such as legislation on age and sex discrimination, which tends to have a linguistic dimension.

## Conclusion

Finally, then, did Johnson stabilize English? Having completed his Dictionary, he concluded, 'With this consequence [stability] I will confess that I flattered myself for a while; but now begin to fear that I have indulged expectation which neither reason nor experience can justify'

(1755, Preface to the Dictionary). Gradual change in language, he conceded, is irresistible, and the most that can be done is 'that we retard what we cannot repel, that we palliate what we cannot cure'.

Rare indeed is the language or variety of a language that is immune to or that can be successfully protected from outside influence or change. Neither does it seem as if the diversity of English has been impaired by attempts to override it. But dictionaries and grammars have not been entirely without effect. Johnson's, for example, helped stabilize English spelling, and another, Noah Webster's *An American Dictionary of the English Language* (1828), with nationalistic intent, successfully promoted an American English. A dictionary can help codify a standard variety of a language and thereby affect usage in certain contexts, but it cannot shield even that standard variety let alone the language in general against change. With regard to language planning as a whole, some kinds are more likely to achieve their objectives than others, with attempts to stem change and override diversity being among the unsafe bets.

The fate of a global language in a mass-media age would seem to be greater diversity and more rapid change – and apparently a greater variety of dictionaries than ever before. More chaos, and more attempts to bring order to it. Dictionaries of, for example, in alphabetical order, art, biography, dialect, dreams, 'gender-free usage', hip hop, idioms, Internet slang, IT, linguistics, proverbs, quotations, slang, 'teen slang', word origins, not to mention the *Oxford English Dictionary Online*, a dictionary as ongoing as the language itself, and the *Encarta World English Dictionary*, first published in 1999 and sponsored by Microsoft. As the *Guardian* (29 July 1999, p. 11) reported, 'Its [Microsoft's] version of the English language – immediately attacked by critics yesterday as being heavily Americanised – is likely to be incorporated in word processing spell-checkers, a market in which Microsoft is also strong. If these combined new moves succeed, they would give the corporation a uniquely powerful chance to influence the language.' As Ali G would say, Wicked! Ironic too, if Microsoft were to succeed where Swift, Johnson, and so many other fixers have not. But as the Icelandic example above indicates, Microsoft has also been not totally insensitive to linguistic diversity. To coincide with the launch of its Office 2007 system, it announced a series of online dictionaries of regional British English dialects for download into Office, whereupon 'you will be able to type in your own dialect words without seeing red lines appear under every word simply because your software doesn't recognise it' (Microsoft United Kingdom website: 'Microsoft Local Dialect', accessed 2008).

*Kewl,* as they say, or rather spell, at Microsoft. For there is even a (very small) dictionary (online) of the 'bizarre and exotic terms and phrases' used by those who worked at Microsoft in the 1990s (*The Microsoft Lexicon,* 1995–8, compiled and edited by Ken Barnes et al., accessed 2008). Accordingly, let me conclude this chapter in the hope that you have found it highly *buttoned down* and *crisp.*

## Further reading

*Proper English? Readings in Language, History and Cultural Identity* (1991), edited by Tony Crowley, is a very useful collection of key texts, spanning 1690–1987, on the regulation of English. A good companion to this is *Linguistic Purism* (1991), by George Thomas, a detailed attempt to describe purism as it affects language. Robert L. Cooper's *Language Planning and Social Change* (1989) is an excellent review of language planning, and *Verbal Hygiene* (1995), by Deborah Cameron, is a thoughtful critical analysis of modern debates about regulation. Slightly more recent is *Language Planning: From Practice to Theory* (1997), by Robert B. Kaplan and Richard B. Baldauf Jr, and Gibson Ferguson's *Language Planning and Education* (2006) has a good, widely ranging overview in addition to its focus on education policy and methods. *Current Issues in Language Planning* and *Language Problems and Language Planning* are two leading journals in the field. John Baugh's *Beyond Ebonics: Linguistic Pride and Racial Prejudice* (2000) tells the story of AAVE and the debate that surrounds it, and the linguist John R. Rickford has made available much valuable material on 'Ebonics' via his website, at: http://www.stanford.edu/~ rickford/ebonics/. Manfred Görlach is the editor of a collection which charts the intrusions of English into other European languages, *English in Europe* (2002), and of its companion, *A Dictionary of European Anglicisms* (2001). *The Oxford History of English Lexicography* (2009), edited by A. P. Cowie, tells you all you need to know about dictionaries of all kinds of English.

# 15  Slippage

## Slips of the Tongue and Other Blunders

---

This chapter includes the following:
- What causes linguistic slips?
- **Syntagmatic** and **associative** relations in language.
- **Assemblage** and **selection errors**.
- Sigmund Freud's theory of slips or **parapraxes**.
- Jacques Derrida's concept of **différance**.

---

Don't we say odd things sometimes? This chapter is about linguistic slips and why we make them. Talking to a colleague, who was also a friend, and a poet, which makes it worse, I said 'disposition' when I meant to say 'deposition'. I said it twice at least. I knew it was wrong, and I knew he knew it was wrong, by the look of puzzlement, but I just couldn't get a handle on its wrongness. It clicked the next day and I felt such a fool, being what the newspapers call a 'language expert' and all. Some decades ago I said 'ambiguous' when I should have said 'ambivalent'. It haunts me still. Every time I say 'ambivalent' I have to check, before and after, that I am not going to say or that I did not say 'ambiguous'. Same goes for 'ambiguous', but vice versa. It has since spread to 'mitigate' and 'militate', and I am keeping an eye on 'hubris' and 'hummus'.

I will admit to worrying that I am embarrassingly prone to such slips. I feel it has some connection with my total inability to remember a person's name when they are introduced to me. However, being a 'language expert' I can at least categorize my slips. There are: (i) slips of the tongue, like saying 'Fried' when I meant to say 'Freud'; (ii) miswritings – unforgivable, inexplicable memory failure over spellings, for example; (iii) mishearings, such as the following headline on the radio: 'Israeli troops all along the West Bank have been put on paella', which on second hearing turned out to be 'Israeli troops all along the West Bank have been put on high alert'; and (iv) misreadings, such as a sign outside an antiques store saying 'Trousers Welcome', which on closer inspection proved to be 'Browsers Welcome', and, in the TV listings,

*The Wild Brunch*. And as a side-category there might be odd word-induced visions, such as that prompted by a friend talking of her son's *rhinitis* (picture: a teenager with a rhinoceros's head, sneezing). Whenever someone says 'That's irrelevant', I see tusks and huge flappy grey ears. Imagine my horror when I saw the following notice on the door of my local medical centre: 'We only have skeleton staff on duty at this time.'

Thankfully, I know now that all of these incidents are entirely normal symptoms of language. It's not my fault, it's language's, as the present chapter will demonstrate. There *would* be something wrong with me, and with my language, if these incidents *did not* happen.

People say odd things. Like the youngster I saw interviewed on television who said 'just because we're not the same doesn't mean we're different'. Or the woman I overheard in a coffee bar saying 'For the sake of Gaia I think every other generation should not have children.' And another who said 'Well, time isn't the be-all and end-all of everything.' These are odd things to say, though they are caused by a momentary loss of logic as much as by the foibles of language. The idioms of a language, however, can easily derail our sentences. For example, the TV sports summarizer I heard say 'I'm putting my neck out on a bit of a limb here', and the soccer player who, in reply to a radio interviewer's question, said 'Every now and then the boss blows his top but at least it keeps him on his toes', or the politician who said 'We are looking at egg on face to an incredible depth.' And the ex-soccer-manager-turned-pundit who said 'Not many players would've hit him in the eye ... that he could've put his hat on ... that played well.' It would not be right for me to give the impression that soccer managers, players, and pundits are particularly likely to be phrasally challenged, but here are some more of their technical hitches: 'He's in a no-win situation – unless he wins'; 'He's never found wanting very often'; 'He isn't not still one of the best frontmen in football'; and, less of a hitch, more of a poem, 'The onus is not really on us to be honest'. In the name of balance, here is an intriguing turn of phrase from a golf commentator, speculating on the prospects of the 2008 European Ryder Cup team: 'Can they dig themselves out of the hole they've dug for themselves?'

Then there is the simple slip of the tongue. For example, my friend who, instead of asking for a children's toy called a 'water snake' in her local shop, found herself asking the male assistant if he had a 'trouser snake'.[1] Or the BBC radio newsreader who spoke of Martina

---

[1] Oblivious to what she had just said, she followed it innocently with 'Have you got a red one?'

Navratilova winning her tennis match 'in straight sex'. Or the soccer commentator who, during the opening match of the 1990 World Cup, referred to the Cameroon team as 'the macaroons'. Or the waitress in a local coffee house who, curiously, as I was leaving, said 'Hi' when she surely meant to say 'Bye'. In everyday life each of these would probably be called a '**Freudian slip**', an error revealing an unconscious or hidden thought, usually to the embarrassment of the speaker.

There are other types of slips of the tongue besides the Freudian. Take the mechanic telling me of a car so dirty and leak-ridden that when he opened its bonnet he found 'a large crustacean all over the engine'. Or the participant in a radio current-affairs discussion whom I heard saying 'It beggars the question.' Or the manager of a local boys' soccer team, telling parents about a forthcoming tour, saying that 'the boys' behaviour will be exempt'. These are **malapropisms**. The term derives from the fictional Mrs Malaprop, a character in Richard Sheridan's play *The Rivals* (1775) who habitually made wrong word choices, as in 'He is the very pineapple of politeness!' Such mistakes involve the substitution of a similar-sounding word for the correct one – as in 'crustacean' for *crust*, 'beggars' for *begs*, 'exempt' for *exemplary*, and 'pineapple' for *pinnacle* – sometimes because of ignorance (as in the case of Mrs Malaprop), sometimes because of a temporary or inadvertent slip (as, I trust, in the case of the student who, in an exam, referred to the eminent linguist 'Billy Crystal', meaning David Crystal), which means that a malapropism may also be a Freudian slip. I would rather not think that the student who, in an essay on sexism in English, wrote 'The term *bachelor* is very positive, indicating a virile young man, whereas *sphincter* means a sad old woman', had committed a 'Freudian malapropism', but I suppose it is possible. This malapropism is a written one, a slip of the pen.

Although we associate the phrase 'Freudian slip' mostly with slips of the tongue, Freud himself was interested in a variety of errors, mishaps, forgettings and misrememberings. It is in *The Psychopathology of Everyday Life* (originally published in German in 1901) that Sigmund Freud (1856–1939) discusses these phenomena, which he calls **parapraxes**. According to Freud, parapraxes are motivated by unconscious, repressed thoughts surfacing in our everyday behaviour.

A **parapraxis** can be a slip of the tongue. For example, Freud records a professor saying, in a lesson, 'I can hardly believe that, since, even in Vienna with its millions of inhabitants, those who understand the nasal cavities can be counted *on one finger*, I mean on the fingers of one hand', and, on another occasion, 'In the case of the female genitals, in spite of many *Versuchungen* [temptations] – I beg your pardon, *Versuche* [experiments]...' (1901, p. 122). Interestingly, in the index of para-praxes at the back of my copy of *The Psychopathology of Everyday Life*, the German *Versuche* is glossed not as 'experiments' but 'experients', an error worthy of inclusion under the 'Slips of the Pen and Misprints' section of the same index. Another ready candidate would be 'pubic scrutiny' for *public scrutiny*, which I came across in a text published by the Broadcasting Standards Commission in Britain. Another, unusual one I found in the inlay booklet of a music CD, which said, referring to a particular period in the artist's career, 'At the time his critical and commercial sock was at a low.' Figure 16 shows a non-native-speaker slip of the pen, from the window of a mini-market on a small Greek

**FIGURE 16**   NOTICE IN SHOP WINDOW, PAXOS, 2008

island. Michael Erard, in an article for *New Scientist* (2008), reports on slips, mispronunciations, and simplifications in global English among non-native speakers: 'non-native speakers are stripping out parts of English that cause misunderstandings with other non-native speakers' (p. 3 of online version), though in this case I would expect the use of 'troll' for *trolley* to be a one-off error not a trend.

Likewise, 'ear Michael' in the instructions for a *headphone microphone* made in China that my son bought.

A parapraxis can also be a misreading. For example, Freud notes his own tendency when on holiday in an unfamiliar town to read the word 'Antiquities' on every shop sign displaying a word of the slightest similarity. 'This betrays the questing spirit of the collector', says Freud (1901, p. 158), generously. It reminds me of my misreading outside an antiques store: 'Trousers Welcome'. I prefer not to attempt a Freudian interpretation.

A parapraxis can also combine forgetting and **paramnesia** or false recollection, as when Freud forgot the name of a painter, *Signorelli*, and could only think of the names of two other painters, *Botticelli* and *Boltraffio*. Freud's analysis (1901, pp. 38–44) of this central example links it to his repression of thoughts about death and sexuality. How?

To comprehend the connection one has to know (i) that immediately before being unable to recall *Signorelli*, Freud had been discussing with his travelling companion some customs of the Turkish people living in *Bosnia* and *Herzegovina*, (ii) that these customs, in Freud's thoughts, related to death and sexuality and (iii) made him think of the bad news – the suicide of one of his patients – that he had recently received while staying in a village called *Trafoi*, and (iv) that this made him wish to change the topic of conversation, to the work of the painter whose name he found he could not recall. His explanation is that his repressed thoughts displaced the name *Signorelli*, so that Freud forgot the name (which he wished to remember) while the repressed thoughts (which he wished to forget) pushed to find a way to the surface. This they did via language, which connected *Botticelli* and *Boltraffio* with his repressed thoughts and with *Signorelli*. The *Signor-* part of *Signorelli* is the same as a term of address in Italian, which connects it with the *Her-* part of *Herzegovina*, which sounds the same as the German term of address, *Herr*. The *-elli* part of *Signorelli* connects with the *-elli* in *Botticelli*. *Bo-* in *Botticelli* and *Boltraffio* connects with *Bo-* in *Bosnia*, and *-traffio* connects with *Trafoi*. Thus, a sound similarity connects *Signorelli* and *Botticelli*, and sound similarities and similarities in the functions of words connect the three painters' names with the place names, and Freud associated the place names with thoughts of death and sexuality. These thoughts find expression in *Botticelli* and *Boltraffio*, and force aside *Signorelli*.

One might well suspect that a similar series of connections could probably be made between any three words. Indeed, we might go further and suggest that words are intrinsically connectable, but this does not invalidate Freud's analysis.

Not all of Freud's parapraxes occur in language – there are, for example, 'bungled actions', as when Freud gave his thumb 'a most painful' pinch (1901, p. 235) on hearing a patient announce his intention of marrying Freud's eldest daughter – but a great many are linguistic. What all parapraxes have in common is that they are unintentional actions or performances caused by motives unknown to our conscious minds. They have their roots in repressed thoughts in the unconscious mind. Needless to say, Freud's interest is in the workings of the human mind, particularly in the dynamic relationship between the unconscious and the conscious parts of the human mind. His interest is in discovering the motives for parapraxes, not in investigating what it is about language that makes it amenable to parapraxes.

But Freud did draw on work on language slips by language scholars (*work* by language scholars, that is, not slips), in particular an 1895 study of German slips by Rudolf Meringer and Carl Mayer. In 1895, the specialized study of language was known as **philology**, in which the emphasis was on the history of languages. However, the study of language underwent a metamorphosis following the publication in 1916 of Ferdinand de Saussure's *Course in General Linguistics*, which emphasized the importance of studying the structures of languages at single points in time. Language scholars – whether philologists or modern, post-Saussurean linguists – have tended to have, in the matter of language slips, different interests from those of Freud. Their general aims have been to discover configurational patterns among the great variety of slips in order to learn more about how the human brain stores and retrieves linguistic items, and in order to test hypotheses about the underlying grammatical organization of language. Individual linguists have sometimes disagreed with Freud, but the viewpoints of Freud and of linguistics in general regarding language slips are not incompatible. One could say that they are complementary. And it is Saussure who provides us with a model of language that explains its fundamental amenability to slips.

Freud suggests that, unlike foreign words and names, such as *Signorelli*, the ordinary material of our native language 'appears to be protected against being forgotten' (1901, p. 94). But this protection is not absolute, and our use of our native language succumbs frequently to other disturbances – slips of the tongue, slips of the pen, misreadings, and so on. Saussure provides us with an explanation of the protection against forgetting that our native language has, an explanation which also, it turns out, accounts for slips. The same explanation helps account for the connectability of *Signorelli*, *Botticelli* and *Boltraffio*. Put simply, it is in the nature of language that words leak into one another. No word is independent. Bizarre though it may seem, a word is inhabited by other words. Any one word is inhabited or haunted by all the other words in the same language. The title of this chapter, 'Slippage', refers to the errors of language known as slips and to their explanation: the view that, by their very nature, the units of language will slip into each other.

Some connections are obvious: Did you hear about the truck that spilled its load of raspberry preserve? Police told motorists to expect a *traffic jam*! What do astronauts bring their lunch to work in? *Launch boxes*! A **pun** is a play on words that are the same or similar in sound but different in meaning, or on the differing meanings of the same word. You would not know it from the examples above, but puns can be funny. When the Jim Carrey character in the film *The Mask* (1994) is ordered, by an officer of the law, to 'Freeze!' and he is immediately encased, in mid-air, in ice, we laugh. Less funny is the reason why we laugh at this 'Freeze!' Two meanings are brought together into simultaneity. The figurative colloquialism of the TV and cinema cop is united with the literal, central meaning of the word. *The Mask*'s 'Freeze!' combines wordplay with a visual pun. Puns that do not require special effects are very common. We find them routinely in comedy, in literature, in newspaper and magazine headlines, in advertisements, and even on noticeboards outside churches, as in the following: 'God answers knee-mail.' I have something of a soft spot for puns, and in this I am in excellent company. William Shakespeare committed 1062 puns in his works (according to F. A. Bather, 1923, p. 397), punning being a predilection that had 'some malignant power over his mind' (Samuel Johnson, 1765, p. 36). Maybe the funniest puns happen unintentionally. Once, in a lecture on language and gender, talking about the idea that the English language privileges terms for men over terms for women, I actually said 'Men come before women.' Some years ago

I heard a radio newsreader say 'Last night in Londonderry two men were shot in the waterworks area.' In an article in a local newspaper about the police force's attempts to prevent illegal activities at public conveniences, I read 'police have cracked down on the toilets'. But in truth an 'unintentional pun' is a contradiction in terms. Puns are deliberate wordplays. These latter examples are slips, quite possibly Freudian slips, whose funniness, once recognized, depends on the same mechanism used in puns. The sounds of language, then, provide an obvious route for slippage. In puns, a sequence of sound draws together different meanings.

Sounds themselves slip in another well-known way. In a **spoonerism**, sounds occurring in an ordered sequence, in a phrase or in a sentence, are transposed, as in 'chish and fips' for *fish and chips*, and 'sporks and foons' for *forks and spoons*. Spoonerisms are named after the Reverend Dr William Archibald Spooner (1844–1930), Dean and Warden of New College, Oxford, who is reputed to have committed such errors regularly. His 'original spoonerisms' allegedly include 'shoving leopard' for *loving shepherd* and 'minx in spoonlight' for *sphinx in moonlight*. The Reverend Dr may have been unfairly treated. Only a handful of 'original spoonerisms' have been verified, and the kind of slip we now call a spoonerism is probably as old as speech itself. Defined more precisely, a spoonerism is a transposition of the initial sounds of two words in a spoken sequence, as in the following snippet from a radio correspondent reviewing the day's newspapers in Israel: '... the *Jerusalem Coast* parries an article on ...'.

When the former manager of the England soccer team, Bobby Robson, commenting on the merits of two members of the 1998 World Cup squad, said, 'and they're soluble ... and they're solid and reliable', he did not commit a spoonerism. Nevertheless, he did mix up the elements of a spoken sequence. His error is a **blend**. Blends and spoonerisms are two types of **assemblage error**, a category used by Jean Aitchison in her book *Words in the Mind* (2003). Assemblage errors happen when something goes awry in the ordering of the elements of a spoken sequence. There are many types of assemblage error. Two common ones are **anticipation**, where a sound is used in anticipation of a sound from later in a sequence, as in 'into the record brooks goes Tim Brabants' and 'teachers' industrial action over pee ... over pay – that's all from me', and **perseverance**, where a sound is substituted following its use earlier in a sequence, as in 'in older children when the results can be much serier [*serious*]' (details of sources for these, and other original examples in this chapter, are given at the end of the book). You might think, when my son, as a seven-year-old, describing where in France we had stayed on holiday, said 'Bordogne', that he had committed an assemblage error, blending *Bordeaux* and *the Dordogne*. But as far as he was concerned, at that moment, 'Bordogne' *was* the name of a place we had visited. 'Bordogne' is a blend caused by misremembering. It is better placed in Aitchison's other major category of slips, **selection errors**. A selection error happens when the wrong item is chosen from our mental warehouse of words. My son misremembered a foreign name, whereas Aitchison's categories are designed for our native language. Many of the slips of speech reported earlier in this chapter fall quite easily into the selection-error category, like 'disposition', 'ambiguous', 'trouser snake', 'macaroons', 'crustacean', and so forth. Mishearings and misreadings, like 'paella' and *The Wild Brunch*, can also be understood as selection errors. There is a connection between Aitchison's categories and a distinction made by Saussure in his *Course in General Linguistics* (1916). For Saussure, everything in a language is based on relations. He distinguishes (pp. 122–7) two kinds of relations: **syntagmatic relations** and **associative relations** (the latter are sometimes referred to as **paradigmatic relations**). These explain why language is fundamentally amenable to slips.

From Freud we get a psychological explanation for some kinds of slips. From Saussure we get an explanation of the pathways between words that allow and encourage slips. Saussure tells us that each language is a system. The system (or *langue*, as he calls it in the original French) of any language underpins its performance (or *parole*, in the French), and the system is a symbolic system (see Chapter 7, 'Strange Orchestras', for further detail). The system is comprised of symbols which Saussure calls **linguistic signs**, each sign consisting of a **signifier** (or 'sound-image') and a **signified** (or 'concept'; see Chapter 6, 'Signs', for more). A word is a linguistic sign, but there are other kinds as well, for example, grammatical units (like the *-s* that indicates a plural in English), and idioms can be considered linguistic signs. The system is relational – the meaning of each sign is dependent on the sign's difference from other signs, that is, the linguistic signs exist in relation to each other. The relations between them are **syntagmatic** and **associative**. Saussure calls the meaning that ensues from these relations **value**.

Syntagmatic relations arise because, when we speak or write, language is **linear** – in use, language occurs in lines or sequences. The linguistic signs underpinning these sequences are in a relation with each other, and Saussure calls these linear sequences **syntagms** (1916, p. 123). The sequence 'crossing' is a syntagm, comprising the units *cross* and *-ing*. The sequence 'Heavy plant crossing', which I have seen displayed in Britain near construction sites, is a syntagm comprising the units *Heavy, plant, cross*, and *-ing*. Each unit of a syntagm acquires some of its value by being distinct from the other units present in the syntagm – from its syntagmatic relations. The rest of its value it acquires by being in a relationship with units or signs *not present* in the syntagm, and Saussure says (p. 123) that these absent signs are in an associative relation with the present sign. That is, a word will always call to mind other words, even words not present in the syntagm. An association may spring from sound resemblance or identity, as between 'plant', referring to machinery, present in the syntagm 'Heavy plant crossing', and *plant*, meaning a vegetable organism, absent from the syntagm. Each word in any syntagm is, as Saussure (p. 126) puts it, 'like the center of a constellation' of associations. For example, 'crossing', by virtue of its first element, calls to mind *crossed, crosses*, and *across*. By virtue of its *-ing* ending it calls to mind *running, walking, swimming, meaning*, and so on. The meaning that 'crossing' appears to contain may call to mind other signs with similar meanings, like *traverse* and *bridge*, or other signs with contrasting meanings, like *running, walking, swimming, agreeing*. Its sound may call to mind *loss* and *possible*. 'Heavy plant crossing' may call to mind the word *noughts*, because 'cross' occurs also in the syntagm *noughts and crosses*. So we can see that the kinds of linguistic links that Freud discovered among foreign names in his *Signorelli* example also operate, according to Saussure, within each language. Within a language, 'A word can always evoke everything that can be associated with it in one way or another', says Saussure (p. 126). The further out into the constellation we travel the looser is the associative bond between a 'satellite' sign and the first, present sign, but in theory *all* the signs of a language link up in a massive series of associative relations.

Words in a syntagm, says Saussure, are 'chained together' (p. 123). In a language, linguistic signs are also linked in a virtually endless chain of associations. In a language, signs connect like the rings of a necklace, which is an image used by the psychoanalyst Jacques Lacan. And the necklace 'is a ring in another necklace made of rings' (Lacan, 1957, p. 153). Lacan, a theorist who synthesized the ideas of Saussure and Freud, calls this the **signifying chain**. The effects of the chain are odd. For example, the meaning of a sign, of a word, is never fully present in the word itself. The philosopher Jacques Derrida (1930–2004) put it like this, 'the signified concept is never present in and of itself, in a sufficient presence that would refer only to itself' (1968, p. 11). A word always refers to other words. Derrida adds, 'every concept is inscribed in a chain or in a system within which it refers to the other, to other concepts, by means of the systematic play of differences'. A word acquires much of its meaning via the relations of the language system. Its meaning is influenced by other words, that is, the word is haunted by the meanings of other words, though these other meanings also are never fully present in these other words. Meaning is never fully present, and although I talked earlier rather impulsively of separate meanings, no two (or more) meanings in a language are ever fully separate. Meaning is at once differential, that is, influenced by relations of contrast between signs, and deferred, from sign to sign. This is the 'play' that Derrida refers to and for which he coined the term *différance* (see Derrida, 1968), itself a wordplay, to indicate differing and deferring. Derrida draws out an implication of Saussure's model of language, that language essentially is wordplay, play between words. Language essentially involves slippage. Words slip into other words. Language essentially entails ambiguity, or 'multi-guity', or to use the technical term, **poly-semy**, possession of multiple meanings. The slippage that Derrida refers to is semantic, to do with meaning, but Saussure's model also implies that the shapes, the grammatical forms, and the sounds of words are prone to slippage.

In conclusion, slippage has two apparently contradictory effects. First, it aids memory. If the symbols of a symbolic system call each other to mind they are easier to remember, and according to the neuroscientist Terrence Deacon (1997), this fundamental characteristic of human language fits with the learning capabilities of the brains of human infants. Children acquire language remarkably efficiently, and language itself helps them do this by being a mnemonic system. Secondly, slippage disrupts memory, and it disrupts the performance of language. If the symbols connect with each other, then every once in a while or even quite often an element is going to turn up where it is not wanted. Errors will happen. Assemblage errors are influenced by the syntagmatic chain, selection errors by the associative chain. I really should not have worried about my 'disposition' slip. My friend, as a poet, is in the business of slippage. In fact, we all are. Slips are normal.

## Further reading

For an accessible survey, go to *Um . . . Slips, Stumbles, and Verbal Blunders, and What They Mean* (2007), by Michael Erard. His website, at http://umthebook.com/, includes extracts and an excellent bibliography of work on slips. Two substantial collections of essays on language errors are *Errors in Linguistic Performance: Slips of the Tongue, Ear, Pen, and Hand* (1980), and *Speech Errors as Linguistic Evidence* (1973), both edited by Victoria A. Fromkin. A Speech Error Database, built on Fromkin's collection, can be accessed via http://www.mpi.nl/resources/data. Another online collection is at http://eggcorns.lascribe.net/ – *eggcorn* is a term coined to label slips which make a kind of sense in their own right despite being errors, as in 'eggcorn' for *acorn*. I could add 'outsane' to the collection, as in 'the outsane ... outside lane', an example of anticipation I noticed in a radio commentary on an athletics meeting. *Outsane*, I propose, should be the opposite of *insane*. Jean Aitchison's *Words in the Mind: An Introduction to the Mental Lexicon* (3rd edn, 2003) is a helpful guide to what linguists believe about how our brains store and access words, while a thorough analysis of puns is provided by *On Puns: The Foundation of Letters* (1988), edited by Jonathan Culler. Freud's *The Psychopathology of Everyday Life* (1901; 1975 in the Penguin Freud Library) is a fine read. An English translation of Derrida's influential (though demanding) essay 'Différance' (1968) is in his *Margins of Philosophy* (1982), translated by Alan Bass, and Lacan discusses the signifying chain in his 'The Agency of the Letter in the Unconscious or Reason since Freud' (1957) in *Écrits: A Selection* (1977), translated by Alan Sheridan.

# 16 Communication Breakdown

## Modelling What Happens When We Communicate

This chapter includes the following:

- How can the same utterance have different meanings?
- Saussure's **speaking-circuit**.
- **Models of communication** by Shannon and Weaver, and by Thomas Sebeok.
- Explanation of the terms **bit**, **entropy**, **information**, **noise**, and **redundancy** in communication theory.

## Introduction

'Just a perfect day, you made me forget myself, I thought I was someone else, someone good.'

'You know what it's about, don't you?' said a friend to me about Lou Reed's *Perfect Day* (1972). It's a love song, I thought, though the BBC used it in 1997 in a promotional film celebrating the corporation's 75th anniversary, saying, 'The idea behind *Perfect Day* is that the richness of music you can hear on the BBC can evoke images of your perfect day' (BBC *Perfect Day* web-pages, accessed 2001). 'Oh such a perfect day, you just keep me hangin' on.' 'It's about heroin use', said my friend, and it is true that in the film *Trainspotting* (1996) the song plays behind the lead character's overdose. 'You're going to reap just what you sow.' Certainly the torpor expressed by the song fits with this interpretation, which fits in turn with what I know about the kind of songs that Lou Reed writes – though I think that I have heard him say in an interview that *Perfect Day* definitely is a love song. Strange, nevertheless, that *Perfect Day* makes sense as a love song, as an advertisement for a broadcasting corporation, and as a song about heroin addiction. The one song communicates at least a few divergent meanings. Strange but quite routine also, in that this kind of thing happens frequently in communication.

This chapter looks at English by way of a consideration of the connections between language, meaning, and communication, and as an example *Perfect Day* raises a number of helpful and intriguing questions about communication via language. How and why does the song communicate divergent meanings? This is the primary question. But in addition, how important are Lou Reed's intentions in determining the meaning of *Perfect Day*? If he says it is a love song, does that mean that it is not a song about heroin addiction? And how important is our state of knowledge about Lou Reed, his life and work, in determining the meaning of *Perfect Day*? These questions are helpful (as well as intriguing) because in order to answer them one has to figure out what communication is and what kind of relationship there is between communication, meaning, and language.

Human beings communicate in a variety of ways, using a variety of instruments and media. We communicate by gesture, by the positioning of our bodies, by our facial expressions, through touch, via machines, via radio waves, via satellite, electronically, wirelessly, and so on. Most significantly, human beings communicate by language – by speaking, hearing, writing, and reading. The linguist John Lyons said (1977, p. 32) that 'it is difficult to imagine any satisfactory definition of the term "language" that did not incorporate some reference to the notion of communication', adding that 'it is obvious, or has appeared so to many semanticists [**semantics** being the study of meaning], that there is an intrinsic connexion between meaning and communication, such that it is impossible to account for the former except in terms of the latter'. From this point of view, then, neither **language** nor **meaning** can be defined without reference to **communication**, which is another way of saying that language is essentially about communication. (There are riders that one could add to this view – for example, that language is also about the construction of identity, and about making sense of the world.) Lyons is also implying that, for semanticists, meaning that is not communicated is not meaning, in which case *Perfect Day* would have no meaning if nobody, ever, had heard it. But would it have meaning if only Lou Reed and Lou Reed alone had ever heard it? This is another useful question.

Over the last century a number of models have been put forward which attempt to account for communication and types of it. In this chapter, I concentrate on the two basic, central models, each of which tells us a great deal about what happens whenever we use language.

## The 1916 model of communication

The word *communication* entered the English language in the four-teenth century from French, but it originates in Latin *communica-tio/communicationis* 'making common to many'. In communication, it is knowledge that is made common, if we use the term *knowledge* in the broad sense of 'awareness of things'. In communication, knowledge passes between communicators – knowledge is being shared. However, according to our first model of communication, this sharing of knowl-edge depends upon the communicators already being in possession of a considerable sum of shared knowledge. This first model describes communication via a specific medium, that of speech, and the sum of shared knowledge is also specific, that being a given language, but its basic principle that communication depends on shared knowledge has wider applications. The model is called the **speaking-circuit** and it comes from Ferdinand de Saussure's *Course in General Linguistics* (1916, pp. 11–15). Saussure's diagram of the speaking-circuit is reproduced in Figure 17.

Saussure's speaking-circuit is deceptively simple. It describes how we humans communicate when we speak, by providing a breakdown of the simplest communicative act involving speech. But the analysis is not self-contained, for it rests upon a far-reaching theory of the nature of language, and in addition the speaking-circuit has some remarkable implications.

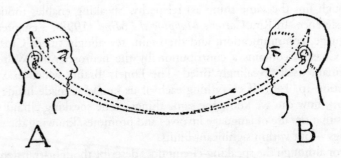

**FIGURE 17**  THE SPEAKING-CIRCUIT (from Saussure, 1916, p. 11)

The speaking-circuit strips spoken communication to its bare minimum. The minimal act features two persons, 'A' and 'B', and it involves the transfer of **concepts** between their brains. For example, according to Saussure, a given **concept** or 'mental fact' (1916, p. 11) is associated in the brain of A with a given **sound-image**. The sound-image is so named because it is the mental picture or 'psychological imprint' (1916, p. 66) of a sequence of linguistic sounds, such as a spoken word. The sequence of sounds is the physical expression of the sound-image. So, a given concept unlocks a given sound-image in the brain of A, and the brain of A then transmits impulses to A's organs of speech, which then produce the relevant linguistic sounds. Person A speaks. The sound waves travel to B's ears, and then enter into a process which is the reverse of what has just happened in A's brain. The sounds that B hears should trigger a sound-image in B's brain, and this sound-image should unlock a corresponding concept, which with luck will be the same as or very similar to the 'original' concept in A's brain. If so, according to the speaking-circuit, a thought has been transmitted from A's brain to B's brain. Remarkable. Communication has happened. It is quite possible now that other concepts will present themselves in the brain of B, and that B will give voice to these. If this happens, a communicative loop has been established: the speaking-circuit.

What Saussure is saying is that every time we utter a word we have in our minds a picture of the sonic shape of the word (the sound-image), and this picture is coupled with a thought which encapsulates the meaning of the word (the concept). In order to speak meaningfully we must have in our brains a store of mental units, each one made up of a sound-image and a concept, and the transference of concepts from mind to mind is enabled by speech and by the links that sound-images provide between speech and concepts. It seems that the speaking-circuit model of communication treats the use of language as equivalent to (though not the same thing as) telepathy. Speaking enables thought-transference. In Rita Carter's *Mapping the Mind* (1998), a chapter on language, communication, and the brain, revealingly titled 'Crossing the Chasm', contains a contribution by the neuroscientist Walter J. Freeman, itself revealingly titled 'The Lonely Brain', which asks the question (p. 146) 'If everything each of us knows is made inside our brains, how can we know the same things?' The speaking-circuit suggests that the use of language involves and promotes 'knowing the same things' – but within significant limits.

For although the speaking-circuit does describe thought-transference via speech, in actual fact the process it outlines is not really equivalent to telepathy. Telepathy, presumably, would allow the transference of any thought or feeling from individual to individual. The speaking-circuit does not describe the transference of just any old thoughts, it describes the transference of only those thoughts allowed by language, that is, only those thoughts which exist *in* language, thoughts which have been made *linguistic*.

It is later in his *Course* (1916, pp. 65–7) that Saussure makes it clear that a given concept and its associated sound-image form a unit in the brain, a mental unit which he calls the **linguistic sign**. In Saussure's theory, oral sounds are made linguistic by being underpinned by the mental units he calls linguistic signs. He renames the concept and the sound-image parts of the sign the **signified** and the **signifier** respectively, thereby pointing up both the unity of the linguistic sign and its dual nature. Saussure's linguistic sign is a mental 'object', and is distinguished from its physical expression in linguistic sounds. Hence Saussure makes a distinction between the physical expression or execution of language, which he calls (in the original French) ***parole*** (1916, p. 13), and the psychological structure which underpins execution – Saussure argues that each language is structured on a system of linguistic signs, and he calls this system ***langue*** (p. 9). This system, or *langue*, exists in the minds of the speakers of a given language. In total it exists only in the totality of minds of speakers of a language. It is therefore, remarkably, a communal, social entity *and* a psychological entity. *Langue* is a system which has a 'potential existence' (p. 14) in each individual's brain but which in practice 'is not complete in any speaker; it exists perfectly only within a collectivity'. *Langue* is based on convention, for it is comprised of linguistic signs, and each linguistic sign is a conventional agreement among a community of speakers. For example, as an English speaker I am party to an agreement that the word *elephant* designates 'a large grey mammal with tusks, flappy ears and a trunk'. In Saussurean terms, the agreement is that the sound-sequence 'elephant' is allied to the signifier *elephant*, which is combined with the signified 'a large grey mammal with tusks, flappy ears and a trunk'. *Langue*, then, is the accumulation of mental, linguistic, agreed conventions of a community of speakers, and in the case of English this is now a huge community. The thoughts that pass between the minds of English speakers (via English speech) must be, according to Saussurean theory, thoughts that are already a part of the underpinning structure or *langue* of English. Each speaker of a given language must possess a shared knowledge of its *langue* with its other speakers before communicating with its other speakers. But how do communicating speakers acquire their shared knowledge of their common *langue* if not by communicating using their shared knowledge? Which came first, shared knowledge or speaking?

This is not a question that Saussure pays great attention to. In his defence, the main aim of the *Course in General Linguistics* was to identify an object of study for linguistics, and this object was *langue*. *Parole* or speaking – the French for speaking-circuit is *circuit de la parole* – was of lesser importance to Saussure, and so too was any theory of the evolution of *langue*. Saussure concentrated on a theory of the structure of *langue*, that is, of the underlying, symbolic, lexical structure of a language. Before addressing the question of the development of *langue*, one would have to decide whether one was talking about the acquisition of a native language by an infant, the acquisition of a second or foreign language by an older learner, or the acquisition of language by *Homo sapiens*. Saussure's very general answer, which would serve as a good starting point for any more detailed explanation, is that the shared knowledge of *langue* and the execution of the shared knowledge by speaking develop continually together. He says (p. 9) that *langue* 'is both a social product of the faculty of speech and a collection of necessary conventions that have been adopted by a social body to permit individuals to exercise that faculty'. In other words, *langue* is a set of agreements among a speech community which makes communication by speech possible *and* which develops through its use in speech. Once under way, the process is a rolling programme of co-development. It would take the establishment of only a modicum of shared linguistic knowledge between individuals for the rolling programme to be set in motion. It continues to happen around us, as speakers of a language. As Saussure points out, *langue* is not complete in any individual speaker, and in my brain there are extensive gaps in knowledge of the linguistic signs associated with, for example, car maintenance and computers. I may hear the words, even picture the sound-images, but the concepts are often just not there. But speaking could remedy this, if I could find patient, sympathetic, comprehensible English speakers whose *langue* is expert in these areas – and I am sure such persons must exist, somewhere. The common knowledge that we would possess would enable us to increase our common knowledge, a speaking-circuit would occur, and in time I would learn to speak with confidence about cars and computers. (Luckily, and remarkably, failure to locate such individuals will not prevent me from driving a car or using a computer.)

Language and its use, then, enable us to 'know the same things'. But can we be *sure* that we know the same things? How is communication by speech verified? This basic question about speech and communication was formulated as early as the fourth century BC by the Greek philosopher Plato, in the dialogue *Cratylus* (as cited by Keller, 1995, p. viii). In the terms of the speaking-circuit, it is as follows: How can person A be sure that the concept in his (or her) brain, that he (or she) transmits to B, ends up as the same concept in B's brain? For example, when I utter the sound-sequence 'telepathy' the corresponding concept in my brain is 'communication of thoughts or feelings by means other than the known senses'. If the concept eventually unlocked in your brain by 'telepathy' is 'a large grey mammal with tusks, flappy ears and a trunk', then we are in trouble. My sentence 'Thoughts can be transferred by telepathy' would lead to some confusion. Of course, **feedback**, a key notion implied in the very term **speaking-circuit** (though not discussed by Saussure), would enable us to sort out this kind of confusion, eventually, providing that there was sufficient common ground in the rest of our communication. But can I ever be certain that the concept linked to 'telepathy' in my brain is identical to the concept linked to 'telepathy' in your brain? In the case of 'elephant', we could go a long way towards verification of concept-identity if we had a large grey mammal with tusks, flappy ears, and a trunk in the vicinity, but ultimately (and in the absence of telepathy) there is no way to verify absolutely that my linguistic concepts are identical to yours. I would have to get into your brain to be sure.

Walter J. Freeman asks (1998, p. 146), 'how can we know the same things?' His own reply is, 'We can learn almost the same things.' Saussure's model is in keeping with this view. It does not require an exact identity of linguistic knowledge among speakers. Saussure says, 'Among all the individuals that are linked together by speech [that is, language], some sort of average will be set up: all will reproduce – *not exactly of course, but approximately* – the same signs united with the same concepts' (1916, p. 13, italics added). Among all the speakers of English there is 'some sort of average', a *langue* in which there is approximate agreement about meaning. Yet I cannot help but notice, at this point, in this chapter, that there is ambiguity in Saussure's statement above. It might mean (a) that different speakers of a language will possess knowledge of differing *amounts* of its signs; or (b) that they might not have all the same signs in common, say, if they speak different dialects; or (c) that different speakers will *perform* signs differently, say, with different accents; or more likely, I think, it means (d) that the same sign will in fact be perceived as *approximately* the same sign by different speakers, and this is the point I have been pursuing. *Langue* does not entail all the speakers of a given language understanding its linguistic signs in precisely the same way.

What we can now see is the beginning of an answer to the question of the divergent meanings of *Perfect Day*. Saussure's theory of *langue*, upon which his speaking-circuit model rests, opens up the possibility that divergence of meaning is in fact a quite normal condition of language in use. Saussure focuses on speech because he believes it to be the primary medium of language, but the essentials of the circuit can be applied to the other chief medium of language, writing. The shared knowledge we need for performing language may be approximate, *almost* the same. The use of language will, therefore, be conducive to divergence of meaning. Communication by speech is made possible by the fixed code of meanings (*langue*) that underpins it, but there is approximation, play, 'almost-ness' in the code, with the result that communication and communication breakdown are never far apart. The ambiguity in the quotation above is evidence of play in the use of the code and suggests that, in matters of meaning, the *intentions* of the speaker/writer may not equate with the *interpretations* of the hearer/reader.

Furthermore, *langue* is both social and psychological, and each speaking individual has internalized a *langue* in some measure, so another way to interpret the speaking-circuit would be to see it as the externalizing of a system of meaning that exists in speakers' brains, so that an individual can easily 'speak' to himself or herself. In which case, *Perfect Day would* have meaning if only Lou Reed and Lou Reed alone had ever heard it, even if he had only ever heard it inside his head. But does talking to oneself count as communication? And are there other factors which can cause the same song, or indeed the same sentence, to have divergent meanings, or that cause intention and interpretation to differ?

The speaking-circuit takes us some way towards answering our *Perfect Day* questions. Its basic principle – that communicating depends on communicators possessing shared knowledge – can be applied to any conventionalized means of communication, linguistic or non-linguistic (such as gestures, rituals, semaphore, morse code, smoke signals). At a stretch, it could even be applied to non-conventionalized communication. For example, the bodily chemicals called *pheromones* transmit messages and at an innate, subconscious level our bodies 'share knowledge' of the 'meanings' of pheromones – though this is a quite different kind of communication, in that it does not involve intention. In some definitions of human communication (for example, Burgoon et al.,

1994, p. 32), communication without intent is not communication. Similarly, in a classic essay on the topic of meaning (1957), H. P. Grice argues that, in communication via conventionalized methods, intention is a pre-requisite for meaning.

The second model of communication approaches the matter from a different angle.

## The 1949 model of communication

Roy Harris, an expert on Saussure, argues that the speaking-circuit model was a product of its time, influenced by the technological innovations of telegraphy, telephony, and broadcasting (Harris, 1983, pp. 155–6). Certainly this influence is evident, but it does not negate the explanatory power of the speaking-circuit, and neither is Saussure's view therefore dated. Indeed, although Saussure's description of brain activity is philosophical rather than technical, his theory fits well with our current, much more specific knowledge of neural operations. Scanning has shown that activity is sparked in different areas of the human brain according to whether we are analysing word meaning, speaking or listening (Carter, 1998, pp. 148–53). The second model of communication is equally a product of its time, originating in the late 1940s in communications engineering. We find it in *The Mathematical Theory of Communication* (1949), by Claude E. Shannon and Warren Weaver. The book consists of a long, technical article by Shannon (first published in slightly different form in 1948), and a shorter, explanatory piece by Weaver. Shannon diagrams his model as in Figure 18.

Shannon begins (1949, p. 3) by noting that 'The fundamental problem of communication is that of reproducing at one point either exactly or approximately a message selected at another point.' He treats this as an 'engineering problem', a problem which has to be tackled when designing an efficient communication system, as in telegraphy, telephony, radio, television, and so forth. Nevertheless, his theory turns out to be highly relevant to meaning and to language.

I will take us through the diagram before explaining and discussing it with the aid of examples. The diagram charts a linear event. The **information source** selects a desired **message** from a set of possible messages. The **transmitter** operates on the message, **encoding** it into a **signal**, in other words, turning it into a form which it can send along

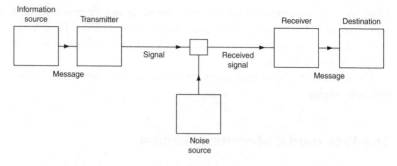

**FIGURE 18**    A MODEL OF COMMUNICATION (from Shannon and Weaver, 1949, p. 5)

the **channel of communication**. As the signal travels along the channel, it may be affected by **noise**. Eventually the signal reaches the **receiver**, which **decodes** the signal back into a message, which should be an exact or approximate reproduction of the initial message. The receiver makes the message available to the **destination**, that is, the person or thing for whom the message is intended.

In telegraphy, for example, the transmitter encodes written words into sequences of interrupted electrical currents of varying lengths (dots, dashes, spaces), which are then sent along the channel, a line or wire, to be decoded by a receiver. In radio, the channel is space and the signal is electromagnetic waves. In communication involving computers, information is encoded into digits, and can be sent down a variety of channels, such as telephone cables, radio waves, and microwaves. In our modern lives, receivers are common – radios, televisions, phones, computers, and so on.

The model can also be applied to communication by speech and writing. In these cases, source and transmitter are at the same location – the human body. So too are the receiver and destination. In speech, the voice transmits sound waves which are received by the ears, and the channel is the **vocal–auditory** channel. In writing, the channel is usually **visual**. According to Shannon and Weaver, in both speech and writing the human brain is the information source and the destination, and the message originates in the brain. According to their model, it is when the message is changed into a signal that encoding takes place, but we know from Saussure's model that language in the brain is already in coded form. The Shannon/Weaver model does not go into the psychological structuring of meaning, but concentrates on the effects on meaning of transmission in a communication system. For example, from the engineering point of view, it is important to quantify the amount of **information** that a channel handles. For Shannon and Weaver, and in mathematical communication and information theory in general, the term **information** has a specific, technical meaning. Weaver says (see Shannon and Weaver, 1949, p. 100), 'information is a measure of one's freedom of choice when one selects a message'. The information content of a message therefore has a relation with probability, or to put it another way, with uncertainty, that is to say, with **entropy**. The more probable or predictable a message is the less information content it has. If I know that a message is going to be sent to me, and if I also know its content before it is sent, then when I receive it, it will not be informative. By contrast, the more freedom of choice involved in constructing a message, the more information content it has, because freedom of choice increases the destination's uncertainty about which message has been selected. But the freedom of choice cannot be without limit. There must be a system in place, a set of possible messages to choose from or a limit on the available choices, and we can see language as such a system. In communication theory, entropy is the measurement of the uncertainty of messages and their parts, and therefore the measurement of their information content. The **bit** (a contraction of **binary digit**) is the unit in terms of which the entropy of a message is measured. A bit is a unit of information. One bit is a choice between two equally probable possibilities, for example, between the digits 0 and 1 in 'digital' systems.

Measuring the information content of English-language messages is complicated by the fact that probability shifts as the message proceeds. A sentence is a stream of linguistic elements and will be affected by grammatical structure and the relative frequencies of words and letters or sounds. For example, as Weaver points out (Shannon and Weaver, 1949, p. 102), 'After the three words "in the event" the probability for "that" as the next word is fairly high, and for "elephant" as the next word is very low.' The u that follows a q in the spelling of English words has a high probability. Shannon calculated that the entropy of a written English text declined from about 4.7 bits at its start to between 0.6 and 1.3 bits per letter by the hundredth letter (reported in Pierce, 1980, pp. 101–4). That is, it became more predictable as it proceeded. Any part of a message or signal which is completely predictable, such as the u that follows q, is said to be **redundant**. A communication system in which there is redundancy is, from one point of view, less efficient than one which has no redundancy. On the other hand, redundancy is essential to counteract **noise**.

**Noise** here is a technical term for disturbances that affect a signal while it is in a channel. Noise is undesirable uncertainty affecting a message: static in an analog radio signal or 'snow' or pixellation or break-up on a television picture are noise. In writing, misprints and spelling errors are examples of noise. In speech, noise can be psychological (for example, a daydream), or some kind of distraction (such as a passing elephant), or noise can be . . . noise – for example, in a lecture theatre, if a lecturer's words are drowned out by the sound of a dozen students coughing. Luckily, the English language has inbuilt redundancy, and in many instances this will enable material lost because of noise to be recovered, as in: 'Today's lecture is about [. . . a dozen coughs] relationship [. . . a dozen snorts and splutters] language, meaning [. . . several sneezes] communication.' Enough of this message remains for its hearers to retrieve the missing parts, which in this context are redundant. If, however, part of the final word had been obliterated, leaving only '. . .-ication', then the limits of redundancy might have been passed in this example, whose ending might well be reconstructed as, say, 'mastication' or 'fornication'. Text messaging and instant messaging exploit redundancy, and some of their ways of doing so (by using acronyms or initialisms, other shortenings, and non-standard spellings) are not innovations, but have well-established precedents, as David Crystal (2008, pp. 41–52) points out. Consonants carry more information than vowels, and txtng exploits this too by omitting vwls. Newspaper headlines also take advantage of redundancy. Newspaper headlines tend to omit 'grammatical words', such as **determiners** (like *the, a, this, that*) and **auxiliary verbs** (like *be, do, have*), and other items, while at the same time aiming for intelligibility. This requires some skill, and miscalculation can result in ambiguity or impaired intelligibility, as demonstrated by the following, mainly from my local newspapers:

999 MEN IN ACCIDENT

CYCLISTS TOLD – STICK TO THE ROAD

CITY SEWER TRAFFIC GRIDLOCK

CITY CORNED BEEF EYELASH HORROR

HOLE IN THE WALL RIPPED FROM PUB

DRIVER BLAMES TRAIN CRASH ON BEE

BABY BONUS VOTES

The redundancy fail-safe mechanism in English has difficulty compensating for the terseness of these headlines, though knowing that 999 is the telephone number of the emergency services in Britain, and that CITY is short for 'Swansea City', and that HOLE IN THE WALL is a colloquialism for an ATM helps. We can call this extra information 'contextual', and the importance of context is further illustrated by the next example, in Figure 19.

**FIGURE 19**

It is an advertising logo and it depends on redundancy. Its full form is recognizable as English, and during its life as a logo it made immediate sense to many people, because to these people its missing parts were redundant. They could make it whole again easily. I will explain this example and return to the subject of context shortly.

To sum up the 1949 model: Weaver likens it to 'a very proper and discreet girl' (p. 116) at a telegraph office accepting a telegram, who pays no attention to whether the telegram is embarrassing, joyous, or sad, that is, no attention to its meaning, at least not in the general, everyday sense of the word *meaning*. What this girl is required to do is 'deal with all possible messages' (p. 116). What Weaver is saying is that the Shannon theory is concerned primarily with the statistical measurement of messages and signals, in order to design efficient communication systems. He emphasizes that the theory's use of the term **information** must be distinguished from everyday uses of the term, and the same applies to **noise** and **redundancy**. Nevertheless, although the aims of the 1949 model are restricted, it does provide a serviceable general theory of communication, as well as a basis for further insights. The concept of noise, for example, opens a way into explaining the difference between a message at the point of transmission and at the point of reception. Noise is always likely to be present in the channel and therefore picked up by the receiver along with the signal, and because of noise the very act of sending a message – the act of communicating – will change a message. Communication is communication breakdown!

In speech and writing, noise will intervene between the intentions of the speaker/writer and the interpretations of the hearer/reader. For example, the 'message' that a literary text carries may travel great 'distances' through time and space, and can undergo 'disturbances' due to cultural and linguistic change – think of the distance between the composition in the late fourteenth century of Chaucer's *Canterbury Tales* and its reception by a present-day reader. In theory, any text, old or modern, can 'arrive' at its destination changed, changed by the effects of noise, and when it arrives at multiple destinations (that is, when it is read by many readers), divergent interpretations will arise as a matter of course. This process contributes to the creative essence of a text. When we take this into account, it seems more normal for performances of Lou Reed's *Perfect Day* to result in divergent meanings than not. A development of this idea informs a famous essay, called 'The Death of the Author' (1968), by the critic and semiotician Roland Barthes. In it Barthes argues that a text is at the mercy of the communicative process, so that 'a text's unity lies not in its origin but in its destination' (p. 148). Barthes's view is that a text and its author are also at the mercy of language, and an author's intentions are immersed in the structural play of approximation and ambiguity inherent in language, denying the text an 'ultimate meaning' (p. 147). For Barthes, authorial intention and all its trappings – 'the author, his person, his life, his tastes, his passions' (p. 143) – cannot control the meaning of a text. If we apply this to *Perfect Day*, the meaning of the song cannot be closed down by Lou Reed's intentions, whatever they may be – which is not to say, however, that his intentions, his life, and so on, are irrelevant to its meaning.

John Lyons, who discusses the 1949 model in his authoritative *Semantics* (1977, pp. 36–41), adds his thoughts on the relationship in linguistic communication (conversation, for example) between the source of a message and its destination: 'the participants in the communicative process will always have some knowledge or beliefs about one another and will be continually adjusting their view of one another (and, in particular, of one another's sincerity and reliability) in the course of their communicative interaction' (p. 40). In other words, the communicative situation can be very fluid and the content of the messages pinging back and forth between participants will be affected by their (ongoing) perceptions of each other and of each other's messages. From this we can recognize that a message is affected by the source's mental construction of the destination and of the destination's likely perception of the message, which is a kind of anticipation known as **feedforward**. This happens whether the destination be an individual, or many individuals (such as an audience in a lecture theatre), or many groups of many individuals (as in mass communication via newspapers, the Internet, cinema, and television, where market research can fuel sources' mental constructions). Also, we can recognize that our interpretation (as destinations) of *Perfect Day* can be affected by our perception and knowledge of Lou Reed (as source).

## Conclusion

In the development of modern communication theory, the 1949 model had a formative role, alongside the model proposed by the social scientist Harold Lasswell, which he summed up as 'Who Says What in Which Channel to Whom with What Effect?' (1948). A number of modified versions of Shannon and Weaver have been proposed, for example, David K. Berlo's SMCR model (1960), which fleshes out the attributes of the source, message, channel, and receiver, and the Westley–Maclean model (1957), which clarifies distinctions between interpersonal and mass communication. But the most inclusive reworking of the 1949 model is given in 'Communication' (1988), by Thomas A. Sebeok (1920–2001), a leading figure in the North American tradition of semiotics. Sebeok's model is particularly useful because it also amounts to an amalgamation of the Shannon/Weaver and Saussure models (Saussure being a founding figure in European semiotics). Sebeok's 1988 diagram of communication is reproduced in Figure 20.

Sebeok retains the linear transmission event and adds to it the semiotic notion of the **sign**, that is, something (such as a symbol of some kind) that stands for something else for somebody. 'A message is a

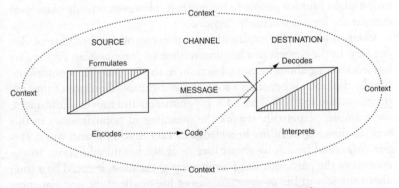

**FIGURE 20**  SEBEOK'S MODEL (1988, p. 29)

*sign,*' he says (p. 23), 'or consists of a string of signs.' As he is concerned primarily with human communication using signs, including linguistic signs, rather than with communications engineering, Sebeok conflates source and transmitter into a single source box, which, however, is divided into two. The shaded half represents the mysterious way in which the human brain formulates a message into a sign or string of signs. Similarly, in the destination box (a conflation of receiver and destination) the shaded area represents the mysterious or as yet 'unfathomed' (p. 26) aspects of the brain's interpretation of the message. Sebeok's initial and final boxes build into the line of communication the notion of a semiotic code of some kind as integral to the formulation and interpretation of messages. One example of such a code would be Saussure's *langue*.

The other major contribution of Sebeok's model is the all-encompassing **context** 'in which the entire transaction is embedded' (p. 29). Context, says Sebeok (p. 29), 'includes the whole range of the animal's cognitive systems (that is, "mind"), messages flowing parallel, as well as the memory of prior messages that have been processed or experienced and, no doubt, the anticipation of future messages expected to be brought into play'. Therefore, despite everything we have learned so far about the act of communication, context 'always decisively influences' (p. 29) the interpretation of a message. Context can determine whether a message can be decoded at all. For example, in the context of 1990s Finland and Sweden, it is highly likely that the message of Figure 19 could be readily decoded as a reduced form of VIKING LINE, a ferry company operating across the Baltic Sea. The company's use of this reduced logo was intended to demonstrate that its name or brand was so well-known, so much a part of Baltic life, that it needed only a slight hint for people to recognize it. However, outside of its local context the logo is less easily decoded.

Context fills out the explanation for the semantic malleability of *Perfect Day*. In the context of a heroin overdose in *Trainspotting*, *Perfect Day* becomes a song about heroin addiction; in the context of a promotional film by the BBC, it becomes a song about the musical output of the corporation; and so on. TV ads, TV programmes, and movie soundtracks, for example, perpetually rework the meanings of popular songs in this way. In the context of my knowledge of Lou Reed's life and work, *Perfect Day* could be a song about love or about heroin addiction. In the context of the particular day I am having at the time, it could be a song about the joys of life or the sadnesses of life or about the consequences of one's actions – or about all of these things. A more recent theory of communication, emerging in the 1990s, known as **relevance theory**, explains, by means of the notion of relevance, the interaction of linguistic meaning and context in producing interpretations. Positioned within **pragmatics** (a branch of linguistics dealing with language in use), arising out of H. P. Grice's work on **inferencing** (linguistic meaning from the hearer's point-of-view), and associated in particular with the work of Dan Sperber and Deirdre Wilson, relevance theory argues that a basic principle of communication is our assumption (as 'destinations') that the information being communicated to us will be relevant to us. Thus we go looking for relevance in the information being communicated. We can take this further: if context includes 'mind' and cognizance of past experiences and messages, then I could 'project' onto *Perfect Day* an interpretation influenced by my inner preoccupations, which adds weight to the view that linguistic communication, based as it is on the psychological code of *langue*, may always involve talking to oneself.

## Further reading

*The Communication Theory Reader* (1996), edited by Paul Cobley, contains a large selection of key writings on communication from the fields of linguistics, semiotics, and literary and media studies. Just as useful is *Communication and Culture: Readings in the Codes of Human Interaction* (1966), edited by Alfred G. Smith, a selection emphasizing work from mathematics and linguistics, and including seminal writings by Warren Weaver, Norbert Wiener (on 'Cybernetics'), and Noam Chomsky. For a general introduction, see *Human Communication* (3rd edn, 1994), by Michal Burgoon, Frank G. Hunsaker and Edwin J. Dawson, and for an accessible introduction to the mathematical theory of communication, see *An Introduction to Information Theory: Symbols, Signals and Noise* (2nd edn, 1980), by John R. Pierce. The principles of relevance theory are presented in *Relevance: Communication and Cognition* (2nd edn, 1995), by Dan Sperber and Deirdre Wilson. Then if you want further to explore work on inferencing, try Stephen C. Levinson's *Presumptive Meanings: The Theory of Generalized Conversational Implicature* (2000), and *Relevance Theory: Applications and Implications* (1998), edited by Robyn Carston and Seiji Uchida. Thomas Sebeok's collection of essays *A Sign is Just a Sign* (1991) is a good starting point for exploration of his work. *Communication and Culture: An Introduction* (2000), by Tony Schirato and Susan Yell, is a useful and wide-ranging guide written from the cultural studies perspective. For an introduction to non-linguistic communication in humans, see *Bodily Communication* (2nd edn, 1988), by Michael Argyle. David Crystal's *txtng: the gr8 db8* (2008) is an excellent study of, and apology for, the text-messaging phenomenon.

# 17 Noam Chomsky and the Generative Enterprise
## Language as It Is if You Don't Have to Bother Talking

---

This chapter includes the following:
- A guide to **transformational generative grammar**.
- Explanation of the **Minimalist Program**.
- An overview of Chomsky's work.
- Chomsky and American linguistics.
- Explanation of the terms **language faculty**, **universal grammar**, **recursion**, **I-language** and **E-language**, **logical form** and **phonetic form**.

---

## Introduction to the Introduction

Here is something that Chomsky said, 'Human language is acquired by exposure, not training...just as breathing is' (as quoted in an article in the *New York Times* in 1975, cited by Barsky, 1997, p. 174). And here is something else that he said, 'The question about language is, "To what extent is it like a snowflake and to what extent is it like a spine?"' (in an interview in Chomsky, 2004, p. 156). Truth be told, over a period of 50 years and more, Chomsky has said so many things about language, and yet one could argue that he also assiduously avoids saying too much, consistently shying away from speculation. His critics, however, claim that speculation is the very basis of Chomsky's hypotheses on language. Much has been said about Chomsky, and his output tends to divide opinion sharply. His work in linguistics has motivated much research by others, a lot of which can be summed up by the characterization 'the Generative Enterprise'. So what is the 'Generative

Enterprise'? What does it say about language? What has it got to do with the English language? What does Chomsky mean by the opening statements above? And who is Chomsky?

## Introduction

Avram Noam Chomsky was born on 7 December 1928 in Philadelphia, Pennsylvania, to immigrant parents from a Russian, ultra-orthodox Jewish background. He began his undergraduate studies at the University of Pennsylvania in 1945, having already developed significant interests in languages, philosophy, logic, and politics. He was awarded his doctorate by Pennsylvania in 1955, for *Transformational Analysis*, actually on the strength of just one chapter of this dissertation. But behind this chapter were nearly 1000 pages of technical notes, out of which he produced *The Logical Structure of Linguistic Theory* (microfilmed in two versions in 1955 and 1956, and published in another version in 1975).

In the same year that he got his doctorate, Chomsky started work at the Massachusetts Institute of Technology (MIT), a scientific university, where he has worked ever since. In 1957, not yet 30, he published *Syntactic Structures*.

This is the book that first propelled Chomsky to fame. Chomsky's work for *The Logical Structure of Linguistic Theory* forms a backdrop to *Syntactic Structures*, though more immediately it arose out of an undergraduate course that he was teaching at MIT. While in part a product of existing trends in American linguistics, *Syntactic Structures* brought about a sea change in the discipline, and showed influences from mathematics, communication theory, psychology, and logic. Robert Lees, in an influential review (1957, pp. 37–8), said that it 'is one of the first serious attempts on the part of a linguist to construct within the tradition of scientific theory-construction a comprehensive theory of language which may be understood in the same sense that a chemical, biological theory is ordinarily understood by experts in those fields'.

Over 50 years on, there is no linguist more famous than Chomsky. He is famous too for his vigorous political activism, informed by a deep mistrust of all brands of centralized government, and is particularly known for his criticism of American foreign policy and aspects of the state of Israel. He has been an extraordinarily prolific writer and public speaker in both politics and linguistics. It is commonly accepted that

*Logical Structure* and *Syntactic Structures* revolutionized linguistics – even invented linguistic theory in the modern sense. Chomsky himself has emphasized the radical break with the past that his work represented, and especially has stressed the revolutionary nature of the later incarnation of the 'Generative Enterprise', that is, the 'Minimalist Program' (MP). And while it is correct that Chomsky's work and the Generative Enterprise have undergone sweeping overhauls since 1957, certain fundamentals remain constant, and even the new moves can be seen to belong to a single, progressive project. The label **Generative Enterprise** is used in the titles of two books based around interviews with Chomsky (1982, 2004), and is one way to describe the research trajectory inspired by his work, now involving scholars in Europe and Japan, as well as in North America. Focusing on Chomsky's output, this chapter will look at the shifts that have occurred in the Enterprise. It will also discuss the constant fundamentals. The relationship between change and perseverance is one of its themes.

One constant fundamental is indicated by the opening quote to this chapter. Chomsky is certain that human language is a biological trait, driven by a '**language faculty**' in the human brain, and emphatically is not merely a cultural phenomenon learned through experience and training. Ask the question, 'Is language a biological organ?' and Chomsky replies (2000a, p. 1), 'it is pretty clear that it is', adding, 'this, I think, gives quite a lot of insight into the essential nature of human beings'.

The comment from Lees points towards another fixed conviction: Chomsky sees his work in linguistics as science, on a par with work in biology, chemistry, and physics, written according to the conceptual, methodological, and formal demands of the scientific method.

The second quote at the beginning of this chapter signals a fundamental question and concern which becomes more explicit as Chomsky's original 'transformational' approach is superseded in the 1980s by the 'principles and parameters' framework and then the '**Minimalist Program**'. Chomsky asks, is language like a snowflake, that is, of perfect and optimal design, or is it like a spine, which is flawed, and prone to problems, but nevertheless is the best that Nature could come up with? What Chomsky wants is a theory that can account for language, and explain it in best and simplest fashion, irrespective of whether language is like a snowflake or a spine, in other words, a theory that is methodologically minimal. He also wants that theory, ultimately, to tell us whether in fact language is like a snowflake or like a spine, in other words, to deal with substantive minimalism, asking in what sense is the human language faculty perfectly designed? These two facets, as we shall see, go together by default. Hence the Minimalist Program stage of the Generative Enterprise.

Much work (though by no means all) in generative linguistics has used the English language as its testing ground. Chomsky has been the leading voice, and this chapter tells the story of his contribution to the Generative Enterprise, and to our understanding of the nature of English specifically and of language as a whole, following him from *Syntactic Structures* to the Minimalist Program, and focusing on these in particular as the journey points that demarcate his career to date. It will include explanation of key terms, a few of which I have already used rather liberally above.

Just before we proceed, I will end this Introduction with another thing that Chomsky said (in 2000a, p. 25) about language. Speaking of certain features (in an example sentence), which although not physically present are nevertheless understood to be there, he said, 'as far as the mind is concerned, they are all there; if you don't have to bother talking, they would all be there'. A remarkable statement? Bear in mind (but perhaps do not say it aloud) that it appears that Chomsky wants a theory that describes language as it is if we don't have to bother talking.

## *Syntactic Structures* (1957): transformational generative grammar

One aspect of Chomsky's style is an impressive line in bracing dismissiveness. He can declare that the greatest dictionary of all, the *Oxford English Dictionary*, is 'much too superficial' (Chomsky, 2000a, p. 12), and that the work of Ferdinand de Saussure is 'in significant measure a serious regression' (private correspondence, 2008). To be fair, lack of context makes these judgements seem starker than they are *in situ*, perhaps, and furthermore, Chomsky is not averse to describing his own earlier work as, in certain ways, in some respects, wrong. So, one might debate the wisdom of appraising his work from its beginnings, when one is aware that, in a sense, everything has changed since *Syntactic Structures*. However, in another sense, and risking a touch of bracingness myself, nothing has changed. Dead ends have been reached, for sure, terms have come, gone, been replaced, quite bewilderingly it seems, adjustments have been made, but throughout there is a persistent endeavour based on an enduring conviction.

With regard to terms, it is best to begin with the description by which the analysis introduced in *Syntactic Structures* became known, **transformational generative grammar**. One word at a time, in reverse order.

The term **grammar**, first, takes us on a short excursion.

At the start of *Syntactic Structures* (p. 11), Chomsky says that a grammar 'can be viewed as a device of some sort for producing the sentences of the language under analysis'. Not for the last time, Chomsky's choice of terminology, though precise, proved open to misinterpretation. Words like *device* and *produce* misled many, says Lyons (1991, p. 42), into assuming that Chomsky thought of a grammar as some sort of software and/or hardware capable of replicating the behaviour of a speaker (an idea that was topical in 1950s linguistics). But these terms are abstract, not literal, and are drawn from mathematics, in keeping with Chomsky's aim of formalizing grammatical description after the manner of mathematical description. And yet, as Chomsky's work proceeds, we find that his notion of **universal grammar** or **UG** equates with his notion of the **language faculty**, or **faculty of language**, often abbreviated to **FL**, and that the FL is indeed a 'device' of biological engineering that forms part or parts of the human brain.

If we look at Chomsky's 1959 review of Burrhus Frederic Skinner's book *Verbal Behavior* (1957), we find early expressions of the UG viewpoint. In this review, the 30-year-old Chomsky rips through the behaviourist theories of Skinner (1904–90), an eminent figure in the field of psychology. **Behaviourism** originated in psychology in the work of John Broadus Watson (1878–1958). Chomsky (1959, online reprint) rejects as futile, impoverished, and even 'astonishing' the behaviourist belief that the acquisition of language in humans can be explained entirely by reference to external factors provided by environment and experience. That is to say, the belief that we learn language, our 'verbal behaviour', solely by means of the training provided by experience, through stimulation and reinforcement. Chomsky (1959) does not deny that 'reinforcement, casual observation, and natural inquisitiveness (coupled with a strong tendency to imitate) are important factors' in a child's acquisition of language, but adds, 'as is the remarkable capacity of the child to generalize, hypothesize, and "process information" in a variety of very special and apparently highly complex ways which we cannot yet describe or begin to understand, and which may be largely innate'. The suggestion of innateness is important, and is enlarged upon elsewhere in the review, showing that Chomsky means by this an inherent, evolved linguistic property of the human brain (the language faculty), that is activated by experience, leading to a child's acquisition of his or her native language. The research that Chomsky had already begun aims to discover the exact nature of this innate mental property, and leads to the Generative Enterprise.

In the review of Skinner, and in *Syntactic Structures*, we see evidence of Chomsky's intense dissatisfaction with the then dominant approach in North American linguistics. That approach was **structuralist** and **descriptivist**, as well as behaviourist.

In essence, the structuralist view of language is concerned with roles and systems. The structuralist is interested in the role that a sound, or a word, or a unit of grammar has in relation to other sounds, words, or units in a language. For example, although the sounds represented by the letters *b* and *p* in the English words *bit* and *pit* are phonetically very similar (they differ only in that *b* is **voiced** and *p* is not), a structuralist analysis shows that these are two separate **phonemes** in English, because the (small) phonetic contrast between the two is used to distinguish words and meanings, in English, as evidenced by *bit* and *pit*. Finnish, on the other hand, does not have separate *b* and *p* phonemes. Different languages make use of the array of possible consonant and vowel sounds to create different phonemic systems. The structuralist is interested in describing such linguistic systems (in pronunciation, vocabulary, grammar) and how they work.

In Europe, twentieth-century structuralist linguistics followed the conceptual lead provided by Saussure's *Course in General Linguistics* (1916). In North America, it became characterized by a more practical concentration on collecting data in the field, and on developing the necessary methodologies for doing so, because of a major interest in describing the previously undocumented indigenous languages of North America. Consequently, the label **descriptivist** has been used for much American linguistics of the 1930s–1950s. Franz Boas (1858–1942) was an influential figure, as was his follower, Edward Sapir (1884–1939), both of them primarily anthropologists.

Another leading figure was Leonard Bloomfield (1887–1949), best known for his 1933 book, *Language*. Bloomfield's linguistics was not only descriptivist, it was also behaviourist. In addition, Bloomfield was influenced by the early twentieth-century, European school of philosophy known as **logical positivism**, which emphasized the importance of observable, verifiable data. Bloomfield aimed to make linguistics more scientific, precise, and rigorous by considering only events and data that could be directly observed or physically measured, and his behaviourist approach rested on explanation in terms of an organism's *responses* to *stimuli* in the environment. For example, saying 'Fetch me that apple' is a linguistic response to seeing an apple while hungry. Problematic areas, like human thought, or 'mind', were of necessity either in some measure redefined according to such principles, or ignored. In this approach, therefore, **semantics** or the study of meaning is seriously weakened, and it was neglected in North American linguistics up to and including the publication in 1951 of *Methods in Structural Linguistics* by Zellig Sabbatei Harris (1909–92), who was Chomsky's mentor.

Chomsky rejected the behaviourist doctrine. Also, his work moved away from the descriptivist view of data – for Chomsky, any account of language derived from analysis of a body or **corpus** of collected material (items of speech, for example) will be limited by the character and size of that corpus. In each language 'there are infinitely many sentences' (Chomsky, 1957, p. 13), and a grammar of a given language must in some way provide the blueprint for all the grammatical sentences of that language. Moreover, he says, in his review (1959) of Skinner:

> It appears that we recognize a new item as a sentence not because it matches some familiar item in any simple way, but because it is generated by the grammar that each individual has somehow and in some form internalized. And we understand a new sentence, in part, because we are somehow capable of determining the process by which this sentence is derived in this grammar.

This takes us back to the terms *grammar* and *generative* in *Syntactic Structures*, but first, let me finish summarizing the transition from mid-twentieth-century American linguistics to Chomsky's work. Chomsky's scientific linguistics, unlike that of Bloomfield, explores the human mind, or the 'mind-brain' as he comes to call it. This exploration is necessary because of Chomsky's conviction about the innate, internalized nature of our language knowledge. Whereas Bloomfieldian linguistics is **empiricist** (concerned with directly observable sense-data), Chomsky's work is **mentalist** (concerned with investigation of the human mind) and **rationalist** (allowing reason rather than sense-data to form the basis of scientific enquiry). As it progresses, therefore, the Generative Enterprise increasingly contributes to the new multi-discipline of **cognitive science**, the science of the mind. And Chomsky focuses on grammar and semantics as the crucial areas of language, neglected by those who preceded him in America. Also, Chomsky's dismissal of Saussure's work as a 'serious regression' is due to Saussure's lack of attention to grammar.

While Chomsky's notion of what he would later call *universal grammar* forms an enveloping setting for *Syntactic Structures*, the term **grammar** introduced at the start of the book refers to that blueprint of an individual language, mentioned above. Remember, the argument goes like this: a language has infinitely many sentences, and a native speaker of a language is able to recognize as grammatical or ungrammatical any new sequence which he or she encounters, because of the internalized 'device' possessed by that speaker, by means of which a grammatical sentence is 'derived' or formed or, using the term (again drawn from mathematics) Chomsky settles on, '**generated**'. He says (1957, p. 13), 'The grammar of L [the language] will thus be a device that generates all of the grammatical sequences of L and none of the ungrammatical ones.' This **generative grammar**, then, is a representation of the nature of a language's grammaticality and of the process by means of which speakers recognize and produce grammatical sentences. It is decidedly, absolutely not a manual for guiding speakers, nor a description based on any corpus of real speech. As Chomsky's work proceeds, it becomes obvious that his grammar of a language is concerned with **syntax** (sentence structure), **morphology** (word structure), **phonology** (sound systems), and **semantics** (meaning). More usually, in other schools of linguistics, grammar is seen as the study of syntax and morphology only. **Transformations** have a place in the generative grammar that Chomsky devises, but we must cover a little more ground before we reach the grammar's transformational component.

In *Syntactic Structures*, Chomsky discusses three models for the description of a language. These are **finite state grammar**, **phrase structure grammar**, and **transformational grammar**. The guide below to *Syntactic Structures* provides basic detail on the Chomskyan way of thinking about language.

## Finite State Grammar

Pinocchio, we know, cannot get away with a lie, for if he lies, his nose grows. In the film *Shrek the Third* (2007), under probing interrogation from Prince Charming, Pinocchio tries neither to lie nor tell the truth about the whereabouts of Shrek. But are his sentences grammatical? 'On the contrary, I'm possibly more or less, not definitely rejecting the idea, that in no way, with any amount of uncertainty, that I undeniably do or do not know where he shouldn't probably be. If that indeed wasn't where he isn't. Even if he wasn't not where I knew he was could mean that I wouldn't completely not know where he wasn't.' The goal for a satisfactory grammar, rather obviously, is that it should define grammaticality in a language. However, if by *grammaticality* we mean the capacity to distinguish grammatical or well-formed sentences from ungrammatical or ill-formed sentences, when (i) the number of sentences in a language is theoretically infinite, because a language is open-ended in its creativity, leading always to new sentences, even peculiar ones like Pinocchio's, and (ii) the length of any one sentence is also theoretically infinite, as we can imagine one of Pinocchio's becoming, then we begin to see the size of the task facing Chomsky. He could set about describing, one by one, the infinitude of sentences, but this will produce a grammar that is 'practically useless' (Chomsky, 1957, p. 18), and not much different from actually saying the infinitude of sentences. And it is an impossible, never-ending task. It would also be an admission of failure, because of Chomsky's hypothesis that there has to be a simpler, elegant key to the infinitude of sentences – to the **creativity** or **open-endedness** of a language – because otherwise human infants would be unable to acquire language. Such a failure has not been countenanced by Chomsky. A major weakness of twentieth-century structuralist linguistics, for Chomsky, is its disregard of this creative aspect of language use. It is also why he is able to call even the most comprehensive list of linguistic items, like the *Oxford English Dictionary*, 'superficial'. Such enterprises are simply not concerned with accounting for our ability to grasp and acquire a language.

The creative infinity that a language has is a **discrete infinity**, that is, it is structured on discrete items – words, or to be more technical, **morphemes** (grammatical units). The morphemes are structured out of **phonemes** (sound units), which are limited in number, and which have no intrinsic meaning, but which can be combined in sequences, enabling the creation of limitless numbers of morphemes and sentences, which do have meaning. If one accepts that a language is creative and open-ended, and that there is a simple, elegant key to its creativity, it is reasonable to suggest that the key (the grammar) must involve only a finite number of operations and also must include the facility to repeat essentially the same operation over and over (like Pinocchio's accumulation of negative verb-forms), and placing parts within parts, thoughts within thoughts. This is **recursion**, the recurrence of elements in a structure, allowing us to insert chunks of language (like, 'who is a wooden puppet') into other chunks (like 'Pinocchio replied ingeniously'), without limit if we wish ('Pinocchio, who is a wooden puppet, whose father was called Geppetto, who [...] replied ingeniously'). The full description of the nature of recursion in language and the pursuit of a truly limited set of grammatical rules are the central quests of the Generative Enterprise.

A finite state grammar is the simplest type of grammar discussed by Chomsky in 1957 that, 'with a finite amount of apparatus, can generate an infinite number of sentences' (p. 24). In the model provided by a finite state grammar, a sentence is generated by a sequence of choices made in a 'left-to-right' direction. The first choice of the first element in a sentence is the leftmost choice. Each subsequent choice is determined in some degree by the preceding elements. Take the following simple examples used by Chomsky (1957, p. 19): *the man comes, the men come, the old man comes, the old old man comes, the old men come, the old old men come*. The leftmost choice is *the*, one of many words that can be used at the start of an English sentence. If the noun chosen to follow *the* is singular, like *man*, this dictates that the verb which follows the noun must be in agreement, and is also singular in form, *comes*. If plural *men* is chosen, it must be followed by a plural verb-form. And so on. It is also possible to insert a qualifier, such as the adjective *old*, which may be introduced more than once, forming a recursive loop. For this group, and the choices involved, a simple *state diagram* can be constructed (Figure 21).

A finite state grammar, then, proceeds through a finite number of internal 'states' from *initial state* to *final state*. In doing so, it defines grammatical sequences. However, on the one hand, the grammar becomes cumbersome when applied to long sentences, and on the other, it is too narrow to account for all (grammatical) English sentences. 'English is not a finite state language', says Chomsky (1957, p. 21), because English has sentences in which there are such dependencies not

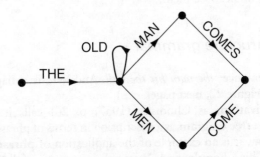

**FIGURE 21** STATE DIAGRAM FROM CHOMSKY (1957, p. 19)

only between adjacent syntactic units, but also between units which are separated by a sequence of other units – and that sequence itself may be sentence-like in character and contain interdependent words which are separated by another sequence of units, and so forth. For instance (and to adapt one of Chomsky's illustrations (p. 22)), in *The man who said that if such-and-such is the case, then this-and-this will happen, is arriving today*, there is a dependency between *The man* and the second *is*, and also between *if* and *then*. This repeated insertion of sentence-like sequences within a sentence is another example of recursion. A consequence of this is **displacement** or **dislocation** – of the local relation between *The man* and *is arriving today*, for example – a point which we shall return to later.

Chomsky concludes (1957, p. 24) that 'we are forced to search for some more powerful type of grammar and some more "abstract" form of linguistic theory', adding, 'on some level, it will not be the case that each sentence is represented simply as a finite sequence of elements of some sort, generated from left to right by some simple device'. To generate non-finite languages such as English, therefore, an abstract linguistic level must be postulated. This is a crucial point. It demonstrates Chomsky's certainty about how any human language works and is understood in the human mind, which is not self-explanatory in the left-to-right ordering of (for example) English sentences as we speak them. In other words, there is a disparity between the apparent structure of sentences as we hear/see them and how we actually understand them – something is hidden from view, but is nevertheless understood to be there. As far as the mind is concerned, it is there; if you don't have to bother talking, it would all be there. For Chomsky, there must be a further, simple, basic, mental linguistic level. *Syntactic Structures* presents his first major attempt to describe it and how it relates to sentences as we hear/see them.

## Phrase structure grammar

Here is a sentence: *the man hit the ball*. And here is a diagram of its derivation (Figure 22, next page).

The **derivation**, as Chomsky (1957, p. 26) calls it, of which Figure 22 is a **tree diagram**, is a description in terms of phrase structure. That is to say, it is an example of the application of **phrase structure grammar**. This Chomsky finds 'essentially more powerful' (p. 30) than the finite state model.

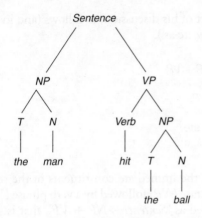

**FIGURE 22**  TREE DIAGRAM FROM CHOMSKY (1957, p. 27)

Chomsky's phrase structure grammar is a version of **immediate constituent analysis**, a mode familiar to the Bloomfieldian linguists. It is a type of *parsing*, that is, a breaking down of sentences into their constituent parts. Constituent analysis does this stage by stage, gradually zooming in until we reach constituents which cannot be broken down any further. Chomsky presents (p. 27) his grammatical derivation of *the man hit the ball* as follows:

Sentence
NP + VP                                    (i)
T + N + VP                                 (ii)
T + N + Verb + NP                          (iii)
the + N + Verb + NP                        (iv)
the + man + Verb + NP                      (v)
the + man + hit + NP                       (vi)
the + man + hit + T + N                    (ii)
the + man + hit + the + N                  (iv)
the + man + hit + the + ball               (v)

While the tree diagram gives a clear, accessible view, the nine-line derivation of the sentence additionally shows the order in which the analysis has been made. The derivation uses the six rules (i–vi) of the simple example phrase structure grammar which Chomsky establishes

(p. 26) at the start of his discussion, as follows (and in which the arrow
→ stands for 'rewrite as'):

  (i)   *Sentence*→ *NP* + *VP*
  (ii)  *NP*→ *T* + *N*
 (iii)  *VP*→ *Verb* + *NP*
 (iv)  *T*→ *the*
  (v)  *N*→ *man, ball,* etc.
 (vi)  *Verb*→ *hit, took,* etc.

In this grammar, the immediate constituents of the sentence are analysed as a noun phrase (*NP*) followed by a verb phrase (*VP*), and this first
rule (i) is expressed as '*Sentence*→ *NP* + *VP*', that is, 'rewrite *Sentence*
as *NP* + *VP*'. Subsequently, we learn that the immediate constituents
of *NP* are *T* + *N* (rule (ii)); that *T* is 'rewritten' as *the* (iv); that *N* is
rewritten as *man, ball,* or any other noun (v); that the immediate constituents of *VP* are *Verb* + *NP* (iii); and that *Verb* is rewritten as *hit*,
or *took*, or any other verb (vi). We already know, from rules (ii, iv, v),
the constituents of *NP* in *VP*. This elementary phrase structure grammar provides basic tools, in the form of rules, by means of which we
can characterize the structural derivation of *the man hit the ball*, and of
other English sentences.

Note that in the full nine-line derivation above there are still only six
rules, for rules (ii), (iv), and (v) each apply twice.

In Chomsky's model, such a grammar begins with an **initial string**
(*Sentence*), then proceeds through a finite set of **instruction formulas**
or rules (1957, p. 29), ending with a **terminal string**, that is, a string
which cannot be further broken down by the phrase structure grammar
(other than by rules which specify phonemes). Each instruction formula
'rewrites' only one element – 'only a single element can be rewritten in
any single rule' (p. 29). In all of this, the goal is clarity and precision, so
that derivations and their tree diagrams enable us to reconstruct (almost
at a glance) the phrase structure of each sentence of the language (each
terminal string of the grammar) (p. 30).

So, in phrase structure grammar a sentence is analysed as a set of
syntactic parts, revealed by means of constituent analysis, and which
can be represented in a tree diagram. In the diagram above, we see
that the sequence *hit the ball* can be traced back to the constituent
*VP*, whereas the sequence *man hit* cannot be traced back to any
single constituent, and does not constitute a syntactic component
in the sentence (Chomsky, 1957, p. 28). In fact, *man* and *hit* are

separated by a constituent boundary. Constituent analysis or phrase structure grammar is commonly used by linguists, and tree diagrams have become prevalent. Phrase structure grammar is used to teach elementary syntax, and, at the other end of the spectrum, it has been developed from the early 1980s into sophisticated theories in competition with the Generative Enterprise, specifically 'Generalized Phrase Structure Grammar' and its successor, 'Head-Driven Phrase Structure Grammar'. Nonetheless, in 1957, in *Syntactic Structures*, after proposing some ways in which his phrase structure grammar could be refined (pp. 28–9, 32–3), Chomsky moves on to transformations.

## Transformations

Here is a transformation:

If $S_1$ is a grammatical sentence of the form

$$NP_1 - Aux - V - NP_2,$$

then the corresponding string of the form

$$NP_2 - Aux + be + en - V - by + NP_1$$

is also a grammatical sentence. (Chomsky, 1957, p. 43)

This is the **passive transformation**, which sets out the relation between **active** and **passive sentences** in English. But what does it all mean, and how does Chomsky arrive at the transformational idea?

Chomsky's (1957, p. 35) view is that, with regard to phrase structure grammar, 'As soon as we consider any sentences beyond the simplest type, and in particular, when we attempt to define some order among the rules that produce these sentences, we find that we run into numerous difficulties and complications.' In this again we see his quest for an elegant, simple theory. The more complex a grammar becomes, the less revealing it is, and the further away it is from providing the key to understanding language acquisition. This belief persists through a half-century of endeavour to his recent work, as we shall see very shortly.

Chomsky (1957, pp. 35–43) chooses three examples to illustrate the inadequacy of phrase structure grammars. This leads him to put forward transformational rules, giving 'an entirely new conception of linguistic structure' (p. 44), and without which phrase structure grammars 'will be so hopelessly complex that they will be without interest' (p. 44). The transformations, therefore, supplement the phrase structure grammar.

His first example is **conjunction**: a productive way to form new sentences in English, such as by the use of the word *and*. Two sentences can be combined into one using this conjunction: *the scene – of the movie – was in Chicago* and *the scene – of the play – was in Chicago* can be combined into *the scene – of the movie and of the play – was in Chicago* (p. 35). In general, this can only happen if, for example, *of the movie* and *of the play* are constituents of their respective sentences (that is, each can be traced back to a single origin), and, moreover, constituents of the same type. A useful grammatical rule can be formulated to cover this phenomenon (p. 36). However, it is not a rule that can be incorporated into a phrase structure grammar, for it does not flow directly on from a single preceding string, but refers necessarily to the whole constituent structure of the existing two sentences. In a sense, then, it is an operation – a 'transformation' – that occurs after the phrase structure grammar. Or, as Chomsky puts it (p. 38), 'the state of the machine [the phrase structure grammar] is completely determined by the string it has just produced (i.e., by the last step of the derivation)', and the conjunction rule 'requires a more powerful machine, which can "look back" to earlier strings in the derivation in order to determine how to produce the next step'.

Chomsky (1957, pp. 38–42) uses the behaviour of **auxiliary verbs** (such as *has, will, be* – auxiliaries modify the main or root verb-form in some way) in English to formulate more rules of the same type, before reaching his third example, the **active-passive relation**, upon which we will dwell a little.

*John admires sincerity* is an **active** sentence. *Sincerity is admired by John* is a **passive** sentence. The terms refer to the role – active or passive – that the **subject** (*John* in the first sentence, *Sincerity* in the second) takes. Although they are syntactically and stylistically different, the native speaker of English intuitively sees these two sentences as semantically equivalent, that is, their meaning is essentially the same. Chomsky shows (pp. 42–3) that the passive auxiliary verb phrase (for example, *is admired*) is quite exceptional among verb forms, and that it would require a whole set of restriction rules in a phrase structure grammar. A more elegant solution is the transformational rule reproduced above at the start of this section. $S_1$ is an active and grammatical sentence, such as *John* [$NP_1$] *admires* [*Aux – V*] *sincerity* [$NP_2$]. *Aux* is the singular *–s* **affix** (add-on) of the verb, in this case. If the stated elements of $S_1$ are inverted and adjusted into the form

$NP_2 - Aux + be + en - V - by + NP_1$, then that (corresponding) string will also be a grammatical but passive sentence: *Sincerity* $[NP_2]$ *is admired* $[Aux + be + en - V]$ *by* $[by]$ *John* $[NP_1]$. Here $be + en$ is the notation that Chomsky gives for the verbal element used for the passive, and *Aux* now is the $-d$ affix. This rule is 'well beyond' the limits of phrase structure grammars, because 'it requires reference to the constituent structure of the string to which it applies and it carries out an inversion on this string in a structurally determined manner' (p. 43). It is a rule which applies to the whole structure of the active sentence, and it specifies the syntactic relation of the two sentences.

We have now reached the point of departure. Chomsky (1957) has demonstrated the limited adequacy of phrase structure grammar, and has presented us with some new rules 'which materially simplify the description of English' (p. 44), and which he calls **grammatical transformations**. 'A grammatical transformation T operates on a given string (or . . . on a set of strings) with a given constituent structure and converts it into a new string with a new derived constituent structure' (p. 44). He goes on to formulate several more transformations (dealing with, for example, negation, and interrogatives), discuss the active–passive transformation further, and begin to devise an order of application of rules in the new, composite grammar. He is optimistic that his grammar will prove to be 'simpler than any proposed alternative' (p. 84), and an overriding principle for Chomsky is simplicity, for reasons already mentioned.

By the end of *Syntactic Structures*, Chomsky has produced (in its early form) his 'device' or grammar 'for generating all and only the sentences of a language' (p. 85), which has led him to describe English 'in terms of a set of levels of representation, some of which are quite abstract and non-trivial' (p. 85). At the same time, put another way, this grammar 'is simply a description of a certain set of utterances, namely, those which it generates' (p. 48). In this grammar, the transformations are the hidden operations that lie beneath our understanding of the sentences we hear and see.

What happened next?

Transformational generative grammar got popular. It continued to be controversial. It got modified. Many linguists took it up. It led to the Generative Enterprise. Chomsky's publications paved the way. His refinement, in *Aspects of the Theory of Syntax* (1965), established what became known as the **standard theory** of generative linguistics, which was revised into the **extended standard theory** by the mid-1970s, incorporating **X-bar theory**, which aimed to simplify the analysis of phrase structure rules. His *Lectures on Government and Binding* (1981) ushered in the **principles and parameters** (**P&P**) framework, which became the **Minimalist Program** by the early 1990s. Throughout these shifts, the explanation of recursion remains a central goal, on the basis that the generation of infinite sentences using finite resources must involve repeated, looped operations.

## The Minimalist Program

Fast-forward to 2002 and an article in the journal *Science*:

> We assume, putting aside the precise mechanisms, that a key component of FLN is a computational system (narrow syntax) that generates internal representations and maps them into the sensory-motor interface by the phonological system, and into the conceptual-intentional interface by the (formal) semantic system ... All approaches agree that a core property of FLN is recursion, attributed to narrow syntax in the conception just outlined. FLN takes a finite set of elements and yields a potentially infinite array of discrete expressions. This capacity of FLN yields discrete infinity (a property that also characterizes the natural numbers). Each of these discrete expressions is then passed to the sensory-motor and conceptual-intentional systems, which process and elaborate this information in the use of language. Each expression is, in this sense, a pairing of sound and meaning.   (Hauser, Chomsky and Fitch, 2002, p. 1571)

As Richard Dreyfuss says in *Close Encounters of the Third Kind* (1977), 'This means something ...'. But what?

In fact, much of the content of the quote above is more familiar than it might at first seem. In this extract from a collaboration with the evolutionary biologists Marc D. Hauser and W. Tecumseh Fitch, we see again the centrality of recursion and of discrete infinity, the idea of a (universal) grammar that is generative, and the notion of a (mental, biological) language faculty – **FLN** here stands for 'faculty of language–narrow sense', distinguished from **FLB** 'faculty of language–broad sense'. The authors propose that FLN is the (human, cognitive) 'computational' system of grammar, and that its core computations are limited to recursion, producing linguistic expressions, and they propose that FLN supplies these to two other 'organism-internal systems', the **sensory-motor** or **SM** system (sense and motion, or articulation and perception) and the **conceptual-intentional** or **CI** system (ideas and purposes, the thought system), each of which imposes its own restrictions on the form of the expressions in order for it to be able to process them. The outcome is language – a joining of sound and meaning, generated by FLN, or universal grammar. FLB is the combination of these three systems. Chomsky has been talking in such terms for some years. His work in the Minimalist Program (MP) of the Generative Enterprise feeds into the collaboration with Hauser and Fitch. The inauguration of the MP is usually taken to be a 1993 essay by Chomsky, but the chief trait of the Program is its pursuit of theoretical economy and simplicity, which, as we have seen, also characterizes *Syntactic Structures*. The underlying conviction in the extract above also goes right back to Chomsky's work in the 1950s.

In the MP, the relationship between syntax and two other components, sound and meaning, is recast in terms of **interfaces** between FLN and the SM and CI systems respectively. Professor Chomsky provides a brief outline of these interfaces:

> Turning to generative grammar, each of us has mastered an internal language (I-language), a system that generates an infinite array of structured expressions, each of which has a meaning and a sound (though it turns out that sound is only one form of externalization of language; sign [sign language] is dramatically similar). Rephrasing, we can say that each expression provides information for thought systems (the conceptual-intentional (CI) interface) and for externalization (the sensorimotor (SM) interface). It is common these days to use the term LF [Logical Form] for the structure generated at the CI interface. That, however, is not the way the term was defined, which leads to confusion. Let's use it in the common rather than the technical way, and call the structure at the SM interface PF [Phonetic Form]. Then we can say that the I-language generates pairs (PF, LF), connecting sound and meaning, roughly in Aristotle's sense.   (Chomsky, private correspondence, 2008)

The term **I-language** was introduced by Chomsky in 1986, in order to clarify the notion of **competence** developed first in *Aspects of the Theory of Syntax* (1965). Every individual has an **I-** or **internalized-language** – it is that mastery or knowledge of language that a human is genetically endowed with. Universal grammar is therefore a theory of I-language. I-language is contrasted with **E-language**, just as previously competence was contrasted with **performance**. E-language is an abbreviation of **externalized-language**, which refers to the collection of sentences enabled by I-language. It is thus a subtly different construct from performance, which referred to the individual's actual use of language in real situations.

Also in 1965, Chomsky introduced the distinction between **deep structure** and **surface structure**. The deep structure of a sentence is a grammatical description concerned with meaning; surface structure is concerned with the sentence's 'translation' into sound. The concepts are precursors to **Logical Form** and **Phonetic Form** respectively, though Chomsky emphasizes that there is only a 'loose relation' between the two sets, and that, 'The terms "deep" and "surface" structure are best eliminated, I think, as a historical residue of earlier efforts to formulate a theory of I-language' (private correspondence, 2008). This is because the apparatus has been in constant refinement since 1957. Many constructs have been and continue to be *re*constructed. Even transformations. In 1981 (p. 18), transformations were reduced to a single rule: **move α** (move alpha), sometimes summed up as 'move anything anywhere'. In effect, move α says that any constituent of a structure can be moved anywhere else in a sentence, and if a particular movement is not possible, that restriction must be explained. So it is really exceptions which must be described rather than rules, and transformations are reconfigured as movements, induced by the 'legibility conditions' imposed at the 'boundaries' between FLN and SM, and FLN and CI.

In the principles and parameters approach launched in 1981, it was assumed that the properties of the language faculty were general **principles**, principles which apply across languages. And it was assumed that there were also 'slight options of variation' (Chomsky, 2000a, p. 14), that is, the range of variants that a principle can assume across languages, termed **parameters**. Behind this is the familiar Chomskyan view that the key to language is elegant, simple, coupled with the concomitant conviction that variation in and across languages is superficial in nature. This line is developed further in the Minimalist Program, which asks the snowflake-or-spine question, that is, 'how good a solution is language to certain boundary conditions that are imposed by the architecture of the mind?' (Chomsky, 2000a, p. 17) The phrase 'architecture of the mind' refers in particular to the SM and CI systems. In order for the human language faculty to operate as a language faculty it must be able to 'communicate' with these systems. It must interface successfully with them. The systems must be able to read what FLN provides. There are restrictions on its design and workings, therefore, which are imposed by other cognitive and physiological limitations, such as our abilities with regard to structured sequences of sound (the

SM system) and to structured expressions of meaning about the world (the CI system). The SM system will require that an expression has a temporal order (2000a, p. 19), in order for perception and articulation to happen. The use of speech as a vehicle for language requires sentences to be linear – a sentence must occur as a linear sequence, one element or unit after another – and in the Chomskyan view this leads to a restructuring and in some respects an effacing of the linguistic patterns that FLN presents to the SM system. The CI system will require 'certain kinds of information about words and phrases and certain kinds of relations among them' (2000a, p. 19). Whether we are dealing with the MP or *Syntactic Structures*, the conviction is that 'it doesn't follow that the structure of the language is determined by the exigencies of how it is received by us' (as John Collins puts it in his book-length guide to Chomsky (2008, p. 56)). In other words, what we concretely hear/see is not identical with what we understand, that is, is not identical with the pre-interface sentence. In the Chomskyan view, as we know, the infinitude of concrete sentences must be underpinned by simplicity. The MP is the current, developing framework for investigating the nature of this simplicity, and it proposes that even the apparent imperfections of language might be explicable as characteristic of an optimal design.

For example, 'One dramatic imperfection in human language is the property of displacement', says Chomsky (2000a, p. 23), 'which seems to be universal' and 'looks rather intricate'. In the sentence *the book seems to have been stolen* (2000a, pp. 23–6), there is a hidden, understood local relation between *book* and *stolen*, which has been displaced by intervening words. But that local relation is still seen by the mind, otherwise we would not grasp the meaning of the sentence. What we hear is *the book seems to have been stolen*, but what we grasp is *the book seems to have been stolen [the book]*. The mind sees the local relation as well as the **displacement**, and the movement between the two can be subsumed, along with all other possible 'transformational' movements, under move α. In a further theoretical development, the phrase is assumed to have been 'copied' from one place and attached somewhere else. According to **copy theory** (Chomsky, 1993), the mind sees all the copies, but the original occurrence has its phonetic content deleted at the SM interface (and is then left unpronounced), and its copy is foregrounded, made more prominent, in its new position. The attraction of such an account is that it shows displacement to be a simple operation, and an optimal FLN solution to interface legibility conditions. Moreover, *parameters* or 'slight options of variation' can be said to apply at the interfaces, and variations which occur across different languages can be said to be superficial and due to variations in the ways in which the SM and CI systems access (and modify) the deeper, and uniform linguistic information.

## Conclusion

Is Chomsky right? To respond in the style of Pinocchio: one cannot not say that there is a need unequivocally to make a judgement, or not make a non-judgement, with regard to the correctness or incorrectness of Chomsky's assumptions, but on the other hand, and so on. Put another way, one cannot say for sure. His hypothesis is persuasive: 'that languages must somehow be extremely simple and very much like one another; otherwise, you couldn't acquire of them' (Chomsky, 2000a, p. 13). But it has always had its opponents. I mention some of them in **Further reading**, below. The approach of the Generative Enterprise is, 'try to abstract general principles and properties of rule systems, take them to be properties of the language faculty itself (of language as such, in other words) and try to show that when you do so, the residue, what is left when you've done that, is much less complex and varied than it looks' (2000a, p. 13). The goal has been constant, but the project's narrative is cyclic, with each major attempt at minimalism breeding a proliferation of analyses, followed by a culling of terms and constructs, a rethink, and then a more radical attempt at minimalism. There is a range of possible verdicts to reach. Hauser, Chomsky and Fitch (2002, p. 1578) conclude by saying that linguists, biologists, psychologists, and anthropologists 'can move beyond unproductive theoretical debate to a more collaborative, empirically focused and comparative research program' of investigation into the FL. It is a statement that both announces the next stage of the mission begun by Chomsky in the 1950s, and, tellingly, carries an echo of his call in the 1959 review of Skinner for 'research, not dogmatic and perfectly arbitrary claims'.

## Further reading

The best extended introduction to the full range of Chomsky's work on language is *Chomsky: A Guide for the Perplexed* (2008), by John Collins. Also useful, and clear, is *Chomskyan Linguistics and its Competitors* (2007), by Pius ten Hacken. Another good guide is *Chomsky's Universal Grammar: An Introduction* (3rd edn, 2007), by V. J. Cook and Mark Newson. As for tackling the primary material, the lengthy, testing but gratifying route would be to read some of the key works in chronological order: *Syntactic Structures* (1957), *Aspects of the Theory of Syntax* (1965), *Lectures on Government and Binding* (1981), and *The Minimalist Program* (1995). If you prefer a more sensible shortcut, use *The Architecture of Language* (2000a), which is the text of a lecture delivered in Delhi in 1996, together with the follow-up discussion. Chomsky is at his most accessible when responding to questions, and *On Nature and Language* (2002) and *The Generative Enterprise Revisited* (2004), both of which contain interviews, are excellent appraisals of the major themes. With regard to critical writings on Chomsky's linguistics, *On Noam Chomsky: Critical Essays* (1974), edited by Gilbert Harman, is a good source for early commentaries, and *Chomsky and His Critics* (2003), edited by Louise M. Antony and Norbert Hornstein, has Chomsky responding to essays on his work by other academics. Charles F. Hockett's *The State of the Art* (1968) is an important critique by a leading linguist unconvinced by Chomsky's theory. In 2005, an article by Daniel Everett, 'Cultural Constraints on Grammar and Cognition in Pirahã' (*Current Anthropology*, Volume 46, Number 4, August–October 2005, pp. 621–46), which drew on Everett's knowledge of the language of the Pirahã tribe of the Amazon, caused controversy in the world of linguistic theory, by arguing that Pirahã did not exhibit recursion. There has been a divided response to the validity of Everett's claims. The best starting point for a tour of the debate is actually Everett's website, which has many helpful links, at: http://www.llc.ilstu.edu/dlevere/. But see also 'Pirahã Exceptionality: A Reassessment' (2007), by Andrew Ira Nevins, David Pesetsky and Cilene Rodrigues, which refutes Everett's analysis. It can be accessed at: http://www-rohan.sdsu.edu/~gawron/mathling/readings/nevinsEtAl_07_Piraha-Exce.pdf. For a succinct biography of Chomsky, use *Noam Chomsky* (2006), by Wolfgang B. Sperlich. *Noam Chomsky: A Life of Dissent* (1997), by Robert F. Barsky, gives a fuller picture, though it is less up to date.

# 18 The Nature of Language
## Linguistic Theory and the Question of Origins

This chapter includes the following:
- The origins of speech.
- Language and the brain.
- Introductions to the **'language instinct'**, the **'symbolic species'**, and the **'FLN/FLB'** theories.
- A brief introduction to the origins of writing.

## Introduction

Somebody somewhere once must have spoken the first words, you would think. Imagine the scene.

*A:* Hi!

*B:* Hi!

*A:* Thank goodness, at last someone I can talk to. For days I've been wandering the savannah looking for someone to talk to about my amazing discovery – language! I can communicate!

*B:* Hi!

*A:* Yes, hi! Here, have a bamboo shoot. Now there's a thing, how did I know that this woody, edible grass is called 'bamboo'? How do I know it's a grass? And why am I speaking English?

*B:* Hi!

*A:* Yes, hi...me *Homo sapiens*, you...well, what are you? *Homo heidelbergensis*?

*B:* Hi!

*A:* Oh dear, I don't think you can speak, can you? When you say 'Hi!' you are merely uttering a short sequence of sounds which, as far as you are concerned, has no meaning. But surely a language depends on

284

an underlying network of relational symbolic signs of a largely arbitrary and conventionalized character which can only have developed through communal agreement? So, how am I able to speak, then? Maybe my brain has an evolved and activated language faculty, enabling me to process syntax, whereas yours does not. If so, how did that happen? But the existence of a language presupposes the existence of a speaking community, does it not? And while we are on that point, surely a speaking community can only emerge through the use of language? How on earth does it all begin? It seems to me to be a classic 'chicken-and-egg' question.

B: Hi!

Imagining the origin of language will perhaps always be a matter of imagining an impossible event – if one is searching for an event. And answering the question of how language originated *will* always involve imagining, speculating. The origin of language is by definition prehistoric, because the definition of *prehistoric* is 'of or relating to the period before written records', and it is generally agreed that writing emerged some time after the advent of speech, which is often seen as the original medium for language, and speech does not fossilize, all of which suggests that speculation cannot be eliminated from the language origins issue. It seems that neither the historical record nor the prehistoric archaeological record can save the search for language origins from speculation and conjecture. This is an uncomfortable situation for linguists.

Famously, at least for linguists interested in the origin of language, the *Société Linguistique de Paris* in 1866 agreed a standing rule barring the topic from its meetings, on the grounds that discussion of it was futile. At the start of the twentieth century, the pioneer of modern linguistics, Ferdinand de Saussure, argued that because 'No society, in fact, knows or has ever known language [that is, a particular language] other than as a product inherited from preceding generations, and one to be accepted as such', then 'the question of the origin of speech [that is, language in general] is not so important as it is generally assumed to be'; indeed, 'The question is not even worth asking' (Saussure, 1916, pp. 71–2). As far as Saussure was concerned, linguistics should be the study of 'the normal, regular life' (p. 72) of existing languages. The best-known linguist of the second half of the twentieth century, Noam Chomsky, commenting on the question of the origin of language, said, 'Here there are some speculations, nothing more, and they do not seem persuasive' (1988, pp. 169–70), and, 'We just do not know enough about human evolution to be able to answer this question' (p. 189). Given the unwelcome lack of hard data and excess of conjecture, why should one bother to discuss the origin of language here and now, especially in a book about only one, particular, present-day language? In the context of the language origins issue, English is a very, very recent phenomenon, being just over 1500 years old, whereas language as a human trait is anywhere from 40,000 to 3 million years old, possibly. In the context of studying the English language ... well, why *does* this book need a chapter on the origin of language?

The blunt answer is that the topic is unavoidable. That is to say, any theory of language, any theory which attempts to explain the nature or workings of language, will presuppose a certain kind of origin for language, although that theory may not address its presupposition at length or even at all. Saussure and Chomsky did not consider the origins issue worth exploring, but each of their theories imagines a beginning for language – or perhaps it is fairer to say that they lead us towards imagining a beginning for language, and (as we shall see) the Saussurean beginning is quite different from the Chomskyan. The Saussurean and Chomskyan views each inform many discussions in modern language study. Furthermore, one can argue that any description of a particular language will imply an opinion on the nature of language in general, and somewhere down the line also a view on the origin of language. Once we start to think about it, views on the origin of language turn up all over the place. One of the most basic assumptions about language is that it defines us as humans. As Chomsky (2000b, p. 3) puts it, 'The human faculty of language seems to be a true "species property", varying little among humans and without significant analogue elsewhere', a statement which carries with it a certain picture of the origin of language. In *The Symbolic Species* (1997), the neuroscientist Terrence Deacon says (p. 14), 'assumptions about the nature of language and the differences between nonhuman and human minds are implicit in almost every philosophical and scientific theory concerned with cognition, knowledge, or human social behavior' (p. 14), and this means that implicit views about the origin of language are pretty ubiquitous. That is why this book has a chapter on the origin of language. It is a topic that is relevant to everything else in the book. Besides, as Deacon says (p. 23), 'Knowing how something originated often is the best clue to how it works.' Or, looking at it slightly differently, the search for origins may well still involve speculation – though less so than when the *Société Linguistique de Paris* banned the topic – but it also casts a very revealing light over all our views about language and languages.

THE NATURE OF LANGUAGE

In this chapter, then, we try to picture the origin of language. We look at what the Saussurean and Chomskyan views of language tell us about its beginnings, and we look at how research in palaeontology, neuroscience, and evolutionary biology has advanced the study of language origins. We consider the origin of speech and (briefly) the origin of writing, while noting that discovering the origin of speech and writing does not necessarily amount to the same thing as discovering the origin of language. We look also at what Chomsky had to say when he eventually got drawn into the debate about origins. In doing all of this we will be looking at the most fundamental qualities of language generally and of any particular language, such as English.

## The 'language instinct' theory

Long, long ago, a long, long time before our present era, I took a beginner's course in linguistics. I remember learning of a number of theories about the origin of language. They were the 'Bow-wow Theory', the 'Pooh-pooh Theory', the 'Ding-dong Theory', the 'Yo-he-ho Theory', the 'Tra-la Theory', the 'Ta-ta Theory', and the 'Deceit Theory'. According to the Bow-wow Theory, language originated in imitation of the noises of animals, that is, it was essentially onomatopoeic. The Pooh-pooh Theory says that language originated in instinctive emotional exclamations; the Ding-dong Theory says that the sounds of language have inherent meaning (for example, a p-sound is violent, an m-sound is calm); the Yo-he-ho, that language arose out of involuntary grunts of effort; the Tra-la, that early language was musical, merely expressive. The Ta-ta Theory is the view that speech organs imitate actions carried out by other parts of the body, and is more normally labelled the 'Gesture Theory', that is, the view that gestural language preceded speech. The Deceit Theory holds that language arose because people wished to obscure their real feelings. The main source for this outline of origins theories was Charles Barber's *The Story of Language* (1972, pp. 27–37), which summarized the work of a number of scholars, Otto Jespersen (1860–1943) being one, though the tradition of quirky nicknames goes back to the nineteenth century. It is a quite disparate collection of theories, and taken individually none is at all adequate as it stands, but neither is it sensible to dismiss any of them out of hand. None of them gets to the heart of the matter, but each to some degree suggests possible fundamental characteristics of early language.

In 1994, the psycholinguist Steven Pinker, in his *The Language Instinct*, put forward a much fuller explication of language, its nature and origins. Pinker's argument amalgamates two persuasive theories, **universal grammar theory** and **evolution theory**. In other words, he brings together the work of two influential scholars, Noam Chomsky and Charles Darwin.

Chomsky is associated with **generative linguistics**, a school of thought which has mutated and evolved since its first formulations in the late 1950s, though a summary of its main, most relevant claims can be presented here. When Chomsky talks of the human **faculty of language** he is referring to a key construct in his theory. It is a faculty possessed by the human brain which enables us to be linguistic beings. Says Chomsky (2000b, p. 4), 'The faculty of language can reasonably be regarded as a "language organ" in the sense in which scientists speak of the visual system, or immune system, or circulatory system, as organs of the body.' It is thus an innate, biological apparatus which equips us for language, more precisely a set of modular units in the brain which are 'dedicated to language' (Chomsky, 2000b, p. 117). This is not to say that such an apparatus or 'organ', as specified in Chomskyan terms, has yet been discovered – it is, I will repeat, a theoretical construct. **Universal grammar** is 'the theory of the initial state of the language faculty' (2000b, p. 73), that is, 'the language faculty before any experience' (Chomsky, 1988, p. 61). Universal grammar aims to describe the syntactic categories, constraints, and processes shared by all human languages. In Chomsky's theory, the term **grammar** – as opposed to the term **universal grammar** – refers to a description of a particular language (English, Swahili, Japanese, Spanish, whatever), that is to say, 'The grammar of a particular language is an account of the state of the language faculty after it has been presented with data of experience' (1988, p. 61). It is this grammar that has been called also a **generative grammar**, because the language faculty, after its activation by experience (by environment, by life), 'generates' all the expressions of a particular language used by an individual. In the generative approach, analysis of a language aims to specify principal devices in **syntax** (sentence formation), such as **phrase structure rules**, which describe basic or **deep structure**, and **transformations**, which modify deep structure to produce **surface structure** variations (for example, the inversion in word order in English which changes a basic sentence structure into a question – *You can read* becomes *Can you read?*). Chomsky's generative approach metamorphosed in the 1990s into the **Minimalist Program**, which continued the quest for universal grammar, but also called into question the notions of deep and surface structure. (You can read more about the development of Chomsky's work in the preceding chapter of this book; in this chapter, we focus on its relevance to the origins question.)

The logic of Chomsky's theory of universal grammar arises out of the observation that there are fundamental similarities between all of the world's languages, and the observation that children acquire language remarkably efficiently and rapidly. The most satisfactory explanation of these phenomena, for Chomsky, is that each human brain must possess a language 'organ', a biological programme for language or **language acquisition device** or universal grammar. **Faculty of language** is another of its labels. In accordance with this view, the Chomskyan linguist believes that the great diversity exhibited by the world's languages 'can be no more than superficial appearance' (Chomsky, 2000b, p. 7).

For Chomsky, the language faculty is a biological fact waiting to be discovered. Just as nineteenth-century chemistry provided the abstract theories that led to the discovery of the atom and the molecule, linguists must postulate abstract structures 'for which we have to search for the physical basis' (Chomsky, 1988, p. 186). Chomsky deduces that the language faculty 'is an expression of the genes' (2000b, p. 4), but suggested that finding out exactly how this happens is 'a distant prospect for inquiry' (2000b, p. 4). Steven Pinker, however, argued (1994) that there was much to be gained from merging Chomsky's ideas with evolution theory, in order to account for the origins of the language faculty – and it is from this that his phrase 'the language instinct' develops. Language, for Pinker, is 'a biological adaptation to communicate information' (1994, p. 19); it is an instinct because the biological make-up of our brains compels us to be linguistic.

Pinker maintains that language can be accounted for by the central notion in Darwin's theory, **natural selection**. This is because, according to Pinker (1994, pp. 358–64), the human language faculty fits into Darwin's category of 'Organs of extreme perfection and complication', and Darwin is concerned to demonstrate that even such complex, sophisticated organs can be formed by natural selection (Darwin, 1859, pp. 217–24). All that natural selection needs in order to do its work are variation in a species and a great, great amount of time. **Natural selection** is the name for the view that species evolve with the help of minuscule changes happening unceasingly across great periods of time, in a process which inevitably supports the 'preservation of favourable variations and the rejection of injurious variations' (Darwin, 1859, p. 131) – because the latter are 'bred out' (they are by their very character liable to being bred out) and the former are 'bred in'. Taking the eye as an example of a perfected, complex organ, Darwin acknowledges that it is 'scarcely ever possible' (p. 218) to discover the gradations by which such an organ has been perfected through time by studying only its ancestry in one species. But the diversity of 'eyes' among the whole group of arthropod species (crustaceans and so on), from 'an optic nerve merely coated with pigment' to eyes of 'a moderately high stage of perfection' (p. 218), permits us to conceive of possible gradations in the evolution of the eye in vertebrate species.

According to Pinker, the language instinct (our biological drive to speak) is like the eye – complex, perfected, and brought about by natural selection. The physical realization of the language instinct is in 'intricately structured neural circuits, laid down by a cascade of precisely timed genetic events' (Pinker, 1994, p. 362), and this sustains our ability to grasp syntactic and phonological (or sound) structures, to acquire vocabulary, and it underpins our speech perception and the other parts of the language instinct, each of which in Pinker's view is an adaptation produced by natural selection. An initial favourable variation has led to a long line of progressive neurological changes tied into the evolution of language.

This leaves questions begging, like exactly how does the brain deal with language? And when did humans first become linguistic?

## Language origins and the brain

The human brain has two halves or hemispheres, a left hemisphere and a right hemisphere, which are covered in a layer of grey tissue called the cerebral cortex. This main mass of the brain is the cerebrum. Underneath the cerebrum are, in evolutionary terms, older parts of the brain – the limbic system and the cerebellum or 'little brain', and further down still, the brainstem, which evolved over 500 million years ago. Already we see that over (immense periods of) time, the human brain has changed remarkably. It is the highly developed cerebrum that distinguishes us as human.

Much of what we know of the workings of the human brain comes from studying individuals suffering from brain impairments or injuries, and more recently from the use of advanced scanning techniques such as positron emission tomography (PET) and functional magnetic resonance imaging (fMRI), both of which map areas of brain activity. The nerve cells that create brain activity are known as neurons (100 billion of them in each brain), which are connected up in large neural networks and are adapted to carry electrical signals. The neurons are surrounded by glial cells (1000 billion of them), that support the neurons and execute numerous other functions. The information required to produce these cells is genetic – it comes from our genes. One of the chief themes of research has been the **localization** of brain functions, that is, linking different kinds of cognitive function to different areas of the brain, for example, identifying which parts of the brain deal with visual images, which deal with execution of body movement, which deal with language, and so on. Two well-known language areas were first identified in the nineteenth century. The neurologist Paul Pierre Broca (1824–80) discovered **Broca's area**, at the side and towards the front of the left hemisphere of the cortex. Individuals with damage to this area can understand speech but have difficulties in speaking (this condition is known as *Broca's aphasia*). The neurologist Carl Wernicke (1848–1905), not unnaturally, discovered **Wernicke's area**, located in the left hemisphere, at the side, behind Broca's area. Individuals with damage to Wernicke's area can produce fluently constructed speech but use wrong or inappropriate words and cannot monitor their speech (*Wernicke's aphasia*). Thus it has been suggested that Broca's area is concerned with speech production and Wernicke's with speech comprehension. Other areas of the left hemisphere have been linked to other linguistic functions, such as listening, writing, and reading. In a minority of people, particularly among people who are left-handed, these language areas are located in the *right* hemisphere of the cortex. Nevertheless, left or right hemisphere, the existence of these language areas would support the view that not only are the functions of the brain localized, but they are also **lateralized**, that is, specific functions have developed within one or the other hemisphere, a view we will come back to shortly.

Broca's area forms a raised lump on the surface of the human brain, with the result that it leaves its imprint on the human skull, and thereby gives us the possibility of fossil evidence of language – imprints of Broca's area on fossil skulls. A skull known by its catalogue number in the National Museum of Kenya, ER 1470, discovered by Bernard Ngeneo, a fieldworker employed by the palaeoanthropologist Richard Leakey in 1972 near Lake Turkana, north-eastern Kenya, and dated at about two million years old (Leakey, 1994, p. 129), was examined by the neurologist Ralph Holloway, who made a cast of the interior of the skull. The cast indicated that the brain that once occupied the skull had Broca's area and also that there was a slight asymmetry in its left–right configuration (Leakey, 1994, p. 129, and Holloway, 1983, pp. 109 and 113), in other words, a suggestion of lateralization. Says

Holloway (1974, p. 110), 'this very ancient and relatively large brain was essentially human in neurological organization', while Leakey concludes (1994, p. 129) that it was likely that the owner of the brain had been able to communicate 'with more than the pant–hoot–grunt repertoire of modern chimpanzees'. Does this prove that speech goes back at least two million years? Not conclusively. Why not? Because, disappointingly, as Pinker (1994, p. 310) puts it, 'the role of Broca's area in language is maddeningly unclear'. While there is a correlation between a certain kind of linguistic disorder and damage to Broca's area, the correlation is not absolute. For example, the symptoms of Broca's aphasia can be produced by damage to other parts of the brain, and damage to Broca's area alone, in itself does not usually lead to protracted and severe aphasia. In addition, monkey brains can also have a small area homologous to Broca's area (and another homologous to Wernicke's), which seems to be used for controlling the muscles of the face and vocal tract and for processing sensory information (Pinker, 1994, p. 350). So we cannot be sure about the functions of KNM-ER 1470's Broca's area.

Similarly, we cannot be certain about the roles of your or my Broca's and Wernicke's areas. There is evidence that they are involved in linguistic functions, but there is also evidence that linguistic functions are associated with a scattering of brain regions, and that the functions of a damaged area can be taken over by another area if damage occurs at an early age. Pinker says (p. 317), 'We will never understand language organs and grammar genes by looking only for postage-stamp-sized blobs of brain.' The language 'organ', for Pinker, is there in 'the wiring of the intricate networks that make up the cortex, networks with millions of neurons' (p. 317), and the 'grammar genes' would be the stretches of DNA that specify the proteins that work the neurons that work language (p. 322). (Pinker imagines (in some detail) the actions of a network of neurons dealing with the phonetic, grammatical, and lexical aspects of the third-person, singular, present tense regular verb inflection of English, that is, -s as in *Bill walks* (pp. 318–20).)

Pinker's view still holds even if not only the localization but also the lateralization of brain functions turns out to be less clear-cut than it has seemed. In an article in *New Scientist* (3 July 1999, pp. 26–30), surveying research on lateralization, John McCrone reported on brain-scanning experiments that showed activity in both hemispheres during language tasks: 'Areas on the left dealt with the core aspects of speech such as grammar and word production, while aspects such as intonation and emphasis lit up the right side' (p. 28). The suggestion was that it is processing styles rather than functions that distinguish the two hemispheres, though even this may be a simplification. McCrone concluded (p. 30), 'It is how the two sides of the brain complement and combine that counts.' While localization and lateralization can be identified, the brain is an integrated whole, with very many interconnections between the regions. Greenfield and Leek (1999, p. 49) say, 'Whatever is innate [in the brain, with regard to language acquisition] seems to have a more general or abstract quality.'

The work of Terrence Deacon adds weight to the view that it is unwise to see the language functions of the brain as limited to the left hemisphere. He agrees that there *is* lateralization of language functions, but points out also that 'The right hemisphere is not the non-language hemisphere' (Deacon, 1997, p. 311), that is, in Deacon's terms, there are language functions in both hemispheres which do in fact combine and complement each other. For example, patients with extensive right-hemisphere damage can generally speak well but may fail to comprehend the logic of a story or joke (Deacon, 1997, p. 312). The point that Deacon makes is that getting a joke tends to require grasping conflicting senses – there will be an unexpected twist, an 'illogical' logic which catches us off guard, as can happen when two senses are connected by the same form in wordplay (in a pun, for example). This has to do with our understanding of words as symbolic **signs** operating in a symbolic system or network. The meaning or meanings of a word depend not so much on the word's relationship to the thing(s) it refers to but on the role it plays – the place or space it occupies – in the symbolic system, that is, in a language. It depends on its relationships with other words. Jokes often depend on wordplay and wordplay often depends on the fact that two words similar in form can have different or conflicting senses, or that one form can have different senses. The play is possible because of relationships within the system, because of the associations and contrasts between the elements of the system, associations and contrasts which ultimately delimit and define the elements. Understanding language requires us to grasp the principles of a symbolic system and of symbols working associatively, 'playing off' one another. Deacon argues (p. 313) that there are paired neural networks in the left and right hemispheres of the brain, the left concerned with the kind of grammatical analysis that Pinker writes about, the right with symbolic information.

## The 'symbolic species' theory

Now we have returned to the Saussurean view of language, which is that a language is a symbolic system of **linguistic signs** (in summary, words) in which meaning arises out of the interplay of relationships between the signs. Deacon does not invoke Saussure (in fact, in his one reference to Saussure he rather misapprehends his work), but Deacon's view of language is certainly Saussurean and semiotic, that is, it treats language as a sign system (**semiotics** is the study of sign systems). Deacon's account of the origin of language, in *The Symbolic Species* (1997), is very much in keeping with Saussurean theory. He is therefore working with a different perspective on language from that of Pinker and Chomsky (who focus on underlying grammar), and this entails a different analysis of the linguistic functions of the brain and their origin, and a distinctive account of the origin of language.

For Deacon, the increase in brain size relative to body size during human evolution is a crucial factor in identifying when language originated. There is general agreement among scholars that one of the main reasons (if not *the* main reason) for the large human brain is language; but a large brain, in terms of natural selection, is not necessarily a good thing. It's heavy and it's big, growing remarkably during the post-natal period. The evolutionary benefits need to outweigh these drawbacks, and a capacity for language seems to be a principal benefit. If the fossil record of our hominid ancestors were to show a significant increase in brain size relative to body size at some point, this would suggest a period for the initial development of linguistic abilities. Bearing in mind that the fossil record of hominid evolution is still sparse (though much less sparse than at the time of the *Société Linguistique de Paris*'s ban), it shows the following broad trends: (a) a comparatively static estimated body weight from around three million years ago until modern *Homo sapiens*, and (b) a persistent steep rise in estimated brain volume from three million years ago to the present, with what seems to be a first significant enlargement around two million years ago, with the appearance of the type labelled *Homo habilis* (Deacon, 1997, pp. 343–4). It is this first increase that has been taken to mark the origin of the genus *Homo* – the meandering, with-some-extinct-branches evolutionary line that leads from *habilis* to *rudolfensis* to *erectus* to *heidelbergensis* to *sapiens*. Associated with this brain expansion and the genus *Homo* is the appearance in the record between two and two-and-a-half million years ago of stone tools – the beginning of the Stone Age – at sites in east and southern Africa. A simple interpretation of these 'events' is that natural selection led to the modification of the human brain which allowed the use of stone tools and of language to develop. This would fit with a Pinkerian perspective. The accounts of Steven Mithen (1996) and of Robin Dunbar (1996) provide another slant on this: that the advent of bipedalism and of meat-eating (leading to anatomical change which allowed better vocalization), together then with living in larger groups, fostered tool-making and (later) communication through language, and that brain expansion initially is associated with meat-eating and tool-making. Deacon's account, however, is unusual in that it places the beginnings of language early on in the process, before a whole series of other changes, including brain expansion:

> Stone tools and symbols must both, then, be the architects of the *Australopithecus–Homo* transition [*Australopithecus* is an early hominid genus], and not its consequences. The large brains, stone tools, reduction in dentition [compared with apes, early hominids did not have large canines – teeth, that is, not dogs], better opposability of thumb and fingers, and more complete bipedality found in post-australopithecine hominids are the physical echoes of a threshold already crossed.   (Deacon, 1997, p. 348)

The detail of the ordering of events in this account needs more teasing out, but the point to emphasize here is that for Deacon the essential characteristic of language is that it is a symbolic system. The search for the origin of language has usually centred on speech, but Deacon focuses on the origin of symbols. Using the influential semiotic theory of C. S. Peirce, Deacon describes (pp. 70–9) a hierarchy of **signs**: at the bottom, **iconic signs**, which resemble what they stand for (for example, a portrait or other likeness, such as camouflage); **indexical signs**, which are symptoms of what they stand for (smoke *means* fire, for example); and, at the top of the hierarchy, **symbolic signs**, which have a conventionalized relationship with what they stand for (for example, a wedding ring symbolizes marriage, a salute symbolizes respect, homage). Animals, argues Deacon, can grasp iconic signs (they can notice the resemblance between one thing and another) and indexical signs (they can learn to associate one thing with another, even to the extent of associating an alarm call with the presence of a predator), but humans alone have crossed the 'symbolic threshold'. Only humans have learned to establish and use the communally agreed relationship between a symbolic sign and its meaning, such as that between a word and its meaning. Only humans have grasped the inherently systemic nature of symbolic meaning. Deacon says (p. 99), 'symbols cannot be understood as an unstructured collection of tokens that map to a collection of referents because symbols don't just represent things in the world, they also represent each other'. Or, as Saussure said of language

(1916, p. 121), 'In language, as in any semiological system, whatever distinguishes one sign from the others constitutes it.' Meaning arises out of the interplay of relationships between symbolic signs. Each sign is defined by the others in the system. Using symbolic signs requires cognition of a different order, but it does not, according to Deacon, require a language organ in the brain.

Experiments have shown that, with a great deal of support and reinforcement, and in a limited fashion, chimps can use symbols, proving that 'a modern human brain is not an essential precondition for symbolic communication' (Deacon, 1997, p. 401). What happened originally was that our hominid ancestors crossed the symbolic threshold. Unlike the chimps in present-day experiments, they had no teachers. The necessary support, according to Deacon, came from ritual and from a social imperative. The first, fragile symbolic communication would have developed out of ritualistic use of signs of an iconic and indexical character, probably gestures and vocalizations mainly, which would gradually have evolved into a closed set of conventionalized signs (p. 407). In this context, **ritual** would be repetition of the same set of actions in the same circumstances over and over again. To illustrate how repetition of iconic and indexical signs can lead to symbolism, Deacon (pp. 403–5) draws a comparison with the peacemaking rituals of the Yanomamö Indians of Venezuela and Brazil, which involve ceremonial simulations of warlike and peaceful gestures. Like Mithen and Dunbar, Deacon associates the development of language with the group-living that evolved following the shift to meat-eating. But whereas Mithen and Dunbar suggest that speech emerged as a more efficient form of social bonding (more efficient, that is, than grooming), Deacon sees symbolic communication as a necessary countermeasure to a new situation which upset the status quo of hominid society. His argument, briefly, is as follows.

Deacon argues (pp. 384–5) that there are two particularly distinctive features of human society: language, and the fact that males and females tend to maintain exclusive sexual relationships, reinforced by societal codes, within a context of cooperative, communal living. He suggests that group-living was likely in early hominids, pointing out that it is 'not uncommon in the rest of the primates' (p. 387), but unlike other primates early hominids adopted 'pair bonding' – cooperative pairing involving exclusive attachments between a male and a female. There is a correlation between pair bonding and a relatively small difference between male and female body size, and the hominid fossil record shows the difference between male and female body sizes reducing after the australopithecines. This situation – pair bonding within group-living – is destabilized by the addition of meat to the hominid diet, as evidenced by the use of stone tools for butchering carcasses, because this suggests that some members of the group, most likely some males, would be periodically absent, away scavenging or hunting, and this in turn would allow the remaining males to cuckold those absent. Thus a change in behaviour, to tool-assisted meat-eating, created what Deacon calls 'intrinsically unstable reproductive arrangements' (p. 392), which were 'stabilized by a unique form of social communication' (p. 393). That is to say, crude symbolic communication developed, through ritual, in response to a need to 'refer publicly and unambiguously to certain abstract social relationships and their future extension, including reciprocal obligations and prohibitions' (p. 401). In other words, tool-assisted meat-eating 'drove hominids into a niche where symbolic communication was critical' (Deacon, private correspondence, 2001) in order to announce and safeguard exclusive male–female attachments. In summary, meat + communal living + 'marriage' = language.

Deacon estimates that 'use of simple special-purpose symbolic communication (for reproductive partner "negotiation" and food distribution) had become routine by at least two million years before the present' (private correspondence, 2001). Once the symbolic threshold was crossed, probably in the lead-up to *Homo habilis* (that is, over two million years ago), a new behavioural environment was established for natural selection to operate in, and a range of advantageous traits would have developed in response to selection pressures. Some of them, such as bipedality and dexterity, were already in process. Those circuits of hominid brains (particularly towards the front of the cortex) suited to dealing with symbolic communication developed apace. Language itself evolved in tandem with these adaptations. (Deacon argues (1997, pp. 102–15) that the brains of children are especially adapted to acquiring symbolic understanding, and that language is especially adapted to the brains of children.) Eventually, perhaps beginning around one-and-three-quarter million years ago (p. 409), the unusual human vocal tract, with its low larynx, began to evolve, as the importance of vocalizations in symbolic communication increased. (The modern human vocal tract is well adapted to speaking, but at a cost. The high larynx that baby humans and most mammals have allows simultaneous breathing and swallowing, whereas low-larynxed adult humans are at greater risk of choking.) What Deacon describes is a 'co-evolutionary' snowball of behavioural and biological adaptations, which began with symbols and led eventually to the beginnings of speech, with the consequence that 'a general-purpose protolanguage with a complex mixture of speech and gesture became routine by 1.6 million years before the present' (Deacon, private correspondence, 2001). His theory does not require a language 'organ', nor special mutations, nor does it need Bow-wow-pooh-pooh-tra-la-type scenarios. Symbols came first, speech came later.

## The 'FLN/FLB' theory

Chomsky responds, briefly, to Deacon in *On Nature and Language* (2002), and is, mostly, dismissive. His view remains (p. 85) that 'It is hard to avoid the conclusion that a part of the human biological endowment is a specialized "language organ," the faculty of language (FL)', and that this FL 'is an expression of the genes'. In this, he is with Pinker. However, the publication by Chomsky in 2002 of an article co-written with Marc D. Hauser and W. Tecumseh Fitch started a renewed debate on the evolution of FL, and a lengthy exchange with Steven Pinker, and his collaborator, Ray Jackendoff, in the scientific journal, *Cognition* (see Pinker and Jackendoff, 2005; Fitch, Hauser and Chomsky, 2005; and Jackendoff and Pinker, 2005). This, then, is not a discussion about the when and where of language origins, but is a dispute between 'innatists', and quite an involved dispute, about the precise character of the language faculty.

Hauser, Chomsky and Fitch (2002) propose a refinement to the notion of the language faculty, by distinguishing between the faculty of language in the broad sense (FLB) and in the narrow sense (FLN). They propose that FLN computes only the core operation of syntax, namely **recursion**, which accounts for the creative open-endedness of language, that is, the fact that an infinite number of sentences can be generated from a finite set of components and rules. There is no limit in theory, for example, to the number of times adjectives may modify a noun in a sentence, or adverbs modify a verb, or to the number of phrases that may be inserted into a sentence, in English. These are all examples of recursion, which refers to operations which can be repeatedly applied, over and over. FLB, say Hauser, Chomsky and Fitch, is FLN plus other mental systems which are relevant to language, specifically those concerned with production and perception of sound and meaning. Their article summarizes research on communication in other species, and they postulate that it is only FLN that is uniquely human. For example, they say that research shows that some animals (such as cotton-top tamarins) can perceive speech to the extent of being able to extract word-like units within a continuous stream of speech (Fitch, Hauser and Chomsky, 2005, p. 195). They also point out (2005, pp. 198–9) that permanently descended larynges have been discovered in other mammals (the cat family, some species of deer), and they argue (p. 190) that the human FOXP2 gene – which has been implicated in the 'wiring-up' of brain regions for language – 'is nearly identical in form to a homologous [of similar origin and development] gene in other mammals, and the consequences of its expression [production of a protein] are not specific to speech or language'. All of these features belong to FLB, and FLB 'has an ancient evolutionary history, long predating the emergence of language' (2002, p. 1573). This leaves FLN, whose functions, they propose, are determined by conditions imposed by the interfaces FLN has with the other mental systems in FLB. Ultimately, FLN is 'constrained by biophysical, developmental, and computational factors shared with other vertebrates', and it is these pre-existing constraints that have fashioned FLN rather than 'direct shaping by natural selection targeted specifically at communication' (2002, p. 1574). In all of this we see the combination of the comparative evolutionary biology of Fitch and Hauser, and Chomsky's Minimalist Program linguistics (though it adjusts his stance on origins somewhat). Crucially, they conclude that it looks as if the language faculty is not a dedicated biological adaptation after all, that is, FL may have evolved for reasons other than language. In this view, there is no Pinkerian 'language instinct'. Hence the *Cognition* 'conversation' with Pinker and Jackendoff.

Pinker and Jackendoff do not go along with the FLN/FLB distinction as proposed by Hauser et al., though they do agree that some such separation of core and outer properties is useful. They also have a different position on what constitutes uniquely human biological adaptations, arguing that a trait that 'has been modified in the course of human evolution to such a degree that it is different in significant aspects from its evolutionary precursors (presumably as a result of adaptation to a new function that the trait was selected to serve)' (Jackendoff and Pinker, 2005, p. 214), can be considered a uniquely human adaptation. They think (pp. 214–15) that the most likely source for a uniquely human language system is the accumulation of the 'extensive duplications, modifications, expansions, and interconnections of pre-existing primate systems'. The FOXP2 gene, they argue (pp. 215–16), is not only uniquely human but is *primarily* 'language-facilitating', leading to more precise coordination of mouth and face movements. Jackendoff and Pinker offer a '**construction-based**' view of language that stresses the importance of the mind's stored representations of morphemes (individual units of grammar), words, and idioms, representations which associate sound structure with slices of syntactic structure (such as words and idioms) with meaning. Compared with the strict Chomskyan standpoint in generative linguistics, this is a move towards Saussure, though it is influenced by computational linguistics. In the construction-based view, syntax is the solution to the problem of how to combine and express these representations in linear strings (broadly speaking, it 'unifies' them, matches them together); it is not the core generative component of language. The construction-based theory has the 'happy consequence', say Jackendoff and Pinker (2005, p. 223), of making it 'natural to conceive of syntax as having evolved subsequent to two other important aspects of language', these being the symbolic use of utterances (as put forward by Deacon, 1997), and the evolution of phonological (sound) structure as a way of distinguishing and forming words. In all of this from Pinker and Jackendoff, the notion of language as a biological adaptation persists.

## The origins of writing

Usually, the first writing is dated to the fourth millennium BC, on the evidence of clay accounting tablets from ancient Sumer in the Middle East. These tablets were inscribed with symbols which recorded lists of objects and persons. Gradually the Sumerians adopted conventions that now seem intrinsic to writing – basically that it should be organized in lines read in a constant direction – and from their earliest pictorial signs they developed phonetic signs, to represent sounds and grammatical elements. But written symbols go back much further than the fourth millennium BC.

Wherever in the world we find sites of prehistoric cave art we will also see so-called abstract signs: dots, lines, triangular, quadrangular, oval, and other shapes. The examples in Figure 23 are from the

**FIGURE 23**   'ABSTRACT SIGNS' FROM FONT-DE-GAUME CAVE, DORDOGNE, FRANCE (from Daubisse et al., 1994, pp. 16, 28)

Font-de-Gaume cave in Périgord, France (extracted from Daubisse et al., 1994, pp. 16, 28). When I visited Font-de-Gaume, our guide said that these signs were 'abstract' because 'we do not know their meaning'. These written signs of the Upper Palaeolithic period (40,000–10,000 years ago) of the Stone Age, probably do (or did) have meaning, but meaning which we are as yet unable to decipher. One major study

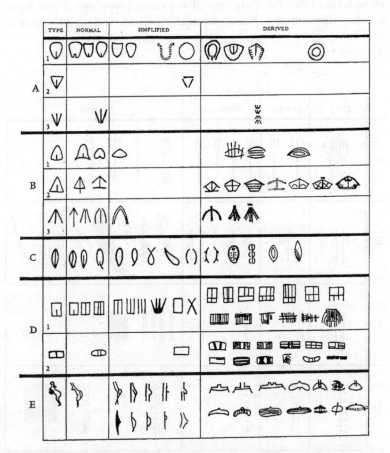

**FIGURE 24**   TYPOLOGY OF FEMALE SIGNS (André Leroi-Gourhan, 1968, p. 513)

The categories: **A and B**, triangular signs; **C**, oval signs; **D**, quadrangular signs; **E**, claviform signs – 'strokes with a semi-circular projection on one side or even simply a short line' (p. 146).

is that by the prehistorian André Leroi-Gourhan (1911–86) in his monumental survey of prehistoric art (1968). He says (p. 137), 'When each set of signs was analyzed separately, it leaped to the eye that the ovals, triangles, and quadrangular signs were all more or less abstract variations on the vulvas which appear among the earliest works of prehistoric art. As for the dots and strokes, it was obvious that they are male signs, although their degree of abstraction is beyond any simple similarity of form.' Leroi-Gourhan arrived at a general typology of cave signs, dividing them into two basic symbolic sets, female and male (Figures 24 and 25).

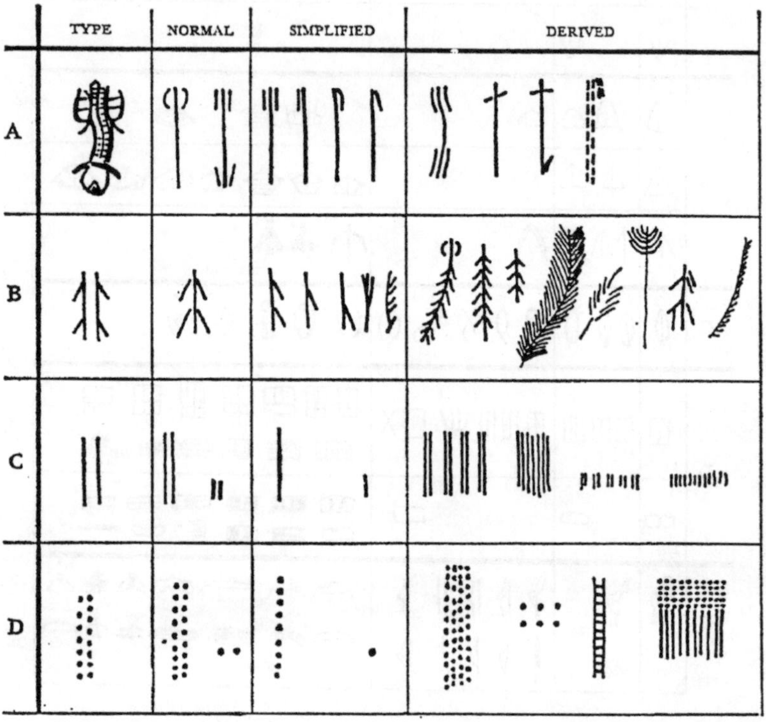

**FIGURE 25** TYPOLOGY OF MALE SIGNS (André Leroi-Gourhan, 1968, p. 514)

**A**, hooked or 'spear-thrower' signs; **B**, barbed signs; **C**, single and double strokes; **D**, dots and rows of dots.

He concluded that the signs, in association with the depictions of animals, formed a symbolic system expressing a binary division of meaning into female and male, and his work provided a stimulus for the semiotic approach to prehistoric art (see, for example, the special issue of the journal *Semiotica*, Volume 100, 2/4 (1994), on prehistoric signs). In Leroi-Gourhan's opinion, at Lascaux, Périgord, which has fantastic paintings and many signs dated to 17,000 years ago, Stone Age people 'came very close to writing' (as reported by Delluc and Delluc, 1990, p. 46). Indeed the archaeologist Marija Gimbutas (1921–94) argued (1999, pp. 43–54) that the abstract signs of the Upper Palaeolithic are the precursors of an 'Old European' script – an alphabet used in linear fashion, and evidenced on pottery and other objects from the sixth millennium BC. According to Gimbutas, the continuity of Old European script was disrupted by the arrival in Europe from the fifth millennium BC onwards of Indo-European languages, which eventually gave us most of the languages of modern Europe, including English.

## Conclusion

And so we draw to a close. The traditional understanding that 'true writing' began with the Sumerians has made controversial the view that prehistoric cave signs are examples of writing. In his highly sensible discussion of the issue, the ethnologist Richard Rudgley says (1998, p. 85), 'It is now more clear that the writing systems that emerged in Mesopotamia [that is, in Sumeria] and elsewhere around 5000 years ago owe their development to innovations that can be traced back to the Neolithic period [up to 10,000 years ago] and, in various respects, even as far as Upper Palaeolithic times.' But he also says (p. 84) that if the sign systems of the Upper Palaeolithic are ever shown to fit into conventional understandings of true writing 'then the entire evolutionary sequence from prehistoric "pre-writing" to civilised "true writing" would, of course, collapse overnight'. However, the semiotic approach, which looks at the evolution of 'written' symbolism, emphasizes a long continuity, stretching as far back as the 'abstract' signs associated with the cave art at Chauvet, Ardèche, France, dated at 35,000 years old (for example, the panel of dots in Figure 26), or even as far back as the patterned engravings on pieces of ochre found at the Blombos Cave, South Africa, dated at over 70,000 years old (*National Geographic*, July 2000, p. 100, and *Science*, vol. 295 (11 January 2002), pp. 247–9).

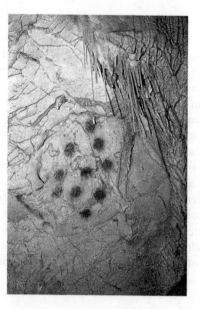

**FIGURE 26**   PANEL OF DOTS FROM CHAUVET CAVE (Chauvet et al., 1996, p. 28)

Similarly, treating language as essentially a symbolic system allows us to go looking for something separate from but nonetheless fundamental to the origins of speech, that is, the 'moment' when our ancestors crossed the symbolic threshold. If we think that there is some kind of language faculty wired into our brain, then the origins story has to explain what the faculty is, how it works, and how it came about. There have been great advances in our knowledge of prehistory, the human brain, and animal communication, and theories of the origin of language are more sophisticated than used to be the case. But imaginative speculation still has a role. That is in the nature of theory-making. Evidence provides the test.

## Further reading

Use Robbins Burling's *The Talking Ape: How Language Evolved* (2005) for a clear and extensive overview. *Eve Spoke: Human Language and Human Evolution* (1998), by Philip Lieberman, is another good starting point. For a shorter account placed within a general description of human prehistory, drawing on advances in genetics, see *Before the*

*Dawn: Recovering the Lost History of Our Ancestors* (2006), by Nicholas Wade; and for something concise and visual, go to *The Human Story: Where We Come From and How We Evolved* (2007), by Charles Lockwood. As well as showing that the 'Tra-la Theory' is far from dead, Steven Mithen's *The Singing Neanderthals: The Origin of Music, Language, Mind and Body* (2005) emphasizes the evolutionary connections between language and music. *The Articulate Mammal: An Introduction to Psycholinguistics* (5th edn, 2007), by Jean Aitchison, puts the origins question into the context of a guide to theories of language and mind. Terrence Deacon's *The Symbolic Species: The Co-evolution of Language and the Human Brain* (1997) is a long but very readable synthesis of knowledge from neuroscience, linguistics, palaeoanthropology, animal communication studies, and other domains. Although you risk Pinker-overdose, follow his *The Language Instinct: The New Science of Language and Mind* (1994) with the other two books in his trilogy on language: *Words and Rules: The Ingredients of Language* (1999) and *The Stuff of Thought: Language as a Window into Human Nature* (2007). For Chomsky, see Further reading at the end of Chapter 17, though I will mention here another good entrée into his views on language: *New Horizons in the Study of Language and Mind* (2000b). The websites of Chomsky, Fitch, Jackendoff, and Pinker also provide much useful further material and explanation of their work. See also a report titled 'Semantic Combinations in Primate Calls', by Kate Arnold and Klaus Zuberbühler, in the journal *Nature* (Volume 441, Number 7091, 18 May 2006, p. 303), describing their research which suggests that putty-nosed monkeys in Nigeria can combine two types of warning call into a third, exhibiting very rudimentary syntax. *Brain Power: Working out the Human Mind* (1999), edited by Susan Greenfield and Peter Leek, is an excellent, well-illustrated introduction to our knowledge of the brain. Andrew Robinson's *The Story of Writing* (1995) is similarly impressive. Richard Rudgley's *Lost Civilisations of the Stone Age* (1998) includes a clear-sighted account of the origins of writing, and the *Cambridge Illustrated History of Prehistoric Art* (1998), edited by Paul G. Bahn, provides a comprehensive survey of prehistoric art in all its forms. However, for its combination of spectacle and analysis, André Leroi-Gourhan's *The Art of Prehistoric Man in Western Europe* (1968) is in a class of its own.

# References for Examples

Some examples in the text are given without references. They are listed here with information about sources.

## Chapter 1

Text (i): from article 'Singing Out at Alwyn's Return', *South Wales Evening Post*, 2 August 1999, p. 11.

'Beginning this season . . .': from 'NCAA Loosens Grip on Holding Penalties', *The Ann Arbor News*: 'Sports', 23 February 1999, p. 4.

Text (ii): from tape-recorded field interview in Talysarn, Gwynedd, North Wales, 21 November 1980.

## Chapter 3

Extract (a): *Peterborough Chronicle 1070–1154*, edited by Cecily Clark, 2nd edn (Oxford: Oxford University Press, 1970), p. 21.

Extract (b): *Peterborough Chronicle 1070–1154*, edited by Cecily Clark, 2nd edn (Oxford: Oxford University Press, 1970), p. 57.

## Chapter 5

New Zealand section: Rob Penhallurick, radio interview by Glenn Williams, *Radio Wammo Breakfast*, KiwiFM, 29 July 2008.

## Chapter 7

*Blackadder the Third* quotation: from 'Ink and Incapability', series 3, episode 2, originally broadcast in 1987; also *Blackadder: The Whole Damn Dynasty, 1485–1917*, by Richard Curtis and Ben Elton (London: Penguin, 1998), p. 265.

# Chapter 10

'We are literally juggling beds': *Call Robin Lustig*, BBC Radio 4, 20 January 1998.
*Life In Cold Blood*: 'Under the Skin' appendix, episode 2 of 5, broadcast on 15 April 2008, BBC4.

# Chapter 11

'Sam Peckinpah's *Salad Days*': *Monty Python's Flying Circus*, series 3, episode 7, originally broadcast in 1972.

# Chapter 13

Sex Pistols interview extract: from transcript in *England's Dreaming: Sex Pistols and Punk Rock*, by Jon Savage (London: Faber and Faber, 1991), pp. 258–9, of interview on *Today*, Thames TV, 1 December 1976.

# Chapter 14

John Major, Conservative Party Conference speech extract: from the *Daily Telegraph*, 9 October 1993, p. 10; speech delivered 8 October 1993.
Ali G extract: from *Ali G, innit* video (1999), Channel Four Television.

# Chapter 15

'Israeli troops...': *Today Programme*, BBC Radio 4, early 1997.
'[J]ust because we're not the same...': *Wales Today*, BBC1 Wales, March 2000.
'I'm putting my neck out...': Philip Matthews, Ireland v. France rugby, BBC1, 6 February 1999.
'Every now and then the boss...': *Today Programme*, BBC Radio 4, early 1997.
'We are looking at egg on face...': Rhodri Morgan MP, trailer for *Week In Week Out*, BBC1 Wales, 17 March 1998.
'Not many players would've hit him in the eye...': Glen Hoddle, post-match analysis, France v. England, Sky Sports 1, 26 March 2008.
'He's in a no-win situation...': Graham Taylor, speaking of manager Avram Grant in advance of Chelsea's Champions League tie with Valencia, *Today Programme*, BBC Radio 4, 3 October 2007.
'He's never found wanting very often': expert summarizer Andy Gray, Manchester City v. Liverpool, *Super Sunday*, Sky Sports 1, 30 December 2007.

'He isn't not still one…': Andy Gray, of Thierry Henry, *Super Sunday*, Sky Sports 1, 4 May 2008.

'The onus is not really on us to be honest': Adie Boothroyd, manager of Watford, on play-off day, Sky Sports News, 11 May 2008.

'Can they dig themselves…': Ken Brown, commentating on the Ryder Cup, BBC1, 20 September 2008.

'[Martina Navratilova won her match] in straight sex': repeated on *Medium Wave*, BBC Radio 4, 16 November 1997.

Cameroons: Eurosport World Cup coverage, Argentina v. Cameroon, 8 June 1990.

'It beggars…': *Broadcasting House*, BBC Radio 4, 11 October 1998.

'He is the very pineapple of politeness!': from Richard B. Sheridan, *The Rivals* (1775), edited by Elizabeth Duthie (London: Ernest Benn; New York: W. W. Norton, 1979), Act III, Scene 3, lines 24–5.

'[P]ubic scrutiny': Broadcasting Standards Commission, BBC1, broadcast after *Watchdog*, 4 December 1997.

'At the time his critical…': from notes by Cliff McLenehan for T.Rex, *The BBC Recordings 1970–1976* (Ilford: New Millennium Communications, 1997).

'[E]ar Michael': from X-360 Headphone Microphone packaging, 2009.

'God answers knee-mail': banner notice outside church in Mumbles, South Wales, UK, 14 May 2008.

'Last night in Londonderry…': 9 a.m. News, BBC Radio 4, early 1997.

'[P]olice have cracked down…': *South Wales Evening Post*, 2 December 1997, p. 3.

'Jerusalem Coast…': *Today Programme*, BBC Radio 4, 10 August 2001.

'[A]nd they're soluble…': Bobby Robson, *World Cup '98: Encore*, ITV, 15 June 1998.

'Into the record brooks…': Gary Herbert commentating on the K1 1000m final, BBC1 coverage of Beijing Olympics, 22 August 2008.

'[T]eachers' industrial action over pee…': newsreader Simon McCoy, BBC News Channel, Saturday 22 March 2008.

'[I]n older children…': Lawrence McGinty, Medical Editor, *ITV Lunchtime News*, 08 November 2007.

'[T]he outsane…outside lane': Steve Backley, athletics coverage, London Grand Prix, Crystal Palace, BBC Radio 5 Live, 26 July 2008.

# Chapter 16

999 MEN IN ACCIDENT: front-page headline from the *South Wales Evening Post*, *circa* 1995.

CYCLISTS TOLD – STICK TO THE ROAD: news-item headline from the *Herald of Wales*, 22 January 1997, p. 8.

CITY SEWER TRAFFIC GRIDLOCK: billboard-headline for *South Wales Evening Post*, 25 October 2001.

CITY CORNED BEEF EYELASH HORROR: billboard-headline for the *South Wales Evening Post*, *circa* 1995.

HOLE IN THE WALL RIPPED FROM PUB: news-item headline in *South Wales Evening Post*, 12 October 2007, p. 12.
DRIVER BLAMES TRAIN CRASH ON BEE: billboard-headline for *The Argus* [Sussex], 22 July 2008.
BABY BONUS VOTES: billboard-headline for *South Wales Evening Post*, 20 July 2008.

# Chapter 17

Pinocchio quote: *Shrek the Third* (2007), Dreamworks Animation LLC.

# Bibliography

The Bibliography lists all the works cited in the text, except for films, songs, and radio and television programmes. Certain references and sources for some illustrative examples are omitted in the text, but are given in the list preceding this Bibliography.

Adams, D. and Lloyd, J. (1983) *The Meaning of Liff* (London: Pan, and Faber and Faber).

Aitchison, J. (2003) *Words in the Mind: An Introduction to the Mental Lexicon*, 3rd edn (Malden, Massachusetts and Oxford: Blackwell).

Aitchison, J. (2007) *The Articulate Mammal: An Introduction to Psycholinguistics*, 5th edn (London: Routledge).

Alibhai-Brown, Y. (1994) 'The Great Backlash'. In *The War of the Words: The Political Correctness Debate*, edited by S. Dunant (London: Virago), pp. 55–75.

Allsopp, R. (ed.) (1996) *Dictionary of Caribbean English Usage* (Oxford: Oxford University Press). [With a French and Spanish supplement edited by J. Allsopp.]

Amis, K. (1997) *The King's English: A Guide to Modern Usage* (London: HarperCollins).

Amis, M. (2008) *The Second Plane: September 11: 2001–2007* (London: Jonathan Cape).

Anderson, B. R. O'G. (1991) *Imagined Communities: Reflections on the Origin and Spread of Nationalism*, 2nd edn (London: Verso).

Andersson, L. and Trudgill, P. (1990) *Bad Language* (Oxford: Basil Blackwell).

*Anglo-Saxon Chronicle*, translated and edited by M. J. Swanton (London: J. M. Dent, 1996).

Antony, L. M. and Hornstein, N. (eds) (2003) *Chomsky and His Critics* (Malden, Massachusetts and Oxford: Blackwell).

Argyle, M. (1988) *Bodily Communication*, 2nd edn (London: Routledge).

Arnold, K. and Zuberbühler, K. (2006) 'Semantic Combinations in Primate Calls', *Nature*, vol. 441, no. 7091 (18 May), 303.

Asimov, I. (1942) 'Runaround', *Astounding Science Fiction* (March 1942), 94–103. [Short story featuring the first explicit statement of Asimov's 'Three Laws of Robotics'.]

Austin, J. L. (1975) *How to Do Things with Words*, 2nd edn, edited by J. O. Urmson and M. Sbisa (Oxford: Oxford University Press). The William James Lectures, delivered at Harvard University in 1955 (1st edn published in 1962; Oxford: Oxford University Press).

Avis, W. S., Crate, C., Drysdale, P., Leechman, D., Scargill, M. H. and Lovell, C. J. (eds) (1967) *A Dictionary of Canadianisms on Historical Principles* (Toronto: W. J. Gage).

Ayto, J. (1999) *20th Century Words* (Oxford: Oxford University Press).

Bahn, P. G. (ed.) (1998) *The Cambridge Illustrated History of Prehistoric Art* (Cambridge: Cambridge University Press).

Bailey, R. W. (1991) *Images of English: A Cultural History of the Language* (Cambridge: Cambridge University Press).

Bailey, R. W. (2004) 'American English: Its Origins and History'. In Finegan and Rickford (eds) (2004), pp. 3–17.

Barber, C. (1972) *The Story of Language*, 5th edn (London: Pan).

Barber, C. (2009) *The English Language: A Historical Introduction*, 2nd edn, revised by J. C. Beal and P. A. Shaw (Cambridge: Cambridge University Press).

Barsky, R. F. (1997) *Noam Chomsky: A Life of Dissent* (Cambridge, Massachusetts and London: The MIT Press).

Barthes, R. (1968) 'The Death of the Author'. In *Image Music Text*, essays selected and translated by S. Heath (London: Fontana, 1977), pp. 142–8. Originally published as 'La mort de l'auteur', *Mantéla* V (1968).

Barthes, R. (1970) *Mythologies*, 2nd edn. Selected and translated from the French by A. Lavers (London: Vintage, 1993; original English publication 1972). First French edition published in 1957 (Paris: Éditions du Seuil).

Barthes, R. (1978) 'Inaugural Lecture, Collège de France'. In *A Barthes Reader*, edited by S. Sontag (London: Vintage, 1993; original English publication 1982), pp. 457–78, translation by R. Howard. Delivered on 7 January 1977, and first published as *Leçon* (Paris: Éditions du Seuil, 1978).

Barthes, R. (1982) *A Barthes Reader*, edited by S. Sontag (London: Vintage, 1993; original English publication 1982).

Bather, F. A. (1923) 'The Puns of Shakespeare'. Reproduced in *Crosbie's Dictionary of Puns*, edited by J. S. Crosbie (London: Futura, 1977), pp. 381–97.

Baudrillard, J. (1976) 'Symbolic Exchange and Death'. In *Jean Baudrillard: Selected Writings*, edited by M. Poster (Cambridge: Polity Press, 2nd edn, 2001), pp. 122–51, translated by C. Levin. Originally published in *L'Échange symbolique et la mort* (Paris: Gallimard, 1976), pp. 19–29.

Baudrillard, J. (1991) *The Gulf War Did Not Take Place*, translated by P. Patton (Bloomington and Indianapolis: Indiana University Press, 1995). First published as *La Guerre du Golfe n'a pas eu lieu* (Paris: Éditions Galilée, 1991).

Baudrillard, J. (2001) *Jean Baudrillard: Selected Writings*, 2nd edn, edited by M. Poster (Cambridge: Polity Press in association with Blackwell).

Bauer, L. (2002) *An Introduction to International Varieties of English* (Edinburgh: Edinburgh University Press).

Bauer, L. and Warren, P. (2008) 'New Zealand English: Phonology'. In Burridge and Kortmann (eds) (2008), pp. 39–63.

Baugh, A. C. (1935) 'The Chronology of French Loan-Words in English', *Modern Language Notes*, vol. 50, no. 2 (February), 90–3.

Baugh, A. C. and Cable, T. (2002) *A History of the English Language*, 5th edn (London and New York: Routledge).

Baugh, J. (2000) *Beyond Ebonics: Linguistic Pride and Racial Prejudice* (New York and Oxford: Oxford University Press).

Baugh, J. (2006) 'Bridging the Great Divide (African American English)'. In Wolfram and Ward (eds) (2006), pp. 217–24.

Baxter, G., Blythe, R., Croft, W. and McKane, A. (2008) 'Modeling Language Change: An Evaluation of Trudgill's Theory of the Emergence of New Zealand English', an online 'pre-print' (at: http://www2.ph.ed.ac.uk/~rblythe3/Preprints/BBCM08.pdf) of an essay published in *Language Variation and Change*, vol. 21, no. 02 (July 2009), 257–96.

Beard, H. and Cerf, C. (1994) *The Official Politically Correct Dictionary and Handbook*, updated edn (New York: Villard Books, produced in conjunction with the American Hyphen Society).

Bell, A. and Garrett, P. (eds) (1998) *Approaches to Media Discourse* (Oxford: Blackwell).

Bennett, Alan (1969) *Forty Years On* (London: Faber and Faber). Reprinted in *Alan Bennett: Plays One* (London: Faber and Faber, 1996).

Bennett, Andrew and Royle, N. (2009) *An Introduction to Literature, Criticism and Theory*, 4th edn (Harlow: Pearson Longman).

Bergvall, V. L., Bing, J. M. and Freed, A. F. (eds) (1996) *Rethinking Language and Gender Research: Theory and Practice* (London: Longman).

Berlo, D. K. (1960) *The Process of Communication: An Introduction to Theory and Practice* (New York: Holt, Rinehart and Winston).

Berrey, L. V. and Van den Bark, M. (1954) *The American Thesaurus of Slang*, 2nd edn (London: George G. Harrap & Co. Ltd).

Bex, T. and Watts, R. J. (eds) (1999) *Standard English: The Widening Debate* (London: Routledge).

Bignell, J. (2002) *Media Semiotics: An Introduction*, 2nd edn (Manchester and New York: Manchester University Press).

Bing, J. M. and Bergvall, V. L. (1996) 'The Question of Questions: Beyond Binary Thinking'. In *Rethinking Language and Gender Research: Theory and Practice*, edited by V. L. Bergvall, J. M. Bing and A. F. Freed (London: Longman), pp. 1–30.

Blair, D. and Collins, P. (eds) (2001) *English in Australia* (Amsterdam: John Benjamins).

Blonsky, M. (ed.) (1985) *On Signs* (Baltimore, Maryland: Johns Hopkins University Press).

Bloomfield, L. (1933) *Language* (New York: Henry Holt).

Blyton, E. (1949) *The Mountain of Adventure*, revised omnibus edn (with *The Sea of Adventure* and *The Ship of Adventure*) (London: Macmillan, 1994). Originally published in 1949 (London: Macmillan).

Boberg, C. (2008) 'English in Canada: Phonology'. In Schneider (ed.) (2008b), pp. 144–60.

Boelens, K. (1979) *The Frisian Language* (Holland: Provincial administration of Friesland and Fryske Akademy).

Boswell, J. (1791 [1934]) *Boswell's Life of Johnson*, edited by G. B. Hill; revised and enlarged edition by L. F. Powell. Six vols. (Oxford: Clarendon Press).

Bowerman, S. (2008) 'White South African English: Phonology'. In Mesthrie (ed.) (2008), pp. 164–76.

Bowie, M. (1991) *Lacan* (London: Fontana).

Bracher, M. (1993) *Lacan, Discourse and Social Change: A Psychoanalytic Cultural Criticism* (Ithaca and London: Cornell University Press).

Bradley, D. (2008) 'Regional Characteristics of Australian English: Phonology'. In Burridge and Kortmann (eds) (2008), pp. 111–23.

Britain, D. (ed.) (2007) *Language in the British Isles*, 2nd edn (Cambridge: Cambridge University Press).

Britnell, R. H. (2004) *Britain and Ireland 1050–1530: Economy and Society* (Oxford: Oxford University Press).

Brogan, H. (1999) *The Penguin History of the United States of America*, 2nd edn (London: Penguin).

Brook, G. L. (1965) *English Dialects*, 2nd edn (London: André Deutsch).

Brown, R. W. and Lenneberg, E. H. (1954) 'A Study in Language and Cognition', *Journal of Abnormal and Social Psychology*, vol. 49, 454–62.

Buchanan, J. (1764 [1766]) *An Essay Towards Establishing a Standard for an Elegant and Uniform Pronunciation of the English Language*, 1766 edn (London: Edward and Charles Dilly). Extract, dated as 1764, in *Proper English? Readings in Language, History and Cultural Identity*, edited by T. Crowley (London: Routledge, 1991), pp. 73–80.

Burchfield, R. W. (ed.) (1996 [revised, 1998]) *The New Fowler's Modern English Usage*, 3rd edn (Oxford: Oxford University Press). First edited by H. W. Fowler in 1926.

Burgoon, M., Hunsaker, F. G. and Dawson, E. J. (1994) *Human Communication*, 3rd edn (London: Sage).

Burling, R. (2005) *The Talking Ape: How Language Evolved* (Oxford: Oxford University Press).

Burns, R. (1786) 'To a Louse, on Seeing One on a Lady's Bonnet at Church'. In *Poems*, selected and edited by H. W. Meikle and W. Beattie, 3rd edn (Harmondsworth: Penguin, 1977), pp. 101–2.

Burridge, K. and Kortmann, B. (eds) (2008) *Varieties of English 3: The Pacific and Australasia* (Berlin and New York: Mouton de Gruyter). [The four-volume *Varieties of English* series is essentially a repackaging of *A Handbook of Varieties of English*, edited by B. Kortmann, E. W. Schneider et al. (Berlin and New York: Mouton de Gruyter, 2004).]

Burridge, K. and Mulder, J. (1998) *English in Australia and New Zealand: An Introduction to Its History, Structure, and Use* (Melbourne and Oxford: Oxford University Press).

Burroughs, W. S. (1959) *The Naked Lunch* (London: Calder & Boyars, 1964; originally published in Paris: Olympia Press, 1959).

Burroughs, W. S. (1961) *The Soft Machine* (Paris: Olympia Press; 2nd version published in New York: Grove Press, 1966; 3rd version in London: Calder, 1968).

Burroughs, W. S. (1964) *Nova Express* (New York: Grove Press, 1992; originally published in 1964).

Burroughs, W. S. (1965) 'William Burroughs: An Interview', *Paris Review*, no. 35, 15–49. [The interviewer is C. Knickerbocker.]

Burroughs, W. S. (1967) *The Ticket that Exploded* (New York: Grove Press, 1987; 1st edn 1967; an earlier version was published in Paris: Olympia Press, 1962).

Burroughs, W. S. (1979) *Blade Runner: A Movie* (Berkeley, California: Blue Wind Press).

Burroughs, W. S. (1984) *The Place of Dead Roads* (New York: Henry Holt, Owl Books; 2nd edn, Orlando: Holt, Rinehart and Winston, 1995).

Burroughs, W. S. (1986a) 'Ten Years and a Billion Dollars'. In *The Adding Machine: Selected Essays*, pp. 47–51.

Burroughs, W. S. (1986b) 'On Coincidence'. In *The Adding Machine: Selected Essays*, pp. 99–105.

Burroughs, W. S. (1986c) 'Technology of Writing'. In *The Adding Machine: Selected Essays*, pp. 32–6.

Burroughs, W. S. (1986d) 'Les Voleurs'. In *The Adding Machine: Selected Essays*, pp. 19–21.

Burroughs, W. S. (1986e) 'The Fall of Art'. In *The Adding Machine: Selected Essays*, pp. 60–4.

Burroughs, W. S. (1986f) *The Adding Machine: Selected Essays* (New York: Arcade, 1993; originally published New York: Seaver Books, 1986).

Burroughs, W. S. (1998) *Word Virus: The William Burroughs Reader*, edited by J. Grauerholz and I. Silverberg, with an introduction by A. Douglas (London: Flamingo, 1999; New York: Grove Press, 1998).

Busse, U. and Görlach, M. (2002) 'German'. In *English in Europe*, edited by M. Görlach (Oxford: Oxford University Press), pp. 13–36.

*Cambridge History of the English Language*, vols I–VI (1992–2001), general editor R. M. Hogg (Cambridge: Cambridge University Press).

Cameron, D. (1992) *Feminism and Linguistic Theory*, 2nd edn (London: Macmillan).

Cameron, D. (1994) ' "Words, Words, Words": The Power of Language'. In *The War of the Words: The Political Correctness Debate*, edited by S. Dunant (London: Virago), pp. 15–34.

Cameron, D. (1995) *Verbal Hygiene* (London: Routledge).

Cameron, D. (1996) 'The Language-Gender Interface: Challenging Co-optation'. In *Rethinking Language and Gender Research: Theory and Practice*, edited by V. L. Bergvall, J. M. Bing and A. F. Freed (London: Longman), pp. 31–53.

Cameron, D. (1997) 'Performing Gender Identity: Young Men's Talk and the Construction of Heterosexual Masculinity'. In *Language and Masculinity*, edited by S. Johnson and U. H. Meinhof (Oxford: Blackwell), pp. 47–64.

Cameron, D. (ed.) (1998) *The Feminist Critique of Language: A Reader*, 2nd edn (London: Routledge).

Cameron, D. (2007) *The Myth of Mars and Venus* (Oxford: Oxford University Press).

Cameron, D. and Kulick, D. (2003) *Language and Sexuality* (Cambridge: Cambridge University Press).

Cameron, D., McAlinden, F. and O'Leary, K. (1989) 'Lakoff in Context: The Social and Linguistic Functions of Tag Questions'. In *Women in Their Speech Communities: New Perspectives on Language and Sex*, edited by J. Coates and D. Cameron (London: Longman), pp. 74–93.

Carston, R. and Uchida, S. (eds) (1998) *Relevance Theory: Applications and Implications* (Amsterdam: John Benjamins).

Carter, R. (1998) *Mapping the Mind* (London: Weidenfeld & Nicolson).

Carver, C. M. (1987) *American Regional Dialects: A Word Geography* (Ann Arbor: University of Michigan Press).

*Cassell Dictionary of Contemporary Quotations* (1996), edited by R. Andrews (London: Cassell).

Cassidy, F. G., Hall, J. H. et al. (eds) (1985–2002) *Dictionary of American Regional English*, vols I–IV (Cambridge, Massachusetts, and London: The Belknap Press of Harvard University Press).

Cassidy, F. G. and Le Page, R. B. (eds) (1980) *Dictionary of Jamaican English*, 2nd edn (Cambridge: Cambridge University Press).

Cavalli-Sforza, L. L. (2000) *Genes, Peoples, and Languages*, translated by M. Seielstad (London: Allen Lane, Penguin Press).

Cawdrey, R. (1604) *A Table Alphabeticall* (London: Edmund Weaver. Facsimile reprint, 1970, Amsterdam: Theatrum Orbis Terrarum; and New York: Da Capo Press).

*Chambers Dictionary* (1998) (Edinburgh: Chambers Harrap).

Chambers, J. K. (1973) 'Canadian Raising', *Canadian Journal of Linguistics/Revue canadienne de linguistique* 18, 113–35. [Reprinted in *Canadian English: Origins and Structures*, edited by J. K. Chambers (Toronto: Methuen, 1975), pp. 83–100.]

Chambers, J. K. and Trudgill, P. (1998) *Dialectology*, 2nd edn (Cambridge: Cambridge University Press).

Chambers, J. K., Trudgill, P. and Schilling-Estes, N. (eds) (2003) *The Handbook of Language Variation and Change* (Malden, Massachusetts and Oxford: Blackwell).

Chandler, D. (2007) *Semiotics: The Basics*, 2nd edn (Abingdon: Routledge).

Chase, S. (1938) *The Tyranny of Words* (London: Methuen).

Chauvet, J-M., Deschamps, E. B. and Hillaire, C. (1996) *Chauvet Cave: The Discovery of the World's Oldest Paintings*, translated by P. Bahn (London: Thames and Hudson). [Earlier, French edn published in 1995.]

Chomsky, N. (1955) *Transformational Analysis* (University of Pennsylvania: PhD dissertation).

Chomsky, N. (1955, 1956) *The Logical Structure of Linguistic Theory* (Cambridge, Massachusetts: MIT Humanities Library, microfilm). [Revised version published in 1975, New York and London: Plenum; and in 1985, Chicago: University of Chicago Press.]

Chomsky, N. (1957) *Syntactic Structures* (The Hague: Mouton).

Chomsky, N. (1959) 'A Review of B. F. Skinner's *Verbal Behavior*', *Language*, vol. 35, no. 1, 26–58. [Reprinted in *Readings in the Psychology of Language*, edited by L. A. Jakobovits and M. S. Miron (Englewood Cliffs, New Jersey: Prentice-Hall, 1967), pp. 142–71. I used the online reprint at: http://www.chomsky.info/articles/1967—.html. The online reprint has no pagination.]

Chomsky, N. (1965) *Aspects of the Theory of Syntax* (Cambridge, Massachusetts: The MIT Press).

Chomsky, N. (1981) *Lectures on Government and Binding* (Dordrecht: Foris).

Chomsky, N. (1982) *Noam Chomsky on the Generative Enterprise: A Discussion with Riny Huybregts and Henk van Riemsdijk* (Dordrecht: Foris).

Chomsky, N. (1986) *Knowledge of Language: Its Nature, Origin, and Use* (Westport, Connecticut: Praeger).

Chomsky, N. (1988) *Language and Problems of Knowledge: The Managua Lectures* (Cambridge, Massachusetts: The MIT Press).

Chomsky, N. (1993 [1995]) 'A Minimalist Program for Linguistic Theory'. Originally in *The View from Building 20: Essays in Linguistics in Honor of Sylvain Bromberger*, edited by K. Hale and S. J. Keyser (Cambridge, Massachusetts: The MIT Press, 1993), pp. 1–52. [I used the revised reprint in *The Minimalist Program*, by N. Chomsky (Cambridge, Massachusetts: The MIT Press, 1995), pp. 167–217.]

Chomsky, N. (1995) *The Minimalist Program* (Cambridge, Massachusetts: The MIT Press).

Chomsky, N. (2000a) *The Architecture of Language*, edited by N. Mukherji, B. N. Patnaik and R. K. Agnihotri (New Delhi: Oxford University Press).

Chomsky, N. (2000b) *New Horizons in the Study of Language and Mind* (Cambridge: Cambridge University Press).

Chomsky, N. (2002) *On Nature and Language*, edited by A. Belletti and L. Rizzi (Cambridge: Cambridge University Press).

Chomsky, N. (2004) *The Generative Enterprise Revisited: Discussions with Riny Huybregts, Henk van Riemsdijk, Naoki Fukui and Mihoko Zushi* (Berlin: Mouton de Gruyter).

Chomsky, N. (2008) Private email correspondence, 19 January 2008.

Cixous, H. (1975) 'Sorties: Out and Out: Attacks/Ways Out/Forays'. In *The Newly Born Woman*, edited by H. Cixous and C. Clément, translated by B. Wing (Minneapolis: University of Minnesota Press, 1986), pp. 63–132. Book originally published as *La Jeune Née* (Paris: Union Générale d'Éditions, 1975).

Cixous, H. (1994) *The Hélène Cixous Reader*, edited by S. Sellers (London: Routledge).

Clack, B. and Clack, B. R. (1998) *The Philosophy of Religion: A Critical Introduction* (Cambridge, UK, and Malden, USA: Polity Press and Blackwell).

Clanchy, M. T. (2006) *England and Its Rulers, 1066–1307*, 3rd edn (Malden, Massachusetts and Oxford: Blackwell).

Clark, C. (1970) – see entry for *Peterborough Chronicle*.

Clark, U. (2007) *Studying Language: English in Action* (Basingstoke: Palgrave Macmillan).

Clarke, S. (2008) 'Newfoundland English: Phonology'. In Schneider (ed.) (2008b), pp. 161–80.

Coates, J. (1993, 2004) *Women, Men and Language: A Sociolinguistic Account of Gender Differences in Language*, 2nd edn, 3rd edn (London: Longman; and Harlow: Pearson Education).

Coates, J. (1996) *Women Talk: Conversation Between Women Friends* (Oxford: Blackwell).

Cobley, P. (ed.) (1996) *The Communication Theory Reader* (London: Routledge).

Cobley, P. (ed.) (2001) *The Routledge Companion to Semiotics and Linguistics* (London: Routledge).

Collins, J. (2008) *Chomsky: A Guide for the Perplexed* (London: Continuum).

Concar, D. (1998) 'Innocent Eye', *New Scientist*, vol. 160, no. 2164 (12 December), 10.

Cook, V. J. and Newson, M. (2007) *Chomsky's Universal Grammar: An Introduction*, 3rd edn (Malden, Massachusetts and Oxford: Blackwell).

Cooper, R. L. (1989) *Language Planning and Social Change* (Cambridge: Cambridge University Press).

*Cosmopolitan*, March 1998. 'How to Talk to a Man So He Really Understands You', by W. Bristow (British edn, March 1998), pp. 102–5.

Coulthard, M. (1985) *An Introduction to Discourse Analysis*, 2nd edn (London: Longman).

Cowie, A. P. (ed.) (2009). *The Oxford History of English Lexicography*. Two vols. (Oxford: Oxford University Press).

Cowie, C. (2007) 'The Accents of Outsourcing: The Meanings of "Neutral" in the Indian Call Centre Industry', *World Englishes*, vol. 26, no. 3, 316–30.

'Cox Report' (1989) – see Department of Education and Science.

Crowley, T. (1989) *The Politics of Discourse: The Standard Language Question in British Cultural Debates* (Basingstoke: Macmillan).

Crowley, T. (ed.) (1991) *Proper English? Readings in Language, History and Cultural Identity* (London: Routledge).

Crystal, D. (1997) *The Cambridge Encyclopedia of Language*, 2nd edn (Cambridge: Cambridge University Press).

Crystal, D. (1999) 'Death Sentence', *Guardian*: 'G2', 25 October 1999, pp. 2–3.

Crystal, D. (2003a) *The Cambridge Encyclopedia of the English Language*, 2nd edn (Cambridge: Cambridge University Press).

Crystal, D. (2003b) *English as a Global Language*, 2nd edn (Cambridge: Cambridge University Press).

Crystal, D. (2008) *txtng: the gr8 db8* (Oxford: Oxford University Press).

Culler, J. (1986) *Saussure*, 2nd edn (London: Fontana).

Culler, J. (ed.) (1988) *On Puns: The Foundation of Letters* (Oxford: Basil Blackwell).

*Daily Telegraph*, 12 February 2001. 'The Denglisch Invasion Gives Germans a Scare', article by H. Cleaver, p. 12.

Dalby, A. (2002) *Language in Danger: How Language Loss Threatens our Future* (London: Allen Lane, Penguin Press).

Daly, M., in collaboration with J. Caputi (1987) *Webster's First New Intergalactic Wickedary of the English Language* (London: The Woman's Press).

Danesi, M. (1994) *Messages and Meanings: An Introduction to Semiotics* (Toronto: Canadian Scholars' Press).

Danesi, M. (1999) *Of Cigarettes, High Heels, and Other Interesting Things: An Introduction to Semiotics* (Basingstoke: Palgrave).

Danesi, M. (2000) *Encyclopedic Dictionary of Semiotics, Media, and Communications* (Toronto: Toronto University Press).

Danesi, M. and Sebeok, T. A. (2000) *The Forms of Meaning: Modeling Systems Theory and Semiotic Analysis* (Berlin and New York: Mouton de Gruyter).

*DARE (Dictionary of American Regional English)* – see Cassidy, Hall et al. (eds) (1985–2002).

Darwin, C. (1859) *The Origin of Species by Means of Natural Selection, or the Preservation of Favoured Races in the Struggle for Life*, edited by J. W. Burrow (London: Penguin, 1968). First published in 1859 (London: John Murray).

Daubisse, P., Vidal, P., Vouvé, J. and Brunet, J. (1994) *The Font-de-Gaume Cave*, translated by A. Spiquel (Périgueux: Éditions Fanlac).

Davidoff, J., Davies, I. and Roberson, D. (1999) 'Colour Categories in a Stone-Age Tribe', *Nature*, vol. 398, no. 6724 (18 March), 203–4.

Deacon, T. (1997) *The Symbolic Species: The Co-evolution of Language and the Human Brain* (London: Allen Lane, Penguin Press).

Deacon, T. (2001) Private email correspondence, 21 September 2001.

de Beaugrande, R. (1991) *Linguistic Theory: The Discourse of Fundamental Works* (London: Longman).

de Boinod, A. J. (2005) *The Meaning of Tingo* (London: Penguin).

de Boinod, A. J. (2007) *Toujours Tingo* (London: Penguin).

DeCamp, D. (1971) 'Towards a Generative Analysis of a Post-Creole Speech Continuum'. In *Pidginization and Creolization of Languages: Proceedings of a Conference, Held at the University of the West Indies, Jamaica, April 1968*, edited by D. H. Hymes (Cambridge: Cambridge University Press), pp. 349–70.

Defoe, D. (1724–6) *A Tour through the Whole Island of Great Britain*, introductions by G. D. H. Cole and D. C. Browning (London: J. M. Dent & Sons, 1974).

de Klerk, V. (1992) 'How Taboo are Taboo Words for Girls?', *Language in Society*, vol. 21, no. 2 (June), 277–89.

de Klerk, V. (ed.) (1996) *Focus on South Africa* (Amsterdam: John Benjamins).

de Joia, A. and Stenton, A. (eds) (1980) *Terms in Systemic Linguistics: A Guide to Halliday* (London: Batsford Academic and Educational).

Delbridge, A. (ed.) (2005) *Macquarie Dictionary*, 4th edn (Sydney and Melbourne: Pan Macmillan Australia).

Delluc, B. and Delluc, G. (1990) *Discovering Lascaux*, translated by A. Moyon (Bordeaux: Éditions Sud Ouest).

Department for Education and Welsh Office Education Department (1995) *English in the National Curriculum* (London: HMSO).

Department of Education and Science (1989) *Report of the English Working Group: English from ages 5 to 16* ('The Cox Report') (London: HMSO). [Much of the material from the Report reappears in *Cox on Cox: An English Curriculum for the 1990s*, by B. Cox (London: Hodder & Stoughton, 1991)].

de Quincey, T. (1821) *Confessions of an English Opium Eater* (Harmondsworth: Penguin, 1971).

Derrida, J. (1968) 'Différance'. In *Margins of Philosophy*, translated by A. Bass (Brighton: Harvester Press, 1982), pp. 1–27. 'Différance': address given before the *Société française de philosophie*, 27 January 1968; published simultaneously in the *Bulletin de la société française de philosophie*, July–September 1968, and in *Théorie d'ensemble* (Paris: Éditions du Seuil, 1968). *Marges de la philosophie* first published in 1972 (Paris: Éditions de Minuit).

Dore, W., Mantzel, D., Muller, C. and Wright, M. (eds) 1996 *A Dictionary of South African English on Historical Principles* (Oxford: Oxford University Press, in association with The Dictionary Unit for South African English at Rhodes University).

Doyle, A. C. (1912) *The Lost World* (London: Hodder & Stoughton).

Dubois, B. L. and Crouch, I. (1975) 'The Question of Tag Questions in Women's Speech: They Don't Really Use More of Them Do They?', *Language in Society*, vol. 4, 289–94.

Dunant, S. (ed.) (1994) *The War of the Words: The Political Correctness Debate* (London: Virago).

Dunbar, R. (1996) *Grooming, Gossip and the Evolution of Language* (London: Faber and Faber).

Eckert, P. and McConnell-Ginet, S. (2003) *Language and Gender* (Cambridge: Cambridge University Press).

Eco, U. (1985) 'How Culture Conditions the Colours We See'. In *On Signs*, edited by M. Blonsky (Baltimore: Johns Hopkins University Press), pp. 157–75.

Eco, U. (1999) *Kant and the Platypus: Essays on Language and Cognition*, translated by A. McEwen (London: Secker & Warburg).

Ellis, A. J. (1869) *On Early English Pronunciation, with Especial Reference to Shakspere and Chaucer*, part 1 (London: Trübner for the Early English Text Society).

Elmes, S. (2000) *The Routes of English 3* (London: BBC Adult Learning).

Emmet, A. (1979) – see entry for Saussure (1971).

*Encarta World English Dictionary* (1999), edited by K. Rooney et al. (London: Bloomsbury).

Erard, M. (2007) *Um . . . Slips, Stumbles, And Verbal Blunders, And What They Mean* (New York: Pantheon).

Erard, M. (2008) 'How Global Success Is Changing English Forever', *New Scientist*, issue 2649 (29 March), 28–32.

Everett, D. (2005) 'Cultural Constraints on Grammar and Cognition in Pirahã', *Current Anthropology*, vol. 46, no. 4 (August–October), 621–46.

Fairclough, N. (1989, 2001) *Language and Power* (London and New York: Longman; 2nd edn, Harlow: Pearson Education, 2001).

Fairclough, N. (1995) *Media Discourse* (London: Edward Arnold).

Fairclough, N. (2006) *Language and Globalization* (London: Routledge).

Fennell, B. A. (2001) *A History of English: A Sociolinguistic Approach* (Oxford: Blackwell).

Ferguson, C. A. and Heath, S. B. (1981) 'Languages Before English: Introduction'. In Ferguson and Heath (eds) (1981), pp. 111–15.

Ferguson, C. A. and Heath, S. B. (eds) (1981) *Language in the USA* (Cambridge: Cambridge University Press).

Ferguson, G. (2006) *Language Planning and Education* (Edinburgh: Edinburgh University Press).

Filppula, M., Klemola, J. and Paulasto, H. (2008) *English and Celtic in Contact* (London and New York: Routledge).

*Financial Times*, 2 January 1997. 'Discrimination Pinned to Accents', p. 6.

*Financial Times*, 31 July 1997. 'Accents Still Count in Jobs', p. 18.

Finegan, E. and Rickford, J. R. (eds) (2004) *Language in the USA: Themes for the Twenty-first Century* (Cambridge: Cambridge University Press).

Fisher, J. H. (1977) 'Chancery and the Emergence of Standard Written English in the Fifteenth Century'. *Speculum*, vol. LII, no. 4 (October), 870–99.

Fishman, P. M. (1978) 'Interaction: The Work Women Do', *Social Problems*, vol. 25, no. 4 (April), 397–406.

Fisiak, J. (ed.) (1995) *Linguistic Change under Contact Conditions* (Berlin: Mouton de Gruyter).

Fitch, W. T., Hauser, M. D. and Chomsky, N. (2005) 'The Evolution of the Language Faculty: Clarifications and Implications', *Cognition*, vol. 97, no. 2 (September), 179–210.

Fitz Nigel, R. (1177) *Dialogus de Scaccario*, edited and translated by C. Johnson (London: Nelson, 1950).

Foucault, M. (1969) *The Archaeology of Knowledge*, translated by A. M. Sheridan (London: Tavistock Publications, 1972). Originally published in 1969 (Paris: Éditions Gallimard).

Foucault, M. (1971) 'The Order of Discourse', translated by I. McLeod. In *Untying the Text: A Post-Structuralist Reader*, edited by R. Young (London: Routledge & Kegan Paul, 1981), pp. 48–78. Delivered as Inaugural Lecture at the Collège de France, 2 December 1970. Originally published in 1971 (Paris: Gallimard).

Foucault, M. (1976) *The History of Sexuality*, vol. 1: *An Introduction*, translated by R. Hurley (London: Penguin, 1978). Originally published in 1976 (Paris: Éditions Gallimard).

Foulkes, P. and Docherty, G. J. (1999) Introduction ('Urban Voices – Overview') to *Urban Voices: Accent Studies in the British Isles*, edited by P. Foulkes and G. J. Docherty (London: Arnold, 1999), pp. 1–24.

Francis, W. N. (1983) *Dialectology: An Introduction* (London: Longman).

Freeman, W. J. (1998) 'The Lonely Brain'. In *Mapping the Mind*, by R. Carter (London: Weidenfeld & Nicolson, 1998), p. 146.

Freud, S. (1901) *The Psychopathology of Everyday Life*, Penguin Freud Library, vol. 5, translated by A. Tyson, edited by A. Richards (London: Pelican, 1975; reprinted Penguin, 1991). Series edited by J. Strachey, assisted by A. Richards and A. Tyson; *Zur Psychopathologie des Alltagslebens*, first published in 1901.

Fromkin, V. A. (ed.) (1973) *Speech Errors as Linguistic Evidence* (The Hague: Mouton).

Fromkin, V. A. (ed.) (1980) *Errors in Linguistic Performance: Slips of the Tongue, Ear, Pen, and Hand* (New York and London: Academic Press).

Frutiger, A. (1998) *Signs and Symbols: Their Design and Meaning*, translated by A. Bluhm (London: Ebury Press).

Gargesh, R. (2006) 'South Asian Englishes'. In Kachru, Kachru and Nelson (eds) (2006), pp. 90–113.

Gerald of Wales (1215) *The Journey Through Wales*, in one volume with *The Description of Wales*, translated by L. Thorpe (Harmondsworth: Penguin, 1978).

Gibson, M. (2007) 'Multilingualism'. In Britain (ed.) (2007), pp. 257–75.

Gil, A. (1619 [1621 corrected edn]) *Logonomia Anglica* (Menston, England: Scolar Press, facsimile reprint of the corrected edn, 1968).

Gill, A. A. (1997) 'Smile – You're on Cameo Camera', *Sunday Times*: 'News Review', 28 September 1997, p. 6.

Gimbutas, M. (1999) *The Living Goddesses*, edited and supplemented by M. R. Dexter (Berkeley, Los Angeles, London: University of California Press).

Gimson, A. C. (2008) *Gimson's Pronunciation of English*, 7th edn, revised by A. Cruttenden (London: Hodder Education). First published in 1962 as *An Introduction to the Pronunciation of English* by A. C. Gimson.

Gold, R. S. (1975) 'Introduction' to *Jazz Talk* (New York: Bobbs-Merrill), pp. ix–xii. Reproduced in *Riffs & Choruses: A New Jazz Anthology*, edited by A. Clark (London and New York: Continuum), pp. 321–4.

Gordon, E., Campbell, L., Hay, J., Maclagan, M., Sudbury, A. and Trudgill, P. (2004) *New Zealand English: Its Origin and Evolution* (Cambridge: Cambridge University Press).

Gordon, E. and Maclagan, M. (2008) 'Regional and Social Differences in New Zealand: Phonology'. In Burridge and Kortmann (eds) (2008), pp. 64–76.

Görlach, M. (1990) 'The Development of Standard Englishes'. In *Studies in the History of the English Language* (Heidelberg: Carl Winter, 1990), pp. 9–64.

Görlach, M. (ed.) (2001) *A Dictionary of European Anglicisms* (Oxford: Oxford University Press).

Görlach, M. (ed.) (2002) *English in Europe* (Oxford: Oxford University Press).

Gott, R. (1993) Review of *Culture of Complaint: The Fraying of America* by Robert Hughes, *Guardian*, 1 June 1993. Quoted in Y. Alibhai-Brown, 'The Great Backlash', in *The War of the Words: The Political Correctness Debate*, edited by S. Dunant (London: Virago, 1994), pp. 55–75.

Gough, D. H. (1996) 'English in South Africa'. Introduction to *A Dictionary of South African English on Historical Principles*, edited by W. Dore et al. (Oxford: Oxford University Press), pp. xvii–xix.

Gould, J. (2007) *Can't Buy Me Love: The Beatles, Britain and America* (London: Portrait).

Graddol, D., Leith, D., Swann, J., Rhys, M. and Gillen, J. (eds) (2007) *Changing English* (Abingdon: Routledge; and Milton Keynes: Open University). [Based on *English: History, Diversity and Change*, edited by Graddol, Leith and Swann (London: Routledge and Open University, 1996).]

Gray, J. (1992) *Men are from Mars, Women are from Venus* (New York: HarperCollins).

Green, J. (1998) *The Cassell Dictionary of Slang* (London: Cassell).

Greenbaum, S. (1996) *The Oxford English Grammar* (Oxford: Oxford University Press).

Greenfield, S. (2008) *ID: The Quest for Identity in the 21st Century* (London: Sceptre).

Greenfield, S. and Leek, P. (eds) (1999) *Brain Power: Working out the Human Mind* (Shaftesbury, Dorset: Element Books).

Grice, H. P. (1957) 'Meaning'. In *Studies in the Way of Words* (Cambridge, Massachusetts: Harvard University Press, 1989), pp. 213–23. First published in *The Philosophical Review*, vol. 66 (July 1957).

Grice, H. P. (1975) 'Logic and Conversation'. In *Syntax and Semantics*, vol. 3: *Speech Acts*, edited by P. Cole and J. L. Morgan (New York: Academic Press), pp. 41–58.

Grimm, J. (1822) *Deutsche Grammatik*, vol. 1, 2nd edn (Göttingen).

*Guardian*, 17 November 1997. 'City of Words: Lost for Words in Francophonia', article by J. Ryle, p. 5.

*Guardian*, 1 July 1998. 'New Linguistic Order for Women', article (on French) by P. Webster, p. 15; also, 'Microsoft Closes Windows as Vikings Hammer at the Gates', article (on Icelandic) by M. Walsh, p. 15.

*Guardian*, 10 September 1998. 'Vowel Play Kills orf Queen's English: British Association Science Festival', article by T. Radford and M. Wainwright, p. 11; reports on J. C. Wells's assessment of late-twentieth-century Received Pronunciation.

*Guardian*, 4 March 1999. 'Scousers Hit Out at Author's Pronouncements on Accent', article by M. Wainwright, p. 9.

*Guardian*, 6 May 1999. 'English Loan Words Create "Durama" in Japan', article by J. Watts, p. 15.

*Guardian*, 29 July 1999. 'My Word!', article by N. McIntosh, *Guardian*: 'Online', p. 9.

*Guardian*, 19 April 2000. 'What's in a Name?', feature article by E. Addley, *Guardian*: 'G2', pp. 10–11.

Hacken, P. t. (2007) *Chomskyan Linguistics and its Competitors* (London: Equinox).

Halliday, M. A. K. (1972) 'Towards a Sociological Semantics'. In *Explorations in the Functions of Language* (London: Edward Arnold, 1973), pp. 72–102.

Halliday, M. A. K. (1975) *Learning How to Mean – Explorations in the Development of Language* (London: Edward Arnold).

Halliday, M. A. K. (2006) 'Written Language, Standard Language, Global Language'. In Kachru, Kachru and Nelson (eds) (2006), pp. 349–65. An earlier version was published in *World Englishes*, vol. 22, no. 4 (2003), 404–418.

Halliday, M. A. K. and Matthiessen, C. (2004) *An Introduction to Functional Grammar*, 3rd edn (London: Hodder Arnold).

Harman, G. (ed.) (1974) *On Noam Chomsky: Critical Essays* (Garden City, New York: Anchor Books/Doubleday).

Harris, R. (1983) 'The Speech-Communication Model in Twentieth-Century Linguistics and its Sources'. In *The Foundations of Linguistic Theory: Selected Writings of Roy Harris*, edited by N. Love (London: Routledge, 1990), pp. 151–7.

Harris, R. (2003) *Saussure and His Interpreters*, 2nd edn (Edinburgh: Edinburgh University Press).

Harris, Z. S. (1951) *Methods in Structural Linguistics* (Chicago: University of Chicago Press).

Hasenfratz, R. and Jambeck, T. (2005) *Reading Old English: A Primer and First Reader* (Morgantown, West Virginia: West Virginia University Press).

Haugen, E. (1966) 'Dialect, Language, Nation'. In *The Ecology of Language: Essays by Einar Haugen*, selected and introduced by A. S. Dil (Stanford: Stanford University Press, 1972), pp. 237–54.

Hauser, M. D., Chomsky, N. and Fitch, W. T. (2002) 'The Faculty of Language: What Is It, Who Has It, and How Did It Evolve?', *Science*, vol. 298 (22 November), 1569–79.

Hazen, K. and Fluharty, E. (2006) 'Defining Appalachian English'. In Wolfram and Ward (eds) (2006), pp. 17–21.

Higham, N. J. (1998) *The Norman Conquest* (Stroud: Sutton Publishing).

Hockett, C. F. (1968) *The State of the Art* (The Hague: Mouton).

Hogg, R. M. (general ed.) (1992–2001) – see *Cambridge History of the English Language.*

Hogg, R. M. and Denison, D. (eds) (2006) *A History of the English Language* (Cambridge: Cambridge University Press).

Holloway, R. L. (1974) 'The Casts of Fossil Hominid Brains', *Scientific American*, vol. 231, no. 1 (July), 106–115.

Holloway, R. L. (1983) 'Human Paleontological Evidence Relevant to Language Behavior', *Human Neurobiology*, 2, 105–14.

Holmes, J. (1984) 'Hedging Your Bets and Sitting on the Fence: Some Evidence for Hedges as Support Structures', *Te Reo*, 27, 47–62.

Holmes, J. and Meyerhoff, M. (eds) (2003) *The Handbook of Language and Gender* (Malden, Massachusetts and Oxford: Blackwell).

Honey, J. (1983) *The Language Trap: Race, Class and the 'Standard English' Issue in British Schools* (Middlesex: National Council for Educational Standards).

Honey, J. (1997) *Language is Power: The Story of Standard English and its Enemies* (London: Faber and Faber).

Honna, N. (2006) 'East Asian Englishes'. In Kachru, Kachru and Nelson (eds) (2006), pp. 114–29.

Hopi Dictionary Project (1997) *Hopi Dictionary/Hopìikwa Lavàytutuveni: A Hopi-English Dictionary of the Third Mesa Dialect*, editor-in-chief K. C. Hill (Tucson: University of Arizona Press).

Huber, M. (2008) 'Ghanaian Pidgin English: Morphology and Syntax'. In Mesthrie (ed.) (2008), pp. 381–94.

Hughes, A., Trudgill, P. and Watt, D. (2005) *English Accents and Dialects: An Introduction to Social and Regional Varieties of English in the British Isles*, 3rd edn (London: Hodder Arnold).

Hughes, G. (1991) *Swearing: A Social History of Foul Language, Oaths and Profanity in English* (Oxford: Blackwell; 2nd edn, with a new postscript, London: Penguin, 1998).

Hughes, G. (2000) *A History of English Words* (Oxford: Blackwell).

Hughes, G. (2006) *An Encyclopedia of Swearing: The Social History of Oaths, Profanity, Foul Language, and Ethnic Slurs in the English-Speaking World* (Armonk, New York and London: M. E. Sharpe).

Hughes, S. E. (1992) 'Expletives of Lower Working-Class Women', *Language in Society*, vol. 21, 291–303.

Hutchby, I. and Wooffitt, R. (1998) *Conversation Analysis: Principles, Practices and Applications* (Cambridge: Polity Press, in association with Blackwell).

Huxley, A. (1954) *The Doors of Perception* (London: Flamingo, 1994). Published in one volume with *Heaven and Hell*; *The Doors of Perception* originally published in 1954 (London: Chatto & Windus).

*Independent*, 10 March 1998. 'Gay and Lesbian Meet on Queer Celluloid', article by C. Darke, *Independent*: 'Eye On Tuesday', p. 5.

Jackendoff, R. and Pinker, S. (2005) 'The Nature of the Language Faculty and its Implications for Evolution of Language (Reply to Fitch, Hauser, and Chomsky)', *Cognition*, vol. 97, no. 2 (September), 211–25.

Jaworski, A. and Coupland, N. (eds) (2006) *The Discourse Reader* (Abingdon: Routledge).

Jaynes, J. (1990) *The Origin of Consciousness in the Breakdown of the Bicameral Mind*, 2nd edn (London: Penguin, 1993; 2nd edn originally published Boston, Massachusetts: Houghton Mifflin, 1990; 1st edn originally published 1977, Houghton Mifflin).

Jespersen, O. (1905) *Growth and Structure of the English Language*, 9th edn (Oxford: Basil Blackwell, 1952; 1st edn published in 1905).

Jespersen, O. (1909) *Modern English Grammar*, vol. 1 (Heidelberg: Carl Winter).

Jespersen, O. (1922) *Language: Its Nature, Development and Origin* (New York: W. W. Norton) (Chapter XIII 'The Woman', pp. 237–54).

Johnson, Sally and Meinhof, U. H. (eds) (1997) *Language and Masculinity* (Oxford: Blackwell).

Johnson, Samuel (1747) *The Plan of a Dictionary of the English Language*. Extract in *Proper English? Readings in Language, History and Cultural Identity*, edited by T. Crowley (London: Routledge, 1991), pp. 42–62.

Johnson, Samuel (1755) Preface to *A Dictionary of the English Language*, vol. I, 2nd edn (London: J. and P. Knapton; T. and T. Longman; C. Hitch and L. Hawes; A. Millar; and R. and J. Dodsley). [Vol. II published in 1756].

Johnson, Samuel (1765) Preface to *The Plays of William Shakespeare*. In *Samuel Johnson on Shakespeare*, edited by W. K. Wimsatt Jr (London: MacGibbon & Kee, 1960), pp. 23–69.

Johnston Jr, P. A. (2007) 'Scottish English and Scots'. In Britain (ed.) (2007), pp. 105–21.

Jones, D. (1926) *English Pronouncing Dictionary*, 3rd edn (London: J. M. Dent & Sons).

Jones, M. C. and Esch, E. (eds) (2002) *Language Change: The Interplay of Internal, External and Extra-Linguistic Factors* (Berlin and New York: Mouton de Gruyter).

Jones, W. (1786) *The Third Anniversary Discourse*, reprinted in *Sir William Jones: A Reader*, edited by S. S. Pachori (Delhi and Oxford: Oxford University Press, 1993), pp. 172–8. First published in *Asiatic Researches*, Vol. 1 (1788), 415–31.

Kachru, B. B. (1985) 'Standards, Codification and Sociolinguistic Realism: The English Language in the Outer Circle'. In *English in the World: Teaching and learning the language and literatures*, edited by R. Quirk and H. G. Widdowson (Cambridge: Cambridge University Press for The British Council), pp. 11–30.

Kachru, B. B., Kachru, Y. and Nelson, C. L. (eds) (2006) *The Handbook of World Englishes* (Malden, Massachusetts and Oxford: Blackwell).

Kachru, Y. and Nelson, C. L. (2006) *World Englishes in Asian Contexts* (Hong Kong: Hong Kong University Press).

Kamwangamalu, N. M. (2006) 'South African Englishes'. In Kachru, Kachru and Nelson (eds) (2006), pp. 158–71.

Kaplan, R. B. and Baldauf Jr, R. B. (1997) *Language Planning: From Practice to Theory* (Clevedon: Multilingual Matters).

Kay, P. and Kempton, W. (1984) 'What is the Sapir–Whorf Hypothesis?', *American Anthropologist*, vol. 86, no. 1 (March), 65–79.

Keller, R. (1995) *A Theory of Linguistic Signs*, translated by K. Duenwald (Oxford: Oxford University Press, 1998).

Kennedy, R. (2002) *Nigger: The Strange Career of a Troublesome Word* (New York: Pantheon).

Kiesling, S. F. (2006) 'English in Australia and New Zealand'. In Kachru, Kachru and Nelson (eds) (2006), pp. 74–89.

Kimura, D. (1999) 'Sex Differences in the Brain', *Scientific American Presents*, vol. 10, no. 2 (Summer), 26–31.

Kirk, J., Sanderson, S. and Widdowson, J. D. A. (eds) (1985) *Studies in Linguistic Geography: The Dialects of English in Britain and Ireland* (London: Croom Helm).

Kortmann, B. and Upton, C. (eds) (2008) *Varieties of English 1: The British Isles* (Berlin and New York: Mouton de Gruyter). [The four-volume *Varieties of English* series is essentially a repackaging of *A Handbook of Varieties of English*, edited by B. Kortmann, E. W. Schneider et al. (Berlin and New York: Mouton de Gruyter, 2004).]

Korzybski, A. (1933) *Science and Sanity: An Introduction to Non-Aristotelian Systems and General Semantics* (Lancaster, Pennsylvania: Science Press Printing Company).

Korzybski, A. (1946) 'An Extensional Analysis of the Process of Abstracting', *Synthese*, vol. V, nos 4 and 5 (September–October), 239–41. [Part of a feature on Korzybski and General Semantics, pp. 230–42.]

Korzybski, A. (1951) 'The Role of Language in the Perceptual Processes'. In *Perception: An Approach to Personality*, edited by R. R. Blake and G. V. Ramsey (New York: Ronald Press Company), pp. 170–205.

Korzybski, A. (1990) *Alfred Korzybski: Collected Writings, 1920–1950*, collected and arranged by M. Kendig, with C. S. Read and R. Pula (New York: Institute of General Semantics).

Krapp, G. P. (1925) *The English Language in America*. Two vols. (New York: Frederick Ungar).

Kretzschmar Jr, W. A. (2004) 'Regional Dialects'. In Finegan and Rickford (eds) (2004), pp. 39–57.

Kretzschmar Jr, W. A. (2008) 'Standard American English Pronunciation'. In Schneider (ed.) (2008b), pp. 37–51.

Kristinsson, A. P. (2008) Private email correspondence, 8 September 2008.

Kurath, H. (1949) *A Word Geography of the Eastern United States* (Ann Arbor: University of Michigan Press).

Kurath, H. and McDavid Jr, R. I. (1961) *The Pronunciation of English in the Atlantic States* (Ann Arbor: University of Michigan Press; reprint Tuscaloosa: University of Alabama Press, 1982).

Labov, W. (1971) 'Hypercorrection by the Lower Middle Class as a Factor in Linguistic Change'. In *Sociolinguistics*, Proceedings of the UCLA Sociolinguistics Conference, 1964, edited by W. Bright (The Hague: Mouton, 1971), pp. 84–113.

Labov, W. (1994, 2001) *Principles of Linguistic Change*, vol. 1: *Internal Factors*; vol. 2: *Social Factors* (Oxford: Blackwell).

Labov, W. (2008a) 'The Mysterious Uniformity of the Inland North'. Paper delivered on 7 August 2008, at Methods in Dialectology XIII, University of Leeds. (The page numbers I give in the text refer to slides in the PowerPoint presentation, available at: http://www.ling.upenn.edu/~wlabov/PowerPoints/PowerPoints.html.)

Labov, W. (2008b) Private email correspondence, 29 August 2008.

Labov, W., Ash, S. and Boberg, C. (2006) *The Atlas of North American English: Phonetics, Phonology and Sound Change* (Berlin and New York: Mouton de Gruyter).

Lacan, J. (1956) 'The Function and Field of Speech and Language in Psychoanalysis'. In *Écrits: A Selection*, translated by A. Sheridan (London: Tavistock Publications, 1977), pp. 30–113. 'Fonction et champ de la parole et du langage en psychanalyse', Report to the Rome Congress held at the Istitutio di Psicologia della Università di Roma, 26 and 27 September, 1953. Published in *La Psychanalyse*, vol. 1 (1956), 81–166.

Lacan, J. (1957) 'The Agency of the Letter in the Unconscious or Reason since Freud'. In *Écrits: A Selection*, translated by A. Sheridan (London: Tavistock Publications, 1977), pp. 146–78. 'L'instance de la lettre dans l'inconscient ou la raison depuis Freud', delivered on 9 May 1957, in the Amphithéâtre Descartes of the Sorbonne, Paris, at the request of the Philosophy Group of the Fédération des étudiants ès Lettres. Written version dated 14–16 May, 1957, published in *La Psychanalyse*, vol. 3 (1957), 47–81.

Lacan, J. (1991) *Le Séminaire de Jacques Lacan, Livre XVII: L'Envers de la Psychanalyse: 1969–1970*, text established by J. A. Miller (Paris: Éditions du Seuil, 1991).

Lacey, N. (2000) *Narrative and Genre: Key Concepts in Media Studies* (Basingstoke: Macmillan).

Lakoff, R. (1973) 'Language and Woman's Place', *Language in Society* , vol. 2, 45–80. Revised reprint in *Language and Woman's Place* (New York: Harper & Row, 1975), pp. 3–50.

Lasswell, H. D. (1948) 'The Structure and Function of Communication in Society'. In *The Communication of Ideas*, edited by L. Bryson (New York: Harper and Row), pp. 37–51.

Leakey, R. (1994) *The Origin of Humankind* (London: Weidenfeld & Nicolson).

Lees, R. B. (1957) Review of *Syntactic Structures*, *Language* 33, 375–407; I used the reprint in *On Noam Chomsky: Critical Essays*, edited by G. Harman (New York: Anchor Books/Doubleday, 1974), pp. 34–79.

Leith, D. (1983) *A Social History of English* (London: Routledge & Kegan Paul).

Leroi-Gourhan, A. (1968) *The Art of Prehistoric Man in Western Europe*, translated by N. Guterman (London: Thames and Hudson).

Levinson, S. C. (2000) *Presumptive Meanings: The Theory of Generalized Conversational Implicature* (Cambridge, Massachusetts: The MIT Press).

Levinson, S. C. (2003) *Space in Language and Cognition: Explorations in Cognitive Diversity* (Cambridge: Cambridge University Press).

Levinson, S. C. and Wilkins, D. P. (eds) (2006) *Grammars of Space: Explorations in Cognitive Diversity* (Cambridge: Cambridge University Press).

Lieberman, P. (1998) *Eve Spoke: Human Language and Human Evolution* (London and Basingstoke: Picador).

Limbrick, P. (1991) 'A Study of Male and Female Expletive Use in Single and Mixed-Sex Situations', *Te Reo*, 34, 71–89.

Liszka, J. J. (1996) *A General Introduction to the Semeiotic of Charles Sanders Peirce* (Bloomington and Indianapolis: Indiana University Press).

Lockwood, C. (2007) *The Human Story: Where We Come From and How We Evolved* (London: Natural History Museum).

Lodge, D. (1984) *Small World: An Academic Romance* (London: Martin Secker & Warburg). [The present book quotes from the Penguin edition of 1985.]

Long, D, and Preston, D. R. (2002) *Handbook of Perceptual Dialectology*, vol. 2 (Amsterdam: John Benjamins).

Lorenzo-Dus, N. (2008) *Television Discourse: Analysing Language in the Media* (Basingstoke: Palgrave Macmillan).

Lyons, J. (1977) *Semantics*, vol. I (Cambridge: Cambridge University Press).

Lyons, J. (1991) *Chomsky*, 3rd edn (London: Fontana Press).

McArthur, T. (1987) 'The English Languages?', *English Today*, 11 (July), 9–11.

McArthur, T. (ed.) (1992) *The Oxford Companion to the English Language* (Oxford: Oxford University Press).

McArthur, T. (1998) *The English Languages* (Cambridge: Cambridge University Press).

McArthur, T. (2002) *The Oxford Guide to World English* (Oxford: Oxford University Press).

McCrone, J. (1999) 'Left Brain, Right Brain', *New Scientist*, vol. 163, no. 2193 (3 July), 26–30.

MacDonald, I. (2005) *Revolution in the Head: The Beatles' Records and the Sixties*, 3rd edn (London: Vintage).

Magritte, R. (1929) 'Les Mots et Les Images' ('Words and Images'), *La Révolution surréaliste*, 15 December, 32–3.

Mallory, J. P. (1989) *In Search of the Indo-Europeans: Language, Archaeology and Myth* (London: Thames and Hudson).

Mallory, J. P. and Adams, D. Q. (2006) *The Oxford Introduction to Proto-Indo-European and the Proto-Indo-European World* (Oxford: Oxford University Press).

Malmesbury, William of (1125) *De Gestis Pontificum Anglorum* (*Deeds of the English Pontiffs*), edited from the Autograph Manuscript by N. E. S. A. Hamilton (London: Longman, and Trübner; Oxford: Parker; and Cambridge: Macmillan, 1870). Passage from the Prologue to Book III, translated by A. Willmott for Penhallurick and Willmott (2000). [There is another not-altogether-faithful but well-known English version of Malmesbury's Latin passage, dating from 1387. It occurs in John of Trevisa's translation and elaboration of Ranulph Higden's *Polychronicon*, a fourteenth-century history of the universe.]

Malotki, E. (1983) *Hopi Time: A Linguistic Analysis of the Temporal Concepts in the Hopi Language* (Berlin: Mouton).

Malotki, E. (2001) Private email correspondence, 9 August 2001.

Marckwardt, A. H. (1958) *American English* (New York: Oxford University Press).

Mather, J. Y. and Speitel, H. H. (eds) (1975). *The Linguistic Atlas of Scotland: Scots Section*, vol. 1 (London: Croom Helm).

Melchers, G. and Shaw, P. (2003) *World Englishes* (London: Arnold).

Mencken, H. L. (1936) *The American Language: An Inquiry into the Development of English in the United States*, 4th edn (New York: Alfred A. Knopf). [The 1st edn was published in 1919.]

Mencken, H. L. (1945, 1948) *Supplement I & II* to *The American Language: An Inquiry into the Development of English in the United States*, 4th edn (New York: Alfred A. Knopf).

Meringer, R. and Mayer, C. (1895) *Versprechen und Verlesen, eine psychologisch-linguistische Studie* (Stuttgart: Göschense Verlagsbuchhandlung).

Mesthrie, R. (ed.) (2008) *Varieties of English 4: Africa, South and Southeast Asia* (Berlin and New York: Mouton de Gruyter). [The four-volume *Varieties of English* series is essentially a repackaging of *A Handbook of Varieties of English*, edited by B. Kortmann, E. W. Schneider et al. (Berlin and New York: Mouton de Gruyter, 2004).]

Mesthrie, R. and Bhatt, R. M. (2008) *World Englishes: The Study of New Linguistic Varieties* (Cambridge: Cambridge University Press).

Miles, B. (1992) *William Burroughs: El Hombre Invisible* (London: Virgin Books).

Miles, B. (1997) *Paul McCartney: Many Years From Now* (London: Secker & Warburg).

Miller, C. and Swift, K. (1981) *The Handbook of Non-Sexist Writing for Writers, Editors and Speakers*, British edn revised by S. Dowrick (London: The Women's Press).

Miller, J. (2008) 'Scottish English: Morphology and Syntax'. In Kortmann and Upton (eds) (2008), pp. 299–327.

Mills, S. (2004) *Discourse*, 2nd edn (London: Routledge).

Milroy, J. (1996) 'Linguistic Ideology and the Anglo-Saxon Lineage of English'. In *Speech Past and Present: Studies in English Dialectology in Memory of Ossi Ihalainen*, edited by J. Klemola, M. Kytö and M. Rissanen (Frankfurt am Main: Peter Lang, 1996), pp. 169–86.

Mitchell, A. G. and Delbridge, A. (1965a) *The Pronunciation of English in Australia* (Sydney: Angus and Robertson).

Mitchell, A. G. and Delbridge, A. (1965b) *The Speech of Australian Adolescents* (Sydney: Angus and Robertson).

Mithen, S. (1996) *The Prehistory of the Mind: A Search for the Origins of Art, Religion and Science* (London: Thames and Hudson).

Mithen, S. (2005) *The Singing Neanderthals: The Origin of Music, Language, Mind and Body* (London: Phoenix).

Modiano, M. (2006) 'Euro-Englishes'. In Kachru, Kachru and Nelson (eds) (2006), pp. 223–39.

Moon, B. (1994) *A Guide to the National Curriculum*, 2nd edn (Oxford: Oxford University Press).

Moore, F. (1744) *A Voyage to Georgia, Begun in the Year 1735* (London: Jacob Robinson).

Mottram, E. (1971) *William Burroughs: The Algebra of Need* (New York: Intrepid Press).

Mufwene, S. S. (1991) 'Is Gullah Decreolizing? A Comparison of a Speech Sample of the 1930s with a Sample of the 1980s'. In *The Emergence of Black English: Text and Commentary*, edited by G. Bailey, N. Maynor and P. Cukor-Avila (Amsterdam: John Benjamins, 1991), pp. 213–30.

Mufwene, S. S. (1996) 'The Founder Principle in Creole Genesis', *Diachronica*, 13, 83–134.

Mufwene, S. S. (1997) 'The Legitimate and Illegitimate Offspring of English'. In *World Englishes 2000*, edited by L. E. Smith and M. L. Forman (Honolulu: College of Languages, Linguistics and Literature, University of Hawai'i, 1997), pp. 182–203.

Mufwene, S. S. (2008a) 'Gullah: Morphology and Syntax'. In Schneider (ed.) (2008b), pp. 551–71.

Mufwene, S. S. (2008b) *Language Evolution: Contact, Competition and Change* (London: Continuum).

Mugglestone, L. (2003) '*Talking Proper': The Rise of Accent as Social Symbol*, 2nd edn (Oxford: Oxford University Press).

Mulcaster, R. (1582) *Elementarie*, edited by E. T. Campagnac (London: Oxford University Press, 1925).

Nagy, N. and Roberts, J. (2008) 'New England: Phonology'. In Schneider (ed.) (2008b), pp. 52–66.

*National Geographic*, July 2000. 'The Dawn of Humans: People Like Us', by R. Gore, pp. 90–117.

National Institute for Japanese Language (2007) *The National Institute for Japanese Language* (Tokyo: National Institute for Japanese Language).

Nevins, A. I., Pesetsky, D. and Rodrigues, C. (2007) 'Pirahã Exceptionality: A Reassessment', at: http://www-rohan.sdsu.edu/~gawron/mathling/readings/nevinsEtAl_07_Piraha-Exce.pdf.

Newbrook, M. (1999) 'West Wirral: Norms, Self-Reports and Usage'. In *Urban Voices: Accent Studies in the British Isles*, edited by P. Foulkes and G. J. Docherty (London: Arnold, 1999), pp. 90–106.

*New York Times*, 25 September 1975. 'Experts Labor to Communicate on Animal Talk', by I. Shenker, p. 45.

O'Donnell, H. (1994) 'Mapping the Mythical: A Geopolitics of National Sporting Stereotypes', *Discourse and Society*, vol. 5, no. 3, 345–80.

Orsman, H. W. (ed.) (1997) *The Dictionary of New Zealand English: A Dictionary of New Zealandisms on Historical Principles* (Auckland: Oxford University Press).

Orton, H. et al. (eds) (1962–71) *Survey of English Dialects: The Basic Material* (Leeds: E. J. Arnold).

Ostler, N. (2005) *Empires of the Word: A Language History of the World* (London: HarperCollins).

*Oxford Dictionary of New Words* (1997), edited by E. Knowles with J. Elliott (Oxford: Oxford University Press).

*Oxford Dictionary of Quotations* (1996), edited by A. Partington, 4th edn (Oxford: Oxford University Press).

*Oxford English Dictionary*, or *A New English Dictionary on Historical Principles* (1884–1933), edited by J. A. H. Murray et al., 13 vols, 1st edn (Oxford: Clarendon Press);

2nd edn, 20 vols, edited by J. Simpson and E. Weiner (Oxford: Clarendon Press, 1989). [Supplements and Additions were also published in 1972–86 and 1993–7.]

Parry, D. (ed.) (1999) *A Grammar and Glossary of the Conservative Anglo-Welsh Dialects* (Sheffield: National Centre for English Cultural Tradition, University of Sheffield).

Partridge, E. (1947) *Usage and Abusage: A Guide to Good English*, 3rd edn (London: Hamish Hamilton).

Patrick, P. L. (2008) 'Jamaican Creole: Morphology and Syntax'. In Schneider (ed.) (2008b), pp. 609–44.

Pearson, H. (1997) 'Stop Jumping on the Vogts Wagon, Give Germans a Break', *Guardian*: 'Sport: This Sporting Life', 3 November 1997, p. 7.

Pease, A. and Pease, B. (2001) *Why Men Don't Listen & Women Can't Read Maps*, 2nd edn (London: Orion).

Peirce, C. S. (1893–1910) 'Logic as Semiotic: The Theory of Signs', selections from mss. dated from 1893 to 1910. In *The Philosophy Of Peirce: Selected Writings*, edited by J. Buchler (London: Routledge & Kegan Paul, 1940), pp. 98–119.

Peirce, C. S. (1992, 1998) *The Essential Peirce: Selected Philosophical Writings*, vol. 1 (1867–1893), vol. 2 (1893–1913), edited by N. Houser, C. Kloesel and the Peirce Edition Project (Bloomington and Indianapolis: Indiana University Press).

Penhallurick, R. (ed.) (2000) *Debating Dialect: Essays on the Philosophy of Dialect Study* (Cardiff: University of Wales Press).

Penhallurick, R. and Willmott, A. (2000) 'Dialect/"England's Dreaming" '. In Penhallurick (ed.) (2000), pp. 5–45.

*Peterborough Chronicle 1070–1154*, edited by C. Clark, 2nd edn (Oxford: Oxford University Press, 1970).

Pierce, J. R. (1980) *An Introduction to Information Theory: Symbols, Signals and Noise*, 2nd edn (New York: Dover Publications).

Pinker, Steven. (1994) *The Language Instinct: The New Science of Language and Mind* (New York: William Morrow; and London: Penguin).

Pinker, Steven. (1999) *Words and Rules: The Ingredients of Language* (London: Weidenfeld & Nicolson).

Pinker, Steven. (2007) *The Stuff of Thought: Language as a Window into Human Nature* (London: Allen Lane/Penguin).

Pinker, Steven. and Jackendoff, R. (2005) 'The Faculty of Language: What's Special About It?', *Cognition*, vol. 95, no. 2 (March), 201–236.

Pinker, Susan (2008) *The Sexual Paradox: Men, Women and the Real Gender Gap* (London: Atlantic Books).

Preston, D. R. (ed.) (1999) *Handbook of Perceptual Dialectology*, vol. 1 (Amsterdam: John Benjamins).

Pullum, G. K. (1991) *The Great Eskimo Vocabulary Hoax and Other Irreverent Essays on the Study of Language* (Chicago and London: University of Chicago Press).

Puttenham, G. (1589) *The Arte of English Poesie*, edited by G. D. Willcock and A. Walker (Cambridge: Cambridge University Press, 1936).

*Radio Times*, 14–20 March 1998. 'The Heat Is On for the King of Cool', Quentin Tarantino interview by B. Norman, pp. 46–8.

Ramson, W. S. (ed.) (1988) *The Australian National Dictionary: A Dictionary of Australianisms on Historical Principles* (Melbourne: Oxford University Press).

Rheingold, H. (1988) *They Have a Word for It* (Louisville, Kentucky: Sarabande Books).

Roach, P. (2004) 'British English: Received Pronunciation', *Journal of the International Phonetic Association*, vol. 34, no. 02 (December), 239–45.

Robinson, A. (1995) *The Story of Writing* (London: Thames & Hudson).

Rodley, C. (ed.) (1997) *Lynch on Lynch* (London: Faber and Faber).

Rudgley, R. (1998) *Lost Civilisations of the Stone Age* (London: Arrow).

Samuels, M. L. (1963) 'Some Applications of Middle English Dialectology', *English Studies*, 44, 81–94.

Sandford, C. (1995) *Kurt Cobain: 1967–1994* (London: Victor Gollancz).

Sapir, E. (1929) 'The Status of Linguistics as a Science'. In *Selected Writings of Edward Sapir in Language, Culture, and Personality*, edited by D. G. Mandelbaum (Berkeley and Los Angeles: University of California Press; and London: Cambridge University Press, 1949), pp. 160–6.

Sapir, E. (1949) *Selected Writings of Edward Sapir in Language, Culture, and Personality*, edited by D. G. Mandelbaum (Berkeley and Los Angeles: University of California Press; and London: Cambridge University Press).

Saussure, F. de (1916) *Cours de linguistique générale*, edited by C. Bally and A. Sechehaye, in collaboration with A. Riedlinger (Paris: Éditions Payot). English translations (*Course in General Linguistics*) by W. Baskin (New York City: The Philosophical Library, 1960), and by R. Harris (London: Duckworth, 1983). (The present book uses the 1960 translation.)

Saussure, F. de (1968, 1974) *Cours de linguistique générale*, critical edition by R. Engler (Wiesbaden: Otto Harrassowitz, 1989–90; reproduction of the edition of 1968–74).

Saussure, F. de (1971) *Words upon Words: The Anagrams of Ferdinand de Saussure*, edited by J. Starobinski, translated by O. Emmet (New Haven and London: Yale University Press, 1979). Originally published as *Les mots sous les mots: Les anagrammes de Ferdinand de Saussure* (Paris: Éditions Gallimard, 1971).

Saussure, F. de (1972) *Cours de linguistique générale*, critical edition by T. de Mauro (Paris: Éditions Payot, 1985; reproduction of the text of 1972).

Saussure, F. de (2002) *Écrits de linguistique générale*, edited by S. Bouquet, R. Engler and A. Weil (Paris: Éditions Gallimard and the Institut Ferdinand de Saussure). English translation (*Writings in General Linguistics*) by C. Sanders, M. Pires and P. Figueroa (Oxford: Oxford University Press, 2006).

Savage, J. (1991) *England's Dreaming: Sex Pistols and Punk Rock* (London: Faber and Faber).

Savage, J. (2007) *Teenage* (London: Pimlico).

Schiffrin, D., Tannen, D. and Hamilton, H. E. (eds) (2001) *The Handbook of Discourse Analysis* (Malden, Massachusetts and Oxford: Blackwell).

Schirato, T. and Yell, S. (2000) *Communication and Culture: An Introduction* (London: Sage).

Schleicher, A. (1863) *Die Darwinsche Theorie und die Sprachwissenschaft* (Weimar).

Schmidt, J. (1872) *Die Verwandtschaftsverhältnisse der indogermanischen Sprachen* (Weimar: Böhlau).

Schneider, E. W. (2003) 'The Dynamics of New Englishes: From Identity Construction to Dialect Birth', *Language*, vol. 79, no. 2, 233–81.

Schneider, E. W. (2008a) 'Synopsis: Phonological Variation in the Americas and the Caribbean'. In Schneider (ed.) (2008b), pp. 383–98.

Schneider, E. W. (ed.) (2008b) *Varieties of English 2: The Americas and the Caribbean* (Berlin and New York: Mouton de Gruyter). [The four-volume *Varieties of English* series is essentially a repackaging of *A Handbook of Varieties of English*, edited by B. Kortmann, E. W. Schneider et al. (Berlin and New York: Mouton de Gruyter, 2004).]

*Science*, 11 January 2002. 'From a Modern Human's Brow – or Doodling?', report by M. Balter, vol. 295, no. 5553, 247–9.

Scragg, D. G. (1974) *A History of English Spelling* (Manchester: Manchester University Press).

Sebeok, T. A. (1988) 'Communication'. In *A Sign is Just a Sign* (Bloomington and Indianapolis: Indiana University Press, 1991), pp. 22–35.

Sebeok, T. A. (1991) *A Sign is Just a Sign* (Bloomington and Indianapolis: Indiana University Press).

*Semiotica* (1994) Special Issue: Prehistoric Signs, vol. 100, 2/4.

Shakespeare, W. (1596) *Romeo and Juliet*, edited by J. A. Bryant, Signet Classic Shakespeare (New York: New American Library, 1964).

Shakespeare, W. (1599) *King Henry V*, edited by T. W. Craik, Arden Shakespeare (London: Routledge, 1995).

Shannon, C. E. and Weaver, W. (1949) *The Mathematical Theory of Communication* (Urbana: University of Illinois Press). Consists of 'The Mathematical Theory of Communication', by Shannon, pp. 3–91 (first published in slightly different form in the *Bell System Technical Journal*, July and October 1948), and 'Recent Contributions to the Mathematical Theory of Communication', by Weaver, pp. 94–117.

Shelley, M. (1818) *Frankenstein; or, The Modern Prometheus* (London: Lackington, Hughes, Harding, Mavor & Jones).

Shelley, P. B. (1840) *A Defence of Poetry*, edited by H. A. Needham (London: Ginn and Company, 1931; an edition which also contains Sir Philip Sidney's *An Apology for Poetry*).

Shin, H. B. and Bruno, R. (2003) 'Language Use and English-Speaking Ability: 2000' (US Census Bureau; available at: http://www.census.gov/prod/2003pubs/c2kbr-29.pdf).

*Sight and Sound*, July 1997. Review (by J. Romney) of *The Lost World: Jurassic Park*, vol. 7, no. 7 (July), pp. 44–6.

Simpson, J. (2008) 'Hypocoristics in Australian English'. In Burridge and Kortmann (eds) (2008), pp. 398–414.

Sinclair, J. McH. and Coulthard, R. M. (1975) *Towards an Analysis of Discourse: The English Used by Teachers and Pupils* (London: Oxford University Press).

Sinclair, J. McH. et al. (1972) *The English Used by Teachers and Pupils*, final report to SSRC, mimeo (University of Birmingham).

Singh, I. (2000) *Pidgins and Creoles: An Introduction* (London: Arnold).

Singler, J. V. (2008) 'Liberian Settler English: Phonology'. In Mesthrie (ed.) (2008), pp. 102–114.

Skinner, B. F. (1957) *Verbal Behavior* (Englewood Cliffs, New Jersey: Prentice-Hall).

Smith, A. G. (ed.) (1966) *Communication and Culture: Readings in the Codes of Human Interaction* (New York: Holt, Rinehart and Winston).

Smith, G. P. (2008) 'Tok Pisin in Papua New Guinea: Phonology'. In Burridge and Kortmann (eds) (2008), pp. 188–209.

Smith, N. and Haabo, V. (2008) 'Suriname Creoles: Phonology'. In Schneider (ed.) (2008b), pp. 339–82.

Spender, D. (1985) *Man Made Language*, 2nd edn (London: Pandora Press). [First edition published in 1980 (London: Routledge & Kegan Paul).]

Sperber, D. and Wilson, D. (1995) *Relevance: Communication and Cognition*, 2nd edn (Oxford: Blackwell).

Sperlich, W. B. (2006) *Noam Chomsky* (London: Reaktion Books).

Stapleton, K. (2003) 'Gender and Swearing: A Community Practice', *Women and Language*, vol. 26, no. 2, 22–33.

Starobinski, J. (1971) – see entry for Saussure (1971).

Story, G. M., Kirwin, W. J. and Widdowson, J. D. A. (eds) (1998) *Dictionary of Newfoundland English*, 2nd edition with Supplement (Toronto: University of Toronto Press).

Strevens, P. (1980) *Teaching English as an International Language* (Oxford: Pergamon Press).

Strevens, P. (1981) 'What *Is* "Standard English"?', *RELC Journal*, vol. 12, 1–9.

Sturrock, J. (2003) *Structuralism*, reissued 2nd edn with a new introduction by J-M. Rabaté (London: Fontana).

*Sunday Times*, 14 March 1993. 'Yer Wot? "Estuary English" Sweeps Britain', article by C. Hymas, pp. 1 and 24.

Sutton, L. A. (1995) 'Bitches and Skankly Hobags: The Place of Women in Contemporary Slang'. In *Gender Articulated: Language and the Socially Constructed Self*, edited by K. Hall and M. Bucholtz (New York and London: Routledge), pp. 279–96.

Svartvik, J. and Leech, G. (2006) *English: One Tongue, Many Voices* (Basingstoke and New York: Palgrave Macmillan).

Sweet, H. (1946) *Sweet's Anglo-Saxon Reader in Prose and Verse*, 10th edn, revised by C. T. Onions (London: Oxford University Press).

Swift, J. (1712) *A Proposal for Correcting, Improving and Ascertaining the English Tongue*, 2nd edn (London: Benjamin Tooke). Extracts in *Proper English? Readings in Language, History and Cultural Identity*, edited by T. Crowley (London: Routledge, 1991), pp. 28–41.

Talbot, M. M. (1998) *Language and Gender: An Introduction* (Cambridge: Polity Press, in association with Blackwell).

Talbot, M. (2007) *Media Discourse: Representation and Interaction* (Edinburgh: Edinburgh University Press).

Tannen, D. (1990) *You Just Don't Understand: Women and Men in Conversation* (London: Virago).

Tanner, H. H., Reiff, J., Long, J. H., Hoerder, D. and Dobyns, H. F. (eds) (1995) *The Settling of North America: The Atlas of the Great Migrations into North America from the Ice Age to the Present* (New York: Macmillan).

Tanner, T. (1971) *City of Words: American Fiction, 1950–1970* (London: Jonathan Cape).

Thibault, P. (1996) *Re-reading Saussure: The Dynamics of Signs in Social Life* (London: Routledge).

Thomas, G. (1991) *Linguistic Purism* (London: Longman).

Thomason, S. G. (2001) *Language Contact: An Introduction* (Edinburgh: Edinburgh University Press; and Washington, DC: Georgetown University Press).

Thorne, B. and Henley, N. (eds) (1975) *Language and Sex: Difference and Dominance* (Rowley, Massachusetts: Newbury House).

Thorpe, L. (1978) – see Gerald of Wales.

Thurber, J. (1953) 'My Own Ten Rules for a Happy Marriage'. In *Thurber Country* (Harmondsworth: Penguin, 1962; collection originally published in London: Hamish Hamilton, 1953), pp. 47–55.

*The Times*, 28 March 2000. 'The Test: Michael Caine', by P. McCann, *The Times*: 'Analysis', p. 7.

Tollefson, J. W. (1991) *Planning Language, Planning Inequality: Language Policy in the Community* (London: Longman).

Tristram, H. L. C. (ed.) (1997, 2000, 2003, 2006) *The Celtic Englishes I–IV* (vols I–III, Heidelberg: C. Winter; vol. IV, Potsdam: University of Potsdam Press).

Trudgill, P. (1975) *Accent, Dialect and the School* (London: Edward Arnold).

Trudgill, P. (1983) 'Acts of Conflicting Identity: The Sociolinguistics of British Pop-Song Pronunciation'. In *On Dialect: Social and Geographical Perspectives* (Oxford: Basil Blackwell), pp. 141–60.

Trudgill, P. (1999) 'Standard English: What it Isn't'. In *Standard English: The Widening Debate*, edited by T. Bex and R. J. Watts (London: Routledge, 1999), pp. 117–28.

Trudgill, P. (2002) 'The History of the Lesser-Known Varieties of English'. In *Alternative Histories of English*, edited by R. Watts and P. Trudgill (London and New York: Routledge), pp. 29–44.

Trudgill, P. (2004) *New-Dialect Formation: The Inevitability of Colonial Englishes* (New York: Oxford University Press).

Trudgill, P. and Hannah, J. (2008) *International English: A Guide to the Varieties of Standard English*, 5th edn (London: Hodder Education).

*Uncut*, April 1998. '*Jackie Brown* Special', no. 11, pp. 44–9. Includes Pam Grier interview by S. Dalton, pp. 48–9.

Upton, C. (2000) 'Maintaining the Standard'. In Penhallurick (ed.) (2000), pp. 66–83.

Upton, C., Kretzschmar Jr, W. A. and Konopka, R. (2003) *The Oxford Dictionary of Pronunciation for Current English* (Oxford: Oxford University Press).

Upton, C. and Widdowson, J. D. A. (2006) *An Atlas of English Dialects*, 2nd edn (Abingdon: Routledge).

Verner, K. (1875) 'Eine Ausnahme der ersten Lautverschiebung', *Zeitschrift für vergleichende Sprachforschung*, 23, 97–130.

Visconti, T. [with Havers, R.] (2007a) *Bowie, Bolan and the Brooklyn Boy: The Autobiography* (London: HarperCollins).

Visconti, T. (2007b) Private email correspondence, 13 November 2007.

Wade, N. (2006) *Before the Dawn: Recovering the Lost History of Our Ancestors* (London: Duckworth).

Wakelin, M. F. (1975) *Language and History in Cornwall* (Leicester: Leicester University Press).

Wakelin, M. F. (1977) *English Dialects: An Introduction*, 2nd edn (London: Athlone Press).

Wakelin, M. F. (1986) 'English on the *Mayflower*', *English Today*, vol. 8, 30–33.

Wardhaugh, R. (2006) *An Introduction to Sociolinguistics*, 5th edn (Oxford: Blackwell).

Wardhaugh, R. (2009) *An Introduction to Sociolinguistics*, 6th edn (Oxford: Blackwell).

Weber, S. (1991) *Return to Freud: Jacques Lacan's Dislocation of Psychoanalysis*, translated by M. Levine (Cambridge: Cambridge University Press).

Webster, N. (1783, 1804) *The American Spelling Book, being the First Part of a Grammatical Institute of the English Language* (Hartford, Connecticut: Hudson and Goodwin; revised edn 1804).

Webster, N. (1789) *Dissertations on the English Language* (Menston, England: Scolar Press, facsimile 1967).

Webster, N. (1828) *An American Dictionary of the English Language*. Two vols. (New York: S. Converse).

Wee, L. (2008) 'Singapore English: Phonology'. In Mesthrie (ed.) (2008), pp. 259–77.

Weinreich, U. (1953) *Languages in Contact: Findings and Problems* (The Hague and New York: Mouton, 1968; originally published as no.1 in the series Publications of the Linguistic Circle of New York, 1953).

Weinstein, B. (1980) 'Language Planning in Francophone Africa', *Language Problems and Language Planning*, vol. 4, no. 1, 55–77.

Weiss, G. and Wodak, R. (eds) (2007) *Critical Discourse Analysis: Theory and Interdisciplinarity* (Basingstoke: Palgrave Macmillan).

Weldon, T. L. (2006) 'Gullah Gullah Islands (Sea Islands, SC, GA)'. In Wolfram and Ward (eds) (2006), pp. 178–82.

Weldon, T. L. (2008) 'Gullah: Phonology'. In Schneider (ed.) (2008b), pp. 192–207.

Wells, J. C. (1982) *Accents of English*, vol. 1: *An Introduction* (Cambridge: Cambridge University Press).

Wells, J. C. (1998) – see entry for *Guardian*, 10 September 1998.

Westley, B. H. and Maclean Jr, M. S. (1957) 'A Conceptual Model for Communication Research', *Journalism Quarterly*, 34, 31–8.

White, R. G. (1868) 'Words and their Uses', *The Galaxy*, vol. 5, no. 3 (March), 334–42.

Whitman, W. (1904) *An American Primer*, edited by H. Traubel (Boston: Small, Maynard).

Whorf, B. L. (1940) 'Science and Linguistics'. In *Language, Thought, and Reality: Selected Writings of Benjamin Lee Whorf*, edited by J. B. Carroll (Cambridge, Massachusetts: The MIT Press, 1956), pp. 207–19.

Whorf, B. L. (1941) 'The Relation of Habitual Thought and Behavior to Language'. In *Language, Thought, and Reality: Selected Writings of Benjamin Lee Whorf*, edited by J. B. Carroll (Cambridge, Massachusetts: The MIT Press, 1956), pp. 134–59.

Whorf, B. L. (1956) *Language, Thought, and Reality: Selected Writings of Benjamin Lee Whorf*, edited by J. B. Carroll (Cambridge, Massachusetts: The MIT Press).

Wilson, S. (2008) 'St. Helena English: Phonology'. In Mesthrie (ed.) (2008), pp. 223–30.

Witherspoon, J. (1781) 'The Druid: No. V', *Pennsylvania Journal and Weekly Advertiser* (9 May).

Wodak, R. and Meyer, M. (eds) (2001) *Methods of Critical Discourse Analysis* (London: Sage).

Wolfram, W. and Schilling-Estes, N. (2006) *American English: Dialects and Variation*, 2nd edn (Malden, Massachusetts and Oxford: Blackwell).

Wolfram, W. and Torbert, B. (2006) 'When Linguistic Worlds Collide (African American English)'. In Wolfram and Ward (eds) (2006), pp. 225–32.

Wolfram, W. and Ward, B. (eds) (2006) *American Voices: How Dialects Differ from Coast to Coast* (Oxford: Blackwell).

Wright, J. (ed.) (1898–1905) *The English Dialect Dictionary*. Six vols. (London: Henry Frowde).

Young, T. (1814) Book review (includes first use of the term *Indo-European*), *Quarterly Review*, X, 255–6.

# Webography

The Webography lists all the websites or webpages mentioned in the text. Items are listed alphabetically according to the main keyword, name, or surname. The information given below is correct at the time of writing.

About.com: French Language, Laura K. Lawless' French Language Blog: 'Courriel – c'est officiel', 12 July 2003: http://french.about.com/b/2003/07/12/courriel-cest-officiel.htm.
About.com: German Language, 'Denglisch: When Languages Collide': http://german.about.com/od/vocabulary/a/denglish.htm.
About.com: German Language, 'The History of German Spelling Reform': http://german.about.com/library/blreform.htm.
*Académie française*: http://www.academie-francaise.fr/.
Association for the Preservation of Virginia Antiquities: Jamestown Rediscovery webpages: http://www.preservationvirginia.org/rediscovery/page.php?page_id=1.
Gareth Baxter, Richard Blythe, William Croft and Alan McKane: 'Modeling Language Change: An Evaluation of Trudgill's Theory of the Emergence of New Zealand English' (2008): http://www2.ph.ed.ac.uk/~rblythe3/Preprints/BBCM08.pdf.
BBC History, on the Vikings and Normans in England: http://www.bbc.co.uk/history/trail/conquest/.
BBC News Despatches, 'Spelling Reform Divides Germany', 12 May 1998: http://news.bbc.co.uk/1/hi/despatches/91398.stm.
BBC News Entertainment, 'Emily Thrown Out of Big Brother', 7 June 2007: http://news.bbc.co.uk/1/hi/entertainment/6729673.stm.
BBC News Middle East, Tim Franks: 'Jerusalem Diary, Monday 7 April [2008]: Language Lessons': http://news.bbc.co.uk/1/low/world/middle_east/7334357.stm.
BBC News Online: http://news.bbc.co.uk/.
BBC *Perfect Day*: http://www.bbc.co.uk/info/perfect/. [Discontinued.]
British Library Archival Sound Recordings: Accents and Dialects: http://sounds.bl.uk/maps/Accents-and-dialects.html.
British Library *Sounds Familiar?* website: http://www.bl.uk/learning/langlit/sounds/index.html.
Noam Chomsky website: http://www.chomsky.info/.
Noam Chomsky: 'A Review of B. F. Skinner's *Verbal Behavior*' (1959): http://www.chomsky.info/articles/1967—.htm.
Coiff1rst: http://www.coiff1rst.com/index_us.php.
cutup machine, by Gary David Leeming: http://gary.leeming.googlepages.com/cutup.
Robert de Beaugrande website: http://www.beaugrande.com/.

Adam Jacot de Boinod: *The Meaning of Tingo* (2005) and *Toujours Tingo* (2007): http://themeaningoftingo.blogspot.com/.

Department for Children, Schools and Families [UK], The Standards Site: http://www.standards.dcsf.gov.uk/.

*Dictionary of American Regional English* (*DARE*): http://dare.wisc.edu/.

*Dictionary of Canadianisms on Historical Principles* and *Bank of Canadian English*: http://faculty.arts.ubc.ca/sdollinger/dchp2.htm.

*Dictionary of Newfoundland English Online:* http://www.heritage.nf.ca/dictionary/.

The Eggcorn Database: http://eggcorns.lascribe.net/.

English and Celtic in Contact, University of Joensuu: http://www.joensuu.fi/fld/ecc/.

Michael Erard website: http://umthebook.com/. See also: http://michaelerard.com/.

Michael Erard: 'How Global Success is Changing English Forever', *New Scientist*, issue 2649, 29 March 2008: http://www.newscientist.com/article/mg19726491.300-how-global-success-is-changing-english-forever.html.

Dan Everett home page: http://www.llc.ilstu.edu/dlevere/.

W. Tecumseh Fitch home page: http://www.st-andrews.ac.uk/~wtsf/.

Victoria A. Fromkin's Speech Error Database: http://www.mpi.nl/resources/data.

Institute of General Semantics: http://www.generalsemantics.org/.

*Guardian*.co.uk, News Technology, 'French Consign "email" to Trash Can', 21 July 2003: http://www.guardian.co.uk/technology/2003/jul/21/france.international-news.

Robert Hasenfratz and Thomas Jambeck: *Reading Old English: A Primer and First Reader* (2005): http://www.readingoldenglish.com/.

Raymond Hickey: *Studying the History of English*: http://www.uni-due.de/SHE/.

Raymond Hickey: *Studying Varieties of English*: http://www.uni-due.de/SVE/.

Ray Jackendoff home page: http://ase.tufts.edu/cogstud/incbios/RayJackendoff/index.htm.

*The Japan Times Online*, Tomoko Otake: 'Japanese: A Language in a State of Flux', 23 September 2007: http://search.japantimes.co.jp/cgi-bin/fl20070923x1.html.

William Labov home page: http://www.ling.upenn.edu/~wlabov/.

William Labov: 'The Mysterious Uniformity of the Inland North' (2008a), paper delivered on 7 August 2008, at Methods in Dialectology XIII, University of Leeds: http://www.ling.upenn.edu/~wlabov/PowerPoints/PowerPoints.html.

Linguistic Atlas Projects of the United States: http://us.english.uga.edu/.

Linguistic Society of America: http://www.lsadc.org/.

*The Linguist List*: http://linguistlist.org/.

*Macquarie Dictionary Online* (*Australia's National Dictionary Online*): http://www.macquariedictionary.com.au/anonymous@919FFD28681692/-/p/dict/index.html.

University of Manchester Working Group On Language Contact: http://languagecontact.humanities.manchester.ac.uk/home.html.

*The Microsoft Lexicon, or Microspeak made easier*, Ken Barnes et al.: http://www.cinepad.com/mslex.htm.

Microsoft UK: Microsoft Local Dialect Programme: http://www.microsoft.com/uk/dialect/default.mspx.

Andrew Ira Nevins, David Pesetsky and Cilene Rodrigues: 'Pirahã Exceptionality: A Reassessment' (2007): http://www-rohan.sdsu.edu/~gawron/mathling/readings/nevinsEtAl_07_Piraha-Exce.pdf.

The New Zealand Dictionary Centre: http://www.victoria.ac.nz/lals/research/nzdc/index.htm.

*Oxford English Dictionary Online*: http://dictionary.oed.com/.

The Peirce Edition Project: http://www.iupui.edu/~peirce/.

Steven Pinker home page: http://pinker.wjh.harvard.edu/.

Max Planck Institute for Psycholinguistics: http://www.mpi.nl/.

John R. Rickford home page: http://www.stanford.edu/~rickford/.

*Routes of English* (BBC Radio 4): http://www.bbc.co.uk/radio4/routesofenglish/.

*Scream* official website: http://www.dimensionfilms.com/scream/. [Discontinued.]

Semiotic Solutions: http://www.semioticsolutions.com/.

Hyon B. Shin and Rosalind Bruno: 'Language Use and English-Speaking Ability: 2000', October 2003, US Census Bureau: http://www.census.gov/prod/2003pubs/c2kbr-29.pdf.

*The Statesman*, Bengal, 'Railway Committee Wants New Tracks to Arrest Jumbo Deaths', Kolkata 28 December 2008: http://www.thestatesman.net/page.arcview.php?clid=6&id=264976&usrsess=1.

Teun A. van Dijk website: *Discourse in Society*: http://www.discourses.org/.

# Index

# 348 INDEX

jazz, 55–6, 68–9
Jespersen, O., 28, 46–7, 147, 287
Johnson, Samuel, 57, 108, 216–17, 223, 229–30, 239
Johnston, P., 73
Jones, Daniel, 194
Jones, William, 20, 25
Joyce, J., 163
*Julius Caesar*, 131–3
*Jurassic Park*, 169–70
Jutes, 12, 19

Kachru, B. B., 89–90
Kamwangamalu, N. M., 83
Kennedy, J. F., 70
Kennedy, R., 205
Kiesling, S. F., 87–8
Kimura, D., 147–8, 150
*Kingdom of Heaven*, 172
*King Kong*, 170
Kirwin, W. J., 76
Korzybski, A., 151–4, 157, 161, 163, 166
Krapp, G. P., 55, 193
Kretzschmar Jr, W. A., 63–4, 67, 193
Kristeva, J., 149, 155
Kristinsson, A. P., 219–20
Kurath, H., 63–6

L1, *see* first language, English as a
L2, *see* second language, English as a
Labov, W., 30–1, 62–3, 67, 211–12, 225–6
Lacan, J., 94, 129–30, 134, 154–6, 202–5, 242
    *see also* master-signifiers; signifying chain; symbolic order
Lakoff, R., 138–41, 143–6
Lance, B., 217
*langage*, 107
    *see also* Saussure, F. de
language
    acquisition of, 130, 222, 243, 250, 266–7, 270, 275, 289, 293, 297

brain and, 147, 238, 248, 250–4, 260, 264, 266–8, 285, 288–97, 299, 304
communication and, 245–61
creativity of, 270, 278, 298
definitions of, 97, 246
dialect and, 1–2, 7–9, 11–16, 34, 191, 226
gender and, 136–50, 231, 239–40
in use, 168, 173–4, 215–16, 222, 252, 261, 278, 285
origins of, 284–300, 303–4
reality and, 103–4, 107, 109, 111–17, 119–35, 139, 143, 163–4
sex and, 112–13, 115–17, 123, 136–8, 141–3, 146–51, 164, 211
variety and, 14–15, 73, 197, 225–6
language change through time, 9–11, 17–47, 63, 65–7, 102–3, 110, 128, 145, 184, 188–9, 198, 216–17, 227, 229–31, 258
language contact, 3–4, 18–19, 26, 34–6, 40–8, 70–3, 76, 80, 85–7, 198
    *see also* contact varieties
language death, 18–19
language faculty, 264–7, 269, 278–82, 285–6, 288–90, 292, 296, 298–300, 304
    *see also* Chomsky, N.
language families, 17–18, 20–7, 54
*Language in Society*, 141
'language instinct', *see* Pinker, Steven
language planning, 216–32
language policy, 223
*langue*, 101–4, 106–17, 119–20, 129–32, 153–4, 158, 166, 179, 202, 241–3, 249–52, 260–1, 285, 293, 295
    *see also* Saussure, F. de
larynx, 297, 299
Lascaux, 303
Lasswell, H. D., 259
Latin, 3, 18–24, 43–4, 47, 53, 112–13, 161, 186, 189, 219, 247